Reconstructing Iraq's Budgetary Institutions
Coalition State Building after Saddam

The invasion of Iraq led to a costly nine-year state-building and reconstruction effort. Reconstructing Iraq's budgetary institutions proved to be a vital element of the state-building project, as allocating Iraq's growing oil revenues to pay salaries and pensions, build infrastructure, and provide essential public services played a key role in the Coalition's counterinsurgency strategy. Consistent with the literature on state building, failed states, peacekeeping, and foreign assistance, this book argues that budgeting is a core state activity necessary for the operation of a functional government. Employing a historical institutionalist approach, this book first explores the Ottoman, British, and Ba'athist origins of Iraq's budgetary institutions. The book next examines American prewar planning, the Coalition Provisional Authority's rule making and budgeting following the invasion of Iraq in 2003, and the mixed success of the Coalition's capacity-building programs initiated throughout the occupation. The budgetary process introduced by the Coalition offered a source of institutional stability in the midst of insurgency, sectarian division, economic uncertainty, and occupation. This book sheds light on the problem of "outsiders" building states, contributes to a more comprehensive evaluation of the Coalition in Iraq, addresses the question of why Iraqis took ownership of some Coalition-generated institutions, and helps explain the nature of institutional change.

James D. Savage is Professor of Politics at the University of Virginia. He received a PhD in political science, an MPP in public policy, and an MA in economics at the University of California, Berkeley. Savage is the author of *Funding Science in America: Congress, Universities, and the Politics of the Academic Pork Barrel* (Cambridge, 2000); *Making the EMU: The Politics of Budgetary Surveillance and the Enforcement of Maastricht*; and *Balanced Budgets and American Politics*. His articles have appeared in publications such as the *Journal of Politics, Review of International Political Economy, Legislative Studies Quarterly, Comparative Political Studies*, and *Public Administration Review*. He is the recipient of numerous fellowships and awards, including the American Political Science Association's Harold D. Lasswell dissertation prize, an Olin-Bradley postdoctoral fellowship at Harvard University, a Council on Foreign Relations–Hitachi International Affairs fellowship, a Fulbright–European Union Affairs fellowship, and a Jennings Randolph Senior Fellowship at the United States Institute of Peace.

Reconstructing Iraq's Budgetary Institutions

Coalition State Building after Saddam

JAMES D. SAVAGE
University of Virginia

CAMBRIDGE
UNIVERSITY PRESS

CAMBRIDGE
UNIVERSITY PRESS

32 Avenue of the Americas, New York, NY 10013-2473, USA

Cambridge University Press is part of the University of Cambridge.

It furthers the University's mission by disseminating knowledge in the pursuit of education, learning, and research at the highest international levels of excellence.

www.cambridge.org
Information on this title: www.cambridge.org/9781107678767

First published 2013

Printed in the United States of America

A catalog record for this publication is available from the British Library.

Library of Congress Cataloging in Publication Data
Savage, James D., 1951–
Reconstructing Iraq's budgetary institutions : coalition state building after Saddam / James D. Savage, Professor, Department of Politics, University of Virginia.
    pages cm
Includes bibliographical references and index.
ISBN 978-1-107-03947-6 (hardback) – ISBN 978-1-107-67876-7 (pbk.)
1. Budget – Iraq.   2. Finance, Public – Iraq.   3. Nation-building – Iraq.   4. Postwar reconstruction – Iraq.   5. Iraq – Economic policy.   I. Title.
HJ2154.3.S28   2013
336.567–dc23   2013013936

ISBN 978-1-107-03947-6 Hardback
ISBN 978-1-107-67876-7 Paperback

For Lenore

Contents

Tables

Figures and Illustrations

Preface

The December 2011 withdrawal of American troops from Iraq ended the nine-year war that cost the United States more than sixty-five hundred military, civilian employee, and contractor deaths; more than seventy-two thousand wounded; $1 trillion in short-term costs and perhaps another $2 billion or more in longer-term obligations in military benefits and health care expenses; America's international credibility; and years of effort at reconstructing Iraq's state and civil society.[1] U.S. Coalition allies also incurred losses, including the United Kingdom's 179 military deaths. For the Iraqis, the war resulted in more than a hundred thousand dead, countless thousands of civilians wounded, and millions of Iraqis displaced from their homes. At the time this is being written, the legitimacy of Iraq's governing coalition remains tenuous. As Prime Minister Nouri al-Maliki attempts to consolidate his power by marginalizing his opposition, he ordered the arrest of Iraq's Sunni vice president, Tariq al-Hashimi; an attempt was made to assassinate the Sunni minister of finance, Rafia al-Essawi; the governor of the Central Bank of Iraq, Sinan al-Shabibi, was suspended; and Muqtada al-Sadr has called for new elections. Street protests and demonstrations that occurred during the Arab Spring reflect the Iraqi people's deep dissatisfaction with the provision of basic public services. More than a million Iraqis remain unemployed. Millions of other Iraqis fled their homeland, perhaps never to return. Corruption is endemic and undermines efforts at developing good governance and the rule of law. Regional and sectional issues threaten Iraq's nationhood and contribute to the resurgence in sectarian violence. In the midst of this familiar list of woes that challenge an embryonic Iraq, why study the Iraqi budgetary process?

---

[1] Associated Press, "Iraq: Key Figures Since the War Began," December 3, 2011. http://news.yahoo.com/iraq-key-figures-since-war-began-205810481.html/.

Whenever I mentioned to colleagues that I was writing about budgeting and Iraq, they presumed the budget in question was the U.S. budget, and that my subject was how many billions of dollars Iraq would cost and how much would be borrowed from abroad to finance the war.[2] As a public budgeting and finance scholar, however, I was curious to learn about what the Coalition was doing to help stand up Iraq's own budget. Everyone knew about the gutting and looting of Iraq's ministries and the desperate need to rebuild the country's infrastructure and for the government to pay its bills. Colin Powell warned President Bush that the invasion of Iraq meant that "You will own all their hopes, aspirations, and problems. You'll own it all."[3] Given my parochial interests, for me this included owning the responsibility of helping the Iraqis budget. So, in 2006 I began searching out and interviewing government officials in the agencies that might logically have a role in such a task. My interest in Iraqi budgeting was soon shared in a more prominent way, for in 2007 the ability of the Iraqis to budget became the subject of President Bush's press conferences and the congressional testimony of General Petraeus and Ambassador Crocker. Building Iraq's ability to spend its budget served the broader counterinsurgency strategy, and "budget execution" became the mantra and metric of the Coalition's various capacity-building programs. The American government, by law, raised Iraqi budgeting to a benchmark for measuring success in Iraq. Whether the Coalition could beat back the insurgency, reconstruct the Iraqi state, and provide urgently needed public services were all tied to the Iraqis' ability to budget. By definition, the term "reconstruction" refers to "the process of rebuilding degraded, damaged, or destroyed political, socioeconomic, and physical infrastructure of a country or territory to create the foundation for long-term development."[4] This book, therefore, is about the Coalition's struggle to reconstruct Iraq's budget, and how the Iraqis have used their budget process to create some sense of political and institutional stability in the midst of a violent insurgency, sectarian division, economic uncertainty, and occupation.

This research is based, in part, on some one hundred interviews and sustained contact with a wide range of U.S. government officials, officials affiliated with Coalition partner government agencies, donor agency officials, contractors, and Iraqi officials. Finding primary source material for this book often proved to be difficult. The debate surrounding the decision to invade Iraq and the nature of the occupation is ongoing, intensely partisan, and divisive. Reputations and careers are at stake. Moreover, it is important to remember that the United

---

[2] On the cost of the war, see James A. Baker III and Lee H. Hamilton, *The Iraq Study Group Report*, New York: Vintage Books, 2006; Linda J. Blimes and Joseph E. Stiglitz, *The Three Trillion Dollar War: The True Cost of the Iraq Conflict*, New York: W.W. Norton & Company, 2008.

[3] Bob Woodward, *Plan of Attack*, New York: Simon & Schuster, 2004, 150.

[4] Dan Snodderly (ed.), *Peace Terms: Glossary of Terms for Conflict Management and Peacebuilding*, Washington, DC: United States Institute of Peace, 2011, 44. Also see James D. Savage, "Iraq's Budget as a Source of Political Stability," *Special Report*, 328, United States Institute of Peace, March 2013.

States has been effectively engaged in a war on terror since September 11, 2001, and this broader security context has been compounded by the invasion and occupation of Iraq. This state of affairs was especially acute as violence in Iraq intensified in 2006, during the 2007 surge, and through the 2008 American election. Many federal government documents remain classified; agency officials are hesitant to speak; interviews are commonly agreed to only if they are conducted off the record. Many of these individuals are civil servants who work in sensitive positions of a highly political nature, and their candor and generosity may best be thanked by avoiding linking their identities with their direct comments.

I am truly indebted to a number of colleagues who offered invaluable advice on strengthening this project. John Gilmour and Melvin Leffler patiently and heroically read my entire manuscript. Martha Derthick, John Duffield, John Echeverri-Gent, Sydney Milkis, William Quandt, Herman Schwartz, Sven Steinmo, and Joseph White, each in their own way and at critical moments, provided me with encouragement and helpful comments.

A number of exceptionally generous individuals contributed to this research: Ali Allawi, Hashim al-Assaf, Michael Barluck, Kamal Field al-Basri, Rodney Bent, Seth Bleiweis, Stuart Bowen, Paul Bremer, James Brewer, Paul Brinkley, Julie Browning, Joseph Cristoff, Ryan Crocker, Dawn Crosby, Ginger Cruz, Jay Doden, Terry Garman, Ashraf Ghani, Robert Giusti, Andy Griminger, Patricia Haslach, Burdin Hickok, James Hunter, James Jeffrey, Christopher Jennings, Ronald Johnson, Van Jorstad, Scott King, Sherri Kraham, Clare Lockhart, Robert Loftus, Stephen Lord, Jared Markland, Larry McDonald, Tony McDonald, Peter McPherson, Chris Milligan, John Mongan, James Moonier, Denise Natali, David Nummy, David Oliver, Erol Özvar, Jeremy Pam, Kyle Peterson, Charles Ries, Lynda Roades, Michael Ruffner, Nadja Ruzica, Yahia Said, Todd Schwartz, Andre Sekowski, Ged Smith, Tom Stall, Allison Stanger, James Stephenson, Jackie Strasser, Kevin Taecker, John Taylor, Kathy Thompson, Laura Trimble, Justin Tyson, Robert Viernum, David Wall, James Wallar, Wade Weems, and Aaron Williams.

Thomas Hartwell most kindly permitted me to use photographs he took of Iraq's Ministry of Finance in 2003.

I am indebted to the United States Institute of Peace for support, through the Jennings Randolph Senior Fellows program, to finish writing this manuscript. The Office of the Vice President for Research and the College of Arts and Sciences at the University of Virginia generously provided financial support for this project.

Lewis Bateman and Shaun Vigil's editorial support and guidance at Cambridge University Press proved to be invaluable.

This book is dedicated to my dear wife, Lenore, whose love, friendship, and joyful smile encouraged me through the long years of researching and writing this book.

Abbreviations

ARDP	Accelerated Reconstruction Development Program
CBI	Central Bank of Iraq
CDP	Capacity Development Plan
CERP	Commander's Emergency Response Program
CPA	Coalition Provisional Authority
CPA OMB	Coalition Provisional Authority Office of Management and Budget
CPI	Commission on Public Integrity
CRC	Civilian Response Corps
CRS	Congressional Research Service
CSO	Bureau of Conflict and Stabilization Operations
CTO	Cognizant Technical Officer
DFI	Development Fund for Iraq
DFID	Department for International Development
DG	Director-General
EPCA	Emergency Post-Conflict Assistance
ePRT	embedded Provincial Reconstruction Team
FMIS	Financial Management Information System
FSO	Foreign Service Officer
GAO	Government Accountability Office
GOI	Government of Iraq
HR	House of Representatives
IAMB	International Advisory and Monitoring Board for Iraq
ID	Iraq Dinar
IFMIS	Iraq Financial Management Information System
IIG	Iraq Inspector Generals
IMF	International Monetary Fund
IRMO	Iraq Reconstruction Management Office

IRRF	Iraq Relief and Reconstruction Fund
ISFF	Iraq Security Forces Fund
ITAO	Iraq Transition Assistance Office
KDP	Kurdistan Democratic Party
KRG	Kurdistan Regional Government
LSP	Legislative Strengthening Program
MOF	Ministry of Finance
MOP	Ministry of Planning and Development Cooperation
MSI	Management Systems International
NCCMD	National Center for Consultation and Management Development
NSC	National Security Council
NSPD-44	National Security Presidential Directive-44
OAT	Office of Accountability and Transparency
OMB	Office of Management and Budget
ORHA	Office of Reconstruction and Humanitarian Assistance
OTA	Office of Technical Assistance
PAC	Procurement Assistance Center
PDS	Provincial Development Strategy
PFM	Public Financial Management
PFMAG	Public Finance Management Action Group
PMO	Projects Management Office
PRB	Program Review Board
PRDC	Provincial Reconstruction and Development Committee
PRT	Provincial Reconstruction Team
PST	Provincial Support Team
PUK	Patriotic Union of Kurdistan
QDDR	Quadrennial Diplomacy and Development Review
RTI	Research Triangle Institute International
SBA	Stand-By Agreement
S/CRS	State/Coordinator for Reconstruction and Stabilization
SIGIR	Special Inspector General for Iraq Reconstruction
TOTS	Training of Trainers
USAID	United States Agency for International Development
WMD	Weapons of Mass Destruction

State Building and the Reconstruction of Iraq's Budgetary Institutions

> The fiscal history of a people is above all an essential part of its general history.... In some historical periods the immediate formative influence of the fiscal needs and policy of the state on the development of the economy and with it on all forms of life and all aspects of culture explains practically all the major features of events; in most periods it explains a great deal and there are but a few periods when it explains nothing.... Our people have become what they are under the fiscal pressures of the state.
>
> Joseph A. Schumpeter

On Valentines' Day 2007, President George W. Bush evaluated the political and economic progress taking place in Iraq by pointing to one significant accomplishment. "The other day," Bush announced, "the Iraqi government passed a $41 billion budget, $10 billion of which is for reconstruction and capital investment. There's a lot of talk in Washington about benchmarks. I agree – 'benchmarks' meaning that the Iraqi government said they're going to do this; for example, have an oil law as a benchmark. But one of the benchmarks they laid out, besides committing troops to the Iraqi security plan, was that they'll pass a budget in which there's $10 billion of their own money available for reconstruction and help. And they met the benchmark. And now, obviously, it's important they spend the money wisely."[1] Bush's pronouncement on the status of Iraqi budgeting came at a time when Baghdad's government and the American-led occupation verged on collapse, overcome by waves of violence that engulfed Iraq. Insurgents bombed the Golden Mosque of Samarra the preceding year, igniting sectarian assassinations, suicide attacks, and roadside bombings that killed as many as thirty-eight hundred Iraqis a week between September 2006 and January 2007, the pinnacle of civilian deaths experienced since the

---

[1] George W. Bush, "Iraq and Iran: The President's Press Conference," Manassas, Virginia, February 14, 2007, Presidentialrhetoric.com, www.presidentialrhetoric.com/speeches/02.14.07.html/.

overthrow of Saddam Hussein.[2] At that moment when the occupation appeared to be most vulnerable, Bush's reference to the Parliament's approval of the budget could be regarded as a desperate search for good news. Bush's statement, however, reflected the reality that by 2007 the Coalition's strategy for countering the violence and reconstructing the Iraqi state centered not only on a surge in American military forces but also on rebuilding the Iraqi government's ability to budget.

The Coalition's emphasis on Iraqi budgetary capacity was actually quite understandable. Iraq, in one sense, is no different from any other state; it needs to budget in order to function. After deposing Saddam's regime, the American-led Coalition struggled to reconstruct the Iraqi state as a way of countering the rising insurgency, and this meant rebuilding the state's budgeting capacity. The insurgency directly attacked Iraq's infrastructure, blowing up and destroying power grids, petroleum production facilities, bridges, roads, water works, and government buildings. These attacks threatened Iraqi lives and security, crippled the government's ability to provide basic services to its people, and contributed to the country's staggering unemployment. Most notably, the delivery of electricity, the provision of potable water, the production of foodstuffs, and the extraction of petroleum continued to fall below their preinvasion levels. The failure to provide these services encouraged civil discontent and unrest, promoted broad disaffection with the government, and furthered the ambitions of the insurgency. As the insurgency and the violence it generated spiked in late 2006, Coalition officials concluded that the Iraqi state's ability to offer these services required the reconstruction of an effective budgetary system.

How, and with what effect, did the Coalition attempt to reconstruct Iraq's budgetary institutions as a core element of its state-building and counterinsurgency strategies? How did budget execution become the overarching metric for evaluating many of the Coalition's capacity-building programs? Which of Saddam's budgetary institutions proved to be susceptible to change and which proved resistant? Under which circumstances did the Iraqis take ownership and employ the Coalition's budgetary institutions to help govern their country? By answering these questions, this book attempts to fill existing gaps in the literature on the Coalition's invasion, occupation, and state-building efforts in Iraq. As Schumpeter suggests, budgeting helps tell the fiscal history of a people. In the case of Iraq, assessing these budgetary reconstruction activities sheds new perspectives on the general problem of "outsiders" attempting to build states, contributes to a more comprehensive evaluation of the American experience in Iraq, addresses the question of why Iraqis took ownership of some Coalition-generated institutions and not others, and helps explain the nature of institutional change.

This book argues that the Coalition's efforts at reconstructing the Iraqi government's budgetary system played a critical role in building the Iraqi state. Although much of the public attention paid to Iraqi budgeting came with the rise

---

[2] Keith L. Shimko, *The Iraq Wars and America's Military Revolution*, New York: Cambridge University Press, 2010, 191.

of the insurgency and the establishment of the 2007 benchmarks, American interest in this area predates the 2003 invasion. American prewar planning did consider the structuring of Iraqi budgetary institutions and organizations, how they should function, and what role they should play in a post-Saddam Iraq. After the invasion, Coalition officials contacted and worked with appropriate Iraqi ministries to engage in stabilization "triage budgeting" to pay civil servants and pensioners. Coalition officials drafted Iraqi budgets, imposed new budgetary rules, and established new budgetary processes. Ambitions for building Iraqi budgeting ran deeper than fighting the insurgency. In addition to reconstructing the capacity of the central state, the Coalition viewed budgeting as a way to promote federalism at the provincial and municipal levels by empowering these governments with the authority to make budgets, select projects for funding, and encourage local participation in the decision-making process.[3] In this way, Coalition officials expected that a reconstructed budgetary system would contribute to the creation of a meaningful federal system and the rise of democratically engaged civil society, all as a part of Iraqi state building.

To fulfill these ambitions, the Coalition committed substantial financial resources and the efforts of numerous American agencies, including the Departments of Defense, State, and Treasury; the Agency for International Development (USAID); and the Office of Management and Budget (OMB); as well as agencies from the United Kingdom and Australia. A host of private contractors complemented these agencies, and international organizations that included the World Bank and the International Monetary Fund (IMF) provided their own solutions for building budgeting capacity. An indicator of the Coalition's concern for Iraq's budgeting capacity is found in one of the eighteen benchmarks established in 2007 for evaluating progress in Iraq. The 17th Benchmark measured the Iraqi government's capacity for "Allocating and spending $10 billion in Iraqi revenues for reconstruction projects, including delivery of essential services, on an equitable basis." "Allocating" referred to success in preparing and adopting a budget; "spending" referenced the ability to execute a budget's spending requirements. Preparing and adopting the budget demonstrated the Iraqis' technical ability to draft a viable budget document and engage in democratic parliamentary deliberations. In this context, Bush addressed Iraq's ability to allocate its budget in August 2007, saying that "Iraq's government still has more to do to meet many of its legislative benchmarks.... The parliament has passed about sixty pieces of legislation, including a $41 billion budget. Despite the slow progress in the Iraqi Parliament – here's the evidence – Iraq as a whole is moving forward."[4]

---

[3] On the importance of budgeting as a tool to build civil society and public participation in governmental affairs, see Anwar Shah (ed.), *Participatory Budgeting*, Washington, DC: World Bank, 2007.

[4] George W. Bush, "President Bush Addresses the 89th Annual Convention of the American Legion," August 28, 2007, http://www.whitehouse.gov/news/releases/2007/08/print/20070828-2.html/.

Spending the budget's allocated funds served as the overriding metric for assessing progress in constructing capital projects, providing basic services, and judging the Coalition's state-building ministerial and provincial capacity development programs. All of this, the Americans reasoned, would contribute to the Iraqi government's legitimacy, strengthen the economy, contribute to bureaucratic effectiveness, and reduce the level of violence as part of an overall counterinsurgency strategy.

Evaluations of the 17th Benchmark indicate the Coalition achieved some degree of success in its budgetary rebuilding efforts, particularly given the many bleak assessments that are commonly offered of the occupation and reconstruction of Iraq. The U.S. Government Accountability Office (GAO) found only three of the eighteen benchmarks met, and four partially met, but one of those partially met was the 17th.[5] As Bush suggested, the Iraqis did indeed allocate their budget. Nonetheless, half of the benchmarks clearly remained unfulfilled. The actual downstream spending of these allocations proved far more challenging and elusive as a result of the diminished capacity of the Iraqi bureaucracy, ongoing violence, and massive corruption. The central government's inability to spend its budget, for example, reflected a dysfunctional bureaucracy unable to engage in the basic administrative acts of contract management and procurement. The struggle to build Iraqi budget execution consumed Coalition capacity-building activities at the ministerial and provincial levels. Not infrequently, the Iraqis resisted Coalition and donor training and advice, which often suffered from the lack of clear goals, standards, coordination, and sensitivity to the expressed needs of the Iraqis. At the same time, however, this focus on budget execution and spending money overwhelmed efforts to build systems that promoted transparency and accountability in the use of government funds. Thus, the 17th Benchmark pointed to the accomplishments as well as the setbacks and failures experienced by the Coalition in Iraq.

As the following sections of this chapter indicate, this study is informed by several bodies of scholarly literature. First, consistent with the postconflict, fragile state, failed state, peacekeeping, and foreign assistance literatures, this research views effective public budgeting as a necessary condition of successful state building. Second, this project relies on theories of historical institutional change to explain the institutional transformation taking place in Iraqi budgeting. Third, as some state-building and foreign assistance scholars suggest, the simple imposition of rules often proves to be insufficient in the creation of institutional change. Successful institutional change is highly contingent on aid beneficiary

---

[5] There are evaluations of this period that find the CPA's oversight of the Iraqi economy to be more successful than examples of other American occupations. See James Dobbins, Seth G. Jones, Benjamin Runkle, and Siddharth Mohandas, *Occupying Iraq: A History of the Coalition Provisional Authority*, Santa Monica: Rand, 2009. Also see James F. Dobbins, "Towards a More Professional Approach to Nation-Building," in *International Peacekeeping*, 15 (2008) 1, 67–83.

ownership and buy-in. Consequently, from a broad, historical perspective, institutional change takes the form of layering, where the struggle to impose a new institutional layer is reflected in the pushback, resistance, and obstruction offered by those benefiting from existing institutions. Institutional change involves ambiguity, complexity, and contingency. The reduction and overcoming of this resistance is reflected in institutional ownership and stakeholding. Those changes that are most successfully adopted are, on the one hand, where the demands for change are highly visible, salient, and subject to a system of monitoring and sanctioning by external actors, and, on the other hand, where the outcome of change is least threatening and most beneficial to domestic actors. Institutional change, in other words, is most likely to occur where there is a coincidence of interests.

BUDGETING IN THE STATE-BUILDING LITERATURE

In the recent literature on state building, public budgeting plays a critical role in the development of good governance and effective administrative capacity. The origins of the contemporary practice and study of externally induced, donor-driven state building is commonly located in the late 1980s and early 1990s.[6] Several very disappointing decades of relying on World Bank and IMF structural adjustment agreements and holding elections to bring warring parties together proved to be insufficient remedies for resolving conflict, creating legitimate government, promoting economic development, and preventing the growth in the number of failing and failed states. These failed states jeopardized the well-being of their own people while they threatened the stability and peace of the world community of states. International organizations and donors reached consensus that successful foreign assistance, peacebuilding, and postconflict operations depended on the introduction of functioning state institutions.[7] These state-building efforts required external intervention by these

---

[6] On the history and evolution of state building, see, for example, Roland Paris, "Peacebuilding and the Limits of Liberal Internationalism," *International Security*, 22 (1997) 2, 54–89; Mixin Pei and Sara Kasper, "Lessons from the Past: The American Record on Nation Building," Carnegie Endowment for International Peace, *Policy Brief*, 24 (May 2003), 1–6; Oisin Tansey, "The Concept and Practice of Democratic Regime-Building," *International Peacekeeping*, 14 (2007) 5, 633–646; Ian Johnson and Ethan Corbin, "Introduction – The US Role in Contemporary Peace Operations: A Double-Edged Sword?," *International Peacekeeping*, 15 (2008) 1, 1–17; Victoria K. Holt and Michael G. Mackinnon, "The Origins and Evolution of US Policy Towards Peace Operations," *International Peacekeeping*, 15 (2008) 1, 18–34; William Flavin, "US Doctrine for Peace Operations," *International Peacekeeping*, 15 (2008) 1, 35–50; David Chandler, *International Statebuilding: The Rise of Post-Liberal Governance*, New York: Routledge, 2010, 60–62.

[7] On the limits of elections, see Dennis A. Rondinelli and John D. Montgomery, "Regime Change and Nation Building: Can Donor's Restore Governance in Post-Conflict States?" *Public Administration and Development*, 25 (2005), 15–23; Roland Paris and Timothy D. Sisk, "Understanding the Contradictions of Postwar Statebuilding," in Roland Paris and Timothy D. Sisk (eds.), *The Dilemmas of Statebuilding*, New York: Routledge, 2009, 1–20.

organizations and their practitioner agents, whose actions would be enforced through aid conditionality. To accommodate this intervention, more generous and elastic definitions of state sovereignty challenged traditional notions of state autonomy, thereby legitimizing the presence of international actors who attempted to fix failing states by building good governance.[8] Good governance, in turn, is a function of a state's administrative capacity that is largely measured by the technical standards of international best practices. Good governance includes good budgeting.

Budgeting is a core state function. Effective budgeting enables the state to plan, prioritize, allocate resources, and manage the bureaucracy. Competent budgeting contributes to efficacious fiscal and macroeconomic policies. Budgeting and the government it serves can be transparent, participatory, and promote democratic decision making, or it can be opaque, hierarchical, and encourage authoritarian rule. Democratic budgetary institutions promote the rule of law, transparent decision making, a culture of bargaining and compromise, deliberation in the allocation of resources, civil society, and accountability in the management of public funds. Budgeting, as a central component of public finance, has long been regarded as a driving factor in the history of state formation.[9] Consequently, Ashraf Ghani and Clare Lockhart see budgeting as the "linchpin of the state." They identify ten key functions that must be fixed in failed states. Budgeting plays a role in two of these functions: the sound management of public finances and effective public borrowing. "The record of state activities lies most clearly in its budget," they write, "which is both the medium and the message. The budget brings the rights and duties of citizenship into balance.... Thus, the discipline of preparation, implementation, and alteration of budgets allows the translation of public goals into measurable programs and projects. Public expenditure takes place through the rules for the procurement of goods and services, accounting, and auditing. Adherence to these rules is a

---

[8] Chandler, *op. cit.*, especially chapter 3; Stein Sundstol Eriksen, "'State Failure' in Theory and Practice: The Idea of the State and the Contradictions of State Formation," *Review of International Studies*, 37 (2011), 229–247.

[9] In addition to the contemporary failed state, peacekeeping, and foreign assistance literature, budgeting and public finance have long been considered a foundational element in state building. See, for example, Fred W. Riggs, "Bureaucrats and Political Development: A Paradoxical View," in Joseph LaPalombara (ed.), *Bureaucracy and Political Development*, Princeton: Princeton University Press, 1963, 120–168; Charles Tilly, "Reflections on the History of European State-Making," in Charles Tilly (ed.), *The Formation of National States in Western Europe*, Princeton: Princeton University Press, 1975, 3–83; James D. Savage, *Balanced Budgets and American Politics*, Ithaca, NY: Cornell University Press, 1988; Margaret Levi, *Of Rule and Revenue*, Berkeley: University of California Press, 1988; John Brewer, *The Sinews of Power: War, Money, and the English State, 1688–1783*, Cambridge: Harvard University Press, 1990; Martin Van Creveld, *The Rise and Decline of the State*, New York: Cambridge University Press, 1999; Sheldon D. Pollack, *War, Revenue, and State Building: Financing the Development of the American State*, Ithaca, NY: Cornell University Press, 2009.

critical indicator of the state's effectiveness and accountability."[10] Graciana del Castillo recommends that when rebuilding "wartorn" states, "Ideally, the government, as the elected representatives of the people in postconflict situations, should be able to set up a consolidated national budget with all revenue and all expenditure, including those related to economic reconstruction.... The national budget should thus include and prioritize all revenue (including grants) and all expenditure (including investment) in the country, making it the centerpiece of the government's reconstruction strategy."[11] James Boyce and Madalene O'Donnell claim that "The capacity to mobilize, allocate, and spend domestic resources is crucial for the success of peacebuilding efforts."[12] Proficient budgeting, they contend, ensures sustainable domestic funding to complement foreign resources, promotes government legitimacy through the provision of needed social services, and enhances government efforts to establish public security. The World Bank takes public finance management seriously enough to make half of all of its conditions for aid tied to reforms in public sector governance, especially changes desired in budgetary processes, financial management, and financial accountability.[13]

On-Budget versus Off-Budget Spending

Moreover, reconstructing a sustainable, coordinated domestic public finance system as part of a state-building exercise is necessary to break patterns of dysfunctional budgeting that occur when multiple sources of off-government budget donor funding compete with on-budget state funding as the provider of public services. The decision about when to distribute assistance funds through on-budget government institutions rather than rely on off-budget mechanisms directly controlled by donors is a perennial question in foreign assistance and peacekeeping operations. The channeling of donor funds off-budget reflects donor concerns that beneficiary governments lack the necessary political and administrative capacity to allocate and execute funds effectively and honestly. Budgetary state building involves building this capacity so that governments can indeed manage both donor funds and indigenous resources in a manner that

---

[10] Ashraf Ghani and Clare Lockhart, *Fixing Failed States: A Framework for Rebuilding a Fractured World*, New York: Oxford University Press, 2008, 135–136. Also see Ashraf Ghani, Clare Lockhart, Nargis Nehan, and Baqer Massoud, "The Budget as the Linchpin of the State: Lessons from Afghanistan," in James K. Boyce and Madalene O'Donnell (eds.), *Peace and the Public Purse: Economic Policies for Postwar Statebuilding*, Boulder, CO: Lynne Rienner, 2007, 153–184.

[11] Graciana del Castillo, *Rebuilding War-Torn States: The Challenges of Post-Conflict Economic Reconstruction*, New York: Oxford University Press, 2008, 286.

[12] James K. Boyce and Madalene O'Donnell, "Peace and the Public Purse: An Introduction," in James K. Boyce and Madalene O'Donnell (eds.), *Peace and the Public Purse: Economic Policies for Postwar Statebuilding*, Boulder, CO: Lynne Rienner, 2007, 6.

[13] World Bank, *Conditionality in Development Policy Lending*, New York, November 15, 2007, 5.

promotes transparency, accountability, and efficiency in public finance. According to Michael Carnahan and Clare Lockhart, problems occur during assistance efforts when nongovernmental donor organizations retain control over the distribution of their financial resources and operate parallel system of budgeting, rather than turn these resources over to the state for allocation.[14] Donors manage their funds this way in order to ensure that their priorities are funded and because they lack confidence in the state to manage donor funds in a manner consistent with international best practices, particularly the state's ability to control corruption and financial malfeasance. The answer to the question of whether to allocate donor funds on- or off-budget is thus often a matter of the sequencing of events and capacity. "In some fragile states where efforts to bolster existing capacity are unlikely to yield desired outcomes, other channels for distributing foreign aid should be used," note Simon Feeny and Mark McGillvray. "These alternative channels by-pass recipient country governments and can therefore assist in relieving absorptive capacity constraints through reducing the administrative burden of foreign aid."[15]

Although these concerns may be and often are justified, Carnahan and Lockhart argue that over the long term the failure to build strong state-centered budgeting produces uncoordinated and inefficient spending that challenges the state's legitimacy as the deliverer of public services. For example, where the process of democratic public budgeting requires deliberation and political approval for setting spending priorities, the capital projects that emerge from these parallel funding sources may be solely determined by donors. These projects often lack recipient country buy-in and ownership of these investments, with the result that they are neglected or abandoned once donor funding ceases. The presence of parallel budgeting creates its own sets of loyalties and dependencies that undermines the state's legitimacy, conflicts with state funding priorities, encourages the state to remain dependent on donor contributions, and deters efforts at building state capacity. Thus, state building must have as one of its central goals the development of sustainable, effective, and accountable public budgets to provide essential services and thereby gain popular legitimacy.

Building this budgetary capacity is essentially a matter of providing technical assistance and training to those units of government that play critical roles in the

---

[14] Michael Carnahan and Clare Lockhart, "Peacebuilding and Public Finance," in Charles T. Call (ed.), *Building States to Build Peace*, Boulder, CO: Lynne Rienner, 2008, 73–102. Also see Graciana del Castillo, "The Economics of Peace: Five Rules for Effective Reconstruction," *Special Report*, No. 286, United States Institute of Peace, September 2011.

[15] Simon Feeny and Mark McGillivray, "Aid Allocation to Fragile States: Absorptive Capacity Constraints," *Journal of International Development*, 21 (2009), 629. On this point, also see James F. Dobbins, who writes, "While donors may initially finance the resumption of government services, it is important to reconstruct quickly the host's capability to allocate that funding and oversee its expenditure, and to expand its capacity to collect its own sources of revenue." James F. Dobbins, "Towards a More Professional Approach to Nation-Building," *International Peacekeeping*, 15 (2008) 1, 79.

budgetary process. This assistance is typically offered by small numbers of technical advisors who are embedded at ministries of finance and planning. These advisors may be deployed, for example, from the U.S. Treasury's Office of Technical Assistance, the United Kingdom's Department for International Development, the World Bank, or the International Monetary Fund, or, frequently, they are contractors. This assistance tends to focus on helping governments formulate their budgets, which may include training ministry staff in developing the economic assumptions employed in the drafting of their budgets. Technical assistance may also be offered in other aspects of running a finance ministry, such as training the government's treasury in cash management techniques, setting up a chart of accounts, and aiding revenue collection units in strengthening tax compliance. Another common ambition of technical assistance is building an automated financial management information system.

Obstacles to Budgetary State Building

Assessments of foreign assistance and state-building efforts point to the staggering obstacles that must be overcome in building capacity in poor, postconflict, and failing states.[16] Paul Collier, for example, asserts that "How governments spend money is at the core of how they function." However, the world's poorest countries continue to fail despite massive amounts of financial and other forms of assistance. "At present," he says, "spending by the governments of the bottom billion is often atrocious."[17] To help remedy this abuse, Collier calls for a "Charter for Budget Transparency" that would identify international best practices to promote the scrutiny of budget formulation and execution, including the publication and the comparison of budgets across governments. Building budgetary transparency is particularly vital "in the resource-rich countries [where] effective public spending is the vital route to development."[18] He contends that spending aid assistance on-budget is acceptable only in the "better-governed countries." Large amounts of donor assistance spent on-budget in weak states may actually induce instability, as rebels and antigovernment forces may seek to control government funds. Collier recommends that because of the weak performance of assistance and state-building programs, the ambitions of such assistance be limited. "Capacity building is too slow a process to meet the acute needs for skills that arise in the early years of the postconflict period.... Capacity building within the public sector is, of course, necessary. However it

---

[16] Mixin Pei and Sara Kasper noted the limited success of U.S. state-building efforts: "Whereas a strong, indigenous state capacity is almost a requirement for success, building this capacity may be a challenge beyond the capacity of even the most well-intentioned and determined outsiders." "Lessons from the Past: The American Record on Nation Building," *Policy Briefs*, Carnegie Endowment for International Peace, 24, May, 2003, 5.

[17] Paul Collier, *The Bottom Billion: Why the Poorest Countries Are Failing and What Can be Done About It*, New York: Oxford University Press, 2007, 149.

[18] *Ibid*, 141.

should probably attempt neither to recreate the civil service as it was nor even to create a conventional structure of ministries."[19] Collier's prescriptions for developing better-governed countries from bad governments and boosting the potency of foreign assistance thus include providing technical training and international standards to guide spending decisions.

William Easterly, another noted skeptic of interventionist foreign assistance and state building who declares that "outsiders" "don't have a clue" about "how to create institutions," argues that undemocratic rulers receive massive amounts of aid funds with little accountability for their use.[20] "What we see happening is that aid shifts money from being spent by the best governments in the world to being spent by the worst. What are the chances that these billions are going to reach poor people?" Donor beneficiaries are often corrupt, and the governments they lead are incompetent. "So donor bureaucracies remain stuck with the recipient government bureaucracy when they try to implement their aid projects, even when that bureaucracy is not customer-friendly to the poor."[21] Highly critical of unfocused capacity-building programs and the IMF, Easterly argues that for all of its aid conditionality and fiscal monitoring, the agency is ineffective in ensuring that "bad rulers," "bad governments," and "deadbeat governments" use their loans and donations properly. The IMF best functions as a bailout creditor. Consequently, donors should avoid rewarding bad governments with financial assistance that simply enables their corrupt ways. Still, Easterly concedes that "Official aid agencies and national government bureaucracies should remain on the list of possible vehicles for delivering development services ... [and] giving advice on good macroeconomic management."[22] This assistance would presumably contribute to moving bad governments into Easterly's category of good governments, which do operate with functioning budgetary institutions and systems. Thus, for Collier and Easterly, legitimate, functioning, transparent, and accountable budgetary institutions are desirable for and even a necessary condition of good governments, but they consider it unlikely that such institutions can be introduced in dysfunctional governments through existing assistance and state-building practices. Bad governments would be largely left to fend for themselves, or left with far more limited technical advising and guidance than are currently offered by donors and international organizations. The incentive for these governments behaving well would be acceptance into the international community.

---

[19] Paul Collier, "Postconflict Economic Policy," in Charles T. Call (ed.), *Building States to Build Peace*, Boulder, CO: Lynne Rienner, 2008, 111–112.

[20] William Easterly, *The White Man's Burden: Why the West's Efforts to Aid the Rest Have Done So Much Ill and So Little Good*, New York: Penguin, 2006, 77. 133. A similar view is expressed in Daron Acemoglu and James A. Robinson, *Why Nations Fail*, New York: Crown Publishers, 2012, 446–455.

[21] *Ibid.*, 134.

[22] *Ibid.*, 370, 369.

Sequencing in Budgetary State Building

This debate about whether to fund assistance on or off the government's budget points to the deeper issue of sequencing in state building.[23] In the very long what-to-do checklist of state building, what policies, assistance programs, and institution-building activities should take priority, and in what order should they be pursued? Peacekeeping, postconflict, and state-building practitioners and scholars have developed extensive lists, hundreds of items long, regarding the sequencing of humanitarian, stabilization, reconstruction, and development intervention and assistance.[24] A not uncommon list begins with establishing security and providing emergency medical relief. Then the list becomes more complicated, particularly as the focus shifts to economic stabilization and reconstruction, even within the narrower task of budgeting. The best practices for budgetary reconstruction offered by international organizations commonly include the development and promotion of effective budget rules, formulation, execution, oversight, and cash management, to name just a few items of financial concern. Optimally, these systems would be successfully installed and activated simultaneously. Many of these reforms assume the existence of a relatively intact state, one with a functioning administrative apparatus. This rarely occurs in postconflict situations. Should reconstruction spending therefore be withheld until the necessary institutional capacity is established? Collier and Easterly's answer that donor money should be spent off-budget, if at all, reflects the frequent lack of indigenous administrative capacity to spend these funds wisely, effectively, and honestly. The consequence of spending large amounts of money quickly where institutional accountability is insufficient is often fiscal waste, mismanagement, and corruption, resulting in a subsequent loss of public confidence in the broader state-building operation. Yet, del Castillo urges that "The

[23] The notion of sequencing, templates, and lists of task is common in state building. See, for example, Marina Ottaway, "Rebuilding State Institutions in Collapsed States," in Jennifer Milliken (ed.), *State Failure, Collapse and Reconstruction*, Oxford: Blackwell, 2003, 245–266; Richard Allen, "The Challenge of Reforming Budgetary Institutions in Developing Countries," WP/09/96 Washington, DC: International Monetary Fund, May 2009; Dennis A. Rondinelli and John D. Montgomery, "Regime Change and Nation Building: Can Donors Restore Governance in Post-Conflict States?" *Public Administration and Development*, 25 (2005), 15–23; and Andrew S. Natsios, "Time Lag and Sequencing Dilemmas of Postconflict Reconstruction," *Prism*, 1 (2009) 1, 63–76. For sequencing in budgeting, see World Bank, *Public Expenditure Management Handbook*, Washington, DC: World Bank, 1998; Tony Addison and Alan Roe, "Introduction," in Tony Addison and Alan Roe (eds.), *Fiscal Policy for Development*, New York: Palgrave Macmillian, 2004, 1–23; and Adrian Fozzard and Mick Foster, "Changing Approaches to Public Expenditure Management in Low-Income Aid-Dependent Countries," in Tony Addison and Alan Roe (eds.), *Fiscal Policy for Development, New York*: Palgrave Macmillian, 2004, 97–129.

[24] One U.S. Army preinvasion study identified 135 tasks involved in rebuilding the Iraqi state, including six in public finance. Conrad C. Crane and W. Andrew Terrill, "Reconstructing Iraq: Challenges and Missions for Military Forces in a Post-Conflict Scenario," Strategic Studies Institute, U.S. Army War College, January 29, 2003.

disbursement of reconstruction aid should not be delayed – as is often the existing practice – in waiting for the country to have the right conditions in political leadership, governance, institutions, and human capacity." From this perspective, the urgent need to spend money to reconstruct critical infrastructure and provide essential services is immediate and supersedes the creation of these "right conditions."[25] The state-building challenge facing the Coalition in Iraq was whether it could spend its money and Iraqi money quickly enough to meet urgent needs, while simultaneously building accountability into Iraq's budgetary institutions.

Paying Attention to Budgetary State Building in Iraq

Despite the budget's critical function as a core state activity, it is nevertheless possible to examine a good deal of this foreign assistance, postconflict, and state-building literature and find only limited attention paid to the importance of building an effective budgetary system. "There is a growing literature on post-conflict peacebuilding," Boyce and O'Donnell note, "but little treatment of public finance issues within it."[26] This is particularly true in the case of Iraq, where scholars generally neglect the Coalition's efforts to transform Iraq's budgetary institutions, and the studies that do exist often conclude their analyses with the Coalition Provisional Authority's (CPA) 2004 transfer of sovereignty to the Iraqis. These evaluations and histories of the CPA, particularly those released during the first two or three years following the invasion, are often highly and justifiably critical of this phase of the occupation. They concentrate on the multiple state-building failures associated with the lack of American prewar planning for the breakdown in security following the invasion and the inadequate, uncoordinated, and wasteful stabilization and reconstruction programs conducted during the occupation.[27]

[25] Graciana del Castillo, "The Economics of Peace: Five Rules for Effective Reconstruction," *Special Report*, 286, United States Institute of Peace, September 2011, 12.

[26] James K. Boyce and Madalene O'Donnell, "Peace and the Public Purse: An Introduction," in James K. Boyce and Madalene O'Donnell (eds.), *Peace and the Public Purse: Economic Policies for Postwar Statebuilding*, Boulder, CO: Lynne Rienner, 2007, 1.

[27] This is the case with much of the popular press's assessment of the invasion and occupation, including George Packer, *The Assassins' Gate: America in Iraq*, New York: Farrar, Straus and Giroux, 2005; Rajiv Chandrasekaran, *Imperial Life in the Emerald City: Inside Iraq's Green Zone*, New York: Knopf, 2006; and Charles H. Ferguson, *No End in Sight: Iraq's Descent into Chaos*, New York: Public Affairs, 2008. Also see Eric Herring and Glen Rangwala, *Iraq in Fragment: The Occupation and Its Legacy*, Ithaca, NY: Cornell University Press, 2006. Other not uncommon studies of the CPA that assess its role in building the Iraqi economy but neglect the budget include James Dobbins, John G. McGinn, Keith Craine, Seth G. Jones, Rollie Lal, Andrew Rathmell, Rachel Swanger, and Anga Timilsina, *America's Role in Nation-Building: From Germany to Iraq*, Santa Monica: Rand, 2003, chapter 10; Johanna Mendelson Forman, "Striking Out in Baghdad: How Postconflict Reconstruction Went Awry," in Francis Fukuyama (ed.), *Nation-Building: Beyond Afghanistan and Iraq*, Baltimore: Johns Hopkins University Press,

These studies of the CPA focus on the success of currency conversion, ill-fated attempts to liberalize the Iraqi economy, the Coalition's mismanagement of Iraq's reconstruction, and the failure to establish appropriate financial controls over the dispersion and use of funds. The studies that do address budgeting generally concentrate on the use of American funds rather than on how CPA policies specifically affected Iraqi budgeting or Coalition efforts to rebuild Iraqi budgetary institutions.[28] They tend to be broad in scope and rarely "drill down" into Iraq's ministries and examine how they operate.[29] Their timeline is short, ending with the CPA, and thus they violate a basic rule of state building that such

2006, 196–217; Robert Looney, "The Neoliberal Model's Planned Role in Iraq's Economic Transition," *Middle East Journal*, 57 (2003) 4, 569–586; Robert Looney, "Reconstruction and Peacebuilding Under Extreme Adversity: The Problem of Pervasive Corruption in Iraq," *International Peacekeeping*, 15 (2008) 3, 424–440; and Christopher Foote, William Block, Keith Crane, and Simon Gray, "Economic Policy and Prospects in Iraq," *Journal of Economic Perspectives*, 18 (2004) 3, 47–70

[28] There is a general consensus that prewar planning for Iraq proved to be woefully inadequate, particularly for the transition into what is called Phase IV, postconflict, stabilization, and reconstruction operations. See, for example, Anne Ellen Henderson, "The Coalition Provisional Authority's Experience with Economic Reconstruction in Iraq: Lessons Identified," *Special Report*, No. 138, United States Institute of Peace, April 2005; Larry Diamond, "What Went Wrong and Right in Iraq," in Francis Fukuyama (ed.), *Nation Building: Beyond Afghanistan and Iraq*, Baltimore: Johns Hopkins University Press, 2006, 173–195; Joseph J. Collins, "Planning Lessons from Afghanistan and Iraq," *Joint Forces Quarterly*, 41 (2006) 2, 10–14; Kate Philips, Shane Lauth, and Erin Schenk, "U.S. Military Operations in Iraq: Planning, Combat, and Occupation," W. Andrew Terrill (ed.), Strategic Studies Institute, U.S. Army War College, April 2006; Michael R. Gordon and Bernard E. Trainor, *Cobra II: The Inside Story of the Invasion and Occupation of Iraq*, New York:, 2006; Christina Caan, Beth Cole, Paul Hughes, and Daniel P. Serwer, "Is This Any Way to Run an Occupation? Legitimacy, Governance, and Security in Post-Conflict Iraq," in Karen Guttieri and Jessical Piombo (eds.), *Interim Governments*, Washington, DC: United States Institute of Peace, 2007, 319–343; Nora Bensahel, Olga Oliker, Keith Crane, Richard R. Brennan, Jr., Heather S. Gregg, Thomas Sullivan, and Andrew Rathmell, *After Saddam: Prewar Planning and the Occupation of Iraq*, Santa Monica: Rand, 2008; and Donald P. Wright and Timothy R. Reese, *On Point II: Transition to the New Campaign: The United States Army in Operation Iraqi Freedom, May 2003–January 2005*, Ft. Leavenworth, KS: United States Army Combat Studies Institute, 2008. On the need to incorporate stabilization and reconstruction efforts into military planning, see the U.S. Army's "Stability Operations," *Field Manual FM 3–07*, Washington, DC: Headquarters, Department of the Army, October 2008. Also see, for example, Alan Mangan, "Planning for Stabilization and Reconstruction Operations Without a Grand Strategy," Strategic Studies Institute, U.S. Army War College, March 2005; Brian G. Watson, "Reshaping the Expeditionary Army to Win Decisively: The Case for Greater Stabilization Capacity in the Modular Force," Strategic Studies Institute, U.S. Army War College, August 2005; Thomas S. Szayna, Derek Eaton, and Amy Richardson, *Preparing the Army for Stability Operations*, Santa Monica: Rand, 2007; Robert M. McNab and Edward Mason, "Reconstruction, the Long-Tail, and Decentralization: An Application to Iraq and Afghanistan," Monterey: Naval Postgraduate School, 2007; Greg Kaufmann (ed.), *Stability Operations and State-Building: Continuities and Contingencies*, Carlisle: Strategic Studies Institute, U.S. Army War College, October 2008. Unfortunately, there are few critiques of the CPA viewed from the perspective of efforts to reconstruct Iraqi ministries.

[29] There are a few studies of Iraqi ministries. See, for example, Agresto's assessment of the reconstruction of the Iraqi Ministry of Education during the CPA. John Agresto, *Mugged by Reality:*

efforts are long-term propositions. The Office of the Special Inspector General for Iraq Reconstruction (SIGIR), the Congressional Research Service (CRS), and the GAO provide the most valuable and useful analyses of the financial aspects of Iraqi reconstruction, and many of these excellent reports address aspects of Iraqi budgeting.[30] Yet, SIGIR acknowledges that the focus of its analysis is the financial management of U.S. funds and the behavior of American agencies and contractors rather than what transpires in Iraqi ministries and how the Iraqi budget operates. Neither GAO nor CRS evaluates or reports in much detail on the condition of Iraqi budgeting or on the budgetary process at the ministerial and provincial levels of government. Finally, there are some studies that explore the condition of Iraqi budgeting, but they tend to focus on provincial budgets because their authors worked as contractors at the provincial level of government. Although valuable, they miss the overall Coalition experience in reconstructing the Iraqi budgetary system.[31]

The Liberation of Iraq and the Failure of Good Intentions, New York: Encounter Books, 2007. Agresto is particularly critical of USAID's use of reconstruction funds. "USAID had no understanding of the conditions we were facing at the universities, scant understanding of the needs, and no understanding of what was at stake. And, because it is an agency that, while housed within the State Department, prizes its independence, working with them in a collaborative way, except on their terms, was immensely difficult" (144–145). A set of reports by the United States Institute of Peace on security issues that examine the role of the Ministry of the Interior provide a rare analysis that tracks the activities of a ministry throughout the occupation. See Robert Perito, "The Coalition Provisional Authority with Public Security in Iraq: Lessons Learned," *Special Report*, 137, United States Institute for Peace April 2005; Robert Perito, "Iraq's Interior Ministry: Frustrating Reform," *Peace Brief*, United States Institute for Peace, May 2008; and Robert Perito and Madeline Kristoff, "Iraq's Interior Ministry: The Key to Police Reform," *Special Briefing*, United States Institute for Peace, July 2009.

[30] In addition to various reports to Congress issued by SIGIR, GAO, and CRS, the major publication is Office of the Special Inspector General for Iraq Reconstruction, *Hard Lessons: The Iraq Reconstruction Experience*, Washington, DC: U.S. Government Printing Office, 2009.

[31] The best review of Iraqi budgeting through 2009 is Ronald W. Johnson and Ricardo Silva-Morales, "Budgeting Under Resource Abundance and Hesitant Steps to Decentralized Investment Planning and Budgeting in Iraq," in Charles E. Menifield (ed.), *Comparative Budgeting: A Global Perspective*, Sudbury: Jones & Bartlett Learning, 2011, 203–219. There are other studies that briefly consider Iraqi budgeting, although they tend to end with the CPA and focus on the provincial levels of government, as their authors were RTI contractors working in the provinces. Derick W. Brinkerhoff and James B. Mayfield, "Democratic Governance in Iraq? Progress and Peril in Performing State-Society Relations," *Public Administration and Development*, 25 (2005) 1, 59–73; Derick W. Brinkerhoff, "Building Local Governance in Iraq," in Louis A. Picard, Robert Groelsema, and Terry F. Buss (eds.), *Foreign Aid and Foreign Policy: Lessons for the Next Half-Century*, New York: M.E. Sharpe, 2008, 109–128. Two important Iraqi contributions that appeared late in the occupation are Humam Misconi, "Iraq's Capital Budget and Regional Development Fund: Review and Comments on Execution Capacity and Implications," *International Journal of Contemporary Iraqi Studies*, 2 (2008) 2, 271–291, and Ali Merza, "Oil Revenues, Public Expenditures and Saving/Stabilization Fund in Iraq," *International Journal of Contemporary Iraqi Studies*, 5 (2011) 1, 47–80. Iraqi budgeting is also noted in Eric Herring, "Variegated Neo-Liberalization, Human Development and Resistance: Iraq in Global Context," *International Journal of Contemporary Iraqi Studies*, 5 (2011) 3, 337–355.

This project attempts to fill these gaps in the literature, contribute to the assessments provided by SIGIR and other relevant oversight agencies, and offer a more comprehensive assessment of the Coalition's attempts to reconstruct Iraq's budgetary system as part of its overall state-building efforts. This study examines this state-building project through the prewar planning phase, the CPA's occupation, the 2004 transfer of sovereignty and the Iraqis' management of their own budget process, through to the withdrawal of American combat units in 2011. These contemporary events are best understood by first examining the origins of Iraqi budgeting in the Ottoman empire, English colonial budgeting, and the Ba'athist regime under Saddam Hussein. This is the institutional legacy that the Coalition attempted to change through the imposition of new rules and the introduction of various ministerial and provincial capacity development programs. In this way, the Coalition and relevant international donor organizations operated under the assumption that the exogenous influence of foreign assistance, enforced by military power and encouraged by aid conditionality, could produce meaningful institutional change.

IRAQI STATE BUILDING AS INSTITUTIONAL LAYERING

The building of Iraq's budgetary capabilities is viewed as a form of short- and long-term historical institutional change. The historical institutionalist perspective contends that political action occurs within specific historical contexts, where the sequencing of events influenced by existing power arrangements, incentive structures, rules, values, and ideologies helps explain political outcomes. The development of political institutions – rules, legal frameworks, procedures, agencies, and organizations – takes place over long time horizons, the origins of institutions matter, and path-dependent contingent historical choices become locked in and self-reinforcing.[32] Changes in the direction of these paths do occur, however. "Wars, revolutions, conquest, and natural disasters are the sources of discontinuous institutional change ... a rapid change in rules," Douglass North posited, but, nonetheless, "institutional change is overwhelmingly incremental."[33] The Coalition's invasion and rapid conquest of Iraq resulted in the quick "discontinuous institutional change" that removed Saddam Hussein and his Ba'ath Party from power. This scenario of dramatic regime change coincides with the view that the radical introduction of exogenous forces often acts as a prime mover of

---

[32] For definitions of "institutions," see, for example, Walter W. Powell and Paul J. DiMaggio, "Introduction," in Walter W. Powell and Paul J. DiMaggio (eds.), *The New Institutionalism in Organizational Analysis*, Chicago: University of Chicago Press, 1991, 8; B. Guy Peters, *Institutional Theory in Political Science: The 'New Institutionalism,'* London: Continuum, 1999, 18; Douglass C. North, *Institutions, Institutional Change and Economic Performance*, New York: Cambridge University Press, 1990, 4–5; and Sven Steinmo, "What Is Historical Institutionalism?" in Donatella Della Porta and Michael Keating (eds.), *Approaches in the Social Sciences*, Cambridge: Cambridge University Press, 2008, 118–138.

[33] North, *ibid.*, 89.

institutional change. These external events create critical junctures in the long-term development of institutions from one historical path to another. In this way, the existing equilibrium that maintains the *status quo* is punctuated, thus forcing change and the rise of new institutional dynamics.

Yet, North also notes that change is incremental and consequently long term in the making. Institutions are durable and "sticky." The forces that produce them are invested in their preservation and design them to be resistant to change.[34] This resilience means that change may first appear only on the surface of institutions. The effects of "a rapid change in rules" may not immediately alter the procedures and practices that exist at deeper levels within institutions with sufficient force to change organizational behaviors. More specifically in the case of Iraq, major changes in budgetary rules imposed by the CPA did not change all budgetary procedures and practices at the ministerial and provincial levels of government. Change in this instance occurred at a slower pace when it occurred at all, and it proved to be more difficult to achieve than the success of the briefly fought invasion. In addition to its temporal aspects, change is made more complex when the "responses to exogenous shocks are themselves informed by structures, identities, cleavages, programs, [and] agendas present in the prior period."[35] The impact of external forces by themselves is not sufficient to explain change; how endogenous actors and existing institutions react must also be accounted for when explaining the nature of institutional change.

James Mahoney and Kathleen Thelen lend clarity to these factors that influence the degree, pace, and characteristics of change by identifying four types of institutional transformation. These four types reflect the interaction between exogenous sources of change and the extent to which they are intended to alter existing endogenous institutions. Displacement occurs when existing rules are replaced, often abruptly, in their entirety and new rules are introduced. Conversion occurs when existing rules are reinterpreted and implemented in new ways. Drift occurs when rules remain intact, but changes in the broader social environment alter the impact of institutions. Finally, layering occurs when newly introduced rules are incorporated into existing ones, thus changing the influence of existing rules and subsequent behavior.

In each case, the dynamics between political actors, the relative power they exercise as veto players, and the rules and structures they confront explain the rate, extent, and consequences of institutional change. More specifically, when analyzing political change, Mahoney and Thelen write, "The foundation on which we build here is one that conceives institutions above all as distributional institutions laden with power implications. In our approach, institutions are fraught with tensions because they inevitably raise resource considerations and

---

[34] Paul Pierson, *Politics in Time: History, Institutions, and Social Analysis*, Princeton: Princeton University Press, 2004, 42–44.
[35] Karen Orren and Stephen Skowronek, *The Search for American Political Development*, New York: Cambridge University Press, 2004, 103.

invariably have distributional consequences. Any given set of rules or expectations – formal or informal – that patterns action will have unequal implications for resource allocation, and clearly many formal institutions are specifically intended to distribute resources to particular kinds of actors and not to others. This is true for precisely those institutions that mobilize significant and highly valued resources (e.g., most political and political-economic institutions)."[36] This view of political institutions as distributors of resources is particularly apt in examining the change occurring both in Iraq's budgetary institutions, which serve the function of prioritizing, allocating, and managing fiscal resources, and in the political actors who make claims on these resources.

Nonetheless, applying Mahoney and Thelen's four discrete types of change to the Iraqi case is complicated by the chronology of events that make up the invasion, occupation, transfer of sovereignty, and Iraq's increasingly independent exercise of power. Power relationships and rule structures in Iraq shift over time. The invasion and the CPA's occupation fit Mahoney and Thelen's description of change through displacement. The Coalition military dominated Saddam's forces and the CPA exercised executive law-making authority. In what Mahoney and Thelen would describe as a "radical shift," the CPA imposed new, overarching budget rules and drafted Iraq's 2003 and 2004 budgets. Yet, even during this period the Coalition attempted to graft these rules, processes, and procedures on to existing Ba'athist institutions, which, in turn, consisted of revisions and modifications of Ottoman and British budgetary institutions, in a manner more appropriately classified as institutional layering. In other words, the invasion resulted in some Coalition rule changes that proved to be abrupt, dramatic, significant, and displacing, but these efforts at making change also occurred "within the existing system by adding new rules on top of or alongside old ones."[37]

Modified Institutional Layering

This study sees these simultaneous sources of change as a modified form of institutional layering. Rule change in Iraq occurred in a more radical and dramatic manner than Mahoney and Thelen describe in layering, but these rules were often intended to be integrated into the existing system of rules rather than fully displacing them. Layering in the Iraqi case describes a process of amalgamating new rules with existing ones, and, more importantly, the efforts of making them effective in day-to-day budgeting. Where Mahoney and Thelen

---

[36] James Mahoney and Kathleen Thelen, "A Theory of Gradual Institutional Change," in James Mahoney and Kathleen Thelen (eds.), *Explaining Institutional Change: Ambiguity, Agency, and Power*, New York: Cambridge University Press, 2009, 8. Also see Kathleen Thelen, *How Institutions Evolve: The Political Economy of Skills in Germany, Britain, the United States, and Japan*, New York: Cambridge University Press, 2004, and Sven Steinmo, *The Evolution of Modern States: Sweden, Japan, and the United States*, New York: Cambridge University Press, 2010.

[37] *Ibid.*, 16.

focus on endogenous sources of change, in the case of Iraq rule change originates with exogenous sources. Moreover, where rules are sometimes regarded as undifferentiated and similar in design and effect, this project considers rules to be hierarchical and varied, differing in their origin and source, and ranging in their salience, visibility, and enforceability.[38] Major rules, such as the grand bargains of treaties and constitutions, are likely to be more salient, visible, and enforceable than minor rules, such as bureaucratic directives and informal agreements. Major rules in the case of Iraq included the CPA orders on Iraqi budgeting and the 17th Benchmark, which proved to be relatively salient, visible, and enforceable. In terms of visibility, for instance, the Coalition regarded these budgetary rules as significant instruments of power, to the point that President Bush and the Coalition's civilian and military leadership repeatedly and publicly identified them as overarching metrics for measuring success in Iraq. Nonetheless, the articulation and imposition of new rules alone does not constitute a panacea for creating predictable and preferred institutional change and successful state building. David Waldner, like North, warns that there are limits to institutional "engineering" and that institutions should be seen as indicators rather than causes of change.[39] Institutional change is contingent on the nature of existing institutions, their origins, and other antecedent conditions. Therefore, it is not surprising that efforts to create exogenously generated institutional change may spark resistance, friction, pushback, and conflict.

This understanding of institutional change raises important questions about how the Coalition attempted to transform – and with what effect – Iraq's budgetary institutions to meet international best practices and fulfill the American 17th Benchmark, from the period of prewar planning through to the draw-down of U.S. forces in 2011. What are the budgetary institutions the Coalition attempted to change, and what are the historical origins of these institutions? How did the Coalition plan to address Iraq's budgetary needs and engage its budgetary institutions, principally the ministries of Finance and Planning? What actions did the CPA take to change Iraq's budgetary laws and direct the formulation of Iraq's budgets? How did the Coalition attempt to modernize Iraqi budgetary practices and build Iraqi capacity to execute its budgets? What are the command and coordination issues that challenged the management of these capacity development programs? What role did contractors play in these programs? How did these capacity-building efforts serve the Coalition's overarching military strategy to reduce violence in Iraq? Which of Saddam's budgetary institutions changed and which proved impervious to change? Under what conditions did institutional change occur in Iraq? Answers to these questions are critically important for

---

[38] On the importance of visibility, see Matt Andrews, "Which Organizational Attributes Are Amenable to External Reform? An Empirical Study of African Public Financial Management," *International Public Management Journal*, 14 (2011) 2, 131–156.

[39] David Waldner, "The Limits of Institutional Engineering: Lessons from Iraq," *Special Report*, 222, United States Institute of Peace, May 2009.

understanding and evaluating the legacy of the Coalition's state-building and economic reconstruction efforts.

OWNERSHIP AND BUY-IN

In the literature on state building, foreign assistance, and peacekeeping, the presence of ownership, buy-in, and stake holding is regarded as a decisive condition for overcoming this conflict in the effort to create institutional change. As Clark Gibson, Krister Andersson, Elinor Ostrom, and Sikao Shivakumar point out, "The current emphasis on 'ownership' by nearly all major donors, highlights a tension present in bilateral and multilateral aid processes. This tension arises from the fact that the interests of donors and recipient governments usually do not fully coincide."[40] The route for donors to overcome these tensions may lie not only with gaining the recipient's assent that the aid in question reflects the recipient's best interests, but also that the aid stems from recipient preferences. According to Francis Fukuyama, "The majority of cases of successful state-building and institutional reform have occurred when a society has generated strong domestic demand for institutions and then created them out of whole cloth, imported them from the outside, or adapted foreign models to local conditions."[41] Likewise, "Insufficient domestic demand for institutions or institutional reform is the single most important obstacle to institutional development in poor countries." Externally created domestic demand for Fukuyama takes the form of direct political and military force or aid conditionality exercised by exogenous powers. Domestic demand takes place when endogenous actors come to value and take ownership of those institutions, regardless of the influence of exogenous pressures. Andrew Natsios views ownership as the first "and perhaps the most important" principle of reconstruction and development. "It is essential that the country's people view development as belonging to them and not to the donor community; development initiatives must meet the country's needs and its people's problems as they perceive them, not as distant policymakers imagine them."[42] In the absence of buy-in, the ability of endogenous actors to subvert, sabotage, and minimize the effectiveness of exogenously generated rules is significant. "Whatever the asymmetries of power," observes Miles Kahler, "local actors possess bargaining power and often use it effectively. Even in the aftermath of violent conflict and state collapse, local political actors and their response to the peacebuilding program

---

[40] Clark C. Gibson, Krister Andersson, Elinor Ostrom, and Sujai Shivakumar, *The Samaritan's Dilemma: The Political Economy of Development Aid*, New York: Cambridge University Press, 2005, 68.

[41] Francis Fukuyama, *State-Building: Governance and World Order in the 21st Century*, New York: Cornell University Press, 2004, 35.

[42] Andrew S. Natsios, "The Nine Principles of Reconstruction and Development," *Parameters*, 35 (2005) 3, 7.

will be critical to any explanation of the outcome ... each state building game will incorporate different players with different preferences and bargaining advantages."[43] Moreover, gaining this buy-in, a necessary condition of successful state building, as Jason Brownlee suggests, is more likely when true layering takes place, when "interventions have built upon local institutions and traditions."[44] When promoting economic reforms, the IMF cautions, "A key lesson is that local ownership of reforms is absolutely essential for success. Without local counterparts, capacity building will be much slower."[45] Ownership, in other words, serves as a critical determinant in institutional change and the creation of a new institutional path.

The theoretical and practical importance of the idea of ownership raises the question of why the Iraqis took ownership of some institutions and not others. How have the Iraqis taken ownership and employed the CPA's budgetary institutions since the 2004 transfer of power? On what occasions did the Iraqis buy into the Coalition's budgetary institutions, employ them, make them their own, perhaps modifying, revising, or reforming them, but at the same time retaining them? Although the nature of externally generated rules, in terms of their external salience, visibility, and enforceability, explains some of this ownership, what is the role of the endogenous conditions of Iraqi politics? Domestic demand and support for these major rules grew as they advanced the interests of existing and new claimants for budgetary resources. Institutional change provoked successful resistance when these rules were less salient, visible, and enforceable by external forces, and, most important, when they threatened the bureaucracy's core values, practices, and procedures. External coercion by itself did not produce ownership and institutional change. Thus, this project's thesis is that institutional change in Iraq, specifically change in Iraqi budgetary institutions, is a function of preexisting institutions, the introduction of new rules and processes that became routine and standardized in the short term through imposed and sustained action, and that indigenous ownership and political support proved to be decisive in sustaining these rules. Conversely, the durability and stickiness of preexisting institutions, the inability to impose and sustain new rules and processes, and the lack of indigenous ownership all acted to undermine institutional change.

OUTLINE OF THE BOOK

This project finds that various U.S. agencies did engage in preinvasion planning that addressed Iraqi budgeting and fiscal issues, as reflected in plans for the

---

[43] Miles Kahler, "Statebuilding after Afghanistan and Iraq," in Roland Paris and Timothy D. Sisk (eds.), *The Dilemmas of Statebuilding: Confronting the Contradictions of Postwar Peace Operations*, New York: Routledge, 2009, 292.

[44] Jason Brownlee, "Can America Nation-Build?" *World Politics*, 59 (2007) 2, 339.

[45] "IMF Draws on Postconflict Experience to Help Iraq with Currency and Banking Reforms," IMF *Survey*, 32, 19, November 3, 2003, 317.

future role of the Iraqi Ministries of Finance and Planning; Treasury successfully fulfilled its prewar planning short-term goals for Iraq's operational budget; the CPA successfully produced the 2003 and 2004 Iraqi budgets and created a lasting legal framework for Iraq's budgetary process but dramatically failed to develop credible institutions that promoted budgetary transparency and accountability; the 2004 transfer of sovereignty proved to be a critical juncture that challenged the Coalition's ability to gain access and influence in the Ministry of Finance and prevented Coalition attempts to terminate the Ministry of Planning; ministerial and provincial capacity development programs aimed at promoting Iraqi budgetary capacity and execution were significantly undermined by a lack of physical access to Iraqi ministries due to security conditions and Iraqi bureaucratic resistance, by contractor arrogance and poor performance, and by extensive coordination problems that are endemic to Coalition agencies and contractors; Iraqis support budgetary rules and institutions that serve their need to manage the internal allocation of resources and meet the demands of international organizations and donors, but the data used to confirm budget execution, and hence institutional capacity, are highly suspect; and current Iraqi budgetary institutions are a layered mix of legacy institutions from the Ottoman, English colonial, and Saddam eras, as well as legacy CPA institutions and new institutions being developed by the Iraqis themselves and encouraged by international organizations.

Chapter 2 of this study explores the origins of Iraqi budgetary practices, policies, and institutions. What are the budgetary institutions the Coalition attempted to change, and what the historical sources of these institutions? These Turkish, British, and Ba'athist institutions constitute the collective legacy the Coalition attempted to change through the imposition and layering of its own set of rules. The British invasion and occupation of Ottoman Mesopotamia resulted in decades-long state building that included taking command of Turkish public finances. This state-building activity introduced a parliamentary system of government, produced new budgetary laws, and established the Ministry of Finance. At the same time, the British layered this new edifice on to Ottoman institutions, such as the existing system of Turkish taxation. In the process of making these changes, British occupation authorities complained about the lack of adequate staff and the inability of the Iraqis to spend their budgets, problems echoed by Coalition officials nearly a century later. Saddam Hussein and the Ba'athist Party layered their own institutions on those created by the British by adding new budget laws, establishing the Ministry of Planning, and adopting Soviet-style planning. Saddam kept his budgetary institutions fragmented, stacked, and opaque as part of his system of maintaining and exercising power.

This chapter also begins the study of relevant Iraqi ministries. Ministries of finance serve as critical institutional actors in the literatures on nation and state building and the management of foreign assistance funds. Finance ministries lead in the formulation of economic and fiscal policy, coordinate the drafting of the budget with line ministries, shepherd the budget through the legislature, manage the allocation of funds to the ministries and provinces, and help oversee the effectiveness and legitimate use of government funds. An additional body of scholarship emphasizes the institutional function ministries of finance play as veto players in the creation of fiscal agendas and their role in channeling and disbursing donor funds that are allocated on-budget.[46] Strong ministries of finance, for example, are regarded as more effective managers of public funds and more capable of controlling national fiscal imbalances. This study focuses attention on the Iraqi Ministry of Finance because of its special role in the budgetary process and the setting of national economic policies. This study also examines the role of the Iraqi Ministry of Planning and Development Cooperation, which often contends with the Ministry of Finance for influence in the development of budgetary policy. The existence of this institutional legacy of Saddam's regime helps explain some of the complications inherent in Iraqi budgeting.

Chapter 3 examines American planning for what became an effort in reconstructing Iraqi budgetary institutions. How did the Coalition plan to address Iraq's budgetary needs and engage its budgetary institutions, principally the Ministries of Finance and Planning? Economic prewar planning for fiscal and monetary issues did exist and was centered in the Department of the Treasury. Strong personal relationships between Treasury's leadership, Secretary of State Condoleezza Rice, and Secretary of Defense Donald Rumsfeld furthered Treasury's authority in these matters. Among other sources, Treasury employed the State Department's "Future of Iraq Project" in its planning, which runs counter to the view that the "Project" made little or no difference in what later occurred in Iraq. The Project offered recommendations for currency issues, fiscal and monetary policy, and new responsibilities for relevant Iraqi ministries, including the Finance and Planning ministries. Under Saddam, Iraqi budgetary procedures, budgetary decisions, and the budget remained state secrets. Thus, American planners knew little or nothing about the organizational reporting relationships, functions, conditions, or capabilities of these ministries, or the operations of the Iraqi budgetary process. The relationship between Treasury and USAID, which also engaged in economic planning, played a significant role in the successes and failures of Coalition budgetary reconstruction. General Jay

[46] On the significance of finance ministries, see, for example, James D. Savage, "The Origins of Budgetary Preferences: The Dodge Line and the Balanced Budget Norm in Japan," *Administration & Society*, 34 (2002) 3, 261–284; Mark Hallerberg, *Domestic Budgets in a United Europe*, Ithaca, NY: Cornell University Press, 2004; John Wanna, Lotte Jensen, and Jouke de Vries (eds.), *Controlling Public Expenditure: The Changing Roles of Central Budget Agencies – Better Guardians?* Cheltenham: Edward Elgar, 2003; and Allen Schick, "Why Most Developing Countries Should Not Try New Zealand's Reforms," *The World Bank Research Observer*, 13 (1989) 1, 123–131; and, on disbursing donor funds, Clark C. Gibson, Krister Andersson, Elinor Ostrom, and Sujai Shivakumar, *The Samaritan's Dilemma: The Political Economy of Development Aid*, New York: Cambridge University Press, 2005, 69.

Garner attempted to exercise some coordination over this planning in the weeks leading up to the March 2003 invasion.

Chapter 4 focuses on the CPA's drafting of the 2003 and 2004 Iraqi budgets and the imposition of new budget rules. What actions did the CPA take to change Iraq's budgetary laws and direct the formulation of Iraq's budgets? Consistently understaffed and confronting the massive looting that devastated Iraq's ministries, the Treasury team deployed to Iraq initiated currency conversion and the payment of pensions and salaries. The CPA's funding of these payments suffered from an endemic lack of careful fiscal management of American appropriated funds as well as the Development Fund for Iraq, which contributed to Iraq's ongoing problems with corruption. In the absence of a functioning bureaucracy and budgetary process, a small international group of CPA personnel led by a retired U.S. Navy admiral drafted the 2003 and 2004 Iraqi budgets. Though limited in scope and programmatic detail, these served as the first publicly accessible Iraqi budgets since the Gulf War. The CPA's budgets reflected an activist fiscal policy inspired by American programs such as the Great Depression's Works Progress Authority and the need for a massive fiscal stimulus. Spending money quickly, whether American or Iraqi, overrode concerns for transparency, accountability, and basic cash management. The CPA issued rules covering numerous budgetary and financial management matters. These rules elevated the Ministry of Finance to the position it held during the British Mandate as the primary ministry responsible for developing Iraq's budgetary policies.

Chapters 5 and 6 survey the Coalition's various ministerial and provincial capacity development programs that attempted to bring Iraq's budgeting practices into compliance with international best practices and boost budget execution. How did the Coalition attempt to modernize Iraqi budgetary practices and build Iraqi capacity to execute their budgets? These chapters consider the dependency of American nation building and foreign assistance efforts upon contractors. Chapter 5 analyzes the USAID contract awarded to the firm BearingPoint to install a Financial Management Information System (FMIS) in the Ministry of Finance and throughout the Iraqi government. If successfully deployed, FMIS would automate Iraq's budget and accounting processes to ease budgetary formulation, strengthen accountability, and promote transparency. The computerized FMIS would replace the Iraqi bureaucracy's paper and pencil record keeping, and bring the government into compliance with the international best practices demanded by the Coalition and the international donor community. BearingPoint's inability to fulfill its contract points to the limits of relying on contractors to carry out assistance programs and the challenges of obtaining buy-in from aid recipients

Chapter 6 assesses the Coalition's many attempts to boost Iraqi budget execution. The 17th Benchmark and spending of the Iraqi budget became the leading metric for evaluating both the success of Coalition assistance programs and the overall effectiveness of the Iraqi government to build infrastructure and provide essential services. To meet the benchmark, the Coalition and various donors initiated a variety of capacity-building programs aimed at training Iraqi officials and administrators at the central and provincial levels of government in such administrative skills as procurement, contracting, and project management. Contractors conducted sometimes competing and sometimes complementary training and assistance programs. These included USAID's *Tatweer* and Economic Governance programs, Defense's Task Force on Business and Stability Operations, USAID's provincial capacity-building efforts through its Local Governance Program, and the State Department's Provincial Reconstruction Teams. Examining the administration and effectiveness of these programs offers insight into the challenges of coordinating and managing contractors, the variety of contractor training and assistance strategies at work in Iraq, the role metrics and data play in measuring programmatic effectiveness, and the impediments to gaining aid recipient buy-in.

Chapter 7 considers budgeting from the Iraqi perspective. How have the Iraqis employed and taken ownership of the CPA's budgetary institutions in the formulation and adoption of their budgets? The Iraqis took ownership of the CPA budgetary process after the 2004 transfer of power and employed it in the creation of the 2005 through 2011 budgets. This chapter argues that several conditions encouraged this ownership: The Iraqis retained the CPA's budgetary institutions because of the lasting presence of the occupation, the pressures of aid conditionality, the CPA's layering of their rules on to existing Iraqi institutions, the support of new budgetary claimants who accepted and benefited from these institutions, and the political and fiscal exigencies facing the Iraqis that deepened their reliance on the CPA's budgetary rules, practices, and procedures. These exigencies included wide swings in oil prices and consequently in the size of the government's budget deficits. Ownership of the process included demands made by budgetary claimants that the government adhere to the CPA's rules, as Iraqi parliamentarians reinforced Iraq's commitment to the process by creating oversight committees that mirrored those established by Iraqi parliamentarians during the British Mandate. The Iraqis worked to incorporate and layer elements of the CPA's rules on to their own institutions, and thus in the process enhanced the durability and stickiness of these CPA institutions.

Finally, Chapter 8 concludes this study by offering lessons from the Iraqi case in state building. Under what conditions did institutional change occur in Iraq? Exogenously generated change did take place, sometimes with positive outcomes that may be sustainable. In other cases, as in instances of ministerial capacity building, the Iraqis succeeded in blocking contractors from making changes in organizational practices and procedures. Iraqi willingness to take ownership of these externally driven rules proved to be decisive in explaining when institutional change occurred.

2

The Evolution of Iraqi Budgetary Institutions from the Ottomans and the British Mandate through Saddam

Practitioners commonly warn that those about to engage in state building should first come to know local history, culture, and institutions.[1] Through a deeper understanding of the preferences of those who are the presumed beneficiaries of such activities, the scope of the task is better comprehended, planning is enhanced, errors are potentially reduced, conflict with locals is minimized, and the possibilities of gaining local ownership and buy-in increased. The Americans who planned the invasion and occupation of Iraq, however, knew little or nothing about Iraqi budgetary institutions, their histories, or even their functions within the budgetary process, though they later made significant attempts to change Iraq's budgetary rules and the way these organizations worked and how they related to each other. Understanding the challenges the Coalition faced in attempting to make these institutional changes first requires an appreciation for the rootedness of these institutions in Iraqi history and politics.

When Coalition forces entered Iraq in March 2003, what were the Iraqi budgetary institutions they encountered? What were their origins, incentive structures, hierarchies, established power relationships, networks, procedures, and practices? These institutions included the legal framework governing the budgetary process and the organizational entities that exercised authority in formulating, approving, and managing the budget. These institutions originated with the Ottomans, the British occupation and Mandate, and the Ba'athist regime. These institutions were layered upon each other. Sometimes new rules, processes, and organizations abruptly displaced or were imposed on existing

[1] According to the World Bank, "The two most important rules to follow when dealing with developing countries or countries in transition are: (a) do no harm and (b) know your country. A task manager who is advising a government on improvements to the budget and financial management must first collect information on the current performance of budgetary and financial management systems in that country." *Public Expenditure Management Handbook*, Washington, DC: The World Bank, 1998, 95.

ones. Sometimes these new institutions incorporated or were added to existing institutions rather than fully displacing them. The Iraqis established their first Ministry of Finance during the Mandate, while the Ba'athists later added the Ministry of Planning to the institutions engaged in the budgetary process. In both cases these institutions served the broader political interests of their founders. This chapter examines this legacy of institution building, politics, and policy the Coalition encountered in its own efforts at state building in Iraq.

THE OTTOMANS AND THE BRITISH MANDATE

Iraq did possess formal budgetary rules and institutions prior to the American invasion, many dating from the country's pre-Saddam years. "Before the Saddam regime," declared a World Bank assessment of the Iraqi economy, "the budget system in Iraq was fairly efficient and robust."[2] The evolution of this fiscal system may first be traced to the Ottoman empire and the British occupation that stemmed from World War I.[3]

The Ottomans established an extensive system of taxes throughout the empire to finance its massive military and civil service, which the British discovered upon entering Iraq in 1914. The British described Ottoman Iraq's fiscal affairs as "complicated."[4] Reports sent to London by occupation officials repeatedly expressed surprise that the Turks maintained a separate revenue collection process, fully divorced from their spending units and "the executive authorities."[5] "The Turkish administrative system," said one report, "was thus one of watertight compartments, each in separate correspondence with a head departmental office at Constantinople."[6] This organizational structure made sense to the Turks, however, who sought to promote the twin objectives of centralizing political authority in Constantinople by dividing it at the provincial level, while employing Mesopotamia as a source of revenue extraction for the central government. The Turks created at least five independently administered revenue streams that, aside from the collection of general revenue land and agriculture taxes, were directed

---

[2] "Rebuilding Iraq: Economic Reform and Transition," Middle East Department, World Bank, Washington, DC, February 2006, 11.

[3] On this period, see Donald C. Blaisdell, *European Financial Control in the Ottoman Empire*, New York: Columbia University Press, 1929; Sevket Pamuk, "The Evolution of Fiscal Institutions in the Ottoman Empire," Unpublished manuscript, 2002; Metin M. Cosgel, "Efficiency and Continuity in Public Finance: The Ottoman System of Taxation," *International Journal of Middle East Studies*, 37 (2005) 4, 567–586; Linda T. Darling, "Public Finances: The Role of the Ottoman Centre," in Suraiya N. Faroqhi (ed.), *The Cambridge History of Turkey, Volume 3: The Later Ottoman Empire, 1603–1839*, Cambridge: Cambridge University Press, 2006; and Phebe Marr, *The Modern History of Iraq*, Boulder, CO: Westview Press, 2012.

[4] *Iraq Administrative Reports 1914–1932, Volume 1, 1914–1918*, Cambridge: Cambridge Archive Editions, 1992, 11.

[5] *Ibid.*, 14.

[6] *Iraq Administrative Reports 1914–1932, Volume 5, 1920*, Cambridge: Cambridge Archive Editions, 1992, 8.

toward the Ottoman Ministry of Finance. These taxes included the collection of some twenty petty taxes and customs revenues for the European-operated Ottoman Public Debt Administration, which managed debt payments to European creditors, and quarantine fees collected by the health service on both the living and the dead. An extensive revenue-generating apparatus extended from the Ministry of Finance down through the provincial *vilayet*, governed by a *vali* who was assisted by a *defterdar*, the provincial financial officer, to the lowest levels of tax collection, the *mukhtariyah*, the village administered by a *mukhtar*. The Turks gathered revenues through direct tax collections made by *tahsildars* and the use of *multezim* or tax farmers, a device the British disdained as a sign of "weak government." The Turks imposed a host of direct and indirect taxes on its agrarian economy. They valued agricultural goods and products by counting trees, livestock, and produce, and they required various licenses, fees, and duties. To reduce tribal influence and land holding, the Turks demanded that individual leases be required to demonstrate property ownership, leases that in turn could be taxed. Midhad Pasha, who served as *vali* of Baghdad in 1869, introduced the *jarib* tax, a method of valuing land based on averaging the prior five years of land value by the size of the property holding, with a *jarib* constituting slightly less than an acre of land. The Turks succeeded in breaking a string of budget deficits and created surpluses for two or three fiscal years by raising taxes prior to the occupation. As one British report noted, "The Turkish Administration was, like other things Turkish, excellent in theory, ruined in practice. The idea of the Turks was to tax everything; at least everything on which they could lay their hands. Only the air that the unfortunate dweller in Iraq breathed was free from taxation."[7] Despite this assertion, the British by their own admission left the Turkish tax system fundamentally intact, but they did alter the administrative apparatus that generated and managed Iraq's fiscal system.[8]

The Ottoman budgetary practices the British found in Iraq reflected the policies of the last sultan, Abdulhamid II (1842–1918), who ruled from 1876 to 1909. The Ottoman government borrowed heavily from European sources beginning in 1854, following the Crimean War, but defaulted on its loans in 1875. This act forced the government to make costly repayments that by 1881 resulted in Abdulhamid turning over a quarter of the government's revenues to the Ottoman Public Debt Administration. To prevent a second default, an event that Abdulhamid believed would mean the end of the empire, the Sultan tightened his grip on the management of public finances while pursuing a policy of

---

[7] *Ibid.*, 605.

[8] For example, as late as 1923–1924, the British noted that "The land revenue system [by which is here meant the principles on which the assessment of the government share is made] of Iraq to-day is very much the same as the Turkish system in force in these territories in 1911." Elsewhere: "During the year 1923 the Government passed a law known as the Property Tax Law, which provided for a tax of 10 percent on the rental value of properties situated within municipal areas. This tax was in effect the old Turkish Vergo." *Iraq Administrative Reports 1914–1932, Volume 7, 1920–1924*, Cambridge: Cambridge Archive Editions, 1992, 649, 654.

spending restraint, particularly in the provinces. Although the *vali* exercised administrative authority over the provinces, the *defterdar* and other local public financial officials reported directly to Constantinople. As he centralized fiscal control, the Sultan restricted the use of government funds in Mesopotamia primarily to the maintenance of public order. Some two-thirds of Ottoman spending in the Baghdad, Basra, and Mosul provinces funded military and security forces.[9] Abdulhamid nevertheless recognized that Mesopotamia desperately suffered from massive infrastructure needs and the lack of all forms of public services. During his reign, the Sultan received numerous evaluations of Mesopotamia's economic and political potential. The recommendations that followed regularly recommended the construction of various irrigation, drainage, waterway, bridge, and railway projects. The Sultan, however, rejected these expensive proposals in the name of fiscal restraint. Abdulhamid's reluctance to invest and spend large sums of money in Mesopotamia was also influenced by numerous reports of corruption, bribery, and the routine mismanagement of public funds, including the failure to pay salaries, occurring in the provinces.[10]

The British Occupation and Mandate, 1914–1932

Though the battle with Turkish forces for control of Iraq continued into 1918, in 1915 the British began centralizing revenue management and collection in the territories they controlled through an all-powerful Revenue Administration, sometimes called the Revenue Board. This Board effectively served as the occupation's *de facto* ministry of finance. As the British described the establishment of the unit, "the history of administrative development is in fact the story of the gradual formation of departments as opportunity and the necessities of the case demanded and as officers and staff became available."[11] The necessity of the case compelled the British to centralize public finances, pulling together and in some cases ending the various revenue streams, while breaking through the Ottomans' compartmentalized bureaucracy. The Board's duties included managing revenue collection, formulating budgets, controlling expenditures, and keeping accounts. The Board distributed finance officials throughout the retained Ottoman administrative arrangement of provinces, districts, subdivisions, and villages to oversee the tax collection services and reconcile revenue and expenditures. During the four years following the beginning of the occupation, 1915–1919, the British ran increasingly large budget surpluses, as revenues skyrocketed by more than 900 percent. At the same time, the British acknowledged that their "most conspicuous failure of the first four years is the relatively large surplus regularly accruing" due to their

[9] Gokhan Cetinsaya, *Ottoman Administration of Iraq, 1890–1980*, New York: Routledge, 2006, 17.
[10] Ibid, 59–60. Also see Stephen Hemsley Longrigg, *Four Centuries of Modern Iraq*, Beirut: Lebanon Bookshop, 1968, 298–324.
[11] *Iraq Administrative Reports 1914–1932, Volume 5, 1920*, Cambridge: Cambridge Archive Editions, 1992, 46.

inability to spend the funds provided in the budget.[12] Despite extensive and demonstrable social and economic needs and the desire to rebuild Iraq's wartorn infrastructure, the British lacked the capacity to execute their budgets, other than to make payments to civil officials and maintain the operations of government. One report concluded that "At first, undoubtedly the principal factor conducive to underspending was lack of staff."[13] The British viewed the occupation as primarily a military affair, and those assigned to Iraq overwhelmingly consisted of military personnel who lacked experience in civil administration and the development of public works projects. The foreign officers and other civilians who did serve in Iraq found themselves dependent on the military for transport and communications. To make up the difference in staffing, the British reluctantly relied on Ottoman officials to retain many of their positions in the bureaucracy, who during the British invasion destroyed virtually all important government documents. Those documents that remained, and the new ones generated by the occupation government, required translation between English, Turkish, and Arabic. Consequently, "several normal functions of civil government thus remained in abeyance."[14] The year 1920 proved to be fiscally difficult. That year witnessed uprisings throughout Iraq against the British, which imperiled tax collections, while the government nearly tripled spending, particularly for public works, irrigation, transportation, and telegraph operations. Finally, by 1920, the British established the position of Civil Commissioner, which exercised overall control of Iraq's fiscal activities. The Commissioner, in turn, worked through a Financial Secretary, a Revenue Secretary, and a Customs Secretary. The Financial Secretariat managed the budget, developed financial regulations, prepared accounts, and administered the treasury. The Revenues Secretariat managed all revenues except for customs duties, which fell under the direction of the Customs Secretariat.

Creating the Iraqi Ministry of Finance

The formal transition from British rule to that of King Faisal I and the Hashemite monarchy began in 1921. Upon his accession as king, Faisal formed a cabinet on September 10 that included the position of minister of finance. This date, therefore, marks the founding of the modern Iraqi Ministry of Finance that emerged from the British Financial Secretariat. Faisal appointed Susan Effendi Haskil as the first minister, a man who the British viewed as an exceptional choice for the job, respected, well-versed in the financial systems of different countries, practical, with a firm grasp of financial principles.[15] British approval of Faisal's

---

[12] *Iraq Administrative Reports 1914–1932, Volume 5, 1920*, Cambridge: Cambridge Archive Editions, 1992, 121.

[13] *Ibid.*, 122.

[14] *Ibid.*

[15] *Iraq Administrative Reports 1914–1932, Volume 7, 1920–1924*, Cambridge: Cambridge Archive Editions, 1992, 230.

choice was very important, as England retained extensive influence in Iraq
though the League of Nations' covenant that established Britain's Mandate in
Iraq, and by way of provisions granting the British twenty-five years of rights in
the treaty signed in 1922 between Great Britain and Iraq. These rights included
maintaining their advisers in place throughout the Iraqi bureaucracy, including
the new finance ministry. The treaty's Article 104 declared that the king "will
fully consult with the High Commissioner on what is conducive to a sound
financial and fiscal policy and will insure the stability and good organization of
the finances of the Iraq government so long as that government is under financial
obligations to the government of His Britannic Majesty."[16] The British conceded
in a report to London in 1932 that "throughout this period general control
within the Ministry was exercised by British officials," who imported numerous
Indians to staff them.[17] The Finance Ministry's leadership group and scope of
responsibilities quickly grew from the minister, his British adviser, a secretary,
and two assistant secretaries, one of whom managed the budget with the other
managing financial rules and regulations. Soon, another assistant secretary was
assigned oversight of the Department of Customs and Duties, as this responsibility was transferred to the Finance Ministry from the Customs Secretariat, and
then two more secretaries administered land revenues.

The new Iraqi government also provided for an Accounts and Audit
Department run by an Accountant-General, who managed all of the government's
accounting activities. However, this agency's audits and transformation of
accounts into Arabic were delayed for more than a year because of the inability
of the British to obtain seconded staff from India to support the new unit. Due to
these various startup costs, the Ministry of Finance did not present its first budget
to the Council of State until September 1922, halfway through the fiscal year. To
coordinate public finances, Faisal established a ministerial Economies Committee
that examined the proposed budget to find additional revenues and reduce expenditures in order to balance the budget. The new Iraqi Parliament, which consisted
of a Senate and a Chamber of Deputies, created its own standing committees to
consider legislation. The Finance Committee, in particular, exercised review over
budgetary estimates, with the function of recommending reductions in spending.
The Finance Committee often supported the Finance Ministry's budgets that
imposed budgetary restrictions on the overall government. According to British

---

[16] Henry A. Foster, *The Making of Modern Iraq: A Product of World Forces*, Norman: University of
   Oklahoma Press, 1935, 192.
[17] *Iraq Administrative Reports 1914–1932, Volume 10, 1931–1932*, Cambridge: Cambridge
   Archive Editions, 1992, 85. Stansfield writes, "But British influence continued in Iraq. The
   British-nominated Faisal was still the monarch and presided over a state structured designed
   and instructed by British advisers. The British government also leased two bases for its military,
   and, as part of the treaty negotiations, retained a right to use all Iraqi facilities. British advisers and
   experts also remained in place in Iraq, located at key and sensitive points throughout Iraq's civil
   and military apparatus.... This tying of Iraq to Britain would last, according to the terms of the
   treaty, 25 years." Gareth Stansfield, *Iraq*, Cambridge: Polity Press, 2007, 49.

reports, the majority of parliamentary activity often turned to public finance. Commenting on the 1932 parliamentary term, one report declared that "The Budget was as usual the main issue of the session."

The rule whereby the annual estimates are first referred for examination to a Standing Committee and are then again debated in detail by the Chamber provides an opportunity for criticism of the whole work of Government. Deputies can ventilate their grievances against particular departments by proposing their abolition or the reduction of money allotted to them, and much time in each session is in consequence taken up by the Budget debates.[18]

Both ministerial and parliamentary consideration of the budget could, and did, delay the budget's final passage and execution. The ministers did not submit the Depression-era 1930 budget, for example, to Parliament until half way through the fiscal year.

In 1923, the finance minister gained the additional authority of serving as president of the Cadre Commission, which reviewed the employment conditions, pay grades, and rates of the Iraqi civil service. In 1924, the finance minister approved a new set of accounting regulations developed by the Accountant-General, regulations that guaranteed the Finance Ministry the right to issue regulations governing all financial transactions between government ministries and units. At the urging of the British in 1925, the Iraqis adopted an income tax in 1927, which resulted in the establishment of a Department of Income Tax, also placed under the Ministry of Finance.[19] "The financial control of public administration is now by law vested in the Finance Ministry," the British reported. "The Accountant-General is the Ministry's agent for the control of all public accounts."[20] The Iraqis, with British encouragement, also introduced the dinar in 1932. By 1932, the Iraqis derived primary revenues from, in descending order of importance, customs duties (36.5 percent), agricultural produce (22.3 percent), excise taxes that included domestic oil sales (9 percent), livestock taxes (7 percent), stamp duties (2.7 percent), and property taxes (2.5 percent). Oil royalties provided

---

[18] *Iraq Administrative Reports 1914–1932, Volume 10, 1931–1932*, Cambridge: Cambridge Archive Editions, 1992, 469.

[19] An agreement reached between Iraq and Britain in 1924 obligated the Iraqis to take over budgetary responsibility for the security forces. To meet this obligation, in 1925 the Young-Vernon report offered numerous suggestions for cutting spending and raising revenues, including the income tax, all in an effort to bring the Iraqis into fiscal balance. These recommendations reduced the 1925–1926 budget deficit from £1,432,000 to £367,000. On the Young-Vernon report, see Geoff Burrows and Phillip E. Cobban, "Financial Nation-Building in Iraq 1920–32," June 2010, University of Melbourne, unpublished paper. The British acknowledged that "the law was modeled on the British law and was and still is criticized on the ground of its unsuitability for Iraq." *Iraq Administrative Reports 1914–1932, Volume 10, 1931–1932*, Cambridge: Cambridge Archive Editions, 1992, 89.

[20] *Iraq Administrative Reports 1914–1932, Volume 7, 1920–1924*, Cambridge: Cambridge Archive Editions, 1992, 636.

just .3 percent of revenues.[21] Although the British discovered large reserves of oil near Kirkuk in 1927, the exporting of oil did not begin until 1934.[22] Nevertheless, the British Oil Development Company and the Iraq Petroleum Company began making annual payments of £595,000 to the Iraqi treasury in 1933, which may be regarded as Iraq's birth as a petro state. As the British happily reported, "The Government's cash reserves were therefore large and the country's financial position has been completely rehabilitated. With no capital debt, no floating debt, and a substantial Treasury balance, the Iraqi Government is in a thoroughly healthy financial position, a happy state of affairs very largely due to oil."[23]

The General Accounts Procedure Law Number 28 of 1940

In 1940, under the Hashemite monarchy, the Iraqis codified the accumulated duties of the Finance Ministry and the formulation of the government's budget in the "General Accounts Procedure Law Number 28 of 1940."[24] This law served as the foundation for this period of Iraqi history, and, importantly, it also provided the initial fiscal legal framework for Saddam Hussein's government. Reflecting the fiscal and parliamentary systems inspired by the British, the law outlined the standards for budget preparation, set the government's accounting rules and procedures, clarified the development of audit responsibilities, and established a fiscal year beginning on April 1 and ending on March 31, which differed slightly from the Turks' fiscal year that started on March 14. The law, furthermore, continued the centralization of budget formulation and management in the Ministry of Finance promoted by the British. The budgetary process began with the Finance Ministry collecting the line ministries' revenue and spending estimates by the end of October, evaluating and adjusting them, preparing the overall General Budget of the State, forwarding the budget to the Council of Ministers for study, following which it would be submitted to Parliament for approval.

The law charged the finance minister with maintaining the government's revenue and expenditure accounts. No expenditures could be disbursed from the Treasury without the finance minister's approval, except for "secret and propaganda expenses," while revenues could only be received or collected with receipt vouchers authorized by the minister.[25] Much of the law prescribed the control and auditing of funds, in part by repealing rules still in force, such as the Ottoman General Accounts Procedure Law of 1907. The 1940 law vested

---

[21] *Iraq Administrative Reports 1914–1932, Volume 10, 1931–1932*, Cambridge: Cambridge Archive Editions, 1992, 88.

[22] Charles Tripp, *A History of Iraq*, New York: Cambridge University Press, 2007, 69.

[23] *Iraq Administrative Reports 1914–1932, Volume 10, 1931–1932*, Cambridge: Cambridge Archive Editions, 1992, 500.

[24] "General Accounts Procedure Law, No. 28 of 1940," *Iraq Government Gazette*, Directorate General of Propaganda, Ministry of Interior, Baghdad, September 28, 1941, No. 39.

[25] *Ibid.*, 541.

the finance minister with overall responsibility for all government accounts and provided for an Accounts Board that would draft accounting laws and regulations to ensure the proper handling of public funds. The legislation established extensive checks in reporting requirements, with every payment voucher requiring counter-signatures and all accounts audited at the end of the fiscal year. To ensure the safe keeping of government assets, the law declared that an official who handled funds would be "allotted an iron safe, in which he shall keep any money and anything in the nature of money that he receives by virtue of his post."[26]

The Development Board, 1950–1959

Perhaps the most significant institutional development in Iraqi budgeting before the rise of the Ba'athist Party was the creation of the Development Board. As a result of favorable new oil agreements reached with the Iraq Petroleum Company in 1951, oil revenues grew from 29 million dinars in 1950 to 100 million dinars by 1957. To manage and invest these funds, the Iraqis established the Development Board in 1950 to allocate these resources in a politically insulated fashion, presumably free from influence and corruption. The Board membership consisted of the prime minister, the minister of finance, and six "experts, who included an American and Britain, staffed by an independent secretariat." In 1953, to aid in development decisions, the Iraqis set up a Ministry of Development, whose minister was added to the Board. From 1952 through 1959, the Board allocated 70 percent of Iraq's oil revenues, with the remainder supporting ministerial spending. This arrangement separated the allocation of these oil funds from other capital and operating expenditures, leaving the Board to spend its money principally on large-scale economic development infrastructure projects, while the line ministries supported the operational and infrastructure budgets associated with ongoing social and welfare funding. Coordination problems ensued between the Board's spending and that of the ministries; complaints were raised about the absence of Board spending for the government's education, housing, and health activities, as well as about the limited effect of the Board's spending on the immediate needs of the people. Throughout this period, the Board was hindered in its ability to spend its capital budgets because of the time required to create plans for specific projects, hire firms to construct these long-term infrastructure projects, and build the administrative capacity to manage this entire process. Nonetheless, between 1951 and 1958, the Board spent an estimated 229 million dinars directly on capital projects, and the rate of spending doubled during this period, rising to 74 million dinars in 1957. Approximately half of these funds supported building and communication, a third were invested in the agricultural sector, and the remaining amount was allocated to industry.[27] This infusion of government

---

[26] *Ibid.*, 543.
[27] Penrose, 173, 181.

expenditures produced mixed results; as one evaluation concluded, "The large oil revenues of Iraq made development possible, but they did not ensure it, and apart from the control of the great rivers, which eliminated the ravages of floods, and the creation of a variety of public utility and industrial projects, there was little spectacular change in the economic condition of the country."[28]

Summary

The British built their parliamentary vision for Iraq on top of the Ottoman imperial edifice that dominated Mesopotamia for hundreds of years. Turkish governance minimized provincial expenditures even as it developed a complex, compartmentalized system of revenue extraction designed to support Constantinople. The British found many aspects of Ottoman public finance archaic, inefficient, and corrupt. They worked to replace it with a system of parliamentary form and far greater accountability, albeit a system that they managed under their League of Nations' mandate. The British, nevertheless, necessarily maintained much of the Turks' finances due to the bureaucratic and administrative limits of their occupation. The Hashemite monarchy layered its own institution on top of those of the British in the form of the Development Board, which in its own way acted as a precursor to the Ministry of Planning. In the coming years, the Ba'athists would take their turn at layering Iraq's budgetary and fiscal institutions.

BA'ATHIST BUDGETING

The Ba'ath Party's rise to power in 1968 and Saddam's emergence as president in 1979 are reflected in economic policies that promoted centralized political control, economic rewards and patronage to maintain regime support, and economic nationalism. To fulfill these policy goals, the Iraqis often turned to the Soviet Union as a counter to the West in foreign and economic affairs. The Iraqis, for example, engaged the Soviets in the development of their oil fields to offset the bargaining influence of the Iraq Petroleum Company, in the successful effort to gain control over Iraqi oil resources.[29] The use of centralized economic planning and budgeting reflected some western approaches to economic growth in the developing world as promoted by the United Nations, but the economic policies and revolutionary ideology of the Soviet Union heavily influenced Iraq's use of these methods.[30] This pragmatic identification with the Soviets and

---

[28] *Ibid.*, 191.

[29] Tripp, 200.

[30] On the importance of planning for economic development in a socialist and revolutionary context, consider Oskar Lange's statement: "In the socialist countries and in the countries following a national revolutionary pattern we plan economic development, because economic development would not, under historic conditions existent, take place by itself automatically.

socialism extended to the government's budgetary process, which in its own way furthered Saddam's personal rule and one-party control over Iraq.

Designed to serve Saddam Hussein's dictatorship, Iraq's budgetary process acted to promote political and administrative control through the strategic distribution of fiscal resources. The budgetary system itself rested on a system of parallel hierarchical decision making, institutional compartmentalization, extreme secrecy, and Soviet-style budgetary planning. A number of ministries and allied units participated in budgetary decisions, but ultimately Saddam, directly and through his immediate offices, determined the nature of Iraqi budgetary and economic policies. Moreover, significant budgetary activity that funded prohibited military equipment purchases occurred though a supplementary budgetary procedure that Saddam separated from the normal process.

Saddam's Ministry of Finance and the Ministry of Planning

Under the nominal budget process that emerged from these laws and the evolution of politics during Saddam's regime, the Ministry of Finance and the Ministry of Planning directed the development of the budget. Operating under a January through December fiscal year, the Finance Ministry initiated the process by way of a June message from the finance minister to the various spending ministries that they provide the Finance Ministry with their operational budget requests by November. These requests were submitted to the Finance Ministry's Budget Office, which worked with the ministries to reach mutually acceptable programmatic expenditures. Included in these expenditures were a portion of the budgets for the Ministry of Defense and the Military Industrialization Corporation; the Presidential *Diwan*, Saddam's executive office and chief advisory council, approved the remainder of their funds. Finance Minister Hikmat Mizban Ibrahim al-Azzawi, who served in that position from 1995 through 2003, resolved differences at the ministerial level that could not be resolved by the Finance Ministry and ministerial staff. The sum of these ministerial requests constituted Iraq's regular General Government budget. These programs amounted to probably less than half of the government's expenditures, as the Finance Ministry exercised its authority only over Iraq's operational spending.

Consequently it must be planned." Oskar Lange, "Planning Economic Development," in Gerald M. Meier, *Leading Issues in Economic Development*, New York: Oxford University Press, 1976, 804. On differences between planning in capitalist, socialist, and mixed economies, see Michael P. Todaro, *Development Planning: Models and Methods*, Nairobi: Oxford University Press, 1983, and Albert O. Hirschman, *The Strategy of Economic Development*, New York: W.W. Norton, 1978. On Soviet budgeting and planning, see R. W. Davies, *The Development of the Soviet Budgetary System*, New York: Cambridge University Press, 1958; Abram Bergson, *The Economics of Soviet Planning*, New Haven: Yale University Press, 1964; Fyodor I. Kushnirsky, *Soviet Economic Planning, 1965–1980*, Boulder, CO: Westview Press, 1982; and Donna Bahry, *Outside Moscow: Power, Politics, and Budgetary Politics in the Soviet Republics*, New York: Columbia University Press, 1987.

At least during the 1970s and 1980s, Iraq divided its budget into eight "sectors." The General Authorities sector included the Presidency of the National Council, the Financial Monitoring Administration, the Foreign Affairs and Interior Ministries, Local Authority, and the departments of Justice and the Self-Ruled Region. The National Defense sector covered the Ministry of Defense. The Education, Higher Education, and Scientific Research sector encompassed the Ministry of Education and the Council on Scientific Research. The Information and Culture Services sector included the Ministry of Information and Culture. The Social Services sector covered the Ministries of Labor and Social Services, Youth, and Religious Endowments and Religious Affairs. The Health Services sector included the Ministry of Health. The broad Economic Affairs sector incorporated the Ministries of Agriculture and Agrarian Reform, Industry and Minerals, Oil, Transportation, Communications, Housing, Irrigation, and Trade and Planning. Finally, the Financial Affairs sector included the Finance Ministry and the Central Bank.

Meanwhile, planning and the Ministry of Planning grew in size and importance under the Ba'athists. Soon after the overthrow of King Faisal II, the revolutionary government disbanded the Development Board and in 1959 replaced it with a Ministry of Planning. The Iraqis' turn to a planning ministry stemmed in part from events taking place in Nasser's Egypt, where the Egyptians established their own planning mechanisms following their revolution of 1952 to create a socialist centrally planned economy. The Ba'athists, in turn, received assistance in the development of central planning from the Polish government.[31] The expansion of the Planning Ministry's staff from 639 in 1968 to 2,932 in 1976 reflected its growing influence. By the time of the 1970–1975 five-year plan, the ministry succeeded in adding to its staff numerous planners, economists, statisticians, and engineers, many of whom had been trained abroad, to engage in "scientific" and "comprehensive" planning that employed input-output calculations and economic modeling to develop Iraq's economy. According to Jawad Hashim, the Minister of Planning, the plan incorporated "investments, consumption, production, employment, exports, imports and other economic activities so as to achieve the defined economic and social targets. For the first time, this plan included a set of coordinated monetary, fiscal and trade policies."[32] The plan provided specified targets for Iraq's economic sectors that would be implemented through the government's control over nearly all the major productive units in the economy, including its state-owned

---

[31] Ronald W. Johnson and Ricardo Silva-Morales, "Budgeting Under Resource Abundance and Hesitant Steps to Decentralized Investment Planning and Budgeting in Iraq," in Charles E. Menifield (ed.), *Comparative Budgeting: A Global Perspective*, Sudbury: Jones & Bartlett Learning, 2011, 203–219.

[32] Penrose, 478. See Penrose, 252, on the influence of the Egyptians and the establishment of the Ministry of Planning. On the role of the Planning Ministry and the lack of success of the various plans, see chapters 10 and 18. This study points to the general deficiencies of the Iraqi bureaucracy and its ability to implement their plans.

enterprises, with substantial growth and government investment spending planned to promote the oil, mining, and manufacturing sectors.

As part of this planning process that continued on in future plans, for example, the Planning Ministry issued guidelines in 1984 for the "Fundamentals for the Technical and Economic Feasibility Studies and the Later Evaluation of Development Projects." The Ministry reissued these guidelines in 1990 and continued to distribute them as late as 2010 to the various spending ministries and independent directorates. These guidelines outlined the internal decision-making process the ministries needed to conduct for the selection of projects, and the information about the proposed projects the ministries needed to submit to the Planning Ministry. Projects were divided into two broad categories, those that offered "tangible economic returns," such as oil, energy, agriculture, and transportation projects, and those with "intangible economic returns," including hospitals, schools, and all government buildings. Project feasibility guidelines were further delineated into six major sectors: industrial; agriculture; irrigation, reformation, dams, and reservoirs; transportation; "tangible returns" service projects, including housing, sewage, hotels, and shopping centers; and service projects with intangible returns. Ministries were required to produce elaborately detailed information in support of their project requests. For irrigation and agriculture water projects, the Planning Ministry demanded of the spending ministries thirteen separate areas of information on the current condition of water resources, crops, the nature of the population distribution and workforce, climate, project management, project execution, and extensive cost analysis, including the amount of foreign currency required to finance these projects. Finally, the guidelines identified the criteria used for evaluating the project. These criteria focused heavily on such financial considerations as the return on investment, available foreign currency liquidity, the time required to recoup the investment, and the project's net deducted current value. These proposed projects were next evaluated by the Planning Ministry in consultation with the spending ministries and were then prioritized by the Planning Ministry for inclusion in the capital budget. Numerous other regulations existed for the remaining aspects of the management and financing of these projects, including accounting guidelines for the ministries, contractors, "socialist sector" units, and the banks for the handling and disbursement of funds, once the projects had been approved and their implementation had begun.

Both the Planning Ministry and this form of planning phased in and out during Saddam's regime. The government suspended much of its long-term economic planning due to the stresses and economic uncertainties during the 1980s and 1990s due principally to the Iran-Iraq and Gulf wars.[33] Saddam

---

[33] For descriptions of this period, see, for example, Amatzia Baram, *Building Toward Crisis: Saddam Husayn's Strategy for Survival*, Washington, DC: Washington Institute for Near East Policy, Paper 47, 1998, and Kamil A. Mahdi (ed.), *Iraq's Economic Predicament*, Reading, UK: Garnet Publishing Ltd., 2002.

disbanded the Planning Ministry in November 1994, substituting the Planning Commission in its place. With the goal of improving the allocation of capital resources in order to promote Iraq's economic growth, Saddam reinstituted the five- and ten-year plans in 2001 and reestablished the Planning Ministry in 2002. Saddam named Abd al-Mun'im al-Khattab, the director of the Planning Commission, as the minister of planning. The Ministry of Planning's mandate called for it to develop the government's short- and long-term capital budgets and plans, particularly with the assistance of the ministries of Defense, Oil, Industry, and Agriculture. As with the Finance Ministry and the development of the operational budget, the various ministries submitted their capital project requests to the Planning Ministry for inclusion in the General Government budget.[34]

These five- and ten-year plans were made in consultation with the Economic Affairs Committee. Established by Saddam in 1995, the Economic Affairs Committee exercised broad influence over Iraqi economic policy, including budgetary and fiscal policy, monetary policy, and the management of currency reserves. The finance minister chaired the Economic Affairs Committee, whose membership included the ministers of Agriculture, Industry and Minerals, Oil, Planning, and Trade, as well as the governor of the Central Bank of Iraq. After the Finance and Planning ministries drafted their respective sections of the General Government budget, they submitted their proposals to the committee for approval, after which the budget was sent to the Council of Ministers, then to the Revolutionary Command Council, and then to Saddam for his signature. The Economic Affairs Committee's influence extended beyond the General Government budget. Its Foreign Currency Disbursement Committee reviewed the status of the Central Bank's currency holdings and various ministries' foreign currency requests. Approving these requests depended on the success of Iraq's ability to obtain such currency, often through illegal methods, and thus not counted as revenues in the ministerial budgets.

At the presidential level, budgetary issues, except for those of the various intelligence and secret police organizations that required Saddam's attention and signature, were channeled through his Presidential Office, which consisted of the Presidential Secretariat and the Presidential *Diwan*. Saddam established the *Diwan* in 1979 to provide research and administrative support, and it, in turn, included a Financial Accounts Department. This department prepared the budget's final review for Saddam's approval on all budgetary decisions and budgetary allocations within the ministries, including ministerial requests for supplemental funds outside of the annual budgetary process. Most important, the department staffed Saddam for his approval of the intelligence and security budgets, including those for the Iraq Intelligence Service, the Special Security Organization, the

Iraq Atomic Energy Commission, the Military Industrialization Corporation, the Directorate of General Military Intelligence, and the Directorate of General Security. The *Diwan* also reviewed portions of the Ministry of Defense and the Military Industrialization Corporation budgets, which were partially funded though the Ministry of Finance and the Economic Affairs Committee's budget review process. The budgets for these various intelligence and security agencies, as well as for the *Diwan* and the Secretariat, were "black boxed" and excluded from the General Government budget.[35]

Another participant in this process, the National Security Council, reviewed and made recommendations on these black boxed budgets to Saddam through its consideration of intelligence, security, and military affairs. Members of the National Security Council included Iraq's vice president Izzat Ibrahim al-Duri, who chaired the Council and was the chief of the Presidential Secretariat; Saddam's son Qussay, who led the Republican Guard; the ministers of Foreign Affairs and the Interior; and the director generals of the Directorate of General Security, Directorate of General Military Intelligence, Iraqi Intelligence Service, and the Special Security Organization. When, in turn, these security organizations sought supplemental funding, they could approach either the Chief of the *Diwan*, Ahmad Husayn Khudayir al-Samarra'i, or al-Duri, in his role as Chief of the Secretariat. In addition to seeking extra funds through the *Diwan* or the Secretariat, these ministers and director generals could request a personal audience with Saddam to gain his direct approval. This arrangement thus offered the security organizations and ministries several avenues for obtaining supplemental funds, in a manner that sometimes left either the *Diwan* or the Secretariat unaware that the other had been approached for this funding. In this way, too, Saddam could play off the two chiefs in his Presidential Office against one another through domination and insulation of decision making.

Saddam's personal knowledge and understanding of budgetary details is unclear. A rare recording of a meeting between Saddam and his Cabinet in 1982 during the early years of the Iran-Iraq War reviewed a previous decision in which Saddam ordered a 15 percent reduction in nonmilitary ministries and departments that proposed budget increases above their 1981 allocation, and 10 percent cuts for those that proposed budgets below their 1981 allocations. These reductions reflected the budgetary shift toward military spending, with the Ministry of Defense receiving a 52 percent increase. What is interesting about this Cabinet meeting is how Saddam approached budgetary and economic questions. In the midst of an outline of ministerial budget reductions, Saddam diverted the conversation to how costs could be saved by limiting employee overtime hours to reduce ministerial costs. Saddam's solutions to combating Iraq's rising inflation included importing less expensive children's toys. Saddam noted that he observed during his travels throughout Iraq that farmers

[35] U.S. Central Intelligence Agency, *Comprehensive Report of the Special Advisor to the DCI on Iraq's WMD, Volume 1, Regime Finance and Procurement*, Langley, VA, September 30, 2004, 8.

purchased too many televisions and that redistributing these excessive sets would lower prices. "Because when I was passing by some farmer houses," Saddam informed his Cabinet, "I used to see two sets of televisions. So it appears that some of them had bought a television already, and also took another television from what we had. So this is a goal: seize it." At the same time, however, Saddam clearly imposed his will on his highly differential subordinates. For instance, after a presentation on reductions in funding for locally financed institutions, Saddam forcefully pointed out that two different tables of data were being presented in a manner that confused the conversation. "You should have told us this to save all this discussion! These statements in front of you are old. The new statements are the ones adopted!"[36]

This system of parallel hierarchies and compartmentalization of budgetary actors and programs may have suited Saddam's need for political control and secrecy, but it greatly complicated the government's key budgetary units' ability to coordinate their activities. Saddam considered the budget a state secret. Revealing the budget's contents brought the vengeance of the regime down on the violator, while the absence of a free press curtailed any public discussion of the government's budgetary intentions. This secrecy spread to the daily operations of the various ministries. The Finance and Planning ministries, for example, developed their respective operational and capital budgets in a largely independent manner, which undermined the government's management of expenditures. Although the planning and budgeting for transportation infrastructure, hospitals, schools, and such took place in the Planning Ministry, the Finance Ministry tried to fund the annual operations and maintenance budgets for these activities without always knowing what capital projects the government selected. These commitments obligated the government to fund not just the costs of construction but also expenditures for staffing and maintaining these facilities. These ministries, of course, exercised no control and possessed only minimal knowledge of the security agency budgets.[37]

Law of the Unified General State Budget, Number 107 of 1985

The Iraqis modified their 1940 budget and accounting law by adopting the "Law of the Unified General State Budget, Number 107 of 1985." The law first and foremost formalized Saddam's position in the setting of Iraqi economic policy. Saddam fully appreciated the benefits of dominating fiscal policy, for in 1977 he

[36] U.S. National Defense University, "Saddam Meeting with His Cabinet to Discuss the 1982 Budget," Conflict Records Research Center, CRRC Record Number SH-SHTP-A-000-635, Undated Document, circa 1982. Following the 2003 invasion of Iraq, captured documents were sent to the United States for translation. This is the first translated document on Iraqi budgeting that the CRRC released on October 25, 2011.

[37] U.S. Central Intelligence Agency, *Comprehensive Report of the Special Advisor to the DCI on Iraq's WMD, Volume 1, Regime Finance and Procurement*, Langley, VA, September 30, 2004, 10–14.

gained control over the distribution of Iraq's oil revenues, which he employed to advance his political interests.[38] The 1985 law justified revising Iraq's budgetary framework due to the need "to identify the central party" responsible for developing the budget, and to clarify the responsibilities of the actors and agencies involved in the budgetary process.[39] Where the old law placed the minister of finance and the Finance Ministry at the center of the budgetary process, the 1985 law located this responsibility with the President of the Republic, Saddam Hussein. The president authorized the preparation of the budget, which the law trifurcated into the "public" or operating budget, the investment budget, and the "consolidated" budget for the "socialist sector units, of productive economic activity self-financed," or, in other words, state-owned enterprises. In an interesting effort at promoting interagency cooperation, an unspecified deputy appointed by the President was charged with the authority to employ the ministries of Finance, Planning, and Commerce, as well as the Central Bank of Iraq, in formulating these budgets.

The budgetary process began with Finance and Planning ministerial consultation taking place with the various line ministries, with the proposed public, investment, and consolidated elements of the budget submitted to the Council of Ministers. The law directed the Finance Ministry to take the lead in developing the public budget in consultation with the line ministries and then to submit this draft budget to the Council of Ministers by the end of October. The Planning Ministry took on the same function regarding the creation of the investment budget and annual investment plan, presenting these materials to the Council, together with analyses of the state of the economy and the implementation status of the current investment budget. The public enterprises of the consolidated "socialist sector" drafted their budgets, submitted them to their respective parent ministries, which submitted them to the Finance Ministry for review, and then the budgets were sent to the Council. Consistent with the accounting provisions of the 1940 law, all units of government and all public enterprises provided monthly and annually audited financial statements to the Finance Ministry's Office of Financial Supervision Service. The Service presented an overall statement of accounts to the Office of the President of the Republic and to the National Council. On the president's approval of the spending ministries' budgets, the Finance Ministry's Accounting Service authorized the ministries to establish accounts with the Central Bank of Iraq, the Rafidain Bank, or any of their subsidiaries. After receiving this authority, the ministries could draw down their budget allocations from these bank accounts. The 1985 law also called for an annualized balanced public budget. Thus, while building on the 1940 law, the 1985 law introduced new institutional players into the Iraqi budgetary process. The law formally centralized

[38] Tripp, 209.
[39] "Law of the Unified General State Budget, Number 107 of 1985," *Al-Waqaia Al-Aiaqiya*, March 2, 1986, No. 3083, 58–66.

this process under the direction of the President of the Republic and separated the overall development of the budget between the Finance and Planning ministries, in a familiar Soviet fashion.

Another Saddam-era budgeting law, "First Amendment to the Unified Law of the General State Budget, Number 107 of 1985, Law Number 48 of 1990," essentially recodified and amended the 1985 legislation. The 1990 law reinforced the socialist conception of budgeting by declaring, for instance, that "the consolidated budget for the socialist sector is a planning budget."[40] The new law updated the language of the existing rules on budget preparation, process, accountability, and implementation and reinforced the law's accountability provisions. The law charged the ministries of Finance and Planning with creating a common set of final budgetary figures in order to more effectively balance the government's unified budget.

The Finance Ministry proved to be a weak institution, as it lacked the full authority and the technical capacity to prepare, allocate, and manage the broad range of Iraqi government spending. Within the government, the Finance Ministry often played a secondary role to the Ministry of Planning.[41] The Planning Ministry staff tended to be more technically and analytically sophisticated, consisting largely of economists and planners, whereas the Finance Ministry staff consisted primarily of accountants. Professional rivalries and personal disagreements complicated the coordination that needed to occur between these two ministries, particularly so as the Finance Ministry exercised little or no influence over the capital budget. As noted, the Finance Ministry's role was even more diminished in setting budgets for national defense, intelligence, and state security programs. This compartmentalization extended beyond the budget preparation and approval stages to that of budget execution. Making Iraq's budgetary management more difficult, Iraq lacked a functional treasury with a centralized payment system. Once Saddam approved the General Government and the security agency budgets, funds for the various ministries and agencies were allocated by placing them in numerous state-controlled Rafidain and Rasheed bank accounts, from which the ministries administered their own rates of expenditure.

Compartmentalization, fragmentation, and secrecy acted as centrifugal forces that pulled at budget coordination, but they were countered by Saddam's centralized hierarchy of decision making and the widespread fear of his vengeance. Although the formal process suggests some meaningful deliberation at the ministerial level, such as budget negotiations between the Finance Ministry and the spending ministries, budgetary decisions clearly emanated

---

[40] "First Amendment to the Unified Law of the General State Budget, Number 107 of 1985, Law Number 48 of 1990," *Al-Waqaia Al-Aiaqiya*, August 13, 1990, No. 3320, 378–381.

[41] On the tension between the Finance and Planning ministries, see Naomi Caiden and Aaron Wildavsky, *Planning and Budgeting in Poor Countries*, New Brunswick: Transaction Publishers, 2003.

from the President's Office down to all government agencies. Finance Ministry and Planning Ministry budget officers and even ministers learned to push their decisions upward to avoid blame for making decisions that might run contrary to the regime's preferences. Saddam, of course, exercised his strongest control over Iraq's defense, security, and intelligence agency budgets. In a similar fashion, even though the dispersal of agency funds into bank accounts rather than through a treasury suggested a lack of proper expenditure control, the fear of Saddam's revenge may have restrained the direct misappropriation of funds. To steal from the government meant stealing from Saddam, with often horrific results. Before making the most basic of spending decisions, government officials at every level commonly requested written orders to justify their actions, if necessary, to security authorities. This lack of initiative thoroughly permeated Iraq's bureaucracy, producing long-term adverse consequences for the effectiveness of the government's ability to execute its budgets, as well as for Coalition efforts to reconstitute the Iraqi state.

Ba'athist Economic Policies

The outline of Iraqi fiscal and monetary policy promoted by this budgetary system during the Ba'athist regime is well known. Scholars characterize Iraqi policy during the twenty-year period from the late 1950s through the early 1970s, despite relatively short-term fluctuations, as conservative and restrained. Growth in government spending, particularly for the military, accelerated in the late 1960s under the Ba'athists, but oil revenues permitted Iraq to incur minimal levels of foreign and domestic debt.[42] "Between 1958 and 1966, the army doubled its budget, while expenditure on development projects remained stationary or declined. Expenditure on the army increased in direct proportion to the decline in military professionalism, a decline brought into sharp focus by the 1967 war."[43] The spike in oil prices in 1973 allowed the government to boost spending for infrastructure, oil production, education, and health care. The allocation of these funds served to support the *rentier* aspects of Saddam's rule by favoring allies and certain regions within Iraq. Defense expenditures consumed the bulk of this spending, as it grew in the late 1970s from $3.1 billion in 1975 to some $20 billion in 1980, approximately 39 percent of GDP.[44] Despite this increase in spending, oil revenues kept Iraq's debt-to-GDP ratio at just

---

[42] Kamil Mahdi and Haris Gazdar, "Introduction," in Kamil A. Mahdi (ed.), *Iraq's Economic Predicament*, Reading, UK: Garnet Publishing Ltd., 2002, 16.

[43] Kanan Makiya, *Republic of Fear: Politics in Modern Iraq*, Berkeley: University of California Press, 1989, 22.

[44] Sinan al-Shabibi, "The Iraqi Economy: Some Thoughts on a Recovery and Growth Programme," in Kamil A. Mahdi (ed.), *Iraq's Economic Predicament*, Reading, UK: Garnet Publishing Ltd., 2002, 351.

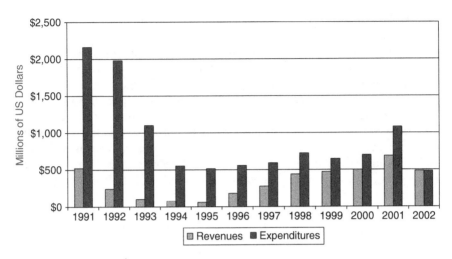

FIGURE 2.1. Iraqi Budgets, 1991–2002
Source: U.S. Central Intelligence Agency

5.2 percent in 1980.[45] Iraq's economy in the 1980s reflected unstable oil production, a drop in petroleum prices, reduced investment and consumption, and
the continued drain of large-scale military spending. The onset of the costly
eight-year Iran-Iraq War in September 1980 and Iraq's decision to persist with
the expenses associated with the prewar-designed 1981–1985 Five Year Plan,
drove the country's indebtedness to 35.4 percent of GDP in 1987. Iraq's debt
service payments grew from some $2.5 billion in 1980 to a cumulative total of
some $24 billion between 1980 and 1990. Iraq reported to the United Nations in
1991 that as a result of the invasion of Kuwait in 1990 and the Gulf War, its total
debt reached $42 billion.[46] Other estimates placed the debt load at $75 billion to
$80 billion.[47] The war and subsequent UN sanctions and embargos stymied
Iraq's oil production, sales, and revenues. As a result, the best available data
indicate Iraq's official revenues for budgetary purposes fell by some 86 percent
from 1991 through 1994, as shown in Figure 2.1; Iraq's official budget expenditures during these ten years fell from a high point of $2.2 billion in constant
dollars in 1991 to less than $500 million in 1997.

Revenues and expenditures then resurged, with an upturn in revenues taking
place in 1996 and 1997. This revenue increase corresponded to the establishment of the UN Oil-for-Food program in 1996. Although UN Resolution 986

---

[45] Ahmed M. Jiyad, "The Development of Iraq's Foreign Debt: From Liquidity to Unsustainability,"
in Kamil A. Mahdi (ed.), *Iraq's Economic Predicament*, Reading, UK: Garnet Publishing Ltd.,
2002, 109.

[46] *Ibid.*

[47] Coalition for International Justice, "Sources of Revenue for Saddam and Sons: A Primer on the
Financial Underpinnings of the Regime in Baghdad," Washington, DC, September 2002, 8.

did not allow for direct cash payments to be made to the Iraqi treasury, government spending did grow slowly over these years to $1.1 billion in 2001.[48] These expenditures included funding for Iraq's food ration program that helped strengthen centralized political and economic control over the population.[49] The budget deficit during this period fell from $1.6 billion in 1991 to $410 million in 2001, the last year for which credible data exists on Saddam's budgets.[50] These budgetary figures do not appear to include the estimated $2 billion per year in hidden funds and assets controlled by Saddam, such as oil revenues derived outside of the Oil-for-Food program.

CONCLUSION

What may be seen from this period in Iraqi fiscal history is that despite the dramatic exogenous shocks of world war, invasion, and occupation by a foreign power, a historical layering of institutions characterized the development of Iraq's fiscal and budgetary system. Ottoman institutions governed Iraq for hundreds of years, and then many of these institutions, such as the government's tax laws, persisted in Iraq for decades after the British invaded Iraq in 1914. As part of their state-building efforts, the British imposed new institutions, organizational structures, and processes on the Iraqis, including the establishment of an increasingly powerful Ministry of Finance in 1921. The British also laid the foundations for an extensive accounting and audit capacity to encourage

---

[48] *Ibid.*, 1. For an alternative view of the consequences of the Oil-for-Food Program on the Iraqis, see Sheila Zurbrigg, "Economic Sanctions on Iraq: Tool for Peace, or Travesty," *Muslim World Journal of Human Rights*, 4, 2007, 2, Article 3. *Rentier* payments stemming from the Oil-for-Food Program included bribes paid to Iraqi officials from foreign corporations seeking contracts funded by the Program. Paul Volcker charged that more than two thousand corporations paid $1.8 billion in bribes and kickbacks to Iraqis. See, for example, Jeremy Lemer and Stephanie Kirchgaessner, "GE to Pay $23.5m to Settle Iraqi Bribe Allegations," *Financial Times*, July 28, 2010, 1; and James Boxell and Jennifer Thompson, "Total Chief Faces Court Grilling Over Iraq Oil-for-Food Corruption Claims," *Financial Times*, August 3, 2011, 1.

[49] Whether Saddam employed the rationing system as part of a reward and punishment system remains debatable. According to one analysis, "A central feature of the state rationing system is that it is comprehensive and non-targeted: everyone is entitled to the ration regardless of means, and the ration and its price are uniform across the country.... Up until that time [1991], there had been a great deal of speculation outside Iraq that the ration system was selectively used by the Iraqi regime as a reward and punishment device against various sections of the population. The 1991 visit discovered no evidence for this.... During our 1996 visit ... the ration system operated exactly in the same way as had been observed in 1991." Haris Gazdar and Athar Hussain, "Crisis and Response: A Study of the Impact of Economic Sanctions in Iraq," in Kamil A. Mahdi (ed.), *Iraq's Economic Predicament*, Reading, UK: Garnet Publishing Ltd., 2002, 56.

[50] U.S. Central Intelligence Agency, *Comprehensive Report of the Special Advisor to the DCI on Iraq's WMD*, Volume 1, *Regime Finance and Procurement*, Langley, VA, September 30, 2004, 13. This report states that "complete data about Iraqi government spending after 2001 are unavailable. A common refrain among government officials and detainees is that many of these records perished during looting and fires after the US invaded Baghdad" (11).

budgetary transparency and accountability. To be sure, the British encountered many obstacles during their Mandate, all of which played out within the broader context of Iraqi hostility toward the occupation.[51] The British acknowledged, for example, insufficient staffing and reliance on seconded territorial personnel for administrative support, delays in the formulation and adoption of Iraqi budgets, the inability to spend and execute budgets, difficulties in balancing the budget before the onset of significant oil revenues, corruption in the bureaucracy, and frustration with an antiquated tax system. Nonetheless, despite their flaws, these budgetary institutions persisted through the Mandate, the Hashemite monarchy, and into Saddam's era. Britain's physical presence obviously contributed to the maintenance of their forms of governance past the formal transition of power to King Faisal. Yet, the Iraqis also accepted and gained ownership of many of these English-inspired institutions, adding to them, as in the form of Iraqi-initiated ministerial and parliamentary committees that participated in the budgetary process. These developments emerged over several decades and stemmed from a long-term political and economic investment of personnel and resources by the British and the Iraqis and were not simply the immediate result of the British invasion.

The budget system that emerged under Saddam served to maintain political control over the institutions of Iraqi government, particularly the military, intelligence, and state security agencies. Iraq's budgetary laws stemmed from their English emphasis on the role of the Ministry of Finance as the central actor in the budgetary process, and later the Ba'athists layered new rules on to this process to reflect the Soviet model of economic planning. These formal rules, however, do not convey the full extent of how Saddam exercised absolute control over budgetary decisions, determined the allocation of revenues derived from the Oil-for-Food Program, or limited the Finance Ministry's influence over other ministries, especially the Planning Ministry. In practical terms, the division of budgetary responsibilities between the Finance and Planning ministries, the compartmentalization of decisions, the secrecy and lack of shared budgetary and economic information between decision makers and institutions, the reliance on a decentralized banking system rather than on a central treasury to allocate funds to ministries, and eventually the need to manage secret and illicit revenues, all undermined the administrative and economic efficiency of Iraq's budgetary system. Saddam's budgetary system, thus, symbolically and in practice, represented a distinct alternative to contemporary international best practices. At the very least, the system lacked democratic deliberation and approval, transparency, and comprehensive accountability. Moreover, Saddam relied on a planning and budgeting system that challenged the marketplace thinking of the Coalition forces that invaded, occupied, and imposed change on Iraq's budgetary institutions.

---

[51] See, for example, Toby Dodge, *Inventing Iraq: The Failure of Nation Building and a History Denied*, New York: Columbia University Press, 2003.

3

Prewar Planning for Iraq's Economic and Budgetary Reconstruction

There is a general consensus that prewar planning for postconflict stabilization and reconstruction operations in Iraq proved to be woefully inadequate.[1] This assessment may be summarized this way: The United States went into the business of state building in Iraq reluctantly and ill-prepared. As a presidential candidate, George W. Bush claimed the Clinton administration overextended and misdirected American foreign affairs. Bush declared that as president he

---

[1] Assessments of American prewar planning for the invasion and the Phase IV occupation of Iraq tend to be highly critical. See, for example, George Packer, *The Assassins' Gate: America in Iraq*, New York: Farrar, Straus and Giroux, 2005, chapter 4; Anne Ellen Henderson, "The Coalition Provisional Authority's Experience with Economic Reconstruction in Iraq: Lessons Identified," *Special Report*, No. 138, United States Institute of Peace, April 2005; Karin von Hippel, "State-Building After Saddam: Lessons Lost," in Brendan O'Leary, John McGarry, and Khaled Salih (eds.), *The Future of Kurdistan in Iraq*, Philadelphia: University of Pennsylvania Press, 2005, 251–267; Larry Diamond, "What Went Wrong and Right in Iraq," in Francis Fukuyama (ed.), *Nation Building: Beyond Afghanistan and Iraq*, Baltimore: Johns Hopkins University Press, 2006, 173–195; Joseph J. Collins, "Planning Lessons from Afghanistan and Iraq," *Joint Forces Quarterly*, 41 (2006) 2, 10–14; Kate Philips, Shane Lauth, and Erin Schenk, "U.S. Military Operations in Iraq: Planning, Combat, and Occupation," in W. Andrew Terrill (ed.), Strategic Studies Institute, U.S. Army War College, April 2006; Christina Caan, Beth Cole, Paul Hughes, and Daniel P. Serwer, "Is This Any Way to Run an Occupation? Legitimacy, Governance, and Security in Post-Conflict Iraq," in Karen Guttieri and Jessica Piombo (eds.), *Interim Governments*, Washington, DC: United States Institute of Peace, 2007, 319–343; Nora Bensahel, Olga Oliker, Keith Crane, Richard R. Brennan, Jr., Heather S. Gregg, Thomas Sullivan, and Andrew Rathmell, *After Saddam: Prewar Planning and the Occupation of Iraq*, Santa Monica: Rand, 2008; Donald P. Wright and Timothy R. Reese, *On Point II: Transition to the New Campaign: The United States Army in Operation Iraqi Freedom, May 2003–January 2005*, Ft. Leavenworth, KS: United States Army Combat Studies Institute, 2008; and David A. Lake. "Two Cheers for Bargaining Theory: Assessing Rationalist Explanations of the Iraq War. *International Security*, 35 (Winter 2010/11) 3, 7–52. For a review of the U.S. military's aversion to stability and reconstruction nation building operations, see Brian G. Watson, "Reshaping the Expeditionary Army to Win Decisively: The Case for Greater Stabilization Capacity in the Modular Force," Strategic Studies Institute, Carlisle, PA, 2005.

would avoid Clinton's overseas interventions and "would be very careful about using our troops as nation builders. I believe the role of the military is to fight and win war and, therefore, prevent war from happening in the first place.... I believe we're overextended in too many places."[2] This position coincided with Bush's neoliberal domestic agenda, an aversion within the U.S. military for nation-building operations, and the prevailing "Washington Consensus" on international development assistance that favored a limited state and the promotion of market-based economies. The term "Washington Consensus," coined in 1989, referred to ten economic policy reforms that included deregulation, privatization, trade liberalization, and, first and second on the list of reforms, fiscal discipline and pro-growth budgetary policies.[3] The planning for the postconflict Iraq reflected this thinking. In preparation for the invasion of Iraq the Americans expected to decapitate Saddam's political leadership and capture weapons of mass destruction (WMD) but provide only short-term humanitarian relief. Failing to find WMDs, the Bush administration's purpose for liberating and occupying Iraqi became the establishment of a democratic political system acceptable to American ideological preferences and regional interests. The lead role for planning the invasion and coordinating the activities of civilian agencies rested with the Defense Department. The Defense Department's leadership generally ignored the postconflict planning that did take place within the agencies, most famously the State Department's "Future of Iraq Project." The Defense Department neglected to prepare for "Phase IV" postconflict reconstruction, and instead focused on short-term humanitarian assistance.[4] The

[2] Quote from the Bush-Gore October 3, 2000, presidential debate. John J. Hamre and Gordon R. Sullivan, "Toward Postconflict Reconstruction," *The Washington Quarterly*, Autumn 2002, 90. On Bush, also see Victoria K. Holt and Michael G. Mackinnon, "The Origins and Evolution of US Policy Towards Peace Operations," *International Peacekeeping*, 15 (2008) 1, 18–34; and Stewart Patrick, "A Return to Realism? The United States and Global Peace Operations Since 9/11," *International Peacekeeping*, 15 (2008) 1, 133–148.

[3] John Williamson, "A Short History of the Washington Consensus," in Narcis Serra and Joseph E. Stiglitz (eds.), *The Washington Consensus Reconsidered: Towards a New Global Governance*, New York: Oxford University Press, 16–17. On the Washington Consensus and neoliberal economics, see Neil King, Jr., "Bush Officials Draft Plan for Free-Market Economy in Iraq," *Wall Street Journal*, May 1, 2003, A1; and Eric Laursen, "Privatizing Iraq," *In These Times*, http://www.inthesetimes.com/site/main/article/325/. On the Washington Consensus, see, for example, Francis Fukuyama, *State-Building: Governance and World Order in the 21st Century*, Ithaca, NY: Cornell University Press, 2004; and Carl J. Schramm, "Expeditionary Economics: Spurring Growth After Conflicts and Disasters," *Foreign Affairs*, 89 (May/June 2010) 3, 89–99.

[4] On the lack of attention paid to the Future of Iraq Project, see, for example, Bensahel et al., *op. cit.*, 31–33; and Larry Diamond, "What Went Wrong and Right in Iraq," in Francis Fukuyama (ed.), *Nation-Building: Beyond Afghanistan and Iraq*, Baltimore: Johns Hopkins University Press, 2006, 175. On the lack of adequate planning for Phase IV, see Michael G. Gordon and General Bernard E. Trainor, *Cobra II: The Inside Story of the Invasion and Occupation of Iraq*, New York: Vintage, 2007. For one interesting prewar American study that noted the importance of public budgeting and finance for the reconstruction of Iraq, see Conrad C. Crane and W. Andrew Terrill, "Reconstructing Iraq: Challenges and Missions for Military Forces in a Post-Conflict Scenario,"

occupation of Iraq would be relatively brief, with the government quickly turned over to sympathetic Iraqi expatriates. The American-led Coalition, often staffed by young, inexperienced neoconservatives, failed to anticipate the postinvasion security challenge and was completely unprepared for the immense reconstruction and state-building efforts that awaited it.[5] The reality of "regime change" in Iraq, therefore, came to mean a dangerous, costly, long-term exercise in nation building, in which the Coalition focused much of its energy on a state-building project directed at reconfiguring Iraqi political organizations, rules, and processes.

Much of this assessment is valid. Yet, contrary to the view that only minimal or fragmented planning occurred, some organized prewar economic planning did take place. What did it entail and what effect did it have in Iraq? Prewar discussions and planning for American postconflict intervention in the Iraq economy began in 2002 and continued until the eve of the invasion. "There was not one single plan," recalled Larry McDonald, Deputy Assistant Treasury Secretary for Technical Assistance Policy. "There were many plans. When you talk about reconstituting institutions of state, and we are just talking about the Finance Ministry, which is a very complex thing which has a lot of components, when you add on to that all the other Iraqi ministries, each one of those efforts [to stand up a given ministry] was a huge plan that had many subcomponents. People speak in shorthand about whether there was a plan for Iraq. I think it is more relevant to speak of plans. There were plans, there were a lot of plans, created at different times by different agencies and levels of government. Some of the plans had to do with reconstituting basic services of the Finance Ministry, the Central Bank, and the main financial institutions, Rafidain and Rasheed, and some of the main aspects of Iraq's financial sector."[6] The Treasury Department assumed this responsibility of taking the lead in planning and executing these economic aspects of the Coalition's reconstruction effort. As this chapter indicates, there were numerous influences on Treasury's planning, including the State Department's fabled "Future of Iraq Project."

THE FUTURE OF IRAQ PROJECT

In 2002, Iraqi expatriates operating under the auspices of the State Department's The Future of Iraq Project issued a series of reports that called for a broad transitional effort to modernize the Iraqi economy by directing it toward a

Strategic Studies Institute, U.S. Army War College, January 29, 2003, 6. These recommendations were not incorporated into Defense Department planning.

[5] The presence of young, inexperienced neoconservatives was promoted, for example, by Rajiv Chandrasekaran, "Ties to GOP Trumped Know-How Among Staff Sent to Rebuild Iraq," *Washington Post*, September 16, 2006, A1; and Rajiv Chandrasekaran, *Imperial Life in the Emerald City: Inside Iraq's Green Zone*, New York: Knopf, 2006.

[6] Interview with William Larry McDonald, October 16, 2006.

market-based economic system.[7] Various critiques of the planning stage of the Iraq war often suggest that the Project played a minimal role in influencing the actual reconstruction efforts pursued by the Coalition. Paul Bremer, for example, indicated that he was unaware of the Project before he entered Baghdad, and that when he finally did read the Project it did not serve as a practical guide for reconstructing Iraq.[8] The Project may very well have produced limited or no effect on many aspects of prewar planning, and was discarded by others with the beginning of the actual occupation. Nonetheless, there is evidence that it did indeed influence the thinking of some central actors in their consideration of what needed to be accomplished in postconflict Iraq, especially as the Coalition addressed the new government of Iraq's economic, fiscal, and budgetary policies. As events unfolded, the Coalition's efforts on the ground did indeed reflect some of the Project's general recommendations in these economic areas.

The Future of Iraq Project consisted largely of a number of targeted reports. The economic report included a section on the "Economy and Infrastructure" that addressed government finance. As a petroleum state, the report noted, Iraq's revenue base relied almost exclusively on oil revenues. Fluctuations in oil market prices drove the size of government spending. At the pinnacle of his political strength in the 1980s, during periods of rising oil prices, Saddam's government, according to the report, operated without fiscal restraint. This enabled the state to expand its presence in the economy and society, determine investment decisions, provide extensive subsidies, maintain minimal direct and indirect taxation, and drive out independent market forces in the private sector. The government's fiscal condition, however, greatly deteriorated following the first Gulf War due to the international economic sanctions imposed on Iraq, the lack of an alternative export economy, diminished foreign currency reserves, marginal foreign investment, and the government's lack of a substitute tax base. Because of its reliance on petroleum revenues, the state failed to build an administrative capacity to collect alternative domestic revenues. Moreover, as the economy declined, the regime considered it unwise to impose upon the population a new system of domestic taxation sufficient to compensate fully for lost oil income.

---

[7] This recommendation for a new market-based Iraq is most comprehensively addressed in U.S. Department of State, Economy and Infrastructure (Public Finance) Working Group, "The Future of Iraq Project," Washington, DC, 2002.

[8] For example, Packer writes that the Defense Department minimized the Project. George Packer, *The Assassins' Gate: America in Iraq*, New York: Farrar, Straus and Giroux, 2005, chapter 4. Interview with Paul Bremer, June 27, 2007. On the Future of Iraq Project: "I don't remember seeing it." Bremer also wrote, "Sometime after arriving in Baghdad, I read press reports about a State Department study on the future of Iraq, claiming it provide a full plan for postconflict activities in the country." Ryan Crocker and Bremer dismissed the Project for this purpose. L. Paul Bremer, *My Year in Iraq: The Struggle to Build a Future of Hope*, New York: Threshold Editions, 2006, 25. Also see L. Paul Bremer III, "Where Was the Plan? *New York Times*, March 16, 2008.

Iraq's public finances needed to be reconstituted to provide for a more rational allocation of expenditures, the report declared, while broadening the government's revenue base. Following Saddam's fall, the report proposed that a new Ministry of Finance and Economy be delegated the responsibility of "formulating and implementing" fiscal policy and the "annual government budget" to rebuild Iraq's fiscal capacity.[9] This would require a thorough inventory of financial resources, infrastructure needs, and the provision of public goods and services. The report noted that government spending constituted a major component of total aggregate demand in the economy and urged that public expenditures be reduced to promote the private sector. Spending on Iraq's military and state security apparatus, in particular, could be cut. Nevertheless, the report also warned that significant government funding and public investment would be necessary to provide the Iraqi people with a wide range of public services and support, including, but not limited to: police and security services; adequate food supplies; emergency and ongoing health care; education; a legal and judicial system; a broad selection of public infrastructure projects, including the construction of schools, hospitals, and water and sewage facilities; and a reconstituted bureaucracy. The report called for major new public investment to rebuild Iraq's oil refineries, electrical generation plants, and petrochemical and fertilizer industries. Despite the demand for a new market economy, this vast reconstruction effort would be heavily financed by public funds. Much of this support would come directly through subsidies and expenditures distributed from the central government's budget, with the remaining funds allocated by a not-yet-created public-private Iraqi Development and Reconstruction Bank.

The report also called for the fiscal empowerment of Iraq's eighteen provincial governments. Noting that these local governments totally depended on central government funding under Saddam, the report encouraged the governorates to provide funding for schools, roads, and parks. To accomplish this, these local governments would be forced to develop their own budgets and generate their own revenue bases, in which "taxes can be easily collected" by imposing new wholesale, property, fuel, and utilities taxes, as well as various administrative and vehicle registration fees.[10] Newly established local councils, meanwhile, would exercise veto power over all aspects of local district public finances within the governorates. Although advocating for local government fiscal development, the report nonetheless remained largely silent about the nature of future central government fiscal assistance to the provincial governments.

[9] U.S. Department of State, Economy and Infrastructure (Public Finance) Working Group, "The Future of Iraq Project," "New Currency, Fiscal and Monetary Policies, Guidelines for the Transitional Government of Iraq," Washington, DC, December 22, 2002, 3.

[10] U.S. Department of State, Economy and Infrastructure (Public Finance) Working Group, "The Future of Iraq Project," "Structure and Authority for Iraqi Local Governance," Washington, DC, December 12, 2002, 2/2.

The reconstructed national government would be responsible for broadening its revenue base. These new revenue sources were needed to avoid Iraq's dependency on price fluctuations in the oil market, with the resulting uncertainty predicting revenues and thus controlling budget deficits. Diversifying the revenue base also contributed to the breakup of Saddam's system of managing economic decision making though his control over the allocation of oil revenues. The government, especially the proposed Ministry of Finance and Economy, would create the administrative and judicial capacity to enforce new tax codes and collect revenues. The report acknowledged the reality of taxpayer noncompliance and bureaucratic corruption. Furthermore, although "the majority of the people will probably welcome the US-led forces as liberators," the report warned that it would be economically and politically unwise to impose new taxes during the disruption likely to occur during the first six months following Saddam's deposition.[11] The new tax code should impose a variety of income, corporate, inheritance, value-added, and land taxes. To counter likely noncompliance and taxpayer hostility, and recognizing "the existing wide disparity in income and wealth," the proposed income tax imposed a progressive set of brackets of 10, 15, 25, and 40 percent.[12] Finally, the report predicted that the transitional government's major reconstruction investments in Iraq's petroleum industry would generate substantial new revenues. This would be facilitated by the likelihood that Saddam would be unlikely to destroy Iraq's oil fields.

The Future of Iraq Project outlined recommendations for building a new Iraq, including numerous proposals that would have economic and especially budgetary implications. Many of the Project's assumptions about how the Coalition would be enthusiastically welcomed in Iraq and how Iraq's security budget could be cut to favor public investment turned out to be fanciful. Still, other recommendations regarding the empowerment of the Finance Ministry, the introduction of a new currency, the urgency of providing significant funding for investment, and the need to boost government revenues through greater oil production were incorporated into the Coalition's short- and long-term statebuilding and reconstruction efforts. The discussions surrounding the Project occurred throughout much of 2002, and aspects of these planning discussions would soon be repeated in agencies other than the State Department as the chance of an invasion increased later that year. Deliberations taking place at the Treasury Department considered a number of the Project's recommendations, some of which were carried out in Iraq.

[11] U.S. Department of State Economy and Infrastructure (Public Finance) Working Group, "The Future of Iraq Project," "New Currency: Fiscal and Monetary Policy, Tax System," Washington, DC, December 22, 2002, 2.

[12] U.S. Department of State Economy and Infrastructure (Public Finance) Working Group, "The Future of Iraq Project," "Tax Policy: Guidelines for the Transitional Government of Iraq," Washington, DC, January 1, 2003, 2–3.

U.S. TREASURY PREWAR PLANNING

On January 20, 2003, the White House released National Security President Directive-24, authorizing the Department of Defense to establish an "Iraq Postwar Planning Office" to coordinate U.S. postconflict operations in Iraq. To discuss the implications of the directive and the establishment of what would become the Office of Reconstruction and Humanitarian Assistance (ORHA), Deputy National Security Advisor Steven Hadley called a National Security Council (NSC) interagency deputies meeting for January 22. Retired Army Lieutenant General Jay Garner, Defense Secretary Donald Rumsfeld's designated leader of ORHA, announced at the meeting that relevant U.S. agencies should focus on addressing Iraq's short-term humanitarian needs and that these agencies would report directly to him. Garner then called for the agencies to develop counterpart Ministerial Advisory Teams that would be attached to each of Iraq's twenty-three ministries. A typical team would consist of U.S. agency officials, coalition partners, and Iraqi expatriates, who would serve as ministerial advisors and provide these ministries with direction and support until the establishment of a new Iraqi government. After being assembled, these agency teams would be stationed in Kuwait and they then would follow the military into Iraq after the invasion.[13]

Among those attending the NSC deputies meeting was John B. Taylor, Under Secretary of the Treasury for International Affairs. A distinguished economics professor and a colleague of Secretary of State Condoleezza Rice at Stanford University, Taylor directed Treasury's Iraq economic stabilization efforts. Taylor proved to be ideally suited for the part, if for no other reasons than his political connections. Shortly after the deputies meeting, Rice invited Taylor to lunch. Not only did Taylor know Rice well from Stanford, he was also a long-time friend of Defense Secretary Rumsfeld. These connections with Rice and Rumsfeld served Treasury's interests with both the Department of State and Department of Defense, for at lunch Rice informed Taylor that Treasury would play a critical role in Iraq and be "operationally responsible" for stabilizing Iraq's public finances.[14] From the earliest days of the prewar planning process, Treasury's status and functional responsibilities were relatively privileged and defined, and the technical nature of conducting economic policy ensured that it would play a dominant role in the earliest phase of the occupation of Iraq. In this way, Treasury escaped "the decision to marginalize the State Department and USAID" in favor of the Defense Department's leading role for managing the forthcoming occupation.[15]

---

[13] Nora Bensahel, Olga Oliker, Keith Crane, Richard R. Brennan, Jr., Heather S. Gregg, Thomas Sullivan, and Andrew Rathmell, *After Saddam: Prewar Planning and the Occupation of Iraq*. Santa Monica: Rand, 2008.

[14] John B. Taylor, *Global Financial Warriors: The Untold Story of International Finance in the Post-9/11 World*, New York: Norton, 2007, 205.

[15] Interview with John B. Taylor, March 21, 2007.

In response to Rice's charge, Taylor and the Treasury Department developed an economic strategy that relied on fiscal and monetary actions to avert a financial, monetary, and bureaucratic breakdown after the fall of Saddam. Preliminary discussions within Treasury and with other U.S. agencies took place beginning in the fall of 2002 on how to manage the economic issues that accompanied a likely attack, such as providing Turkey with financial assistance in exchange for its permission to launch an American assault on northern Iraq from its soil. "The idea that Iraq was potentially on the table and that we needed to think about post-conflict," Taylor recalled, "was probably at least by September–October 2002, not later than that. And so deliberating in all different respects of what to do [began at that time]."[16] In the beginning, said Taylor, there was "a sense of really having to plan in a great degree of uncertainty.... There was a lot of time spent gathering the facts about what the situation was like." Looking for information on the status of Iraq's economy, Taylor's search included hiring a former CIA analyst to produce a report on Iraq's economic and financial system. He engaged in discussions with Iraqi expatriates, including some of the authors of the economic and public finance chapters in the State Department's Future of Iraq Project. Among the more notable of these Project authors with whom Taylor conferred were Sinan al-Shabibi, Nasreen Sideek, and Sabri Zire al-Saddi. Shabibi, a former senior economist with the United Nations' Conference on Trade and Development and a former senior official at Iraq's ministries of Planning and Oil, became governor of the Central Bank of Iraq in 2003. Sideek served as Minister of Reconstruction and Development in the Kurdistan regional government and later in 2003 was appointed Minister of Public Works, the first female minister under the provisional Iraqi government. Saadi wrote extensively about Iraq's currency and foreign exchange problems under Saddam. Consistent with the Project's recommendations, all three encouraged Taylor to replace Iraq's two sets of dinars with a new currency after Saddam's fall as part of a process of removing Saddam's image from public places while controlling inflation. "A difficulty in designing such a currency reform plan," Taylor noted, "was that we did not know which Iraqis would head up financial matters in a transitional government; and whoever was in charge, we did not know what their position would be on matters related to currency. That was one reason why our interaction with the Iraqi expats in the Future of Iraq Project was important. We wanted to make a choice that would be accepted by the Iraqi people."[17] Though Taylor readily agreed with the need for currency conversion, an extensive debate would emerge within the U.S. government about how to introduce the currency and what form it should take.

Incorporating a number of suggestions from the Project, including the introduction of a new currency and a reconstituted and strengthened Ministry of

---

[16] *Ibid.*

[17] John B. Taylor, *Global Financial Warriors: The Untold Story of International Finance in the Post-9/11 World*, New York: Norton, 2007, 210.

Finance, the planning discussions taking place at Treasury focused on the monetary task of replacing Saddam's dinars with new currency, and the immediate fiscal task of requiring prompt payment of salaries to Iraqi civil servants and pensioners. This latter effort recognized the urgency of maintaining a functioning bureaucracy and state apparatus to provide emergency services and help prevent a humanitarian crisis after Saddam's demise. Treasury also sought to avert the problem of massive unemployment and the scenario of elderly pensioners cut off from their primary source of financial support. To accomplish this goal, Taylor recognized the need to enhance the position of the Ministry of Finance in the Iraqi government, "certainly elevating it," noted Taylor, giving it "more visibility than the other ministries.... It had to be raised in importance.... Otherwise it would get shunned and you wouldn't have the budget controls and the idea of a central budget function out of the Ministry of Finance." "Probably the first thing I wanted people to do [in Iraq]," Taylor recalled, "was to get a budget created for the Ministry of Finance, so it could think about allocating resources. I insisted that [our people] do a mock budget here [in the United States] for their ministry, so they could think about their resources and how they would allocate them.... The overall budget for the government was going to be put together by the Ministry of Finance. There weren't going to be any side-budget or off-budgets, there is going to be *the* budget."[18]

In March, Treasury Secretary John Snow and Under Secretary Taylor presented the agency's proposals to President Bush for approval. What Snow presented to Bush addressed not a general strategy of economic development, but a more targeted effort to pay civil servants and replace the dinar. The presentation consisted of a three-slide PowerPoint show titled "Currency Decision for Post-Saddam Iraq" that described a two-phase emergency plan. The first slide read, "As soon as control over the Iraqi government is established we will use United States dollars to pay civil servants and pensioners. Later, depending on the situation on the ground, we would decide about using the new currency."[19] As Snow and Taylor outlined, multiple currencies would be allowed to circulate at flexible exchange rates with the dollar, and civil servants and pensioners would be paid based on lists of pensioners obtained from the Ministry of Finance. "A more detailed plan was put together," Taylor explained, "about what we would do purposively to create financial stability so there would

---

[18] Interview with John B. Taylor, March 21, 2007.
[19] John B. Taylor, "Iraq: Dollars for Dinars," *Hoover Digest*, Stanford University, 2, 2007. http:// www.hoover.org/publications/hoover-digest/article/6078/, Bensahel et al. write that during the prewar planning stage, at the February rock-drill, there were "unresolved issues," including "salaries for civil servants." Yet, it is also noted that "First and foremost, CPA had to start paying Iraqi civil servants.... In late 2002, U.S. Treasury officials worked out a payments strategy." Bensahel et al. are not clear what was unresolved in February, but they do indicate that Treasury planned for the issue, and that cash payments were made as quickly as possible by the CPA. Bensahel et al., 64, 198–199.

not be a collapse in the economy." The slides outlined how the funds would be obtained for these payments. With one week's notice, the Treasury could ship $100 million from Saddam's frozen accounts in U.S. banks to Baghdad, with salaries and pensions paid at their current rate "in real terms." These funds could be allocated under emergency powers granted by the USA Patriot Act and would not require congressional approval. President Bush responded that he preferred that these payments be "more than what they were getting paid under Saddam." As Taylor recalled, "We adjusted the plan accordingly."[20] The President gave his approval to Snow and Taylor on March 12, 2003, a little more than two weeks before the March 30 invasion of Iraq.

TREASURY'S OFFICE OF TECHNICAL ASSISTANCE

To carry out this plan, Taylor responded to General Garner's direction given at the January 22 NSC deputies meeting to establish Ministerial Advisory Teams. The Treasury's team in Iraq would act as the lead agency for the Ministry of Finance, the Central Bank of Iraq, and the country's commercial banks. Taylor's grouping of his team around these institutions reflected his concern that ORHA's energies would largely be focused on the Ministry of Defense and the various security agencies, with little attention paid to Iraq's economic and financial systems. By combining his team to cover these multiple efforts, Taylor hoped to give his group more visibility and influence in decision making. "We felt the finance area was more important than other areas," Taylor claimed. "In other parts of ORHA you have the agriculture person, the transportation person, but we wanted to have a more significant [arrangement] for these economic, finance [issues], so we put them altogether ... to give visibility to this."[21]

Though many units within Treasury were called on to offer financial expertise for the planning effort, the primary membership for Taylor's Ministerial Advisory Team came from Treasury's Office of Technical Assistance (OTA). Established in 1990, OTA's twenty-two-person staff provides technical assistance to foreign governments to improve their financial and fiscal institutions and systems, especially their central banks and monetary systems and issues related to banking, cash, and debt management. These governments typically range from those emerging from state-centered to more market-based economies, such as those of the former Soviet Union, postconflict countries engaged in financial reconstruction emerging from internal and external sources of conflict, and developing nations that seek to strengthen their existing economic systems. OTA teams normally are posted in long- and short-term assignments to assist ministries of finance and central banks, where they are directly embedded in these institutions. OTA's teams focus on five major areas of assistance: budget policy and management; tax policy and administration;

[20] *Ibid.*
[21] *Ibid.*

government debt issuance and management; financial institutions policy and regulation; and financial enforcement. Budget policy and management includes providing assistance to ministries of finance with designing budgetary rules and processes, expenditure and revenue forecasting, account structuring and auditing, budget execution, professional staff development, cash management and debt tracking, budgetary support for substantive policy arenas, computer and technical development, and procedures to strengthen budgetary transparency. Tax policy and administration includes providing assistance to ministries of finance and revenue-generating organizations on designing tax rules and codes, tax compliance systems, and administrative and dispute resolution procedures. Government debt issuance and management includes providing assistance to ministries of finance and central banks with managing government securities and debt management strategies, financial markets, central bank action, and donor sources and funds. Financial institutions policy and regulation includes providing assistance to ministries of finance, central banks, and financial regulators on financial rules and codes, banking oversight and supervision, payments systems, deposit insurance systems, and bank restructuring and privatization. Financial enforcement includes providing assistance to ministries of finance, central banks, and financial regulators on combating financial and securities fraud, corruption, money laundering, terrorist financing, and organized financial crime.

Building Treasury's OTA Team for Iraq

Drawing on these responsibilities, Under Secretary Taylor appointed Van Jorstad, a former OTA director, to serve as Treasury team leader and liaison with the Department of Defense. George Mullinax served as senior advisor to the Bank of Iraq and liaison with Iraq's state and commercial banking system; he was charged with the immediate task of converting Iraq's currency. David Nummy acted as Treasury's senior advisor to the Ministry of Finance; he was charged with the immediate task of paying Iraqi civil servants. Nummy's new responsibilities reflected extensive experience in budgeting and fiscal issues. At the time of his appointment, he served as a senior advisor for Budget Policy and Management in Treasury's OTA, where he worked as a technical advisor for governments and ministries of finance in such locations as the former Yugoslavia, the former Soviet republics, and Afghanistan. Nummy also served as Assistant Treasury Secretary for Finance and Management and as a staffer with the Senate Budget Committee. Another important OTA staffer Nummy added to the team advising the Iraqi Ministry of Finance was Laura Trimble, who worked extensively with ministries of finance in such locations as Bosnia, Kosovo, and Serbia.

Treasury's limited knowledge of how Saddam's government functioned greatly handicapped Nummy's planning for how Treasury would work with the Iraqi Finance Ministry and ensure that it continued to operate once Coalition forces entered the country. Simply put, American authorities knew little about the ministries' staffing or organization or the condition they would be in after the invasion. "Unlike almost every other country we had worked with, we knew nothing about Iraq," recalled Nummy. "All of our attempts to find information either inside the US government or outside the US government yielded no information whatsoever. We had no idea how the banking system worked, no idea how the government really worked, no idea how the tax system worked. . . . Nonetheless we did some planning, trying to put together how many people we would need for that effort, and in the Ministry of Finance function, which was my responsibility, we came up with five or six people [for our team]."[22] Still, based on prior experience, OTA assumed that Iraq's ministries would be largely intact physically, technically competent at the staff level, and functional after the invasion, though it was expected that the top Ba'athist leadership would flee or be removed.

Lacking specific information about the Finance Ministry, the Central Bank, and what they would likely confront on their arrival in Iraq, Nummy, Trimble, and the Treasury team relied on their experiences abroad to meet the challenges and tasks that would likely await them. "Most transition countries basically have very similar characteristics," Laura Trimble explained. "You have a very non-transparent budget. Big [categories of spending] lines that say next to nothing. So you really have no idea other than maybe at the institutional level [what type of spending is taking place]; [the budget] doesn't have any further gradations [of spending levels]. So you want them to present their budget in a way that has transparency. In budget execution, unlike the United States, you don't have a single treasury. Money is scattered to the bank accounts of the spending ministries. So you know what the ministry of finance has disbursed, but you don't get any good reports on the spending. So you really have no sense of how the recipient ministries have used their budget money. So there is a big effort always to claw back central control of budget execution, that the ministry of finance becomes the single payer, so that you don't have a lot of idle cash sitting about in the spending ministries' bank accounts, and you're borrowing money like crazy, because the central government doesn't have it, they have no ability to do cash management. . . . That seems to be a real characteristic of countries with weak ministries of finance."[23] Another complication facing the Treasury team, Trimble noted, stemmed from institutional arrangements that resembled those of communist countries, where there is "also a ministry of planning that does a lot of the analysis, what we consider budgetary analysis. So the ministry of finance is the budget request complier, then doing some indexing to squeeze [the spending] within existing revenues, not doing any sort of analysis [and prioritization] of what programs [should be funded], just indexing, and dispersing cash to the spending ministries."[24] This division of ministerial

[22] Interview with David Nummy, October 24, 2006.
[23] Interview with Laura Trimble, October 24, 2006.
[24] *Ibid.*

responsibilities in a Soviet-style arrangement typically leads to an empowered planning ministry, a relatively weak finance ministry, coordination and budget execution problems, and jurisdictional conflicts between line ministries. Consequently, there existed throughout the U.S. government a strong antipathy toward ministries of planning because they were seen as contributing to these bureaucratic and process problems. More to the point, the American government held little interest in promoting Soviet-type economies and their supporting institutions in its assistance and postconflict programs. This would also hold true for Iraq.

As the Treasury team prepared for its operations in Iraq they would be guided by their own individual and collective experiences, not by a set of Treasury guidelines or by U.S. government official doctrine for working with postconflict ministries of finance. Although organizations such as the World Bank and the International Monetary Fund identified various international best practices, no American template existed for standing up a budget process or a ministry of finance or for how best to allocate funds and collect revenues in a postconflict economy. "You just know what a budget should be," suggested Trimble, "the ways a budget should be created, how the decision making process should work."[25] "The technical aspects of standing up a ministry of finance or central bank, at their core, are pretty hard to mess with," offered Van Jorstad. "There are international standards that are well-defined and well-developed."[26] One reason for this lack of template is that the American system is somewhat unique, lacking as it does a ministry of finance by dividing a typical finance ministry's functions between the Treasury and the Office of Management and Budget (OMB). The OTA group focused on six interconnected priorities they learned needed to be addressed from these prior experiences. First, said Nummy, the team needed to "get a handle on the budget, not only what the budget process had been, but what kind of process could you generate to determine what their needs are going to be in the near-term."[27] Second, government employees needed to be paid as quickly as possible. "All of our experience was that if you want to get a country functioning, you have to get the civil service back to work as quickly as possible, and the only way you can do that is to pay them." Third, pensioners and "all the elements of the economy that depended on the government for their income" required payment. Fourth, effective budgeting depends

---

[25] Interview with Laura Trimble, October 24, 2006.

[26] Interview with Van Jorstad, October 20, 2006. The World Bank and the IMF have published a voluminous number of normative studies on budgetary institutions, rules, institutions, and policies. For example, see Teresa Ter-Minassian, Pedro P. Parenta, and Pedro Martinez-Mendez, "Setting up a Treasury in Economies in Transition," WP/95/16, Washington, DC: International Monetary Fund, February 1995. International best practices are also outlined by the organization Public Expenditure and Financial Accountability (PEFA), whose membership includes the World Bank, IMF, the European Commission, and the United Kingdom's Department for International Development.

[27] Interview with David Nummy, October 24, 2006.

on ensuring that some type of tax revenue stream exists. "Again, [in Iraq there was] zero information on how the tax system worked." "It's rare that in a postconflict situation that you will be generating any revenue for a while, but you have to understand how the system worked." Fifth, the team needed to identify the government's debt situation, the quantity, denominations, and amount owed, and to which entities the government was obligated to make payments on the debt. The sixth priority was ensuring the stability of the currency. "If the currency completely collapses," Nummy observed, "it is difficult to manage the chaos ... but [in Iraq] we didn't know the currency stock, whether it was backed up with anything, we didn't even know the denomination of the currency notes."

Uncertainty about Iraqi institutions and processes diminished Nummy's expectations for what actually might be accomplished, leaving the team to consider how it would likely need to focus on triage and emergency action for its first few months in-country. "If you look at the phases of budgeting in postconflict, the first phase is you just try to quantify what you need for the next six months," said Nummy. "So, you look at what you have to pay people, what are the expenditures that just have to be covered for the government to function at a minimal level. Then try to figure out how you are going to pay for that, and in most postconflict countries you look to donors. Then, once you define what you need for basic survival, once we figure out the revenue source ... then in the next six months, in the next budgeting cycle, you start thinking, 'How can we improve this process permanently.'"[28] Given this tight timetable, Nummy set out these goals for the team's first forty-eight hours on the ground: it should "establish the foundations for an interim administration" and provide for the security of the Finance Ministry records, especially those for gold, cash, securities, and bank deposits. By the end of the first week in Iraq, the team should evaluate all Finance Ministry activities, including its provision for the disbursement of funds.

The Treasury Department incorporated Nummy's recommendations into a broader economic plan titled "Contingency Plans for Reconstruction of Iraq's Financial Institutions and Financial Markets." Concentrating on the Ministry of Finance, the Bank of Iraq, and Iraqi commercial banks, the plan identified Treasury's strategy and tactics for achieving five broad objectives for Iraq, including rapidly evaluating the condition of Iraq's economic and financial institutions, securing Iraqi assets, and standing up Iraqi institutions "that can be handed over to the Iraqi people as soon as possible." As Treasury's Van Jorstad recalled, "Our focus initially under the ORHA umbrella was to take certain actions within the first 90 to 120 days to stabilize the economic situation."[29] Although the plan contained elements suggestive of a long-term agenda, such as creating rules and laws that promoted free markets, much of the plan, in

---

[28] *Ibid.*
[29] Interview with Van Jorstad, October 20, 2006.

the spirit of OHRA's attention to triage and emergency relief activities reflected the need for a relatively short-term effort in stabilizing Iraq's fiscal institutions.

INTERAGENCY COORDINATION AND TREASURY'S REACH-BACK OPERATION

As part of Treasury's prewar planning, Under Secretary Taylor established a "reach-back" operation in March 2003 in the guise of the Iraq Financial Task Force within Treasury's Office of International Affairs. This task force complemented the on-the-ground chain of command that would exist in Iraq by supplementing extensive interagency discussions and meetings held throughout the federal government. Taylor organized this reach-back operation to support the Treasury and other agency teams assigned to help stabilize the Iraqi economy by monitoring and coordinating their activities, by providing technical assistance and guidance from Washington, by supporting the teams on the ground when they needed additional resources or the approval of higher-level authorities, and by serving as a liaison with international organizations such as the World Bank and the IMF. The reach-back process also sought to ensure that the strategy pursued by the economic-financial teams on the ground remained consistent with broader overall strategy and could be altered accordingly. Taylor determined that the task force should be open to representatives from all relevant agencies, such as USAID, OMB, the State Department, and the Federal Reserve. These agency representatives, in turn, would report back to their own chains of command. W. Larry McDonald, Deputy Assistant Treasury Secretary for Technical Assistance Policy, chaired the group. "If we had a typical interagency thing, chaired by NSC," Taylor recalled, "it would be too much micromanaged, and the financial experts wouldn't have as much autonomy as needed. But I didn't want this to view this as our turf. So I suggested that any agency that wanted to detail someone to our taskforce was welcome.... So that way it would be very open."[30] Taylor's openness extended to allied Coalition agencies such as the Australian Department of Finance and Deregulation and the United Kingdom's Treasury Department, both of which would play central roles in the development of Iraq's early budgets. There emerged, McDonald recalled, a "large and complex landscape of assistance providers and people who would have a role in processing and reviewing and deciding what is to be done."[31]

---

[30] Interview with John B. Taylor, March 21, 2007.
[31] *Ibid.* Bensahel et al. write, "Many members of ORHA thought that they needed more time in Washington to solidify their relationships with other U.S. government agencies, especially since the revised ORHA structure called for the entire organization to deploy to the theater without leaving a back office in Washington" (*op. cit.*, 65–66). Treasury, perhaps in contrast to ORHA and other agencies, did establish a reach-back effort.

The Uneasy Relationship: Treasury and USAID

Among these assistance providers, together with Treasury, USAID would be charged with the task of reconstructing the Ministry of Finance's fiscal and technical resources and developing Iraq's provincial budgetary capacities. The Foreign Assistance Act of 1961 established USAID as an independent agency charged with coordinating and centralizing the American aid activities that emerged at the end of World War II. Postwar and early Cold War agencies and programs, such as the State Department's International Cooperation Administration and the Agriculture Department's Food for Peace Program, offered relatively short-term emergency relief. By contrast, USAID gained responsibility for creating more comprehensive, targeted, and often longer-term development programs that include technical training and cooperation as a broader strategy of foreign assistance. Where Treasury's OTA assistance focuses on financial and economic, primarily technical, assistance, USAID's portfolio is broader in scope. The agency's assistance ranges from rural and agricultural development to global health initiatives to education and literacy programs to promoting democracy and the design of government institutions. At the same time, USAID also provides fiscal and monetary policy advice and budgetary technical training and support to legislatures, ministries of finance, central banks, financial regulators, and statistical agencies as part of its assistance programs to promote economic growth. Both agencies, for example, expected to play a role in improving the preparation, development, and execution of Iraq's budgets by the Ministry of Finance and by its spending ministries. Both agencies expected to play a role in improving the administrative and technical skills of Iraq's budgetary officials throughout the government's ministries. This description of USAID's budgetary technical assistance in many ways replicates that of Treasury's OTA. The two agencies often find themselves working in the same conflict and postconflict reconstruction efforts. Through formal and informal interagency discussions and agreements they attempt to arrive at a division of labor detailing how they will approach their shared mission of, say, reconstituting a ministry of finance for a given country.

Despite their similarities in how they approach economic and financial assistance missions, there are two fundamental differences that distinguish the agencies. First, the Treasury Department is a cabinet agency, and USAID is not. Cabinet status gives Treasury a seat at political tables where USAID is not always invited, where key decisions are made and information is shared. According to USAID officials, the agency must obtain approval from the Treasury Department before they may contact the IMF or the World Bank. Not surprisingly, differences over organizational tasks emerge between OTA and USAID. "OTA has carved out a niche that has traditionally belonged to AID," declared a USAID officer. "It's a domestic agency that's gotten into the foreign aid business. One of our pet peeves was that we could initially hire the same individual and put him in country for a year for about half of what OTA costs."[32] Regardless of the merit of USAID's claims about providing less expensive technical assistance, and although USAID predates OTA's establishment by thirty years, Treasury's cabinet status offered OTA an upper hand in interagency discussions regarding the American presence in Iraq. Treasury's senior position, as well as John Taylor's personal standing with Bush administration officials, ensured that Treasury served as the lead agency for planning the reconstruction of Iraq's budgetary and financial system.

Second, the two agencies differ in their capacity to engage in large-scale assistance efforts. Whereas OTA generally provides assistance to central banks and ministries with relatively small teams of professionals, USAID enjoys the authority and funding to offer large, long-term contracts that include specifications and deliverables, with private firms paid as much as hundreds of millions of dollars to conduct USAID missions. Consequently, even if Treasury takes the policy lead for a country mission, some aspects of the overall success of the mission are likely to depend on USAID and its contractors to carry out the work. This reliance on contractors stems from the ongoing thinning of USAID Foreign Service Officers (FSO) and the decentralization of foreign assistance and development activities to other agencies in the executive branch. USAID, with its handful of personnel, often acts as little more than a manager and weak overseer of private contractors. In 1975, USAID employed forty-three hundred permanent staff, thirty-six hundred in 1985, three thousand in 1995, and twenty-two hundred in 2007. As one senior USAID official recounted:

If you go back to the Vietnam War, USAID had approximately 15,000 Foreign Service Officers.... It was a rather robust organization.... Most of the people hired for Vietnam, about 5,000 were riffed [reduction in force] after Vietnam.... About 1990, USAID had about 3,000 FSOs, by 1997 it was slightly under a thousand, the average age was 47 years. There were only three under the age of 30. Something like 60–65 percent of the Foreign Service Officers were eligible for retirement. Efforts by AID to increase those numbers over the last decade have been stillborn. Congress basically balks at it. AID is one of the only agencies that have one budget for programs and another budget for operating expenses. Congress has kept AID on a very short leash.... We've been outsourcing this stuff for now for twenty-five or thirty years. We still have experts, but we have damn few of them. We contract out for those services.... We are not going to turn the clock back. AID is not going to get a budget from Congress. If you took the number of AID people there are, and added in the number of contractors and NGOs to whom we provide contracts and grants to maybe twenty, thirty, forty thousand people.... It's far cheaper to keep a Foreign Service Officer overseas than a contractor.... You bring people in when you need them, and it allows you to reduce the size of your footprint.... You can do the job more effectively with fewer Foreign Service Officers.[33]

So, as a rather standard response for a country mission, especially for such a large task as Iraq might present, USAID's planning for Iraq in 2002 and 2003

[32] Interview with USAID officer, May 1, 2008.
[33] Interview with USAID officer, May 1, 2008.

focused largely on preparing contracts for their assigned ministries and sectors of work.

The process of planning and formulating contracts for Iraq depended greatly on the prior experiences of USAID missions in approximately a hundred countries, but particularly those in conflict and postconflict zones and in Eastern Europe. Eastern European experience was valued because of the political and economic transitions that had taken place there. Iraq's economy was understood to be heavily socialized with a system of extensive subsidies extended to all aspects of Iraqi life, and this system would change dramatically with the fall of Saddam. To promote a market-based economy and give the range of duties assigned to USAID, ten contracts valued at $1.5 billion were awarded for such projects as "Agriculture Reconstruction and Development," "Business Skills Training," "Revitalization of Iraqi Schools and Stabilization of Education," and "Iraqi Health Systems Strengthening." Another set of contracts addressed the Iraqi economy, relevant political institutions, and the development of the provincial governments. The broad goals of USAID's "Economic Governance" included reconstructing the operations of the Finance Ministry. An element of guessing what the conditions USAID would find in Iraq would be like went into the formulation of these contracts. "We weren't really aware of what would be there when we got there. Would there be a lot of destruction, would there be a little bit of destruction? We weren't certain of the operating conditions," recalled Chris Milligan, who participated in USAID's planning process as early as October 2002, then worked closely with General Garner setting up ORHA, and later became USAID Deputy Mission Director in Iraq. "So what we did was put together contracts that would allow us flexibility in responding to the needs as we found them on the ground. One of the things we were working on was putting together a broad economic support contract, which was eventually awarded to the firm BearingPoint in the summer of '03."[34] The execution of that contract, as events proved, played a central role in the Coalition's attempts to reform Iraq's budgetary institutions and processes.

ORHA'S FEBRUARY 2003 "ROCK DRILL" CONFERENCE

A month before the invasion, Jay Garner organized a two-day interagency conference in late February to follow up on the January NSC deputies meeting.[35] Each agency designated to play a role in Iraq participated in the event to review

[34] On USAID's general approach to development, see Andrew S. Natsios, "The Nine Principles of Reconstruction and Development, *Parameters*, 2005, 35, 3, 4–20. Interview with Chris Mulligan, October 24, 2006. On USAID planning, also see Bensahel et al., *op. cit.*, 33–35.

[35] Nora Bensahel, Olga Oliker, Keith Crane, Richard R. Brennan, Jr., Heather S. Gregg, Thomas Sullivan, and Andrew Rathmell, *After Saddam: Prewar Planning and the Occupation of Iraq*. Santa Monica: Rand, 2008. One review of the drill by the United States Institute of Peace noted, "Economic transformation under military occupation seems like the type of endeavor that would benefit from advance planning. Yet many officials involved in Iraq's reconstruction were

the status of interagency and agency planning for Iraq. General Garner called this the "rock drill meeting" in order to "turn over all the rocks" and resolve any problems that lurked in the plans. Attention was paid to how the various agencies planned to organize their Ministerial Advisory Teams and fulfill their missions. As shown in Table 3.1, each of Iraq's twenty-three ministries was assigned one and sometimes two lead agencies in their teams, plus other relevant agencies depending on a ministry's scope of responsibilities. "Iraq had more ministries than we have agencies," Larry McDonald observed, "so it was not always one-to-one."[36] Six agencies acted as the lead agency for the twenty-three teams: Defense, State, Justice, the Army Corps of Engineers, Treasury, and USAID. Treasury acted as the sole lead agency for the Central Bank of Iraq with George Mullinax acting as Senior Advisor. Treasury and USAID were assigned to the Ministry of Finance, with Treasury taking the lead with David Nummy acting as Senior Advisor. USAID also acted as the lead agency for the ministries of Agriculture, Education, Health, Housing and Construction, Labor and Social Affairs and as co-lead for the Transport and Communications ministry.

Remarkably, the State Department received the assignment as the lead agency for the Ministry of Planning. Although the State Department's staff includes economists, the agency is not known as for its management of capital budgets and planning ministries. This delegation divided the oversight of Iraq's budget between the State Department and the Planning Ministry's control over the capital budget, and the Treasury Department and the Finance Ministry's control over the budget's operating or recurring programs. The Coalition's lack of information and understanding of how the Iraqi ministries actually worked and how the Iraqi budgeting system functioned contributed to this divided assignment. ORHA apparently considered the Planning Ministry to be responsible for broad economic development activities, rather than the detailed decision making associated with capital planning, capital budget allocations, and the necessary working relationship a planning ministry should maintain with a finance ministry. As one Treasury officer suggested, "People thought [the Ministry of Planning] was overall economic development. They did not understand that they approved the capital budget. I think if they had known the guts of it, it would never have gone that way."[37] Larry McDonald explained that Treasury may not have offered to become the lead Coalition agency for the Planning Ministry due to the U.S. government's objection to government-planned rather than market-based

struck by how little planning went into the effort. The senior officials tasked to head major reconstruction operations were not brought together to develop a strategy until early February 2003, the month before the invasion of Iraq. Their limited pre-occupation planning was shaped more by speculation than by information about the state of Iraq's economy." Anne Ellen Henderson, "The Coalition Provisional Authority's Experience with Economic Reconstruction in Iraq," *Special Report*, 138, United States Institute of Peace, April 2005, 6.

[36] Interview with William Larry McDonald, October 16, 2006.

[37] Interview with Treasury Department official, February 23, 2009.

TABLE 3.1. *Planned Ministerial Advisory Teams, February 2003*

Iraqi Ministry	U.S. Lead Agency
Agriculture	USAID
Central Bank	Treasury
Culture	State
Defense	Defense
Education	USAID
Electricity	U.S. Army Corps of Engineers
Finance	Treasury, USAID
Foreign Affairs	State
Health	USAID
Higher Education and Scientific Research	Defense
Housing and Reconstruction	USAID
Industry and Materials	Defense
Information	Defense
Interior	Justice
Irrigation	U.S. Army Corps of Engineers
Justice	Justice, State
Labor and Social Affairs	USAID
Military Industrialization	Defense
Oil	U.S. Army Corps of Engineers
Planning	State
Religious Affairs	State
Trade	State
Transportation and Communications	USAID, State, and U.S. Army Corps of Engineers

Source: Nora Bensahel, Olga Oliker, Keith Crane, Richard R. Brennan, Jr., Heather S. Gregg, Thomas Sullivan, and Andrew Rathmell, *After Saddam: Prewar Planning and the Occupation of Iraq*, Santa Monica: Rand, 2008, 60–62.

economies. "It might have been one of those cases where there was no other U.S. government agency that felt like it was the counterpart. Certainly the Treasury Department does not feel like it is the counterpart of the Ministry of Planning. In fact, as an institution we tend to be against ministries of planning. We don't see the importance of ministries of planning as much as we see the importance of some other kinds of ministries. So State was certainly not getting any competition from us on it."[38]

---

[38] Interview with William Larry McDonald, January 30, 2009. One senior State Department official recalled about the allocation of ministerial assignments, "I was involved in the assignments. As a career civil servant, it was very highly politicized, very highly politicized. A lot of in-fighting between the different agencies, with DOD as the ultimate decision-maker. In some cases it had to do with who they wanted to assign to a given ministry." Interview with State Department official, January 26, 2009.

With only a few weeks to carry out their final planning before the various American agencies were to send their advanced teams to Kuwait prior to the invasion of Iraq, the conference discussions revealed that not all agency plans were equally well considered. One review of the conference suggests, for example, that only a handful of agencies had the opportunity to analyze the State Department's Future of Iraq Project and therefore considered whether to incorporate elements from the Project into their own plans. Many conference participants were either unaware of the Project's recommendations or whether the Project's proposals remained in effect. Furthermore, though Jay Garner wanted to add the Project's director, Tom Warrick, to the ORHA staff, he was prevented from doing so by the Defense Department.[39] Treasury's broad search for information on the economy in Iraq, however, included seeking out expatriate members of the Project to learn of their recommendations. Another retrospective weakness observed in the collective planning process was that few of the plans provided for the type of reach-back operation John Taylor established for the agencies engaged in reconstructing those aspects of the Iraqi economy that had been assigned to Treasury. The absence of reach-back planning extended to plans for the entire ORHA organization, which called for ORHA to be deployed to Iraq without a unit assigned to carry out reach-back activities in Washington. Moreover, a number of agencies failed to mobilize their personnel adequately for the mid-March deployment to Iraq. Thus, although questions of how to implement its goals in Iraq remained, such as how to pay civil servants, Treasury's planning appeared to be among the best of these prewar agency planning efforts and postconflict roles, just a few weeks before the beginning of the invasion.

Finally, during these interagency discussions, representatives from the Treasury Department and other civilian agencies identified for the Defense Department the assistance they required to begin their humanitarian and reconstruction efforts. Among the concerns expressed by Treasury officials was that certain targets be spared from the forthcoming bombing campaign. "We had two very key lists," recalled Van Jorstad, who attended the conference. "One was a do-not-target list. We tried to impress upon the military there was not a great deal to be gained by bombing the Ministry of Finance, the Central Bank, and the Ministry of Planning. The second list was 'Protect and Preserve.'" "In other words, after they had actually gained control, especially of Baghdad, that they would protect and preserve those entities. Those were the three ministries or entities that were most important to the Treasury."[40] Despite these warnings, only the Ministry of Oil received military protection.

---

[39] George Packer, *The Assassins' Gate: America in Iraq*, New York: Farrar, Straus and Giroux, 2005, 123–125.
[40] Interview with Van Jorstad, October 20, 2006.

CONCLUSION

The U.S. Treasury Department played the lead role in the Iraqi budgetary reconstruction process, and personnel from its Office of Technical Assistance were among the earliest American officials on the ground after the invasion. Alerted in the early fall of 2002 to a likely invasion of Iraq, Treasury's leadership initiated extensive deliberations and planning on a host of monetary and fiscal issues. The nearly complete lack of credible information available to Treasury and to the U.S. government as a whole that overshadowed the entire planning effort, however, is typified by Treasury's need to hire retired CIA personnel to produce a study on how the Iraqi economy operated and the running of its ministries. Nonetheless, Treasury's discussions were informed by OTA's experiences in Central Europe and the former Soviet republics. The search for information included meeting with Iraqi expatriates who participated in the Future of Iraq Project, a number of whom would assume leadership roles in Iraq following the invasion. Treasury officials examined the Project report itself, noting its recommendations on such matters as currency conversion and empowering an independent central bank. Treasury also made some effort, both before and after the invasion, to explore the history of the economic aspects of the American occupations of Germany and Japan.[41] Drawing on these various sources, Treasury did indeed produce a plan that Secretary Snow and Under Secretary Taylor personally presented to President Bush that would introduce a new currency and pay civil servants and pensioners. This latter aspect of the plan, making payments, specifically addressed a critical operational budgetary matter. Not knowing the organization, condition, or capacity of the Iraqi Ministry of Finance and that government's fiscal system, Treasury assumed and anticipated that in a period of postconflict uncertainty special precautions needed to be taken to ensure these vital payments occurred. An OTA group led by David Nummy would, in ORHA nomenclature, assume the role of the Ministry of Finance's Ministerial Advisory Team, make contact with the Ministry, and, working with the Iraqis, focus its energies on this task.

The Treasury Department's efforts throughout this planning process were aided in three important ways. First, because of its involvement in American negotiations with Turkey, the Defense Department was alerted in the early fall of

[41] Senior Treasury officials, for example, attended a presentation by Toshiyuki Yasui, Senior Fellow of the Japan Information Access Project, "Occupying Japan: Five Myths and Realities: Economists' Eyes and Its Possible Implications to Iraq," JIAP Event "Occupying Iraq," April 23, 2003. For more on how the U.S. occupation of Japan transformed that country's budgetary institutions and employed the Ministry of Finance to direct Japan's economic policies, see James D. Savage, "The Origins of Budgetary Preferences: The Dodge Line and the Balanced Budget Norm in Japan." *Administration & Society*, 34 (2002) 3, 261–284. The American government's ongoing search for lessons include this study issued by USAID: Stephen Lewarne and David Snelbecker, "Lessons Learned About Economic Governance in War Torn Economies," PPC *Evaluation Brief* 14, PD-AGC-437, USAID Bureau for Policy Program Coordination, February 2006.

2002 to the likelihood of an invasion. This provided the Treasury with at least three to four months to initiate a planning process. Second, the Treasury Department enjoyed political access stemming from its cabinet rank, but more so by the personal relationships that existed between its leadership and the top ranks of the Bush administration. Snow and Taylor, for example, presented their plans directly to President Bush, and they received his personal approval for their postconflict strategy. Before the March meeting with Bush, Condoleezza Rice informed John Taylor that the responsibility for coordinating Iraqi public finances for the Coalition rested with Treasury. Third, Treasury drew on a veteran staff of technical assistance advisors who previously served in numerous post-Soviet and postconflict Balkan countries. Although conditions in Iraq remained opaque, based on their prior experiences and given the outline of the Treasury plan for Iraq, they could anticipate what to expect and how they would manage their tasks when they arrived in-country.

Much of the overarching planning process has earned harsh criticism, including putting the Defense Department in overall command of the occupation and reconstruction effort, the decision to leave both the military and the civilian agencies who entered Iraq under-strengthened, the failure to provide for security, the failure to anticipate the true material requirements and financial costs of the war, and the minimalist planning and coordination efforts made by Jay Garner. What a more comprehensive ORHA planning effort could not resolve, however, were the basic bureaucratic divisions of responsibility and organizational cultures that separated the agencies. Over time, what hindered Coalition reconstruction efforts were not the presence of twenty-year-old neocons, but organizational stove piping and the reliance on and management of contractors to carry out reconstruction in Iraq. USAID initiated its planning efforts, accessed its own experienced staff, proceeded with developing contracts to cover a broader set of assistance and reconstruction programs, and served as the primary U.S. liaison agency for more ministries than Treasury. Yet, Treasury and USAID were both charged with the responsibility of addressing Iraqi economic issues, and their differences of approaching these tasks reflected their methods of operation. Treasury sent to Iraq small teams of in-house OTA experts, while USAID relied principally on large numbers of contractors. The strengths and weaknesses of each approach soon became evident when Coalition boots hit the ground in Iraq.

4

Boots on the Ground

The CPA and the New Iraqi Budgetary Process

New institutions may be created by enacting rules that set the terms for proper practices, processes, and procedures that become standardized and routine over time. The Coalition Provisional Authority applied this approach by creating budgetary institutions that differed substantially from those employed by Saddam Hussein. How did the CPA undertake this task and with what success? Handicapped by a host of obstacles, including a remarkable lack of information about the existing Iraqi fiscal ministries and their budgetary procedures, the Coalition entered Baghdad during the chaos that accompanied the March invasion. Coalition officials presumed they would encounter a reasonably intact and functioning Iraqi government. Instead, they found destruction, looting, incapacity, and deteriorating security. Under these conditions, the CPA's *ad hoc* budget team stitched together a budget that completed the 2003 fiscal year with new priorities for a post-Saddam Iraq. During its fourteen months in existence, the CPA issued a series of "Orders" that set out rules outlining the government's budget formulation process, the powers of the Ministry of Finance, contracting and procurement procedures, and the basis for provincial budgeting and finance. These rules were imposed on the Iraqis, but they were integrated into the existing system of rules rather than fully displacing them. When the CPA dissolved on June 30, 2004, the Iraqi government preserved significant elements of this new system, and they are regarded as among the CPA's most successful achievements. At the same time, the CPA's mismanagement of Iraqi funds and the failure to develop other critical elements of Iraq's public financial management system contributed to a lack of institutional accountability and transparency, which undermined the government's ability to control corruption. The CPA's ability to make lasting institutional change in meeting international best practices was handicapped by the familiar challenges of state building, including the CPA's own organizational command and coordination limitations, the restricted resources at its command, its inability to engage Iraqis fully into the reconstruction effort, and its own brief longevity and the transfer of sovereignty to the Iraqis. Moreover, existing institutions proved to be often quite durable and resistant to change, as vested interests defended the status quo. This chapter provides an account of these events, beginning with the discovery that Iraq was less than an intact state.

INVASION AND THE LOOTING OF THE MINISTRY OF FINANCE

The actual invasion of Iraq proved to be a rather brief affair, as Coalition forces rapidly cut through a bewildered Iraqi army. The invasion of Iraq began on March 20, 2003, following an extensive and devastating series of "shock and awe" bombing raids conducted by the American and British air forces. Coalition armored and mechanized infantry units quickly overwhelmed Saddam's largely static and disintegrating formations. The Iraqi government soon collapsed, as its leadership abandoned Baghdad and dispersed throughout the country, leaving Coalition military forces to begin the occupation of the capital city on April 9. Although Baghdad was not fully secured, Jay Garner demanded that his Office of Reconstruction and Humanitarian Assistance group be allowed to enter the capital city to begin its work. The first elements of the civilian agencies made their way into the city on April 19, with Garner entering on April 21. The Treasury's Office of Technical Assistance team led by Van Jorstad, David Nummy, and George Mullinax arrived on April 23.

Even as ORHA's personnel assembled to provide humanitarian assistance, events on the ground quickly undermined their prewar planning. Though the precision bombing campaign produced little in terms of direct infrastructure damage, the military failed to guard against the rampant and destructive looting that swept through Baghdad following the fall of Saddam. Descriptions and visual images of the looting are by now well known. With the notable exception of the Ministry of Oil, the various ministry buildings were ransacked, often stripped bare of all usable office equipment, furniture, and files. As Illustrations 4.1 and 4.2 of the Ministry of Finance's computer data center show, many of the agency's already antiquated computers were overturned, smashed, and burned, with the rest stolen. "The primary Ministry of Finance building, the top four floors, was burned," said one of the Treasury officers who first entered Baghdad, "and the primary Central Bank building was completely destroyed. So that made the near-term implementation of what we had planned very difficult."[1] "No one anticipated the destruction," recalled David Nummy. "There is no post-conflict country that I am aware of where literally all the infrastructure of the ministries is destroyed. There was never a post-conflict country I've been in where there was such a total absence of security."[2] The destruction of Iraq's ministerial infrastructure meant that Iraq's bureaucracy lost its organizational coherence and

---

[1] Interview with Treasury Department official, October 20, 2006.
[2] Interview with David Nummy, October 24, 2006.

ILLUSTRATION 4.1. Looting of the Ministry of Finance Computer Data Center
Photo: Thomas Hartwell

ILLUSTRATION 4.2. Looting of the Ministry of Finance Computer Data Center
Photo: Thomas Hartwell

ability to function even at a minimal level of competency; the government effectively ceased to exist. The Coalition then confronted the task of standing up that government, ministry by ministry, in the face of this enormously destructive looting. "The looting set us back two years," a senior Treasury official later lamented.[3]

The looting that accompanied the invasion and the general lack of information about the actual condition of Iraq's government and economy rendered many of the assumptions that underpinned prewar economic reconstruction planning obsolete. "We really didn't know what we were going to find initially," noted a senior USAID officer. "We knew Iraq under Saddam had been obviously a very closed regime economically ... Stalinist. But we expected the economy to be working within its own parameters, but when we got there and saw things first hand, and also that things broke down a lot, and that the people who were running the economy were gone, there was a lot more whole-sale change [required] than we had initially anticipated."[4] Treasury's OTA team assumed that they would find the Finance Ministry and its facilities, leadership, and staff reasonably intact. "I figured I'd do the same thing that I'd done in the other [postconflict countries]," Laura Trimble noted. "Find the Ministry of Finance, find the budget director, and start going in there every day, and work with that person, looking at how they had done things."[5] The top leadership of Iraq's various ministries consisted of Saddam loyalists who were politically unacceptable, untrustworthy, or incarcerated, or who had fled from Baghdad. The Minister of Finance and Deputy Prime Minister, Hikmat Mizban Ibrahim al-Azzawi, to whom the Coalition assigned the eight of diamonds in its deck of most wanted Iraqi playing cards, proved to be of no assistance after his arrest on April 18. A similar problem emerged with the loss of financial records. "We had very little to go on," remembered Treasury Under Secretary John Taylor. "We knew the systems were antiquated. There had not been much contact with modern computers, and things like that. We had a sense that there were a lot of career people in the Ministry who were knowledgeable people, but not up to speed in terms of the latest technology .... We envisioned that we would go in after Saddam fell, and establish bonds with the civil servants who were there, get the payroll records we'd like to pay, and that's what we were going to do, here are the US dollars, ready to go. But because of the looting, no records could be found at all."[6]

After the looting the Finance Ministry conducted much of its activity in conditions that crippled its administrative capacity. "Working in temporary facilities only accentuated the backwardness of the Iraqi bureaucracy," recalled one CPA official. "The only item on the desk of the Director of Accounts, the key operating individual in the Finance Ministry, the one man with control over

[3] Interview with Treasury Department official, October 16, 2006.
[4] Interview with USAID officer, October 24, 2006.
[5] Interview with Laura Trimble, October 24, 2006.
[6] Interview with John Taylor, March 21, 2007.

every dollar spent in Iraq, was a thick pad of carbon paper. No telephone. No computer. Previously people came to see the Director of Accounts, plead their cases for disbursements over $40, and he subsequently wrote out his decisions and orders in longhand. Even when the phones had worked, the system was that carbon copies of his orders had always been delivered to the other Ministries in Baghdad by couriers in cars. Now their cars had also been stolen or looted. The entire Government was at a halt."[7] The pillaging of the Finance Ministry destroyed many irreplaceable records and ruined the computers and communications equipment that connected it with Iraq's other ministries. Due to the damage inflected on this equipment, Treasury and other agency officials were forced to communicate with Washington's reach-back operations by way of satellite cell phone calls.

In the midst of this devastation and the Iraqi bureaucracy's virtually non-existent administrative capacity, the Treasury team did experience one great bit of good fortune. Slowly, the Finance Ministry's staff returned to work. With them they brought many of the government's files, the most important of which, given the team's immediate concerns, were the civil service salary and pensioner payments data. Fearing the worst during the invasion, the professional staff hid these files in their homes and then returned them as the immediate conflict subsided. These data provided the Treasury team with the information they needed to distribute the frozen $1.7 billion in Iraqi assets held in U.S. banks that President Bush released by executive order on March 20, 2003. More than 274 tons of U.S. dollars in small bills were airlifted to Iraq and quickly allocated by Treasury and Finance Ministry officials to civil servants and pensioners. According to John Taylor, "The Iraqis supplied extensive documentation of each recipient of a pension or paycheck. Treasury officials who watched over the payment process in Baghdad in those first few weeks reported a culture of good record keeping. On April 29, Jay Garner ... reported to Washington that the payments had lifted the mood of people in Baghdad."[8] The Treasury Department's prewar plans called for making these payments and exchanging Saddam's dinars for new postconflict currency. Seven printing presses produced the new dinars, which were delivered to Iraq in twenty-seven jumbo jet plane loads and then over several months were distributed throughout the country. In this way, declared Taylor, "a collapse of the financial system was avoided."[9]

CPA BUDGETING FOR IRAQ

In June, Taylor testified before the Senate Foreign Relations Committee, where he outlined Treasury's accomplishments that emerged from "the contingency

---

[7] Interview with Treasury Department official, December 12, 2007.
[8] John B. Taylor, "We Did Get the Money to Iraq," *International Herald Tribune*, February 27, 2007, 6.
[9] *Ibid.*

plans laid out months in advance of the war." "We began," Taylor said, "selecting members for our team of Treasury advisors back in January; the first wave was deployed to Kuwait in March and arrived in Baghdad in April. We have since sent over a dozen additional advisors with expertise in areas ranging from budgets, to payments systems, to monetary policy."[10] Salary and pension payments made to more than 1.5 million Iraqis and the stabilization and conversion of the currency highlighted Treasury's successes. Yet, developing an Iraqi budget remained among the high-priority tasks still facing Treasury and the CPA. "Prior to the war," observed Taylor, "no Iraqi government budget was published. The lack of transparency and accountability in fiscal operations made it difficult to determine how resources were allocated or how revenues were raised."[11] When it came time to direct the reconstitution of the Iraqi budgetary process and the formulation of a short-term budget for the current fiscal year, however, this task fell to the CPA, not Treasury.

Making the 2003 Iraqi Budget

The March invasion occurred three months into the regular Iraqi fiscal year, leaving the Coalition with the task of either implementing Saddam's still-secret budget or creating a new budget that fit Coalition priorities for the rest of the fiscal year. The overall responsibility for CPA economic policy, including Iraq's budgetary policy, passed from a largely Treasury-led effort with USAID support under ORHA, to Ambassador L. Paul Bremer, Bush's appointee to lead the CPA, who arrived in Iraq on May 12, 2003. Bremer, in turn, relied on Peter McPherson as his senior economic advisor and director of the CPA's Office of Economic Policy. McPherson, who previously served as director of USAID under President Ronald Reagan from 1981 through 1987 and later as deputy Treasury secretary under Reagan and President George H. W. Bush, also directed what became the CPA Ministry of Finance. This unit advised the Iraqi Ministry of Finance and the Central Bank of Iraq on such topics as tax and central banking policy.

To oversee the CPA's budgetary needs, McPherson appointed David R. Oliver, Jr., as director of the CPA Office of Management of Budget (CPA OMB). The CPA OMB's functions included managing the CPA's own budgets, assessing Iraq's reconstruction requirements and preparing cost estimates, and developing the CPA's supplemental appropriations requests to the White House and the Congress. With the Iraqi Finance Ministry's physical infrastructure

---

[10] John B. Taylor, "Reconstruction in Iraq: Economic and Financial Issues," JS-452, Office of Public Affairs, United States Department of the Treasury, June 4, 2003, 2. Also see John B. Taylor, "Reconstruction of Iraq's Banking Sector," "A Briefing Sponsored by the Bankers Association for Finance and Trade and the Arab Bankers Association of North America," JS-895, Office of Public Affairs, United States Department of the Treasury, October 10, 2003.

[11] *Ibid.*, 3.

looted, its office equipment destroyed, and its personnel scattered, Oliver's role expanded, and the CPA OMB came to serve as a *de facto* Ministry of Finance, charged with creating a budgetary process and a budget that made sense to the Coalition. Later, when McPherson left Iraq, Oliver assumed the director duties of both the CPA OMB and the CPA Ministry of Finance. The personnel from these two units often overlapped, depending on the staffing arrangements at the time. Oliver's background as a former rear admiral in the U.S. Navy and four years as the director of the Navy Office of Financial Management and Budget served him well as chief budget officer in Iraq. Of all the budgets in the federal government, none is larger in dollar value; more complex in planning, preparing, and processing; and more demanding to administer than the Department of Defense budget. Within the Defense Department's various service budgets, none is more multidimensional and challenging than the Navy's, which includes the Marine Corps budget, with its responsibility for funding all forms of warfare, personnel, operations and maintenance, research, and procurement. The budgets under Oliver's charge ranged at least ten times larger in dollar value than that of Iraq's 2003 budget. In addition to the technical side of budgeting, the Defense budget is highly political, in terms of developing the budget inside the executive branch, gaining its adoption by Congress, and responding to congressional oversight. By selecting Oliver, the CPA benefited greatly from his Navy experience in drafting the first Iraqi budget, particularly because that budget and Iraq's priorities focused heavily on national security issues, and because he understood the politics of the American budgeting system and how the flow of funds from the United States would come to Iraq. Evaluating Oliver's contribution, Paul Bremer recalled that he "excelled at squeezing every dinar and penny out of our limited funds. If he said we were in financial trouble, I could bet on it."[12] Finally, it is worth noting as an aside that the first two directors of the U.S. Bureau of the Budget who drafted the first federal executive budgets in U.S. history were both retired Army generals. So selecting Oliver to direct the new Iraqi budget was very much in the American tradition.

Oliver faced a daunting set of challenges. First, he could rely on only a very small staff consisting of some half-dozen to ten professionals, which already experienced significant turnover from the ORHA group, to develop the budget. By the time Oliver arrived in Iraq in July, David Nummy and Lara Trimble, for example, were in the process of leaving the country. With Nummy and Trimble went the Treasury Department's key advisors in stabilizing the Finance Ministry since the onset of the invasion. By June 2003, twenty-five OTA staff rotated through Iraq in four different phases. This churn at the staff level, combined with the limited number of advisors in Oliver's charge, constrained the CPA's ability to analyze programs at a meaningful level, develop credible budgetary and fiscal projections, or make significant changes in the way the Ministry's bureaucracy

[12] L. Paul Bremer III, *My Year in Iraq*, New York: Threshold Editions, 2006, 109.

conducted its activities. As Oliver recalled, "You can't get enough people over there to do the work. I thought there should be ten to thirty times as many people over there, and I asked for them and couldn't get those people .... There were only 600 American civilians in Iraq, and I only had four to ten people."[13] The actual composition of the team, nonetheless, did offer Oliver some advantages, as the majority of his budget group consisted of personnel seconded from the Australian and British treasuries. These Commonwealth financial advisors greatly aided Oliver because, despite the modifications imposed by Saddam, the legal framework and practices of the budgetary system reflected years of British presence in Iraq. "The underlying laws were from British colonial rule .... The audit law was very much crafted on the Westminster audit system," noted Laura Trimble.[14] "This meant," said one of Oliver's Commonwealth advisors, "that Iraqi bureaucratic structures and systems were much closer to those in Great Britain and Australia than in America."[15] Some of the older Iraqis schooled at Oxford and Cambridge and trained in England and thus felt a greater affinity for the English and Australians than for the Americans. This shared background eased the way for effective working relationships.

Though differences certainly existed between the U.S. federal government's budgetary processes and procedures and those of the Australians and British, Oliver's small team appears to have coordinated effectively. According to an Australian member of the group, "In my view, the team was competent, professional, and worked well together. I don't recall any significant differences within the CPA on budget formulation process."[16] Still, by the time Oliver began work on the 2004 budget, many of his staff who worked on the 2003 budget cycled out of Iraq. The OTA presence in formulating the budget, for example, was largely replaced by a detail of four or five U.S. Office of Management and Budget personnel drawn largely from the agency's budget review division. "It was absolutely a different team" that drafted the 2004 budget, recalled one of

---

[13] Interview with David Oliver, June 9, 2007. Also see Dave Oliver, "Restarting the Iraqi Economy," November 2003, unpublished manuscript, and Justin Tyson, "Budget Implementation in Post-Conflict Countries: Iraq Case Study," 2006, unpublished manuscript. Tyson, seconded from the United Kingdom's Treasury, served on Oliver's staff from July through December 2003. On the number of OTA staff rotating through Iraq, see U.S. Department of Treasury Office of the Inspector General, "International Assistance Programs: Review of Treasury Activities for Iraq Reconstruction," Audit Report OIG-06-029, Washington, DC: Department of the Treasury, March 23, 2006, 6.

[14] Interview with Laura Trimble, October 24, 2006.

[15] Interview with United Kingdom Treasury Department official, December 3, 2008. For more on the contribution of Australian and British contributions to these budgeting activities, see the United States Institute of Peace "Iraq Experience Project" interview with Rodney Bent, September 14, 2004. After David Oliver left Iraq, Bent served as Director of the CPA OMB and senior advisor to the Ministry of Finance and the Ministry of Planning and Development Cooperation and for a time as co-director with Tony McDonald of the Australian Treasury.

[16] *Ibid.*

the budget officers. "We could have had a more robust team. I don't think it was sufficient."[17]

A second challenge facing Oliver was that much of the Ministry of Finance's top executive leadership proved to be of little help in making budgetary decisions. "You had a whole bunch of guys who understood how to do the detail work," Oliver recalled, but "the problem was, is that budget had been done at the top level, they were done by people who had gone away, either had been killed or fled. So you didn't have anybody who understood the big picture."[18] Saddam-era ministries were very top-down, run by a few key officials who reported directly to Saddam, and their absence meant that the next tier of leaders, mostly directors-general, though technically competent, were not the individuals making overarching policy decisions. Though the Finance Ministry retained much of its top leadership and they aided the Coalition in managing the Ministry's regular operations, Oliver, nonetheless, was placed in the role of *de facto* finance minister and would be the one making those "big picture" strategic fiscal decisions about budget allocations.

Fortunately for Oliver, the Finance Ministry escaped the direct effects of the CPA's widely criticized de-Ba'athification directive, CPA Order 1 "De-Ba'athification of Iraqi Society," signed by Paul Bremer on May 16, 2003. The Order directed that senior Ba'ath Party leaders were "banned from future employment in the public sector."[19] The top three management layers in each ministry were to be examined to determine their membership in the party, with full party members, even those at the junior membership level, removed from their positions in government. The Order thus not only meant the removal of the finance minister, Saddam's man Hikmat Mizban Ibrahim al-Azzawi, and his immediate party-loyalist aides from their positions, but also the Ministry's directors-general. The directors-general managed the major divisional units in the Ministry, such as the director-general for the budget, who coordinated and prepared those elements of the government's budget under the Ministry's jurisdiction, and the director-general for accounts, who oversaw the disbursement of funds. Cutting this deeply into the Ministry could indeed have crippled its leadership capacity among its professional ranks. Yet, as Ali Allawi, who served as finance minister during the Iraqi transitional government between 2005 and 2006, recalled, "The De-Ba'athification Order played very little role in the Ministry of Finance."[20] Though critics of Bremer's Order commonly claim that it gutted the Iraqi bureaucracy of its administrative leadership, what is sometimes forgotten is that the application of the order varied among Iraqi institutions.

[17] Interview with U.S. Office of Management and Budget official, October 24, 2006.

[18] Interview with David Oliver, June 9, 2007.

[19] Coalition Provisional Authority Order 1, "De-Ba'athification of Iraqi Society," Baghdad, May 16, 2003.

[20] Interview with Ali Allawi, May 15, 2007.

The Ministry of Finance was relatively unscathed by de-Ba'athification. David Oliver commanded the CPA's OMB unit, but he did not arrive in Iraq until the first week of June. This meant that the responsibility for implementing the May de-Ba'athification order at the Ministry rested with the Treasury OTA team that preceded both Oliver's arrival and the activation of the Iraqi Governing Council, which later assumed responsibility for implementing the de Ba'athification order. By the time of Oliver's arrival in June, the OTA team had worked with the Iraqis at the Ministry for more than two months. After interviewing the Ministry's leaders to determine their histories with the Ba'ath Party, an OTA official recalled how he applied the Order to the Ministry's deputy finance minister and the various directors-general:

The order said that if you were at some of the highest levels of the Ba'ath Party, you could not hold any position in government at all, but if you were a member at all, you could not be at the top levels of the ministry. So what that meant in the case of the Ministry of Finance is that it would have wiped out all the directors-general. At the point this order was issued, we were already revising the pay system for civil servants, we were already paying civil servants, we were paying pensioners, we were starting to work on getting the budget together, all of those activities that we worked really hard to get started, were built completely around these directors-general. So, had that order been executed as it was, all of that would have come to an end. So I went back to the list, talked to the directors-general, and what I discovered was that the person who had been the director-general for administration had been a more active member of the party ... he had played the role of conduit between the party and the Ministry of Finance. Part of his job was to enforce party orders. So I did ask that guy to leave the Ministry .... We went through the process of having him formally retired. I didn't do anything beyond that.[21]

---

[21] Interview with Treasury Department official, May 9, 2008. The official also stated, "When I first got there and encountered the previous officials at the Ministry of Finance, I had a conversation with every single one of them about what they had done at the Ministry of Finance, what their background was, whether they had been a member of the Ba'ath party, and at what level. What I discovered is that at the director-general level, is that the majority of them had a background that you would find in any country. These were people who had gone to work at the Ministry of Finance at a young age, were educated, had a degree that was relevant to their job, had worked for many, many years, risen through the ranks, and they had great mastery over their jurisdiction. The minister had been captured and a couple of the directors-general had disappeared, but I was able to make contact with nine or ten of the previous directors-general. The ones I talked to, in my mind, were clearly career civil servants and had been promoted for the right reasons. They were incredibly vital to getting the Ministry of Finance operating again. So I had a conversation with them about what level they were in the Ba'ath Party. With one exception, every single one of them was either at the very lowest level or at the next to the lowest level. A lot of them told me that in 2000 or 2001 they were not members, but that they had been approached and told they had to join if they wanted to retain their job at the Ministry. The Party was going to make sure that everyone who had a senior job was a member of the Party. So a lot of them joined simply to keep their job. A lot of them said they had gone to a meeting every six months because that is what was required. There was no evidence that any of them really had been active in the Party. My personal previous experience had been in Eastern Europe, and I discovered ... lots and lots of people in government that had the same exact experience with the Communist Party. So based on that experience, none of this surprised me [in Iraq]."

Thus, only one director-general lost his job due to the de-Ba'athification Order. The Finance Ministry's deputy minister Hashim Obeid, the second-in-command, not only remained at the Ministry, he became the Acting Finance Minister through August 2003. "He was a career civil servant that had risen through the ranks of the Ministry and very knowledgeable in Ministry affairs," reported a Treasury official. "While a member of the Ba'ath party, he was very low level and confided that he had been required to join in order to retain his leadership position at the Ministry, despite being a career employee."[22] Reported another Treasury officer, "He was extremely technically competent and operated [at the Ministry] before the sanctions of the first Gulf War ... and he was critical to [the paying of civil servants and pensioners]."[23] Though a competent bureaucrat in administering the Ministry's day-to-day operations, Obeid proved to be reluctant to make policy decisions. Thus, although the Ministry of Finance retained the top tier of its senior professional management despite de-Ba'athification, because of the traditional administrative passivity shown by the Ministry's leadership, David Oliver and the CPA OMB needed to set priorities, authorize procedures, and draft the new Iraqi budget.[24]

Although the Finance Ministry essentially escaped de-Ba'athification, its experience proved to be the exception rather than the rule for the Iraqi government. One Coalition participant in the making of the 2004 Iraqi budget recalled that with the typical dismissal of ministers and their directors-general taking place in most ministries, "your effective civil servants who were capable of making management decisions were removed, and you were left with career bureaucrats who were largely only capable of taking direction, and that made things very difficult. When we got to June 2004 and we were forced to come up with our first budget, we'd gone out to the necessary line ministries and regional governors asking them to submit their budgets, and they were incapable of doing so. They'd never done anything like that, and if anyone had done anything like that they were long gone. So, in many cases we had to help them with teams of consultants for each ministry or different branch of the Ministry of Finance, help them come up with their capital planning budget, and so on, and it was a very arduous process."[25] Budgeting required an administrative capability not only in the Finance and Planning Ministries, but also in the line ministries. De-Ba'athification crippled their leadership ranks and the ability of these ministries to budget.

---

[22] Interview with Treasury Department official, August 20, 2010.
[23] Interview with Treasury Department official, August 25, 2010.
[24] An example of Oliver's direction is his memo to Mr. Hashim Obeid, Acting Minister, Ministry of Finance, and Mr. Muhanna Jassim Al-Battat, Director General of Accounts, "Procedure for Settlement of Outstanding Obligations of Budget Organizations (Centralized Finance) and of State-Owned Enterprises (Self-Financed)," August 1, 2003. The memo outlines detailed procedures for the preparation of bank reconciliation statements, the disposition of unused checks in frozen bank accounts, and the auditing of accounts by the Board of Supreme Audit.
[25] Interview with U.S. Office of Management and Budget official, October 24, 2006.

Third, the poor quality of Iraqi budgetary and economic information complicated the drafting of the first post-Saddam budget. Some Finance Ministry workers returned selected databases to the Ministry following the invasion, particularly the files necessary for paying civil servants and pensioners. The CPA, however, still lacked reliable expenditure figures by programs and ministries for 2001 and 2002, meaningful projections of petroleum sales and the resulting generation of government revenues, and the information necessary to make macroeconomic estimates. "So many of the numbers were just wrong," recalled a USAID staffer who described how the Iraqis calculated their economic assumptions:

This was a discussion [I had] with a Ministry of Planning official, who basically was talking about economic policy and how it worked, because he had worked in the statistical organization [COSIT – Central Organization for Statistical Information and Technology], he actually headed that unit within the Ministry of Finance. He was talking about how they did economic policy. It was not like you analyze the situation, think about what you can do, set an inflation target and go from there. It was more of, okay inflation is going to be this, and you work backwards. So I think going in, this was a very big challenge for us, because the Ministry of Finance had been very weak under the previous regime. It was really the Ministry of Planning and the Ministry of Oil that were the ministries that had the true strength over political [decisions] and in terms of staff. We went there as AID along with DFID [the United Kingdom's Department for International Development] to work with the Ministry of Finance, viewing them as being the natural lead on so many issues – it really needed a tremendous effort to rebuild the Ministry of Finance .... The staffing wasn't there, the capacity wasn't there.[26]

"Lack of data is a big problem," added another USAID senior officer. "The numbers under Saddam weren't really that good. So you don't even know what your baseline is. All you can do is from when you walked in the door. You probably see all those newspaper articles saying 'things are worse than before.' No, we don't know, those numbers [have no credibility]."[27]

The Iraqis lacked a unified budget with a final bottom line of total government expenditures and revenues. The budget, instead, consisted of multiple compartmentalized programs and their budgets, with ministerial spending dispensed from Iraq's Rasheed and Rafidain state banks. Oliver discovered that nineteen different payroll systems paid the government's civil servants and pensioners. In a May meeting with CPA Director Paul Bremer, Oliver described the legacy of Saddam-era budgeting: "Central budgeting became chaotic because the Ba'athists subverted normal fiscal procedures. As far as we can tell only about 8 percent of the government's spending was channeled through the Ministry of Finance .... It looks like the vast majority of government spending was controlled directly by various offices attached to the presidency ... and Saddam's hand-picked cronies. And under Saddam the budget was a state secret – just like the Russians. We can't find any useful records of this massive 'off budget'

---

[26] Interview with USAID official, October 20, 2006.
[27] Interview with USAID official, October 24, 2006.

spending."[28] The Iraqis compartmentalized and hid data from themselves and the outside world. Budgetary and other economic data, such as gross domestic product, inflation, and unemployment rates, were state secrets, and those who used these data in an unauthorized manner could be severely punished. Faced with these challenges, Oliver and his team pieced together as much credible data as they could, rounded figures when required, and made generous guesstimates and assumptions when necessary.

Fourth, Oliver was under tremendous pressure to produce a budget to kick-start the government's reconstruction efforts. He arrived in Iraq on June 6, and a budget needed to be issued immediately. "If you don't have a budget," noted Oliver, "the country doesn't know what to spend. The ministries are just stopped."[29] The condition of the Iraqi economy proved to be far worse than assumed by prewar planners. Much of Iraq's workforce stood idle and unemployed, and the country's infrastructure suffered from long-term neglect and lack of maintenance. Roads, public buildings, and the electrical grid were in disrepair, and Iraq's all-important oil drilling and refinery facilities, the government's virtual sole source of revenues, functioned with outdated equipment and at suboptimal levels. "The logic," Oliver declared, "was what you needed to get the economy started was to get the electricity to work, potable water, you need the hospitals working, you have got to get security, you've got to get the oil pumping the money that [funds the government]. You need to provide as much money as the country can absorb ... and you need to cover the first 18 months."[30] The urgency to spend government funds to stimulate the economy clearly influenced Oliver's approach to the rapidity of the process. "I got out a budget as quickly as we could .... If there is something really wrong [in the funding for the programs], come back in 30 days. So we got that out so people could start spending. The real crux of it was forcing money out .... I worried more about pushing money out than I worried about anything."[31] This drive to spend trumped Oliver's concerns about how effectively these funds might be used, and it overwhelmed the CPA and the Iraqi government's limited capacity to account for how the funds would be employed. The CPA's imperative to spend later generated charges of waste, fraud, mismanagement, and corruption.

Despite these challenges, even in the swiftness with which the budget would be conceived, Oliver made important changes to the formulation of the Iraqi budget. Saddam left behind a secretive, stove-piped, autocratic budgetary process, in which spending ministries contributed little to decision making. The publication of the budget and its public dissemination as directed by Oliver proved to be one of the most important changes from Saddam's practices, a change the CPA regarded as a significant symbolic triumph over the old regime.

---

[28] L. Paul Bremer III, *My Year in Iraq*, New York: Threshold Editions, 2006, 66.
[29] Interview with David Oliver, June 9, 2007.
[30] *Ibid.*
[31] *Ibid.*

Oliver, however, rejected imposing an American model of budget formulation on the Iraqis. There would be no use of budget functions, baseline budgeting, program budgets, or performance budgeting. He never considered requiring the Iraqis to use the complex Program, Planning, Budgeting, Execution System employed by the Defense Department. Iraq simply lacked the trained personnel, the bureaucratic resources, the institutional rules, and the political checks and balances that enable the American system to function as it does. The Iraqis still crafted their budgets by hand, literally with paper and pencil. To draft the budget, Oliver and his staff learned what they could of how the existing budgetary process operated, how the Ministry of Finance functioned internally, and how the various ministries related to each other under Saddam's regime.

Due to the limited personnel at his command and the pressure to issue a budget as quickly as possible, Oliver relied on the basic elements of the existing system. Oliver's team could neither budget by themselves nor hope to change the process in a fundamental way given the limited time available to them. "What I was trying to do," Oliver recalled, "was use the Iraqi system so that the Iraqis could carry it out."[32] Oliver sought to encourage budgetary participation and deliberation inside the line ministries, between these ministries and the Finance and Planning ministries, and between the ministries and the CPA. To accomplish this, he called on the line ministries to develop their budgets in consultation with their CPA advisors and then to present their budgets to the Finance and Planning ministries for review. Consistent with the CPA's desire to move Iraq toward a more market-based economy, Oliver relied principally on the Finance Ministry rather than the Planning Ministry during the review and drafting of the budget. "I did not use the Ministry of Planning because I thought they were not as competent [as the Finance Ministry]. The Finance Ministry was in charge. Also, the Planning Ministry is really a socialistic appeal right to central planning, which is not appropriate. And I was going to turn away from that."[33] Though Oliver encouraged deliberation among the ministries, the CPA made the spending decisions. One reason for doing so, he claimed, was to protect the Iraqis from assassination. "Senior Iraqis were in significant danger .... Therefore, I established the policy that I would order all changes and actions I desired the Finance and Planning Ministries to undertake. I vetted these orders with these Iraqis whose judgments I valued, but my final guidance was both written and directive .... I suspected that eventually there would be targeted violence against those assisting the Coalition."[34]

Drafted during a few weeks in July, the 2003 budget was intended by the CPA to serve as an interim budget for the half-year, July through December.[35] As shown in Table 4.1, total expenditures were projected at $6,099.6 billion

[32] *Ibid.*
[33] *Ibid.*
[34] *Ibid.*
[35] Republic of Iraq, "Budget Revenues and Expenses, 2003, July–December," Ministry of Finance, Ministry of Planning, Coalition Provisional Authority, July 2003.

TABLE 4.1. *Coalition Provisional Authority 2003 Iraqi Budget (all figures are in millions of U.S. dollars)*

Spending Allocations	Million U.S. Dollars
Operations	2,002.1
Investments	352.7
Reconstruction	256.8
Social safety net	1,350.0
Electricity reconstruction	192.0
Police	150.0
LPG & gas	135.0
Currency reprinting	100.0
Construction Fund	100.0
Military de-mobilization	60.0
Program Review Board	35.0
Other spending	1,366.0
Total allocations	$ 6,099.6
Revenues	
Oil	$ 3,455.0
State-owned enterprises	373.6
Fees, taxes, charges	59.1
Total revenues	$ 3,887.7
Deficit/Surplus	$ –2,211.9

Note: 2003 Budget covers July to December 2003.
Source: Coalition Provisional Authority 2003 Iraqi Budget.

with revenues estimated at $3,887.7 billion, leaving a deficit of $2,211.9 billion. In one of the most important tables in the budget, "Expenditures by Organization," Oliver made a first-cut attempt to specify operational and capital expenditures by ministry, a total figure amounting to $1.4 billion, plus $1.14 billion for salaries and civil service pensions. The "Operating Expenses by Input" table identified functional categories of funding for "service and goods requirements," "assets maintenance," and obligations for Kuwait war reparations. Another table, "Other Proposed Expenditures," identified programmatic spending, such as social safety net programs, the police, and expenses associated with reprinting currency. The budget listed eight "key initiatives" for the Iraqis, including general reconstruction, defense, public health, electrical, communications, water, and sewage improvements, costing $1.4 billion.

The inclusion of tax revenues in the budget reflected extended discussions taking place between the CPA and the Iraqi leadership. The budget assumed total revenues of $3.887.7 billion, including $3.455 billion in projected oil revenues, $374 million in revenue transfers from state enterprises to the government, and $59 million in income stemming from other fees and taxes. These revenue estimates were best-guess figures.

Neither the Iraqis nor the CPA could truly foretell the future value of oil revenues, given fluctuations in the world oil market, or the level of Iraqi oil production. The budget consequently assumed oil revenues would fund more than $1 billion in new infrastructure for the Ministry of Oil through off-budget financing. The estimate of $374 million derived from the revenues generated from some two hundred state-owned enterprises came at a time when many of these enterprises were damaged, dysfunctional, and dependent on government subsidies. Furthermore, Saddam maintained his regime by providing a system of popular subsidies for a wide range of staple products funded by petro dollars, rather than collecting unpopular domestic taxes. Iraq simply lacked a competent reliable internal revenue service. Assuming any meaningful tax collection other than oil revenues, therefore, was very much a leap of faith. Finally, the budget identified a variety of other sources that would finance the government and the reconstruction effort, such as $2.5 billion in seized and vested assets from Saddam's holdings, $1.2 billion from the United Nation's Development Fund for Iraq, and $2.475 billion in U.S.-appropriated Iraqi relief funding that would be managed by USAID.

For David Oliver, broadening the Iraqi tax base beyond oil revenues was an important step in moving the Iraqis away from a state-driven economy, as well as a matter of good public finance. In a meeting between the CPA-appointed Iraqi Governing Council, Paul Bremer, Oliver, and the CPA's chief economic advisor Peter McPherson, the Iraqis debated whether taxes should be imposed. As Oliver recalled,

What happened is philosophically we had this discussion with a group of Iraqi economic policy advisors and also with the Governing Council that you wanted to have taxes. You wanted to have taxes so you had buy-in from the people. This was an intensely long discussion, four hours, because a bunch of Iraqis said 'We're rich, we have oil. There's no reason to have taxes.' And Ambassador Bremer and Peter McPherson and I talked about philosophically you wanted to have taxes. Now they had taxes before on natural gas, electricity, and water, because the houses were metered. So we wanted to keep that as a method to have those people employed as they went around [reading meters], because they were so subsidized. At some point you were going to be changing that, but you first wanted to be rewarding [market behavior], and [then] taxing it.[36]

In a similar manner, the CPA sought to activate existing provisions for income taxes, which had largely been ignored by Saddam's regime, and begin their collection. The imposition of non-petroleum-based taxes thus reflected a fundamental desire to move the Iraqis toward a more liberalized economy, to unite them fiscally by way of the shared sacrifice of paying taxes, as well as to provide some needed employment for civil servants.

After the budget's July release, the CPA and the Ministry of Finance conducted a review to make revisions. Oliver permitted significant capital spending

---

[36] Interview with David Oliver, June 9, 2007.

increases for the Oil Ministry to boost production and additional funds for the Interior Ministry to increase the size of the police force, while the Ministry of Culture sustained the largest budget reduction. The review assumed a sizable drop in revenues from the Agriculture Ministry's state-owned enterprises "to reflect pessimism in [the] likely amount to be collected."[37]

The 2003 budget, in summary, produced a rudimentary set of tables that provided only the broadest guidelines for spending. The budget consisted of titles of ministries and expenditure elements without detailed descriptions of how the funds were to be used or programs implemented. No breakdown existed for personnel expenses, the number of civil servants being funded, or provincial allocations. The budget gave no indication of future or multi-year spending. Significantly, only $2.6 billion of the projected $6.1 billion in expenditures would be channeled through the ministries, with the remainder directed by the CPA, primarily through its Program Review Board (PRB). Uncertainties surrounding oil production and the questionable capacity of Iraqi revenue collection undermined the credibility of the budget's revenue estimates.

Perhaps the most thoughtful external critique of the 2003 budget came from the Open Society Institute's Iraq Revenue Watch. The Revenue Watch group, funded by the international financier George Soros, an avowed critic of President Bush's Iraq policies, acknowledged the difficult conditions under which the CPA worked in drafting the budget. Nonetheless, Revenue Watch noted that, for example, the budget neglected to explain how spending would be financed by Iraqi funding sources, such as the Development Fund for Iraq (DFI) that the CPA began managing in May 2003, and that the CPA needed to provide greater transparency for the PRB's spending decisions. The CPA created the PRB to determine which projects would be funded by DFI and American reconstruction funds. The group applauded the budget's funding of Iraq's Board of Supreme Audit but called for the development of guidelines that would guarantee the Board's autonomy and the generation of timely audit reports.[38]

A more biting critique of this budget came several years later from Ali Allawi, who served as Iraq's finance minister from 2005 to 2006. "The budget," Allawi concluded,

was an amateur and unrealistic affair, hastily put together by ministries that had no idea of modern budget preparation requirements, and a CPA staff that was barely aware of the true needs of the Iraqi state. The Iraqi ministries of Finance and Planning were drawn into a process that in the previous regime had been discharged in the utmost secrecy .... The imprint of the Planning Ministry was all over the budget, clearly establishing the ministry

---

[37] CPA Ministry of Finance and Iraq Ministry of Finance, "Summary of Changes to Ministry Budgets Arising from 30 Day Review, Major Changes to Ministry Budgets for 2003," July 26, 2003.

[38] Svetlana Tsalik, "Iraq's First Public Budget," *Revenue Watch*, Report No. 1, 2003; Svetlana Tsalik, "Keeping Secrets: America and Iraq's Public Finances," *Revenue Watch*, Report No. 3, October 2003.

as a powerful rival to the CPA's technical and advisory staff. The CPA chose the line of least resistance, and where it mattered the most, the old ways were kept going for the sake of expediency. The Governing Council was supposed to have responsibility for budget-setting but was denied appropriate information by the CPA. In any case, the Iraqi-funded budget was a bit of a red herring. Iraqi budgetary rules or constraints did not govern the real expenditures.[39]

Many of Allawi's observations are valid. The 2003 budget did indeed emerge from a hasty effort at budget formulation that incorporated dubious estimates for both taxing and spending. The budget's flaws were rooted in the poor condition of the Iraqi government the Coalition discovered when it entered the country, and from the CPA's own constrained staffing, technical, and information capacities. As Allawi stated, "The CPA could not rely on the Iraqi ministries themselves for a guide to the reconstruction needs of the country. The ministries had been gutted and could not produce effective spending plans and proposals."[40] Consequently, as Allawi charged, Oliver and his staff consciously maintained the outlines of the top-down budgetary decision-making process emblematic of Saddam's regime, as the CPA retained full control over the budget's priorities and parameters. Where Allawi's comments invite reevaluation is his assessment of the Ministry of Planning's standing in the process. Allawi is correct about the relative skill sets of the two ministries, with the Planning Ministry staff possessing the greater analytic and planning skills needed to develop Iraq's capital budgets. Oliver and the CPA, however, clearly acted to raise the Finance Ministry as the dominant ministry responsible for setting Iraq's budgetary and fiscal policy. The Planning Ministry, for example, played a relatively minimal role in the thirty-day review of the 2003 budget, and the Finance Ministry emerged as the central ministry during the preparation of the 2004 budget.

Making the 2004 Iraqi Budget

After finishing the 2003 budget, David Oliver and his team immediately began work on the 2004 budget.[41] Their efforts to complete the budget were spurred by the forthcoming October Madrid Donors Conference that required estimates for Iraqi reconstruction costs and debt relief, which the budget, in part, would provide. A World Bank/United Nations report projected these costs would reach $36 billion over three years. Grants and loans totaling some $33 billion were pledged by the United States, the World Bank, the IMF, Japan, the European Union, and other donors. On October 29, Congress funded the American pledge

---

[39] Ali A. Allawi, *The Occupation of Iraq: Winning the War, Losing the Peace*, New Haven: Yale University Press, 2007, 194.

[40] *Ibid.*, 195.

[41] Republic of Iraq, "2004 Budget," Ministry of Finance, Ministry of Planning, October 2003. Note that where the 2003 budget's list of institutional authors included the Coalition Provisional Authority, the 2004 budget lists only the Finance and Planning ministries.

of $18.4 billion for the Iraq Relief and Reconstruction Fund (IRRF) in an $83.1 billion supplemental appropriations bill that supported military and reconstruction activities in Iraq and Afghanistan. Iraq's vast reconstruction needs drove the 2004 budget. Greater attention would be paid to capital and investment requirements than in the 2003 budget, in which the operating side of the budget drew more consideration. Though more care would be taken in drafting the 2004 budget than the 2003 budget, the CPA's need to spend money as rapidly as possible to reconstruct Iraq and build its security forces drove the budgetary process.

The 2004 budget stands as the only full-fiscal-year budget prepared by the CPA. "The 04 budget was so far above what the Iraqis were used to," claimed a proud CPA OMB official who helped lead the drafting of the budget. "It had line ministries, the number of employees; then we set up a new employee grade scale. The other system was unsustainable. It was run out of the palace by Saddam to reward Ba'athist favorites."[42] The budget did indeed address many of the criticisms justly directed toward the 2003 version, as Oliver and his CPA readily acknowledged, and by doing so it established expectations for the drafting of future budgets by the Iraqis. The Iraqis participated in the formulation of the 2004 budget, for example, to a much greater degree than they did in the drafting of the 2003 budget. "We spent a lot of time talking with [the budget director-general] about the line items in that budget. We were with them all the time," recalled the OMB staffer. "It was a lot of back and forth consultation with them," particularly on capital budget items.[43] The 2003 and 2004 budgets also proved to be more publicly accessible and transparent than any of those produced during the Saddam era.[44]

As the CPA finished the 2003 budget and began its August thirty-day review, the CPA and the Finance Ministry initiated work on the 2004 budget. Finance and line ministries normally work on several budgets simultaneously, so that the preparation and implementation of different fiscal year budgets overlap. So, even as ministries manage and execute the budget of the current fiscal year they may be engaged in drafting the budget for the forthcoming fiscal year. This was true in Iraq. On July 24, the Finance Ministry issued guidelines to the line ministries on how to prepare their budget proposals that would be submitted to the Finance Ministry by August 15.[45] These guidelines directed the ministries to create a network of committees at the ministerial level and within each ministerial directorate to consider recurrent operational and investment capital

---

[42] Interview with U.S. Office of Management and Budget official, October 24, 2006.

[43] *Ibid.*

[44] The CPA's 2003 and 2004 Iraqi budget documents may be found at: http://www.iraqcoalition. org/budget/budget2004.html/. Public availability of budget documents since the June 2004 transfer of power proved to be quite limited until approximately the 2008 and 2009 budgets, when the Ministry of Finance finally developed a Web site.

[45] Ministry of Finance, "Instructions of [sic] Preparing the Budget for Year 2004," Baghdad, July 24, 2003.

spending priorities. More detailed supplementary guidelines issued later ordered the ministries to develop multi-year spending and revenue proposals covering the years 2004, 2005, and 2006. Ministries were directed to provide actual expenditure levels for 2002, and spending requests above 2002 and 2003 levels would have to be justified through 2006. Ministries were required to submit spending levels by geographical region and recommendations for alternative forms of revenue raising, and to provide suggestions for ways to reduce spending. The guidelines set an exchange rate of 1,500 dinars to a U.S. dollar. The guidelines also called on the ministries to begin developing a form of performance budgeting, whereby they would create measures of successful program performance, such as an increase in the number of people receiving potable water, in order to initiate a more efficient allocation of resources. Ministries were ordered to identify, prioritize, indicate the number of Iraqis hired, and provide information on projected capital construction projects. The guidelines terminated the existing four-tiered civil servant salary payment system in favor of a new salary system created by the Treasury Department. State-owned enterprises were directed to fill out detailed forms that outlined the nature of their subsidies, assets, revenues, payment systems, balance sheets, and repayment plans.

Finally, the guidelines described the short timetable for the 2004 budget process. After the line ministries submitted their budgetary plans to the Finance Ministry by August 15, review hearings would take place with the Finance and Planning ministries, as well as with the World Bank and United Nations officials. A week at the end of September was set aside for final deliberations with the Iraqi Governing Council. "There was one gathering of twenty to forty senior Iraqis, and we talked to them," recalled David Oliver. "Then I went over and briefed the Budget Committee at the Council, and then the Council made changes with the whole budget they thought necessary. They got the whole briefing, and we spent hours doing that."[46] Despite this discussion with the Council, an Australian senior official serving on Oliver's staff observed that "It would have been preferable to have arranged the timetables to allow interim Iraqi ministers to have greater involvement in the process." Nevertheless, the staffer added, "It should be noted that the 2004 budget process was already underway when interim Iraqi ministers were appointed."[47] The budget, however, needed to be approved quickly, in preparation for the October Madrid Donors Conference where Iraq would present its National Development Strategy. From a fiscal perspective, the Strategy called for integrated national government budgets, fiscal decentralization, and stronger financial management and accounting of public spending.

The October 2003 version of the 2004 budget and the March 2004 revised version provided a far more detailed picture of the Iraqi economy than the 2003

[46] Interview with David Oliver, June 9, 2007.
[47] Interview with Australian Treasury official, July 27, 2007.

budget.[48] The 2004 budget began by assessing the state of the Iraqi economy and Saddam's economic legacy. Relying on data supplied by the Ministry of Planning, the budget illustrated how Iraqi per capita GDP peaked in 1979, the year before the outbreak of the war with Iran, then fell and later recovered in 1989, only to fall again after the invasion of Kuwait and the United Nations embargo. The data also showed that investment in all forms of gross capital formation virtually collapsed after 1982, which explained the abysmal condition of Iraq's infrastructure. After denouncing Saddam's centrally planned economy and the need to learn from the postcommunist experiences of former Soviet bloc countries, the budget promised balanced budgets, declaring that "Responsible fiscal policy is a key component of Iraq's economic strategy. The 2004 Budget was prepared on the basis that Iraq needs to demonstrate that it can operate with the resources available to it. The 2004 Budget does not rely on increased borrowing or printing money."[49]

The "key challenge" in developing the budget was the lack of a clear budget base, or the level of the previous year's expenditures, in order to determine the proper level of spending for the forthcoming fiscal year, and to create a budget "baseline" to show the longer-term budgetary consequences of current spending. The absence of credible budget data from prior years remained the core of the problem. To create the base, Oliver and the CPA separated the budget into its "on-budget" and "off-budget" components. The on-budget funding supported the ministries and agencies, while off-budget expenditures came from "self-financing" sources. This distinction helped analytically, but putting the numbers together remained difficult. As the budget document explained, "Of the appropriations 'on-budget,' a variety of exchange rates were used, as a means of providing subsidies, and little detail exists on how or where military or Presidency appropriations were spent. Further, the vast bulk of public expenditure under the previous review was 'off-budget,' reflecting goods received under the Oil-for-Food program. The manipulation of this program by the former regime presented a significant challenge in preparing the 2004 Budget."[50] To solve this challenge, programs and agency budgets needed to be separated into sometimes new categories. This categorization also affected programs funded though the U.S. budget. Unlike the 2003 budget, reconstruction programs funded through U.S. appropriations amounting to $2.5 billion were classified as "off-budget" because of their "self-financing" from the U.S. budget.

The budget addressed many of the deficiencies in information and analysis identified by critics of the 2003 version. First, the budget figures were presented in dinars rather than dollars, as had been done in the 2003 budget. Second,

[48] Republic of Iraq, "2004 Budget," Ministry of Finance, Ministry of Planning, October 2003; Republic of Iraq, "Revisions to 2004 Budget," Ministry of Finance, Ministry of Planning, March 2004.

[49] Republic of Iraq, "2004 Budget," Ministry of Finance, Ministry of Planning, October 2003, 5.

[50] *Ibid.*, 11.

TABLE 4.2. *Coalition Provisional Authority 2003 and 2004 Iraqi Budgets (all figures are in billions of Iraqi Dinars)*

	Billion Iraqi Dinars		
Spending Allocations	2003	2004*	2004**
Operations	7,362.3	19,026.7	25,432.3
Investments	1,869.9	1,118.4	3,797.5
Total allocations	9,232.2	20,145.1	29,889.8
Revenues			
Oil	4,096.5	18,000.0	21,262.9
State-owned enterprises	337.5	562.5	0
Reconstruction levy (import duties)	0	450.0	172.5
Excise	0	15.0	3.0
Civil service pension contribution	0	0	101.4
Other revenues	162.0	231.3	188.5
Total revenues	4,596.0	19,258.8	21,729.1
Deficit/Surplus	−4,636.2	−886.3	−8,160.7

Note: 2003 Budget covers July to December 2003.
* October 2003 version.
** March 2004 revised version.

rather than the single-year budget figures included in the 2003 budget, the 2004 version attempted to create a multi-year baseline for long-term planning. The budget predicted a steady increase in both revenues and expenditures through 2006. Revenues, as shown in Table 4.2, would jump by about 10 trillion dinars ($6.6 billion) a year from 2004 through 2006, and spending would climb, but at a slightly lower rate, which would result in small budget surpluses in 2005 and 2006. Revenues from state-owned enterprises; hotel, excise, and land taxes; and user charges were delineated. The budget outlined three years of ministry operating and capital expenditures and broke down total operating expenditures by inputs, such as staff, salary, assets maintenance, and service requirements. A detailed list identified operating expenditures by outputs, such as ministerial operating expenditures, regional development projects, nation-building projects, pensions, Kuwaiti War reparations, and interest on foreign debt and treasury notes. Particularly revealing, the budget provided figures for the number of civil servants and their aggregate cost by ministry. Saddam's four-tiered salary structure for civil servants would be replaced by a thirteen-tiered structure, which among other things would increase spending for these payments. The various ministries would make these payments once their employees were reassigned into the new format. The budget set the total number of civil servant employees at 1,047,718, with 6,633 serving in the Finance Ministry and 1,050 in the Planning Ministry. The budget, furthermore, outlined in greater detail than in the 2003 version how the government would be financed through the DFI and through vested and seized assets.

A significant increase in oil revenues and other capital inflows led to the drafting of a revised March 2004 budget. Total projected revenues, as shown in Table 4.2, grew by nearly 13 percent from 19.258 trillion Iraqi Dinars (ID) ($12.8 billion) to 21.729 trillion ID ($14.5 billion), with total expenditures increasing from 20.1 trillion ID ($13.4 billion) to 29.9 trillion ID ($19.9 billion). Included in this increased spending were new demands for civil servant salary and pension payments, greater-than-expected payments for domestic debt obligations, and, increased allocations for Kuwaiti War reparations. The revised budget also recognized that no revenues would be collected from state-owned enterprises, either because they were unprofitable or because the revenues were uncollectible. This new budget provided a more delineated set of data that offered added insights into Iraq's public finances and the activities of the government's ministries. For example, the reconstruction projects funded by the Ministry of Municipalities and Public Works, the Ministry of Electricity, and the Ministry of Health, were listed by name and expenditure level. Nonetheless, these figures, and the rest of the economic and budgetary numbers included in the two 2004 budgets, as in the 2003 budget, were often best estimates, subject to poor data, changes in economic conditions, the ability to collect revenues, variations in external sources of capital inflows, and fluctuations in oil prices. Another factor, as David Oliver candidly stated, was separating out real government expenditures from corruption and side payments. "The budget for Iraq, if you take out the graft and the money that was going for bribes, we determined it was about $14.5 billion."[51]

CREATING IRAQ'S FINANCIAL MANAGEMENT LAW

The drafting of the 2003 and 2004 budgets resulted in procedures that, although rudimentary in nature, promoted participation, deliberation, and engagement over budgetary choices within the Ministry of Finance, between the ministries, and with Iraqi leaders. By bringing together ministerial officials to discuss budget priorities, Oliver helped to break down some of the compartmentalization and lack of communication among budgetary actors that Saddam's regime encouraged. Nonetheless, these procedures tended to be informal and *ad hoc*. Relying on the budget laws created during Saddam's era that were inspired by the Soviet Union and built on colonial laws enacted by the British and before them the Ottomans, Iraq still lacked a set of overarching budgetary rules that complied with contemporary internationally accepted best practices. To rectify this deficiency, on June 2, just weeks before he left Iraq and the CPA came to an end, Paul Bremer signed CPA Order Number 95, the "Financial Management Law and Public Debt Law." This Order, together with Bremer's Order Number 71 "Local Governmental Powers" and Order Number 87 "Public Contracts," met these

---

[51] Interview with David Oliver, June 9, 2007.

international standards, and they continue to serve as the foundation for Iraq's budget process.[52]

Order Number 95 spells out the principles for Iraqi budgeting; the functions of the Ministry of Finance; and how Iraq's budget is to be prepared, adopted, executed, audited, and reported. The Order also rescinds the existing Iraqi budgetary laws, the 1940 law as revised in 1985 and 1990. The Order first took shape in the CPA Office for Economic Policy and the CPA's Ministry of Finance, the CPA unit that paralleled the Iraqi Ministry of Finance, and it was drafted by contributing staff from the CPA's General Counsel's Office, U.S. OMB, Treasury OTA, the Federal Reserve, and the United Kingdom's Bank of England and its Treasury. The Iraqi Governing Council's Finance Committee extensively reviewed and edited the draft and adopted the final version before Bremer signed the law as a CPA order.

The order begins with a set of principles that underlie Iraqi budgeting and are consistent with internationally agreed-on standards and budgetary rules. They also stand in stark contrast to the manner in which Saddam managed his secret and highly compartmentalized budget and fiscal system. First, the principle of transparency requires that budget information be classified and organized in a manner that promotes accountability and "policy analysis."[53] Second, the budget should embrace the principle of comprehensiveness, so that the budget offers a complete understanding of government operations for legislators, who can then vote on these programs. Third, in accordance with the principle of unity, government resources should be "directed to a common pool" so that expenditures can be allocated consistent with the priorities of the state.[54] These principles are followed by a long list of definitions that by themselves have great significance for the budgetary process. The law set the fiscal year on a calendar year basis, from January 1 through December 31, and it defined the government's chart of accounts to be "a structured list of accounting codes used to classify and record budget revenue and expenditure transactions."[55] To reinforce the principles of comprehensiveness and unity, in contrast to Saddam's fragmented accounting and payments system, the definitions noted that the "Treasury Consolidated Account" consists of the government's consolidated cash balances, and the "Treasury Single Account" is the bank account, or linked bank accounts, through which all revenues and payments are made.

---

[52] Coalition Provisional Authority Order 95, "Financial Management Law and Public Debt Law," Baghdad, June 2, 2004; Coalitional Provisional Authority Order 71, "Local Governmental Powers," Baghdad, April 6, 2004; Coalitional Provisional Authority Order 87 "Public Contracts," Baghdad, May 14, 2004. See all CPA Orders, Regulations, and Memorandum at http://www.iraqcoalition.org/regulations/#Orders/.

[53] Coalition Provisional Authority Order 95, "Financial Management Law and Public Debt Law," Baghdad, June 2, 2004, "Annex A, Section 1, Purpose," 1.

[54] *Ibid.*

[55] *Ibid.*, "Annex A, Section 2, Definitions for the Purposes of This Law," 1–4.

CPA Order 95 elevated the Ministry of Finance's central role in the budgetary process to levels unseen since the 1940 "General Accounts Procedure Law Number 28." By design, the order reinforced the Finance Ministry's role in the budgetary process, raising it above Saddam's Ministry of Planning. Rodney Bent, who served as a CPA OMB director, recalled, "Because there was this bifurcation between the Ministry of Finance and the Ministry of Planning, the other senior advisors, the Australians in particular, wanted to make the Iraqi Ministry of Finance similar to what you see in Western countries. A much more powerful ministry than what the Iraqis were used to. The Iraqis didn't see it that way. The Ministry of Finance was just much less important than the Ministry of Oil or the Ministry of the Interior. [The Finance Ministry] writes your checks and pays your salary, but that's all they do."[56] The order empowered the finance minister to issue regulations, guidelines, and directions to implement the new budget law. The finance minister would submit the draft budget to Council of Ministers for its approval, and then the minister would submit that budget by October 10 to the legislature for its approval. The finance minister controlled the Treasury Consolidated Account, opened bank accounts, and administered the Treasury Single Account that would be maintained by the Central Bank. Significantly, while reporting to the Council of Ministers, the order gave the finance minister operational responsibility for managing and reviewing the investment position of the Development Fund for Iraq, the government's petroleum revenue account. Disbursements from the account required two signatures, one of which would be that of a Finance Ministry official designated by the minister.

The Finance Ministry served as the central actor in the budget's formulation. The ministry created the economic forecasts around which the budget would be prepared. The Central Bank would act in "consultation" with the ministry in making these projections. According to the order, the creation of the new budget began in May with the ministry issuing a report on fiscal policy priorities for the coming year. The Finance Ministry would consult with the Ministry of Planning and Development Cooperation, as the Ministry of Planning formally came to be called, on the capital and investment elements of the budget. In June, again in consultation with the Planning Ministry, the Finance Ministry would issue fiscal guidelines to the spending ministries as they developed their own budget proposals, which they would submit to the Finance Ministry in July. A ministry's full budget proposal would be sent to the Finance Ministry, with copies of the capital budget proposal also sent to the Planning Ministry. The Finance Ministry would then review these proposals to develop its final version of the draft budget. The Finance Ministry's draft budget would identify "irreconcilable" disagreements it

---

[56] Interview with Rodney Bent, October 24, 2006. Bent served in Baghdad from October 2003 to April 2004 as director of the CPA OMB and as senior advisor to the Ministry of Planning and Development Cooperation.

shared with the spending ministry over their budgetary priorities and provide its solution for resolving these conflicts. Remarkably, the order goes on to state: "In determining the proposed solution, the Ministry of Finance *may* consult with the Ministry of Planning and Development Cooperation regarding the prioritization of capital expenditures."[57] Even in the realm of capital spending, the Finance Ministry would thus be granted greater authority than the Planning Ministry in determining budgetary priorities. During this adjustment between spending ministries and the Finance Ministry in the draft budget, any increases in the aggregate spending level required the approval of the Finance Ministry and the Council of Ministers. Finally, in September the finance minister would present the final proposed budget to the Council of Ministers for its approval, and then present it by October 10 to the legislature. If not approved by the Parliament by December 31, the Finance Ministry would allocate the budget on a monthly basis of one-twelfth of the previous year's budget total until the new budget passed. This truly critical provision enabled the Finance Ministry to fund the Iraqi government even if the Parliament failed to reach a political or technical agreement on the budget.

The Finance Ministry would also prepare supplementary budgets and direct them through the budgetary process. The order makes the Finance Ministry responsible for budget execution. Budget execution includes proper cash management, the monitoring of cash flows, internal controls over fund transfers between ministerial accounts, recording of transactions, internal audits, and the allocation of funds from the budget. The order also assigned the Ministry the task of managing the regional treasury offices and administering the opening, recording, and reconciliation of government bank accounts. Order 77 established the Board of Supreme Audit, whose responsibilities included combating corruption, waste, and fraud, while Order 95 authorized the Board to conduct annual audits of the national budget and all supplementary budgets.[58] The Finance Ministry, in turn, would assist the Board with these audits and provide it with all necessary information for that purpose.

The "Public Debt Law" section of the order authorized the Ministry of Finance to manage, issue, and purchase securities and other financial instruments to finance the government's debt. Although the law does state that the Central Bank, acting as the government's agent, shall manage the issuance and redemption of securities, the Finance Ministry plays the central role in this process. The finance minister, not the Central Bank, sets the maturity date, offering price, interest rate, method of computing the interest rate, dates for paying principal and interest, form of security, and currency in which the debt is to be issued. To buy, redeem, or pay the interest on these

[57] Coalition Provisional Authority Order 95, "Financial Management Law and Public Debt Law," Baghdad, June 2, 2004, Annex A, Section 7, Budget Preparation," 11.

[58] Coalition Provisional Authority Order 77, "Board of Supreme Audit," Baghdad, April 18, 2004.

securities, the minister is granted "a permanent and indefinite appropriation of public funds."[59]

Order 95 and Order 71, "Local Government Powers," do provide for some degree of provisional budgetary autonomy and fiscal federalism. After noting that Iraq's government should be democratic, republican, pluralistic, and federal, Order 71 states that each governorate may create a Governorate Council. The councils, in turn, would receive funds from the national budget. The order permitted the councils to set priorities for the provinces, and it allowed them to raise their own funds by way of independently generated fees and taxes. Both Orders 95 and 71 granted councils the right to amend local projects identified in ministerial budget proposals, as long as the amendment was approved by a two-thirds council vote and the change did not raise the spending limit called for in the budget. Order 95 allowed councils and regional governments to borrow and issue loan guarantees, subject to a recommendation by the Ministry of Finance and approval by the Council of Ministers. Finally, each council could create smaller units of government, such as regional and municipal councils. The councils could also raise local taxes and fees and "identify" local budget needs in the national budget.

The orders issued by the CPA are sometimes described as ideologically driven, divorced from reality, ineffective, or simply ignored.[60] Certainly the provisions in these orders that sought to control corruption proved to be ineffective. Yet, even critics of the CPA noted the institutional legacy of the CPA's budget rules. Though deeply unimpressed by the CPA's 2003 and 2004 budgets, former Iraqi finance minister Ali Allawi pointed to the immediate and long-term value of the budgetary process the CPA imposed on the Iraqis: "The most important economic and financial reform that the CPA introduced, however, was the promulgation of

[59] Coalition Provisional Authority Order 95, "Financial Management Law and Public Debt Law," Baghdad, June 2, 2004, "Annex B, Public Debt Law, Section III, Authorities and Duties Pertaining to Outstanding Debt Securities," 3.

[60] Consider the assessment of CPA orders in George Packer, *The Assassins' Gate: America in Iraq*, New York: Farrar, Straus and Giroux, 2005, 317–320: "Bremer issued a blizzard of legal orders covering everything from the registration of NGOs to the appointment of inspectors general in the ministries.... The determination to get the job done overrode everything else, and no one asked whether the CPA had any business writing codes for Iraq that created ... transparent accounting procedures." Packer goes on to quote a demystified CPA staffer, "The quality of the fairyland that was created was very lovely. All these were great laws, but they just had no application in the real world." Rajiv Chandrasekaran wrote, "Before Bremer left, he signed a hundred orders in all. Some were essential.... But many others were aspirational or just plain unnecessary in a nation wracked by a violent insurgency.... Many in the Emerald City assumed that if you wanted to change something, you changed the law, just like in the United States. But Iraq didn't work that way." In Rajiv Chandrasekaran, *Imperial Life in the Emerald City: Inside Iraq's Green Zone*, New York: Knopf, 2006, 239–240. James Dobbins et al. noted the Iraqis' resistance to some of the orders. "There was consistent pushback from some Iraqis on enforcement of CPA's decrees. Ali Allawi, who served as Minister of Defense and Minister of Finance, later wrote that' the legality' of Bremer's Orders was always a contentious issue." James Dobbins, Seth G. Jones, Benjamin Runkle, and Siddharth Mohandas, *Occupying Iraq: A History of the Coalition Provisional Authority*, Santa Monica: Rand, 2009, 15.

the Financial Management Law. This was a profound and far-sighted piece of legislation that set the framework for writing balanced budgets, with public accountability for all government expenditures. The Law played a vital part in establishing the parameters of budget preparation and made unauthorized expenditures – the band of Iraqi budget managers – a culpable act. The fact that its provisions were subsequently breached did not detract from its importance as a powerful tool for ordering Iraqi's public finances."[61] "Order 95," declared a senior United Nations official who worked with the Finance and Planning Ministries in 2008, 2009, and 2010, "is the heart of Iraqi Public Finance."[62]

THE PRESSURE TO SPEND MONEY AND THE CPA'S LACK OF FINANCIAL ACCOUNTABILITY OF IRAQI FUNDS

Sources of Funding for Iraq

Coalition and donor authorities considered spending large amounts of money crucial for Iraqi reconstruction. Before the invasion the State Department's Future of Iraq Project report predicted the need for a massive fiscal reinvestment in Iraqi infrastructure. "Most of oil revenues, e.g., 75%," the report stated, "should be allocated to finance the infrastructure projects. The rest, i.e., 25% should be allocated to the government's annual budget."[63] After the invasion, the CPA repeatedly raised its estimates of Iraqi reconstruction needs, with Ambassador Bremer, as he put it, "setting aside my conservative economic instincts." Within weeks of his arrival in Iraq, Bremer recalled, "We announced a major stimulus program centered on an emergency $100 million public works program."[64] Funding for Iraq's government and the country's reconstruction efforts during the immediate post-Saddam years came from a number of sources. Donor organizations administered some of this funding, such as the World Bank and the United Nations Development Group's management of donations from twenty-six donor states. The U.S. government through the CPA administered the spending of a great majority of these reconstruction funds. They included donor funds from international organizations, contributions from foreign governments, Iraq's own assets held overseas and oil revenues commandeered by the United Nations, and American emergency appropriations.

The primary source of American-generated and CPA-managed reconstruction financing consisted of the Iraq Relief and Reconstruction Fund (IRRF). The

[61] Ali A. Allawi, *The Occupation of Iraq: Winning the War, Losing the Peace*, New Haven: Yale University Press, 2007, 264–265.
[62] Interview with United Nations officer, November 18, 2009.
[63] U.S. Department of State, Economy and Infrastructure (Public Finance) Working Group, "The Future of Iraq Project," "Tax Policy: Guidelines for the Transitional Government of Iraq," Washington, DC, 2002, 2.
[64] L. Paul Bremer III, *My Year in Iraq*, New York: Threshold Editions, 2006, 68.

initial contribution to the IRRF, known as IRRF-1, stemmed from the $2.5 billion FY 2003 emergency supplemental appropriations signed by President Bush on April 16, 2003. The American government intended these funds to support humanitarian relief assistance, training and equipment for Iraqi security forces, and a variety of reconstruction projects. As the Coalition came to recognize the breathtaking scope of Iraq's reconstruction, this funding clearly proved to be inadequate to the task at hand. Prewar and postinvasion promises that the Iraqis could fund the great majority of their reconstruction needs from their own budgetary resources proved illusionary. In April 2003, for example, Andrew Natsios, the director of USAID, declared that "the American part" of reconstruction spending "will be just $1.7 billion. We have no plans for any further-on funding for this."[65] Quickly, however, as Ambassador Bremer observed, "Reality on the ground made a fantasy of the rosy prewar scenario under which Iraq would be paying for its own reconstruction through oil exports within weeks or months of liberation. We were clearly involved in a long-term project of nation-building here, like it or not."[66] Bremer directed Peter McPherson, his senior economic advisor and David Oliver, the CPA budget director, to "come up with 'WPA-type' spending projects."[67] Although often criticized for its neoliberal economic policies, the CPA's spending plans proved to be Keynesian in influence, extensive in scope, and very, very expensive. As McPherson recalled, "There's no question that we said, 'Look, we've got an emergency. We've got a country that is basically not operating . . . and we've got to get money infused into the economy.' We talked a lot about those early WPA days . . . . We spent money on a lot of things that the purists, the free market economy people, would not have approved of."[68]

---

[65] U.S. House of Representatives, Committee on Government Reform – Minority Staff, Special Investigations Division, "The Bush Administration Record: The Reconstruction of Iraq," Washington, DC: U.S. House of Representatives, October 18, 2005, 1. An example of this humanitarian stabilization funding came from USAID's Office of Transition Initiatives. Between April 2003 and March 2004, the Office issued $41 million in grants, including funds to Iraqi ministries to refurbish their offices following the looting that occurred after the invasion. Between April 2003 and March 2006 the Office spent $337 million. Significantly, the Office convinced USAID's leadership not to set quantitative targets for the use of the funds, thus undermining the evaluation of its effectiveness. As USAID's final evaluation report on the Office's activities notes, "While it is clear that OTI was on target in its program, it is difficult to judge the magnitude of objective achievement because OTI did not define end states or develop indicators to track progress toward these outcomes." Peter Boyle, *Strategy and Impact of the Iraq Transition Initiative, OTI in Iraq (2003–2006), Final Evaluation*, Social Impact, Inc., and USAID, Washington, DC, September 30, 2006, v.

[66] Bremer, *ibid.*, 112.

[67] *Ibid.*, 68. In keeping with that New Deal imagery, Peter McPherson described some of the projects the CPA initiated this way: "I funded irrigation ditches, which had been neglected, with thousands of almost WPA work done on irrigation ditches." Interview with Peter McPherson, July 13, 2007.

[68] Interview with Peter McPherson, July 13, 2007.

Relying on the October 2003 World Bank and UN Development Group needs assessment that the reconstruction of Iraq's fourteen government and economic sectors required $55 billion to $75 billion, Bremer and his team radically trimmed this amount into a request politically acceptable to the White House. On September 3, President Bush submitted a request to Congress for $20.3 billion in new IRRF funding, IRRF-2, of which $15.2 billion would be spent on electrical services, water and sewer construction, and the repair of oil facilities, with the balance used to enhance Iraq's security services. Congress approved $18.4 billion of this total, and on November 6, 2003, Bush signed the FY 2004 emergency supplemental appropriations bill. IRRF-2 served as the largest pot of American reconstruction funding, which the U.S. government added to in the post-CPA years through annual emergency supplemental appropriations and spending programs such as the State Department's Economic Support Fund, from which the Coalition spent $4.5 billion in Iraq between 2006 and 2010. Nonetheless, due to the restrictive procurement regulations that governed the contracting of U.S. appropriations and the slow buildup of contracting administrative capacity, the CPA spent just $366 million of the $18.4 billion in IRRF funds between October 2003 and June 2004.[69] This meant that the CPA urgently needed to find more accessible, less restricted funds to finance critical Iraqi reconstruction projects and pay salaries and pensions. The CPA found these monies in the petroleum revenues deposited in the Development Fund for Iraq.

On March 23, 2003, the United Nations Security Council created, through Security Council Resolution 1483, the Development Fund for Iraq. The resolution required that the export sales from Iraqi petroleum and natural gas products still held in the Saddam-era UN Oil-for-Food Program and other Iraqi financial assets held abroad be deposited in the DFI. These funds, though they would be recorded by the Central Bank of Iraq, would, in turn, be held in Federal Reserve Bank of New York accounts and be allocated by the CPA. These funds ostensibly would be spent on reconstruction projects, humanitarian programs, and the costs of operating Iraq's government. The UN resolution also created the International Advisory and Monitoring Board for Iraq (IAMB) to ensure that these funds were appropriately managed, disbursed in a transparent manner, and audited, consistent with international standards and practices. On June 9, the UN adopted Security Council Resolution 1546, which declared that upon the transfer of sovereignty from the CPA to Iraq the Iraqi government would solely determine the allocation of the $29.4 billion

---

[69] On the State Department's Economic Support Fund expenditures, see Office of the Special Inspector General for Iraq Reconstruction, "Most Iraq Economic Support Funds Have Been Obligated and Liquidated," SIGIR 10–018, Arlington, VA, July 21, 2010. On the spending of IRRF money, see Eric Herring and Glen Rangwala, *Iraq in Fragments: The Occupation and Its Legacy*, Ithaca, NY: Cornell University Press, 2006, 77.

held in the DFI and other cumulative assets, though the IAMB would continue to monitor these funds.[70]

CPA Spending of the Iraqi Budget and the Oversight of the DFI

Revelations of gross CPA mismanagement of Iraqi DFI funds produced shocking stories of exorbitant financial waste, administrative carelessness, corruption in contracting, and the failure to track billions in missing dollars.[71] Numerous reports described how the CPA distributed bundles of cash without any form of accountability, approved questionable billing claims for hundreds of millions of dollars, and awarded dubious contracts to a nonexistent private firm to audit DFI funds. The Coalition's prewar lack of knowledge and misunderstandings about what would be experienced in Iraq, the absence of a thoughtful prewar reconstruction and spending plan, and a thoroughly understaffed and unprepared occupational government certainly contributed to the widespread mismanagement of DFI funds. The Coalition faced a dysfunctional Iraqi government, looted ministries, missing documents, a broken contracting system, and growing security risks. Critical months passed between the March invasion

---

[70] The $29.4 billion was the amount held in the DFI account as of the beginning of 2008. U.S. Government Accountability Office, "Stabilizing and Rebuilding Iraq: Iraqi Revenues, Expenditures, and Surplus," GAO-08-1144T, Washington, DC, September 16, 2008, 7. According to the GAO: "As of March 2005, U.S. appropriations, Iraqi revenues and assets, and international donor pledges totaling about $60 billion had been made available to support the relief and reconstruction and government operations of Iraq. U.S. appropriations of more than $24 billion for relief and reconstruction activities have been used largely for security and essential services – including the repair of infrastructure, procurement of equipment, and training of Iraqis – and have been relocated over time as priorities have changed. Iraqi revenues and assets, which totaled about $23 billion in cumulative deposits, were turned over to the new Iraqi government in June 2004 and have largely funded the operating expenses of the Iraqi government. International donor funds have been primarily used for public and essential service reconstruction activities; however, most of about $13.6 billion pledged over a 4-year period is in the form of potential loans that have not been accessed by the Iraqis." U.S. Government Accountability Office, "Rebuilding Iraq: Status of Funding and Reconstruction Efforts," GAO-05-876, Washington, DC, July 2005, 6.

[71] Office of the Special Inspector General for Iraq Reconstruction, "Audit Report: Oversight of Funds Provided to Iraqi Ministries through the National Budget Process," Report No. 05-004, Arlington, VA, January 30, 2005; Mark Gregory, "So, Mr. Bremer, Where Did All the Money Go?" BBC News, November 9, 2006, http://news.bbc.co.uk/2/hi/business/6129612.stm; "Audit: U.S. Lost $9 Billion in Iraqi Funds," CNN.Com, January 31, 2005, http://edition.cnn.com/2005/WORLD/meast/01/30/iraq.audit/index.html?iref=allsearch; James Glanz, "An Audit Sharply Criticizes Iraq's Bookkeeping," *New York Times*, August 12, 2006, A6; Jeremy Pelofsky, "U.S. Sent Giant Pallets of Cash into Iraq," *Washington Post*, February 6, 2007, A1; Jennifer Parker, "Waste in War: Where Did All the Iraq Reconstruction Money Go?" ABC News, February 6, 2007, http://abcnews.go.com/Politics/print?id=2852426; Donald L. Barlett and James B. Steele, "Billions over Baghdad," *Vanity Fair*, October 2007, 336–380; Evelyn Pringle, "When Bremer Ruled Baghdad: How Iraq Was Looted," *Counterpunch*, April 21, 2007, http://www.counterpunch.org/pringle04212007.html/.

and July, when David Oliver could cobble together a budgetary process and a plan for spending Iraqi funds in the 2003 Iraqi budget. Yet, the intense pressure to spend money to pay civil servants, reconstruct Iraq, and contain rising violence overwhelmed the CPA's decidedly secondary efforts to monitor and account for some $9 billion in Iraqi funds.

In the absence of a budget and functioning government, the CPA established a rudimentary allocation process to provide a crude vetting of the rapidly growing number of competing and uncoordinated demands for reconstruction funds. The Program Review Board served as Iraq's *de facto* finance and planning ministries, prioritizing and approving reconstruction projects funded from U.S. government appropriations, commandeering Iraqi vested funds and the DFI. CPA Regulation 3 directed the PRB to recommend to Ambassador Bremer projects for DFI funding, while CPA Memorandum 4 provided a set of contracting rules for DFI projects that would be funded "in a transparent manner to meet the humanitarian needs of the Iraqi people, for the economic reconstruction and repair of Iraq's infrastructure, for the continued disarmament of Iraq, and for the costs of Iraqi civilian administration, and for other purposes benefiting the people of Iraq."[72] Despite this lofty declaration and the outline of best contracting practices, the PRB attempted to operate in the confusion that accompanied the invasion. "When we started this thing, there really were no plans for how we would spend money, how we would safeguard money, and control money," recalled Sherri Kraham, the CPA's Director of Program Review and Deputy Director of the CPA OMB, who also at times chaired the PRB. "So it was all very *ad hoc* .... It was a really difficult process. There were no communications, no phone lines, and no way for the ministries to reach out to their counterparts in the governorates .... Essentially, we ran the Iraqi budget through the Program Review Board."[73]

Early PRB meetings consisted of some twenty members who represented the United Kingdom, Australia, the military, USAID, and various ministerial advisors. This number grew over time, to some fifty members by the end of the CPA in June 2004. Few Iraqis participated in this process, especially in the initial meetings. Existing PRB minutes for 2003, for example, indicate that Iraqis attended just two meetings. Kraham explained that the absence of Iraqis occurred despite repeated invitations to Iraqi officials. "We had these PRB meetings where we were overseeing all these various Iraqi resources; we were overseeing how we were going to spend Iraqi funds. Some of this was going to ministry budgets, but we couldn't get them to attend our meetings. I heard various things. 'Oh, it's hard to get into the Green Zone. They're going to be threatened. We can't find the right

---

[72] Coalition Provisional Authority Memorandum 4, "Contract and Grant Procedures Applicable to Vested and Seized Iraqi Property and the Development Fund for Iraq: Implementation of Regulation Number 3, Program Review Board," Baghdad, August 19, 2003, 2.
[73] Interview with Sherri Kraham, January 26, 2009.

people.' There were so many reasons, but they were just basically absent. We really couldn't get them to come. It wasn't for a lack of trying."[74]

The PRB approved hundreds of projects worth billions of dollars, with the dollar amounts growing in size as the CPA disbanded in June 2004. One PRB participant described the standard decision-making process. "Anyone would have five minutes in the sun to discuss it. Then an up-or-down vote. If approved, the project would get a PRB number. Once it got that number the contracting process began. This was handled by the Program Management Office (PMO) under Admiral David Nash, which was staffed by DOD contracting officers.... Contracts are written and then move to the Joint Area Support Comptroller, who would be responsible for ordering payments when presented with the completed contracts."[75] The dollar amounts approved by the PRB were measured in the hundreds of millions of dollars, especially as the CPA came to an end and tried to spend the DFI funds under its control. During the May 15, 2004, PRB meeting, for example, the board recommended allocating $125 million for the Iraqi Revenue Stabilization Account, $25 million for the Victim's Compensation Fund, $200 million for the Public Distribution Ration system, $500 million for the Iraqi Security Forces, $315 million for the Electricity Sector, $65 million for Vocational Training, $460 million for Oil Infrastructure Reconstruction, and $65 million for Agriculture Reconstruction and Development.[76] Although Regulation 3 charged PRB with the authority to allocate these funds, it also declared that "The Board shall not be responsible for overseeing the manner in which approved spending requirements are executed."[77] As Peter McPherson interpreted this provision, "the explicit clear understanding was that this budget review board had no oversight function ... the ability to get the money out, to track it, was never very good."[78]

The task of tracking the DFI money began in New York, where the New York Federal Reserve Bank sent twenty-one shipments of cash valued at $11.981 billion to Iraq in 2003 and 2004.[79] These funds, bundled into packages denominated into $1, $5, $10, and $100 bills, weighed a total of 363 tons. Once in Baghdad, authorities placed the cash in a vault located in Saddam Hussein's palace inside the Green Zone. After PRB recommendations to Bremer and with his approval, various CPA officials, Iraqi ministry representatives, and military personnel presented their written authorizations for the release of the cash at the palace. In return for a written receipt of funds, these claimants then hauled away

[74] *Ibid.*
[75] Interview with Treasury Department official, April 22, 2009.
[76] Program Review Board Minutes, Baghdad, May 15, 2004.
[77] Coalition Provisional Authority Regulation 3, "Program Review Board," June 18, 2003, 5.
[78] Interview with Peter McPherson, July 7, 2009 and July 13, 2007.
[79] See, for example, Donald L. Barlett and James B. Steele, "Billions over Baghdad," *Vanity Fair*, October 2007, 336–380.

bags, sacks, and boxes filled with dollars.[80] Coalition military personnel delivered pallets of cash to ministries in Baghdad and to provincial treasuries to pay civil servants, pensioners, and reconstruction contractors. Following the release of this cash, virtually no credible records were kept in this cashed-based economy with its unautomated banking system on whether these funds were used appropriately and who received them.

SIGIR's Evaluation of the CPA's Budgetary Oversight

The Office of the Special Inspector General for Iraq Reconstruction (SIGIR) issued a stunning assessment of the CPA's oversight of the $8.8 billion in DFI funds distributed to the Iraqi ministries, most of which went to pay salaries and pensions.[81] The CPA financial management staff, including the CPA OMB, suffered from extensive understaffing and turnover, with some key positions remaining vacant for months at a time, and other personnel billets typically turning over every three months. SIGIR assessed financial accounting and accountability, not budgetary formulation and process.

The PRB was unable to provide SIGIR with a set of principles for approving projects and programs. The CPA lacked documentation that identified budget spending plans, disbursements, or cash payments. CPA Ministry of Finance/OMB staff, who numbered just five or six persons, failed to examine the internal fiscal controls maintained by the ministries or to assess how Iraqi expenditure of DFI funds were used or compared to expectations, claiming that "reviewing budget execution was not their responsibility."[82] After the PRB recommended to

[80] Andrew Alderson, the director of the CPA's Economic Planning and Development Department, who managed the CPA budget for Basra province in 2004, commented on the CPA's cash management: "Just before flying off I had some trouble getting $5 million in cash from Baghdad. Usually I just flew up to the capital and collected the cash myself and brought it back.... But on this occasion there was a security lock-down in Baghdad and they were nervous about handing it over. So they decided to write out a cheque instead.... This was a US treasury cheque for $5.8 million and was made out to me personally. It was as good as having cash in my pocket.... The finance office was tucked away behind a nondescript door. Pat and I entered to find a US staff sergeant waiting like a quartermaster behind his desk. Behind him were several large plastic carrying cases, the kind we normally used for shipping documents.... Please sign the back of it and sign that you have received the funds. 'OK,' I said and signed my name. The sergeant now lifted $100,000 'bricks' of 100-dollar bills from the containers and counted out 58 of them. This was almost too easy." Andrew Alderson, *Bankrolling Basra: The Incredible Story of a Part-Time Soldier, $1 Billion, and the Collapse of Iraq*, London: Robinson, 2007, 156–157.
[81] Office of the Special Inspector General for Iraq Reconstruction, "Audit Report: Oversight of Funds Provided to Iraqi Ministries through the National Budget Process," Report No. 05-004, Arlington, VA, January 30, 2005.
[82] *Ibid.*, 6. According to Rodney Bent, who served as a director of the CPA OMB after David Oliver left Iraq, "What I told the IG was if you want the records go to the Iraqi Ministry of Finance. We at CPA in the Emerald City didn't have the records like that in the Iraqi Ministry of Finance. They weren't in English.... You don't use the budget office to look at procurement problems." Interview with Rodney Bent, October 24, 2006. The SIGIR report also states, "CPA senior

Bremer which projects should be funded, the management of DFI and other funds rested with the Defense Department's PMO. Despite this formal responsibility, CPA officials informed SIGIR that they relied on the Iraqi Board of Supreme Audit and the ministerial inspector generals to monitor and audit DFI funds, although they were clearly incapable of carrying out these functions.

Though the great majority of the DFI funds allocated to the ministries went to salary and pension payments, SIGIR site checks of Iraqi records suggested that significant funds were paid to ghost employees. SIGIR found the official payroll for one ministry listed 8,206 names, but just 602 names were confirmed as actual employees, while at another ministry only 624 of 1,417 names proved to be valid. SIGIR found that although CPA Memorandum 4 required the review of all ministerial contracting procedures, only two ministries, Finance and Electricity, underwent such a review by the end of June 2004. This review of the Finance Ministry, however, was critical because DFI funds came from the CPA to the Ministry for allocation to the line ministries to fund salaries and programs in a manner consistent with the Iraqi budgets. Nonetheless, SIGIR found that "the CPA issued procurement and contracting policy but did not implement procedures to determine compliance with the policy or monitor contracting actions in the Iraqi ministries .... 5 of 7 CPA senior advisors [each advising a separate ministry] and staffs did not provide adequate oversight of Iraqi ministry contracting operations."[83] In October 2003, the CPA awarded a $1.4 million contract to NorthStar Consultants, a private firm located in California, to audit the distribution and use of DFI funds. The CPA issued this contract to a firm in which neither the owner nor the personnel were trained as certified public accounts, but the business engaged in home remodeling. The firm failed to produce the audits and review of ministerial financial controls called for by the contract. SIGIR concluded that as a result of these cumulative breakdowns in financial oversight, "the CPA did not establish or implement sufficient managerial, financial, and contractual controls to ensure DFI funds were used in a transparent manner. Consequently, there was no assurance the funds were used for the purposes mandated by Resolution 1483."[84]

The audits conducted by the firm KPMG for the IAMB generally concurred with SIGIR's findings.[85] In March 2004, the IAMB approved the contract extended by the CPA to the accounting firm KPMG to conduct audits as required

advisors' responsibilities for oversight of DFI financial and contracting actions in the Iraqi ministries were not clear. During discussions with nine senior advisors and/or senior consultants, CPA personnel stated that responsibilities over DFI funds were not clearly communicated to them." *Ibid.*, 5.

[83] *Ibid.*, 9.

[84] *Ibid.*, ii.

[85] Following KPMG's selection in March and the signing of the contract with KPMG in April 2004, just months before the CPA's dissolution, the accounting firm issued three sets of reports covering the CPA period. KPMG published the first set to the IAMB covering the period up to December 31, 2003, on July 15, 2004. The second set covered January 1 through June 28, 2004, and was published on October 14, 2004. The third set covered June 29, 2004, through December 31,

by UN Resolution 1483. KPMG's assessment of the CPA's management of DFI funds identified deficiencies in the metering of oil extraction, which had implications for determining DFI revenues. KPMG found lapses in PRB procedures and record keeping, and inadequate recording of DFI funds by ministerial treasuries at the provincial level.[86] The Ministry of Finance maintained two sets of unreconciled accounts.[87] KPMG concurred with SIGIR's assessment of the NorthStar contract; the firm was directed away from auditing to creating a new cash-based accounting system that failed to meet international best practices.[88] CPA officials relied on existing Iraqi control institutions, including the Ministry of Finance, the Board of Supreme Audit, and ministerial inspector generals, to monitor DFI funds and expenditures.[89] KPMG indicated its difficulty in gaining access to Iraqi officials, leaving it to base many of its findings on a single day's visit to six ministries in August 2004.[90] Given this sample, KPMG positively noted that "all payroll disbursements were in accordance with the accounting records and other supporting documentation" and that with some exceptions proper internal controls and signing procedures existed in the contractual bidding and awarding process.[91]

The CPA's Response to SIGIR

The CPA leadership responded to the SIGIR report and to subsequent congressional hearings held by the House Committee on Oversight and Government Reform in some detail. Paul Bremer asserted that SIGIR ignored the wartime and political context confronting the CPA. The conditions under which SIGIR operated prevented it from implementing a budgeting and accounting system consistent with international best practices. Waiting to pay civilians and pensioners until a satisfactory payroll system existed "would have taken many months, if not years. More than a million Iraqi families depended on the Iraqi government for their salaries. When the CPA arrived in Iraq after Liberation, unemployment was over 50%. Not paying the civil servants would have been destabilizing and would have increased the security threat to Iraqis and to

2004, and was published on May 23, 2005. The first set is brief, given KPMG's limited presence in Iraq until the last months of the CPA.
[86] KPMG Bahrain, "Development Fund for Iraq: Report of Factual Findings in Connection with Disbursements for the Period 1 January to 28 June 2008," Kingdom of Bahrain, September 2004, 14.
[87] *Ibid.*, 9.
[88] KPMG Bahrain, "Development Fund for Iraq, Appendix: Matters Noted Involving Internal Controls and Other Operational Issues During the Audit of the Fund for the Period to 31 December 2003," Kingdom of Bahrain, June 29, 2004, 4.
[89] KPMG Bahrain, "Development Fund for Iraq: Report of Factual Findings in Connection with Disbursements for the Period 1 January to 28 June 2008," Kingdom of Bahrain, September 2004, 7.
[90] *Ibid.*, 11.
[91] *Ibid.*, 12.

Americans."[92] The political context limited the CPA's authority and ability to order the Iraqis to adopt such systems. Bremer continued to list the familiar challenges facing the CPA that he claimed SIGIR neglected to identify, including a dysfunctional Iraqi government, the lack of communications, and the absence of a meaningful budgetary system. SIGIR, moreover, neglected to report the CPA's accomplishments in creating the Iraqi budgets and helping to build the Iraqi institutions that did promote transparency and fight corruption.

Treasury Under Secretary John Taylor asserted that distinctions needed to be made between the financial stabilization effort that took place during the first few months of occupation, when Treasury OTA and U.S. military personnel made emergency payments and managed the currency exchange between old and new dinars, and later in the occupation when DFI funds were transferred by the CPA "to the Finance Ministry, where it was used to finance government operations including salaries and construction."[93] Of the 363 tons of cash airlifted to Iraq in 2003 and 2004, 274 tons represented the emergency stabilization period taking place in the spring of 2003, with the balance reflecting the later period. "One of the most successful and carefully planned operations of the war," Taylor declared, "has been held up in this hearing for criticism and even ridicule .... Praise for the brave experts in the U.S. Treasury who went to Iraq in April 2003 and established a working Finance Ministry and central bank, praise for the Iraqis in the Finance Ministry who carefully preserved payment records in the face of looting ... and yes, even praise for planning and follow-through back in the United States."[94] In addition to Bremer and Taylor, David Oliver argued that the urgency of the moment clearly outweighed concerns for accountability. When asked by a BBC reporter if he knew what happened to the DFI funds, Oliver replied, "I have no idea, I can't tell you whether or not the money went to the right things or didn't – nor do I actually think it is important .... Billions of dollars of their money disappeared, yes I understand, I'm saying what difference does it make?"[95] Emergencies of the moment, Oliver maintained, required that DFI funds be sent immediately, before an understaffed CPA could impose optimal procurement and accounting procedures on the Iraqis. "The coalition – and I think [the CPA consisted of] between 300 and 600 people, civilians and you want to bring in 3,000 auditors to make sure the

[92] Office of the Special Inspector General for Iraq Reconstruction, "Audit Report: Oversight of Funds Provided to Iraqi Ministries through the National Budget Process," Report No. 05-004, Arlington, VA, January 30, 2005, 34.

[93] John B. Taylor, "We Did Get the Money to Iraq," *International Herald Tribune*, February 27, 2007, 6. Taylor referred to hearings held by Chairman Henry Waxman and the House Committee on Oversight and Government Reform on February 5, 2007, when Bremer, Bowen, Oliver, and Ambassador Timothy Carney testified.

[94] *Ibid.*

[95] Donald L. Barlett and James B. Steele, "Billions over Baghdad," *Vanity Fair*, October 2007, 375.

money's being spent?"⁹⁶ "We got that [budget] out so people could start spending. The real crux of it was forcing money out," said Oliver. "I worried more about pushing money out than I worried about anything."⁹⁷

In October 2011, SIGIR issued a new audit of the handling of DFI funds. SIGIR reported that during its administration, the CPA could access $20.7 billion in DFI money from the Federal Reserve Bank. Between August 2003 and June 2004, the CPA received eleven shipments of cash totaling $10.2 billion. A sampling of four of those shipments valued at $5.8 million that were turned over to the Iraqis indicated that although some tracking of these funds occurred, great discrepancies took place in the manner of the transfers. Rather than being deposited in the Central Bank of Iraq as required by CPA regulations, these funds were passed directly to various Iraqi officials. On two separate occasions, for example, $1.6 billion in cash was handed over to Kurdistan Regional Government officials and $150 million in cash was turned over to the minister of finance, with both transfers taking place at the Baghdad airport. The Finance Ministry lacked any accounting for these funds passed on to its minister.⁹⁸ According to Iraq's Board of Supreme Audit, once the government of Iraq received these and other DFI funds, "There is no control in MOF [the Ministry of Finance] or other ministries over the assets transferred by CPA to some of administration in Iraqi ministries financed by DFI and other sources, so MOF and other ministries had not recorded the received and spent amounts in their

---

⁹⁶ *Ibid.*

⁹⁷ Interview with David Oliver, June 9, 2007.

⁹⁸ Office of the Special Inspector General for Iraq Reconstruction, "Quarterly Report to the United States Congress," Arlington, VA, October 30, 2011, 109. A senior SIGIR official explained the purpose and methods of the audit: "Tracing that directly to the DFI and the management of the DFI is a much more difficult case. What we are trying to do is step-by-step determine where the money went and who was in charge of it. It was $20 billion total that the U.S. was responsible for, of that about $10 billion got converted into cash and flow into Baghdad, about $10 billion got moved electronically to different accounts, and at some point became money that the GOI [controlled]. Of the cash, a large portion of it went to contracts, some of it directly went to ministries, and we traced where all of that went. What we were looking at in this particular audit was that there was $6.6 billion on the books remaining on the day when the CPA dissolved, and heretofore we could not find good documentation what happened to that. So we dove a little bit deeper, and we worked with the Federal Bank, we worked with the Central Bank of Iraq, we got a bunch of records, and we managed to reconcile to the point that we think that most of it was actually properly converted and put into the Central Bank of Iraq for use by the Iraqi government, or was kept in the safe. So we can track all of it. The only thing that was done outside of the regulations was one transfer of $150 million and one transfer of $400 million directly to the minister of finance at the airport. So rather than it being deposited in the Central Bank and then given to the Ministry of Finance, it was just directly given to the Ministry of Finance, or the minister of finance. But it's difficult now, because the Ministry is saying it doesn't have the records, and the minister of finance [then] died of a heart attack last year. Did that money actually go for projects?" Once the CPA transferred its DFI funds to the Iraqi government, the Iraqis became responsible for managing and accounting for this money. Interview with SIGIR official, November 21, 2011.

records. MOF and CPA had paid amounts to the administration without informing the account department of the certain ministries. This caused weakness of control and monitoring of these ministries over the transferred amounts."[99]

The debate over the competency of CPA's financial management continued on after the release of the SIGIR and KPMG reports. The Rand Corporation's history of the CPA published in 2009, for example, concluded that SIGIR's expectation that greater accountability for DFI funds could have been achieved given the exigencies of the time to be "unrealistic." "There was no alternative to using Iraqi institutions for this purpose and no possibility of installing new mechanisms throughout the Iraqi government for financial accountability overnight."[100] Special Inspector General for Iraq Reconstruction Stuart Bowen responded to that claim, saying "If you are spending billions of dollars and the difficulty is that it is chaotic because of security problems, that demands greater oversight, not less. Higher standards. If you know, if you recognize in your immediate surroundings that executing a reconstruction program is difficult, then stewardship requires, militates more in favor of stronger oversight standards rather than abandoning them."[101]

As Bowen's reports indicated, the Coalition failed to anticipate in its planning, even as a contingency, the magnitude of the spending required to fund the stabilization and reconstruction of Iraq. Consequently, it neglected to prepare for developing strong contracting, procurement, cash management, and auditing capabilities for both the Coalition and Iraqis to limit budgetary waste, mishandling, and corruption. Optimally, systems of budget formulation, allocation, execution, and accountability would be successfully installed and activated simultaneously. This did not occur, in part for the reasons outlined by the Rand Group. The result is that the CPA's legacy will always be associated with spending excess and mismanagement, including its deficient oversight of the DFI. The CPA's lack of control over DFI funds, however, is fully consistent with the historically dismal record of American financial management in previous conflict situations, such as World War II and Viet Nam.[102] The United

[99] Supreme Board of Audit, "A Report on Evaluating the CPA's Management of the Iraqi Funds from May 22, 2003–June 28, 2004," Baghdad. Undated, 4. http://d-raqaba-m.iq/pdf/e_sigir.pdf/.

[100] James Dobbins, Seth G. Jones, Benjamin Runkle, and Siddharth Mohandas, *op. cit.*, 181.

[101] Interview with Stuart Bowen, July 15, 2009.

[102] Consider Rundell's description of the Army's financial management, which sounds remarkably similar to Iraq: "The Finance Department's record in World War II was handicapped by inadequate prewar planning.... Nor did the War Department seem to pressure Finance for contingency plans. The result was that when war began the Finance Department had to scramble to meet immediate emergencies and to supply patchwork solutions to a great array of problems. It entered wartime operations with prewar methods, some of which proved adequate and some totally unsuitable.... The Finance Department accomplished its mission in World War II with surprisingly small numbers of personnel." Walter Rundell, Jr., *Military Money: A Fiscal History of the US Army Overseas in World War II*, College Station: Texas A&M University Press, 1980,

States simply does not manage money well when the solution to difficult problems rests with spending large amounts of money quickly to achieve strategic military and political goals.

CONCLUSION

The challenge facing the Coalition Provisional Authority in 2003 and 2004 was making effective and lasting institutional changes in the Iraqi budgeting system Saddam Hussein layered on the institutional alterations Britain imposed on the Ottoman system of public finance. The official document, "An Historic Review of CPA Accomplishments, 2003–2004," essentially asserts that the CPA largely accomplished this task. "The CPA helped the Iraqi government to build market-based economy by ... developing transparent budgeting and accounting arrangements, and a framework for sound public sector finances and resource allocation."[103] When reviewing the Ministry of Finance's successes, the report noted the Ministry's "management" of the 2004 budget and the formulation of the 2005 budget.[104] Under extremely challenging circumstances, the CPA did indeed reform Iraq's budgetary institutions and processes by producing two *ersatz* budgets more comprehensive and transparent than Saddam's compartmentalized and secret budgets. The CPA crafted new fiscal laws that codified international best practices into the Iraqi budget process. These rules restored the Ministry of Finance to the prominence it held during the period of the British Mandate, they provided for the active participation of the Parliament in budgetary decision making, and they outlined the beginnings of fiscal decentralization in a country where none existed. These changes promoted democratic institutions and laid the foundation for a new era of Iraqi budgeting.

Nevertheless, it would be a mistake to overstate the CPA's successes in the area of budgetary and fiscal management. To the extent that it made the effort, for example, the CPA demonstrated decidedly mixed success in engaging the Iraqis in the running of their own budgetary institutions. The Iraqis played a minimal role in the setting of 2003 and 2004 budgetary priorities, and virtually no role in making PRB project and program decisions. CPA officials often explained that this lack of participation stemmed from the culture of fear and the resulting lack of initiative that Saddam instilled in the Iraqi bureaucracy. Treasury Under Secretary Taylor and his staff may have planned for

242, 3. By comparison, Taylor writes that extensive planning for financial management for Viet Nam took place, but "the primary difficulty seemed to be that these plans were not taken seriously." Leonard B. Taylor, *Financial Management of the Vietnam Conflict, 1962–1972*, Department of the Army, Washington, DC, 1974, 10.

[103] Coalition Provisional Authority, *An Historic Review of CPA Accomplishments, 2003–2004*, Baghdad, 2004, 3.

[104] *Ibid.*, 70.

currency exchange and the need to pay salaries, but to implement their plan they assumed the Iraqi bureaucracy would be relatively intact. Consequently, the CPA ended up relying on this same ill-equipped and poorly managed bureaucracy to administer and provide oversight for Iraq's politically sensitive DFI funds, a decision that contributed to the reality and perception of pervasive corruption in Iraq.

The clock ran out on the CPA's efforts at transforming Iraqi institutions. The transfer of sovereignty cut short what Bremer and other CPA leaders believed would be a longer-term exercise of power, certainly when compared to other American efforts at state and nation building. "If you take the Japanese and German models," said Bremer, "which are in many ways the only models of successful American occupation recently, and if you think they are the correct models, then obviously we weren't there long enough .... The politics of Iraq made it impossible, as a political matter, for the CPA to stay for five years. It just wasn't going to happen."[105] Ending the CPA left unfinished its agenda for reconstructing Iraqi budgetary institutions, processes, and practices. CPA leaders, for instance, considered eliminating the Ministry of Planning, which was widely viewed as an institutional vestige of Saddam's Soviet-type economy. "These were the people who did all the budget planning processes," recalled a Treasury official. "There were several efforts made during the CPA and afterwards to disband the Ministry of Planning. It's a Soviet command planning ministry. If you are going to move to a market economy, where does this ministry really serve? Regrettably, there was no effort to get rid of it altogether during CPA. When the Iraqi transition government took over ... it was resuscitated again. Then subsequent governments came along and it was decided the Planning Ministry would deal with foreign donors and become the representative to the World Bank. That entire data base [of reconstruction projects] resides in the Ministry of Planning. That is the data base of your capital budgeting methodology, which accedes some of the authority and control that traditionally would be in the Ministry of Finance. The Ministry of Planning has been a particularly difficult animal to deal with, it continued to live on its fashion, but it continued to live on."[106] Saddam Hussein's Planning Ministry thus survived the CPA. Left unresolved were the pressing issue of building the capacity of Iraq's ministries to spend and execute their budgets in a manner that promoted efficiency, transparency, and accountability.

To accomplish this task, the Coalition aimed to complete the CPA's plan for a new computerized financial management information system that would "track the execution of the budget in accordance with international best standards" as part of a broader capacity development effort focused

[105] Interview with L. Paul Bremer, June 27, 2007.
[106] Interview with Treasury Department official, February 23, 2009.

on budget execution.[107] This new system, one that SIGIR, KPMG, and Bremer hopefully pointed to, would serve as the foundation for a modernized Iraqi government's public financial management system. As KMPG reported, "The current MOF accounting software has limited reporting capabilities, for example the MOF Accounting Department could not provide us with consolidated disbursement report for each Ministry. We were informed by the MOF that a new financial management information system will be implemented by 2005."[108] New computers with a state-of-the-art financial computer program would link the Ministry of Finance with other ministries, enabling the government to adopt a new IMF chart of accounts that would enable the Iraqis to track funds after they were allocated in the budget. The promise of the new financial management information system offered financial accountability and transparency and the containment of budgetary corruption.

The Coalition, however, found inducing the Iraqis to buy into the international best practices associated with a new computer system an extremely difficult objective to achieve in post-CPA Iraq.

[107] Coalition Provisional Authority, *An Historic Review of CPA Accomplishments, 2003–2004*, Baghdad, 2004, 70.
[108] KPMG Bahrain, "Development Fund for Iraq: Report of Factual Findings in Connection with Disbursements for the Period 1 January to 28 June 2008," Kingdom of Bahrain, September 2004, 9.

5

Building Iraqi Ministerial Capacity

The Case of FMIS

The Coalition Provisional Authority reconstituted the Iraqi budgetary process in two significant ways. First, by designing and codifying a budget formulation and approval process that reflected international best practices of democratic governments and, second, by empowering the Ministry of Finance beyond the position it occupied under Saddam Hussein's regime. Efforts to modernize Iraqi budgeting, however, went deeper into the bureaucracy than positioning the Finance Ministry as the central actor in the budgetary process and instituting new budgetary procedures. Finding the Iraqis' technical skills seriously lacking, their management of public finance data inadequate and opaque, and their computer systems deficient or nonexistent, Coalition officials planned to introduce a new financial management information system into the Ministry of Finance that would connect it with all other ministries, and eventually with all levels of government. The Coalition's long struggle to achieve this goal reflects its limitations in realizing institutional transformation in Iraq.

This effort to reconstruct the Finance Ministry depended on the ability of private contractors to modernize the Ministry and train its personnel. No war in American history has been so interlinked and dependent on private contractors in all phases of conflict, from security to reconstruction to training, as in Iraq. The names of the contractors Halliburton, Kellogg Brown & Root, Bechtel, and Blackwater, and the sometimes noncompetitively bid contracts that enriched them, will always be recounted as part of the Iraq story.[1] By 2008, an estimated 190,000 civilian contractors operated in Iraq, more than the number of military personnel present at that time; the number of military personnel peaked at 160,000 in 2007. By the end of 2009, a reported 1,600 civilian contractors, American and other nationalities, had been killed and more than 35,000

---

[1] Criticisms of the role of contractors in Iraq are extensive. See, for example, T. Christian Miller, *Blood Money: Wasted Billions, Lost Lives, and Corporate Greed in Iraq*, New York: Little Brown, 2006.

injured.[2] Much of the actual conduct of American foreign policy, particularly American efforts at promoting economic governance and development in Iraq, rested with private contractors. Giant consultancies, such as BearingPoint, Research Triangle Institute International, Adam Smith International, and Maxwell Stamp PLC, dominated the field and received hundreds of millions of dollars in USAID contracts, as well as contracts from Coalition partners. These contractors, not the State Department, USAID, the Treasury Department, or other federal agencies, provided the majority of the civilian person power used to advise and train foreign government officials, build ministries, oversee economic development projects, promote efforts at democratization, and project American interests in Iraq. Thus, the Coalition's reliance on contractors to play a critical role in reconstructing the Iraqi budgetary and fiscal system should not be surprising.

PENCIL AND PAPER BUDGETING IN THE MINISTRY OF FINANCE

On entering Iraq, ORHA and CPA teams confronted a Finance Ministry and budgetary process about which they possessed virtually no prior information and a ministry housed in looted and stripped facilities, abandoned by its staff, and run by a crippled leadership. Although many of the staff slowly returned to work and the Coalition identified acceptable individuals to serve in the Ministry's leadership positions, the Ministry and its personnel were judged to exhibit, at best, a modest level of administrative effectiveness and capacity.

The Coalition, for example, faced the problem of never quite knowing the size of the Ministry's work force. Although the Ministry listed a staff of 6,633 in the 2004 budget, the number actually remained something of a shadow figure. "A lot of people were brought in under the Ministry of Finance payroll," recalled Ali Allawi, the former Iraqi finance minister, "because the Ministry of Finance was used as a sort of holding station for people in between jobs. In the Saddam period, people who were reallocated within the government ... you were generally assigned to the Finance Ministry until you were reassigned to another [ministry]. So the payroll of the MOF was bloated by people who were in transit, or people who were also dismissed ... ended up on the temporary payroll of the

[2] On the number of contractors, see Anthony Shadid, "Letter from Iraq: 'People Woke Up, and They Were Gone," *Washington Post*, December 4, 2009, p. 1, and Paul Grier, "Record Number of US Contractors in Iraq," *Christian Science Monitor*, August 18, 2008, http://www.csmonitor.com/2008/0818/po2so1-usmi.html/. On the number of contractor causalities, T. Christian Miller, "Sometimes It's Not Your War, But You Sacrifice Anyway," *Washington Post*, August 16, 2009, B2, and Steven Schooner, "Remember Them Too," *Washington Post*, May 25, 2009, A21. These figures include non-American contractor and worker causalities, which are usually unreported by the American media. Also see U.S. Congressional Budget Office, "Contractors' Support of U.S. Operations in Iraq," Washington, DC, August 2008.

Finance Ministry. This policy continued after the war."[3] The Ministry's active personnel roster also included staff that fled, were killed in the invasion, or died later as security conditions deteriorated. Other ministries also included shadow personnel in their rosters, and these duplicitous figures inflated the Iraqi budget. Other than the CPA's de-Ba'athification process, the Coalition never seriously attempted to influence the Ministry's human resources and hiring practices.

Not knowing the true size of the Iraqi bureaucracy, however, paled as a challenge to administrative and budgetary effectiveness compared to the Iraqis' reliance on pencil and paper operations in the Ministry of Finance and throughout the government. Virtually all ministerial activities and transactions were conducted in this manner. Coalition personnel discovered that the Finance Ministry employed FoxPro, a basic, somewhat dated, computer program, for some record keeping purposes, but ministerial accounts and the calculations of budgetary expenditures continued to be managed in the more rudimentary fashion. "There were some really qualified and capable staff," as Ali Allawi noted, "but the majority of the staff was used to doing business on a ledger based system, everything was hand-written. It wasn't very well organized."[4] This reliance on paper and pencil documentation reflects deeply rooted traditional administrative practices in the Iraqi bureaucracy. Coalition officials found decision making under Saddam's regime to be strictly a top-down hierarchical affair, one that produced a distinct lack of initiative and inertia that permeated the Finance Ministry and all of Iraqi government. Ministerial bureaucrats feared to make even the most fundamental decisions without explicit written orders signed by their superiors. As one senior USAID officer reported, "There was this whole culture there, don't do anything, don't take initiative, and we are still struggling with that in the ministries, to undo that mindset."[5] The need to get signed documents meant that officials refused to accept faxes and other copied instructions, which greatly lessened their interest in electronically generated paperwork and the use of computers. Consequently, all the data, documents, and written fiscal negotiations between the Finance Ministry and other ministries that were used in the development of the Iraqi budget required the physical

---

[3] Interview with Ali Allawi, May 15, 2007. Some have suggested this reliance on paper documents and signatures is deeply rooted in Arab culture. "In Arab countries, every one of the signatures on those indispensable bureaucratic pieces of paper represents power to some particular holder. The decision to dispense or to withhold the signature vitally adjusts power between one person and the next must be treated accordingly, well prepared, and paid for." David Pryce-Jones, *The Closed Circle: An Interpretation of the Arabs*, Chicago: Ivan R. Dee, 2009, 94.

[4] *Ibid.*

[5] Interview with USAID employee, May 1, 2008. This bureaucratically submissive culture in the face of harsh leadership is hardly unique to Iraq. The historian Max Hastings reported that a similar culture existed in Stalin's Russian Army: "In an army in which fear played so large a part, many officers were reluctant to accept orders by telephone. They demanded written instructions, which could be preserved and produced if matters went awry. . . . Individual initiative was discouraged." Max Hastings, *Armageddon: The Battle for Germany, 1944–1945*, New York: Vintage Books, 2004, p. 125.

delivery of these items by courier, back and forth, from one location to another in Baghdad.

This transmission of information proves to be even more complicated in the delivery of documents between the Finance Ministry and the provinces. The Ministry, for instance, requires that provincial governments provide monthly trial balance sheet reports on their spending of central government funds. Gathering these data is a time-consuming affair, as described by a Treasury OTA officer who spent more than two years in Iraq:

Each month, each spending unit [in the provinces], and there are about 500 of them – a spending unit receives central government funds directly in some fashion – they do a monthly trial balance. That has to be done in paper. The Ministry of Finance does not accept faxes, they do not accept scanned documents. So that monthly trial balance sheet, signed off by the provincial governor, complete with bank statements, is either put in the mail or in a courier package to go to Baghdad. So, that document, whether it comes from Kirkuk or Basra or Anbar, has to go down the highways, through checkpoints, to get to the Ministry of Finance administration building, where it is taken to a mail room, and then it goes to the Director General of Accounting, and they are reviewed. Once that occurs, then that balance goes over to another bunch of people, who key the information in this FoxPro database. This is called consolidation. From that consolidation unit, the accounting folks go through and prepare the consolidated reports that get disseminated.... It is a slow process, it is a labor-intensive process.... So while [preparing] the budget is proceeding at some sort of orderly pace, the ability to report on the budget in some sort of orderly pace is highly suspect.... The monthly trial balance is due the tenth working day of the following month. So at best you are going to have a two-month lag.... It could be that the May report might include the bulk of March activities, but it could also include January or February because of the time it takes to get there. This is merely a factor that it is a paper-based system, it is a physical document that has to travel through time and physical space, requiring physical signatures.[6]

This paper and pencil approach pervades the Iraqi government. It inhibits the prompt sharing of data among ministries and other governmental units, contributes to miscalculations in fiscal transactions, delays critical budgetary decisions, runs counter to international best practices for promoting transparency, and deters efforts to control graft and corruption throughout the execution stage of the budgetary process.

Coalition staff also found the Finance Ministry lacking the necessary technical skills to engage effectively in fiscal policy making. Stemming from the Saddam era, the Ministry of Planning and Cooperative Development's skills in economic modeling and forecasting, particularly for long-term capital project construction and economic investment allocations, far exceeded those of the Finance Ministry. The Finance Ministry's personnel skills tended toward the pencil and paper accounting talents required to complete budget ledgers and fill out various forms. Asking the Finance Ministry to do more, which the CPA

---

[6] Interview with Treasury Department official, December 19, 2007.

clearly intended, meant that new skill sets needed to be developed, and perhaps new, more analytic units created within the Ministry.

USAID, THE BEARINGPOINT CONTRACT, AND THE FISCAL MANAGEMENT INFORMATION SYSTEM (FMIS)

At the beginning of the occupation the primary task of addressing many of the Finance Ministry's perceived administrative weaknesses fell to USAID. Whereas other American agencies, such as Treasury's OTA and the Office of Management and Budget, played critical roles in formulating the 2003, 2004, and 2005 Iraqi budgets, only USAID possessed the ability to issue large-scale contracts and hire the number of firms and personnel needed to rebuild the Ministry's administrative capacity. Treasury OTA and OMB might detail personnel to Iraq, but always in numbers too few to penetrate deeply into the central bureaucracy. Moreover, as security in Iraq deteriorated, regular U.S. government personnel found themselves restricted to the Green Zone, leaving USAID's contractors, who possessed lower security clearances, to make the increasingly dangerous visits to the Finance Ministry's various buildings. USAID began its involvement with Iraq during the prewar planning stage. Recognizing that the agency would be responsible for a long list of reconstruction responsibilities that touched on virtually every aspect of Iraqi society, USAID leaders initiated work on a series of contracts on a set of diverse programs and projects that included economic governance.

USAID awarded its contracts to modernize the Finance Ministry and transform the Iraqi economy to the BearingPoint consulting firm. The politically well-connected firm, headquartered in McLean, Virginia, and staffed by fifteen thousand employees, including thirty-six hundred based in the Washington, DC, region, advised governments on a broad range of political, technical, and economic issues. USAID's contracts to BearingPoint gave it a vital role in promoting American overseas development efforts throughout the world, particularly in the Middle East. With management offices located in Pakistan, Qatar, and the United Arab Emirates, the firm's contracts for that region included a $14 million contract to aid the government of Jordan, a $124.7 million contract to aid Egypt, and a $218 million contract to aid Afghanistan. In a highly controversial decision, on July 24, 2003, USAID awarded BearingPoint a $79.6 million technical assistance contract for services in Iraq, known as Economic Governance I, followed by an additional Economic Governance II contract awarded on September 3, 2004, for $223.3 million.[7] The Economic Governance contracts placed the firm clearly in the center of

[7] USAID initially intended to issue its economic development contract, which BearingPoint helped create, on a sole-source basis to the firm, but complaints by competitors Booz Allen Hamilton, Deloitte & Touché, and IBM Global Services forced USAID to submit the contract to a limited competition. According to the USAID Office of Inspector General's review of the contract, "the

Iraq's economic activities, involving BearingPoint in such issues as fiscal reform, the operation of the central bank, currency reform, the setting of commercial banking regulation, and the development of Iraqi trade and tariff policies.

Within the category of fiscal reform the contract identified five tasks and multiple benchmarks that would be used to measure BearingPoint's accomplishments. First, BearingPoint would create a Macroeconomic and Fiscal Analysis Unit in the Finance Ministry. This unit would, among other duties, produce macroeconomic projections, analyses, and reports on revenues and expenditures. Second, BearingPoint would develop options for Iraq's revenue policies, such as the introduction of new property, consumption, and value-added taxes. Third, BearingPoint would review and assess Iraq's revenue administration and collection capabilities, including the development of a new taxpayer identification system, auditing mechanisms, returns processing procedures, and an automated tax information system. Fourth, the firm would build a system of intergovernmental fiscal relations, including the creation of a revenue-sharing formula, a grants allocation system, and the production of quarterly reports on provincial and local fiscal conditions. Fifth, the contract called for BearingPoint to engage in "Budget Planning, Administration and Financial Management Information System Budget Tasks."

This last task, the broadest in scope of the five, called on BearingPoint to support the Finance Ministry in every aspect of budgetary planning, formulation, execution, auditing, and program evaluation. The firm would develop a 2004 Iraqi budget covering all aspects of government and public enterprise spending, and create a planning process for the drafting of the 2005 budget. BearingPoint's charge engaged the firm in the ongoing responsibilities of the Planning Ministry as well as the Finance Ministry. BearingPoint would provide "detailed guidance" on investment and capital projects to the line ministries and

extensive involvement of BearingPoint in USAID's development of this contract creates the appearance of unfair competitive advantage and we have concluded that USAID did not document and explain how this issue was resolved before proceeding with the award." Memorandum from Bruce N. Crandlemire to Gordon H. West and Timothy Beans, "USAID's Compliance with Federal Regulations in Awarding the Contract for Economic Recovery, Reform and Sustained Growth Contract in Iraq" (AIG/A Memorandum 04–005), Office of the Inspector General, USAID, Washington, DC, March 22, 2004, p. 1. Repeated interviews with U.S. government officials indicate that the contract was competitively bid in name only. James Cox, "BearingPoint Gets Contested Iraq Contract," *USA Today*, July 21, 2003. http://accounting.smartpros.com/x39807. xml/. Also see, on defense of USAID contracting practices, Jeffrey Marbourg-*Goodman, "USAID's Iraq Procurement Contracts: Insider's View," Procurement Lawyer*, 39 (2003) 1, 10–12. BearingPoint was particularly well connected to the Republican Party, as the firm's employees gave more donations to President Bush's 2004 reelection campaign than any other contractor in Iraq. Stephen Foley, "Shock and Oil: Iraq's Billions and the White House Connection," *The Independent*, January 14, 2006. http://www.commondreams.org/cgi-bin/print.cgi?file=/headlines07/0114-02.html/. Also see Antonia Juhasz, *The Bu$h Agenda: Invading the World, One Economy at a Time*, New York: Regan Books, 2006, 195, which points to the BearingPoint contract as an example of a "revolving door" relationship between contractors and the Bush administration.

all other levels of government. Significantly, BearingPoint would seal the budgetary divide separating the two ministries. The contract called for the firm to create a new harmonized budget through "the operation of the Ministry of Finance joint budget planning unit and the institutionalization of a unified annual budget planning process for recurrent and capital expenditures."[8] The firm would establish a Public Enterprise Monitoring Unit within the Finance Ministry that would oversee Iraq's state-owned enterprises and support a Finance Ministry Internal Audit Section that by the end of 2004 would conduct audits throughout the Iraqi government and its provinces. The firm would train Ministry staff in the latest budgeting techniques. Finally, the contract called on BearingPoint to install a Fiscal Management Information System throughout Iraq, a "fully automated budget planning, reporting, and tracking system at the central, provincial, and municipal/district levels."[9] The contract required BearingPoint to "evaluate FMIS software package options and acquire, configure, customize, and implement the most appropriate FMIS package," with the system being fully activated in the central government by December 2004 and throughout all Iraqi governmental units by July 2005.[10]

The Fiscal Management Information System served as the centerpiece of this highly ambitious economics governance contract. This new computer and software system would resolve the challenges posed by the Iraqi government's pencil and paper administrative culture. For the first time in Iraq's history, its public entities would be connected by a modern automated computer system that would transfer fiscal and financial data initially among the ministries and eventually to its provincial and local governments. Through FMIS a new treasury would be created within the Ministry that would enable the government to organize its records into a single treasury account and centrally disburse funds. FMIS would strengthen the Ministry's management of the government's cash flow that since the days of Saddam relied on a diffuse system of multiple accounts entrusted to Iraq's line ministries and banks to allocate funds. FMIS would speed the formulation of the budget, promote a coordinated fiscal policy, enhance debt management, improve transparency, and thereby inhibit corruption. Through the FMIS project, the Ministry would establish a credible chart of accounts that would categorize all budget and spending items, thus permitting the Ministry to better direct, monitor, and predict spending patterns, as well as develop a more efficient procurement process and promote the effective auditing of government funds.

---

[8] USAID Contract RAN-C-00-03-00043-00 awarded to BearingPoint. Signed July 24, 2003.
[9] *Ibid.*, p. 56.
[10] Ibid., p. 57. On the role of FMIS in development strategies, see, for example, Carmen Caba-Perez, Antonio M. López-Hernández, and David Ortiz-Rodríguez, "Governmental Financial Information Reforms and Changes in the Political System: The Argentina, Chile and Paraguay Experience," *Public Administration and Development*, 29 (2009)5, 429–440; and Lourdes Torres, "Accounting and Accountability: Recent Developments in Government Financial Information Systems," *Public Administration and Development*, 24 (2004) 5, 447–456.

A successful FMIS would serve as the foundation for the Coalition's efforts to invigorate Iraq's budgetary system. The document "An Historic Review of CPA Accomplishments," for example, lists seven CPA "successes" in building up the Ministry of Finance, including the development of the 2004 budget, the creation of CPA Order 95, the Financial Management Law, and the implementation of a new pension and payroll system. One of the seven identified CPA accomplishments is the "integration" of the FMIS, "a computerized system to track the execution of the budget in accordance with international standards," in the Finance Ministry.[11] In August 2005, more than a year after the original Economic Governance I contract called for the task to be completed, USAID director Andrew Natsios wrote to Secretary of State Condoleezza Rice that as part of the agency's "structural indicators" for reforming Iraq, "USAID has activated the Financial Management System at 42 of 182 spending sites improving transparency and efficiency through the replacement of manual-based files with electronic-based files and establishing monthly fiscal accounts (with remaining sites scheduled to come on-line in January 2006)."[12] USAID's 2005 Annual Report proudly declared that the FMIS "during 2005 gives the MOF a budget execution system covering over 85% of the government's budget, significantly enhancing the MOF ability to control finances in line with the Financial Management Law and international standards."[13] "FMIS was certainly a priority that was acknowledged by everyone," a senior USAID officer recounted. "There was a common consensus on that all the way around. Because if you can't account for the money, and clearly there was no accounting for money under the previous government, that worked to the advantage of the previous government. That's where FMIS comes into play, because it's going to be a tool for everybody to have a sense [of where the money is being spent]."[14] FMIS acted as the "fundamental backbone of what we were trying to achieve," recalled another USAID staffer.[15]

The IMF and FMIS

FMIS served another purpose. Discussions with donors immediately after the March 2003 invasion indicated a broad desire for greater Iraqi budgetary transparency and accountability. Therefore, not only would FMIS address what the Coalition perceived as Iraq's immediate needs for an automated budgetary system, it also helped fulfill the demands placed on Iraq by donors, especially

[11] Coalition Provisional Authority, *An Historic Review of CPA Accomplishments*, 2003–2004," Baghdad, Iraq, 2004, p. 70.
[12] Andrew S. Natsios, "Information Memo for the Secretary." August 31, 2005.
[13] USAID, *2005 USAID Annual Report*, Section "USAID/Iraq Economic Growth Projects," Washington, DC, 2005, p. 2.
[14] Interview with USAID official, October 24, 2006.
[15] Interview with USAID official, January 10, 2007.

the IMF. The financial agreements reached between the IMF and Iraq called on the Iraqi government to modernize its budgeting systems and create a credible fiscal policy. In September 2004, Minister of Finance Adil al-Mahdi and Central Bank Governor Sinan al-Shabibi submitted a request to the IMF for Emergency Post-Conflict Assistance (EPCA). On September 29, the IMF Executive Board approved an Iraqi purchase of 297.1 million in IMF Special Drawing Rights. This permitted Iraq to receive $435 million in postconflict assistance loans and enabled the Iraqi government to obtain approval from its Paris Club creditors to reduce their claims against Iraq.[16] Although the performance criteria for these loans is normally far less restrictive than other IMF loans, applicant governments are nevertheless required to provide a request statement that identifies their current economic condition and how they plan to develop a stable macroeconomic policy.

The Iraqi letter of intent and supporting memoranda outlined a set of policies that included improving its fiscal position and strengthening its budgetary process. The Iraqis promised to maintain the 2004 budget's spending targets and not exceed the projected deficit level of an estimated 43 percent of GDP developed by the CPA. The 2005 budget drafted by the newly elected Iraqi government would restrain recurrent or operational spending as it projected growth in oil revenues to reduce the deficit to 23 percent of GDP. For both fiscal years the deficits would be fully financed from external sources, including the Development Fund for Iraq and American bilateral and international multilateral assistance. The request also pledged to reform the management and transparency of the government's budget and budgetary accounting systems. New regulations would be passed to fortify the financial management laws enacted by the CPA, the authority of the Supreme Audit Board would be strengthened, the Iraqi Treasury would introduce a single accounting structure, the Finance Ministry would conduct mid-year reviews to better control rates and levels of spending, and the government would extend the Financial Management Information System throughout the entire country.[17]

On December 6, 2005, the new Iraqi finance minister, Ali Allawi, and Central Bank Governor Al-Shabibi followed the 2004 EPCA request with a proposal for an IMF Stand-By Arrangement (SBA). The Iraqi letter of intent requested additional IMF loans totaling 475.4 million in Special Drawing Rights, or $685 million. Like the EPCA, the SBA was intended to strengthen Iraq's ability to structure its debts with international creditors.

---

[16] "IMF Emergency Assistance: Supporting Recovery from Natural Disasters and Armed Conflicts, table 2: Post-Conflict Emergency Assistance, Since 1995," September 30, 2009. http://www.imf.org/external/np/exr/facts/conflict.htm/.

[17] Letter from Dr. Sinan Shabibi and Mr. Adil A. Mahdi to Mr. Rodrigo de Rato, Managing Director, International Monetary Fund, "Iraq: Letter of Intent, Memorandum of Economic and Financial Policies, and Technical Memorandum of Understanding," Baghdad, September 24, 2004. http://www.imf.org/external/np/loi/2004/irq/01/index.htm.

As with the 2004 agreement, Iraq pledged to improve its fiscal position and enhance its budgetary process and management to obtain the SBA. The 2005 deficit would be lowered to 11 percent of GDP, compared to the 23 percent projected for the EPCA, and the 2006 deficit would be lower than that, at 9 percent of GDP. The drop in both years' deficits reflected higher oil prices, leading to larger government revenues that would allow for significantly greater spending. Both recurrent and capital spending would grow in 2006, by 24 and 25 percent, respectively, to accommodate growing security, wages, and pensions on the recurrent side, and reconstruction investment in the capital budget. The Iraqis followed up this request by entering a five-year "International Compact with Iraq" with the World Bank and the United Nations that pledged Iraq would run budget surpluses in 2010 and 2011, even as the budget experienced significant increases in investment expenditures.[18]

In addition to this pledge to control their budget deficits, both in the IMF agreement and the international compact, the Iraqis declared themselves committed to the development of a sound fiscal system and the creation of an automated FMIS system. The Finance Ministry would develop a detailed budgetary classification methodology and chart of accounts that would enable it to better group fiscal transactions into proper categories, organize its programs, and monitor its spending. New implementing regulations would be drafted to support the financial management laws originated by the CPA. Additional audit training and procurement laws would strengthen budgetary controls. The Iraqi government continued to pledge its support for the installation of FMIS and the accompanying Free Balance software. Without an operational FMIS, the IMF staff warned that there would be "the continuation in 2006 of the existing manual system for financial reporting to avoid disruption and changes in existing systems and procedures."[19] Iraq's 2005 and 2006 budgets would therefore

---

[18] Letter from Dr. Sinan Shabibi and Dr. Ali Allawi to Mr. Rodrigo de Rato, Managing Director, International Monetary Fund, "Letter of Intent, Memorandum of Economic and Financial Policies and Technical Memorandum of Understanding," Baghdad, December 6, 2005. http://www.imf.org/external/np/loi/2005/irq/120605.pdf/. "The International Compact with Iraq: A Shared Vision, A Mutual Commitment" offered a broad political, economic, and social vision of what Iraq would attempt to achieve by 2012. The Iraqi government pledged to "align its public finance management with sound international practices," including "Making the Financial Information System (FMIS) operational across all ministries and provinces, including for the management of government contracts and payrolls, as well as for budget planning and accountability" (13). The Compact was announced on July 27, 2006, was formally introduced at the UN on March 16, 2007, and was officially initiated on May 3, 2007.

[19] IMF, "Iraq: Request for Stand-By Arrangement – Staff Report; Staff Supplement; Press Release on the Executive Board Discussion; and Statement by the Executive Director for Iraq," International Monetary Fund, IMF Country Report No. 06/15, January 2006. The IMF staff report noted the promises made by Shabibi and Allawi for budgetary reform, which included the implementation of the FMIS FreeBalance software: "The authorities recognize the importance of enhancing the effectiveness and transparency of budgetary management. They have agreed to an agenda, with technical assistance from Fund and World Bank staff, incorporating: (i) the continuation in 2006

be drafted using pencil and paper in the absence of a computerized system of accounts and data sharing.

The Struggle to Implement FMIS

Despite years of effort by BearingPoint, by the end of 2009 the FMIS system remained unconnected throughout many of Iraq's governmental units, and the Iraqis had yet to rely on FMIS-generated data for budget preparation, adoption, or execution. BearingPoint's inability to activate FMIS was not due to a lack of reported effort. Following the awarding of the contract in late July 2003, the first of BearingPoint's economics and governance team arrived in Iraq on August 6. As BearingPoint's monthly progress reports to USAID suggest, several hundred meetings were then held between the firm, U.S. government officials, other contractors, and Iraqi counterparts at the Finance Ministry, line ministries, and provincial and local governments. Training sessions took place at the ministries, in the International or Green Zone, and in Jordan, particularly when security conditions deteriorated, with Iraqis flown to Amman to take classes. By March 2005, BearingPoint claimed, for example, that "the main IFMIS [Iraq Financial Management Information System], server is now configured and able to connect to all installed budget agencies with Internet connectivity," and that "the IFMIS site staff and IT equipment deployment efforts are both on schedule for completion by the end of April."[20]

Nonetheless, external evaluations of FMIS's progress proved to be far less encouraging. In October 2007, SIGIR offered a largely negative assessment of the contract's status:

of the existing manual system for financial reporting to avoid disruption and changes in existing systems and procedures; (ii) the adoption of fully detailed budget classification and chart of accounts in line with the IMF's Government Financial Statistics Manual (*GFSM*) 2001, within a cash accounting framework by end-June 2006 (structural performance criterion), and initiation of an extensive training program to ensure successful implementation of the new classification for the 2007 budget; (iii) the completion by end-March 2006 of an assessment of the FreeBalance software installed by USAID contractors, and by end-September 2006 a report on a plan to implement any changes necessitated by the assessment; (iv) the preparation of monthly government cash-flow projections by the recently established cash-flow unit; (v) the adoption of implementing regulations for the financial management law in the area of budget preparation by end-March 2006; (vi) the initiation of a training program to strengthen external audit; (vii) the review by end-June 2006 of existing procurement rules to bring them in line with international standards; (viii) the establishment by June 2006 of an audit oversight committee, to become effective on or before December 31, 2006, including the participation of independent international audit experts, to continue the work of the International Advisory and Monitoring Board upon its dissolution in overseeing and making public audits of the Development Fund for Iraq and oil export sales (structural benchmark); and (ix) completion of a census of all public service employees (including military) by June 30, 2006 (structural benchmark)" (13) http://www.imf.org/external/pubs/ft/scr/2006/cr0615.pdf/.

[20] BearingPoint, "The Iraq FMIS: Myths and Realities," Baghdad, March 22, 2005, p. 6.

Although some progress has been reported on IFMIS it is difficult to tell specifically what has been developed and implemented and how much has been expended for IFMIS. Available information shows that the system development and implementation costs are over $38 million. Although contract documents state that IFMIS was to replace the Ministry of Finance's legacy accounting systems, the Ministry continues to operate its legacy systems in parallel with the components of IFMIS. According to US Embassy officials, "nobody noticed" when IFMIS was down for a month, and no one relies on IFMIS to produce reports. Iraqi user requirements have not been identified and incorporated in the system's development. Other ministries, such as Interior and Defense, have developed their own financial management information systems, which are not compatible with IFMIS and cannot transfer financial data from one system to another. As a result, the agency personnel must manually input financial data via terminals in the various ministries.[21]

The USAID's Office of the Inspector General released a similar set of findings a year and a half later in June 2009, when it issued an audit of the entire Economic Governance II contract with BearingPoint. The audit concluded that "In September 2008, after 4 years and $192 million in incurred costs, fewer than half of the originally planned 398 tasks had been performed. In addition, implementation of a major information system (the Iraq Financial Management Information System) was behind schedule, and the system was not yet fully operational."[22] According to Treasury OTA and State Department economics affairs officers, the Iraqis formulated both of their 2008 and 2009 budgets without relying on FMIS.

Four major explanations have been offered for why the FMIS component of the ambitious BearingPoint contract failed to achieve its ultimate objectives. These explanations point to conflicts over the scope and management of the contract, the selection of the software employed to automate the FMIS that proved to be too complex for the Iraqis, the increasingly threatening security environment, and the resistance by the Iraqis to the FMIS system.

1. **Conflicts over the Management of the FMIS Contract:** Problems with the FMIS may first be traced to tensions over the BearingPoint contract that emerged between USAID, CPA, and Treasury OTA. Disputes over the scope, control, and administration of the FMIS component of the contract extended throughout the CPA period and through much of the contract's effective life. Real tension existed between the CPA's leadership and USAID. Where USAID enjoyed

---

[21] Office of the Special Inspector General for Iraq Reconstruction, "Interim Report on Efforts and Further Actions Needed to Implement a Financial Management Information System in Iraq," SIGIR-08-001, Washington, DC, October 24, 2007, p. 2.

[22] USAID Office of the Inspector General, "Audit of USAID/Iraq's Economic Governance II Program," Audit Report No. E-267-09-004-P, Baghdad, Iraq, June 3, 2009, p. 1. An example of a project never implemented is the contract's provision that BearingPoint establish a Macroeconomic and Fiscal Analysis Unit within the Ministry of Finance. According to a senior BearingPoint official, "We never got far with that. We didn't get a positive response from the Ministry in terms of the right resources to do that, and we pulled away from doing that." Interview with Bearing Point employee, December 6, 2006.

relative independence of decision making under General Jay Garner and ORHA, this changed during Paul Bremer's administration of the CPA. "Under General Garner, we were given the lead with several of the ministries, which made sense," a senior USAID official recalled. "The arrival of Ambassador Bremer, a new system was put in place. There were senior advisors for most of the ministries, and USAID gradually lost any privileged position it had before under ORHA. So the organization had inherent conflict. You had people who are flowing from the States who are told they are the senior advisor to a minister or a sector, but the resources to work in that sector are in a different agency. So there's a conflict that's not worked out in one coherent unit, it has to go all the way up the chain [of command]. USAID was also located a mile away from the palace where the senior advisors were supposed to be. Which means that this comes down to personalities rather than systems, and that became a problem."[23] A USAID senior officer suggested that some of the tension stemmed from CPA beliefs that cultural differences separated USAID from the serious work taking place in Iraq: "AID was sort of perceived to be tree-hugging, Birkenstock wearing, peace, love, and happiness kind of folks. That was the image portrayed."[24] By the end of the CPA, Bremer rarely spoke with USAID leadership, leaving their relationship "often on the verge of rupture."[25] "Friction had always existed between the CPA advisers and USAID," reported James Stephenson, USAID's Mission Director in Iraq, "and the situation often deteriorated into one of the groups working at cross-purposes."[26] This clash of command, personalities, and culture reflected serious differences between USAID and Bremer over the direction and scope of the BearingPoint contract.

These competing positions may be traced to what USAID regarded as the mission it prepared for in early 2003 and how Bremer redirected that mission on his arrival in Iraq. During the first few months of 2003 USAID formulated its prewar plans for how the agency would assist in the reconstruction of the Iraqi government. "Part of that [planning] had to do with the idea that initially ORHA and the CPA would have some responsibility for administering Iraqi funds" a BearingPoint contractor recalled. "Part of that initial intent for the FMIS implementation was to assist the CPA in managing those funds." The range of the FMIS project reportedly expanded beyond its initially planned intent, with growing expectations for how it would benefit both the Coalition and the Iraqis. Then, the contractor continued, "It really started losing its original intent. What had started out as a tool for the CPA to use, it blossomed into a tool for the government of Iraq. This automated system is going to increase accountability, transparency, all these wonderful things that automated systems allegedly do. Then you have the IMF and the World Bank coming in,

---

[23] Interview with USAID official, May 1, 2008.
[24] Interview with USAID official, October 24, 2006.
[25] James Stephenson, *Losing the Golden Hour*, Washington, DC: Potomac Books, Inc., 2007, p. 15.
[26] *Ibid.*, 68.

and as part of the Stand-By agreement, the GOI [Government of Iraq] made several commitments [to employ the system]."[27] As the scope of the project expanded, so too did the task assignments and the difficulty of fulfilling them. The project grew from one aiding the Coalition in managing its money to one building up the core fiscal ministries, connecting the fiscal ministries with the line ministries, and then connecting all governmental units at all levels of government, even when these provincial and local "governments" existed in name only.

Tension between the CPA and USAID about the direction of the contract began when the BearingPoint team arrived in Iraq. "Our going-in plan changed very dramatically the moment we got on the ground," recalled another BearingPoint contractor. "The USAID had given us a task order that was very specific about what kinds of things we needed to accomplish in what period of time. This was the contract. We had to have 150 subject matter experts ready to hit the ground by August 6th, which we had. These were people who specifically worked before in postconflict situations in economic governance." When arriving, the team leader was directed to meet with Bremer, who told them they were to "set the contract aside ... and every new scope of the work would be developed by the CPA, but in fact they didn't have the expertise to develop it, so we developed it, but approved by him. So the 150 people we had ready to go, all of the work plans, how we had approached it. ... each of those components, and I believe we had nine different components. ... I arrived on August 6 and on August 7th that was all set aside. We started with a blank piece of paper."[28] The Economic Governance contract, for example, called for BearingPoint to work closely with the Finance and Planning ministries in formulating Iraq's budgets. Yet, the CPA restricted USAID and BearingPoint's access to the Ministry of Finance and excluded the firm from participating in the budgetary process. "In the first year we were there," noted a USAID official, "we were shut out of the Ministry of Finance, except for implementing the FMIS."[29]

USAID expected to manage the Economic Governance contract in a manner far different from what Bremer permitted, once the BearingPoint team arrived in Iraq. Prior to the invasion, prewar planning called for the Treasury Department to manage Iraq's fiscal and monetary policy, and it did so under ORHA and effectively until the creation of the CPA and Paul Bremer's arrival in Iraq in May 2003. Upon Bremer's arrival, and then with his appointment of Peter McPherson as his top economic advisor and Director of the CPA Office of Economic Policy, the CPA exercised this responsibility, which put Bremer and McPherson in conflict with USAID's vision for BearingPoint acting as an overall economic coordinator, as outlined in the Economic Governance contract. As a senior USAID officer explained, "What we had wanted to do was arrive, and the first task was to have BearingPoint do a big map out of what our strategic

[27] Interview with BearingPoint official, October 30, 2006, and December 19, 2007.
[28] Interview with USAID official, February 12, 2008.
[29] Interview with USAID official, May 1, 2008.

approach would have been. We were never able to do that. That was not approved by CPA. There was the impression by CPA was that these are very expensive contactors, and they'll come and spend all the money up, and we won't get anything for it. . . . The deal that was brokered [with CPA] is that you can only do this on a task-order basis, where you write down the activity."[30] Said another USAID official, "We were always directing BearingPoint, but whether the activity was approved or not was up to Ambassador Bremer. . . . Instead of having a holistic, strategic approach, [BearingPoint] was seen as a resource that many people could tap into for their tactical needs. And we tried as hard to get that coordination [over BearingPoint] but it was one of those areas of conflict."[31] From the perspective of the CPA's leadership, however, USAID overstepped its authority. As Peter McPherson, himself a former USAID director, recalled, "My position to my old friend [USAID Director Andrew] Natsios was that even though the contract seemed to see BearingPoint was going to do all of this, there wasn't a chance. My position was we were going to pick and choose BearingPoint contract individuals to do what we wanted them to do. The contract was that they were going to be in charge of it all." Regardless of the contract's terms, the "economic team of McPherson and [David] Oliver was not going to allow that." "What we wanted was, okay, deliver us a tax guy, or a tariff guy, or we need more budget people. [BearingPoint] were never the overall strategists, and there was some tension about that because their contract said they were to be in charge."[32]

Further complaints from USAID emerged concerning the funding of the contract. "The initial difficulty," claimed a high-ranking USAID officer, "was that in the BearingPoint contract, we had approximately $130 million in the contract, and Bremer took a large chunk of money to put into something, leaving approximately $50 million. Eventually we got it back up to $79 million. We literally did not have control of the contract. . . . Bremer gave the final approval [to BearingPoint's responsibilities and activities]. BearingPoint was doing a lot of things that I never would have had them doing. . . . We simply did not have enough resources to put into things we wanted."[33] James Stephenson, USAID's Iraq Mission Director, claimed that "the CPA had taken $35 million from the [BearingPoint] effort. Although we successfully fought to replenish this amount, the contract had largely become a technical assistance slush fund for the senior advisers' pet projects."[34] Another senior USAID officer asserted, "The BP contract was used in more of a short-term focus, almost an ad hoc focus, rather than in the way USAID contracts are generally used, and we had proposed it be used, as a systematic approach. So we found ourselves with a large contract,

---

[30] Interview with USAID official, October 30, 2006.

[31] Interview with USAID official, May 1, 2008.

[32] Interview with Peter McPherson, July 13, 2007.

[33] Interview with USAID official, May 1, 2008

[34] Stephenson, pp. 30–31.

$77 million ... but we were not able to use it in a systematic approach.... We were never given the ability to manage that contract in this manner. We could only do one task at that time, and that task had to have the support of a senior advisor, and then be cleared off by Ambassador Bremer himself. So we were reduced to a piecemeal approach. It was not leading to a synergistic whole."[35] This complaint about the Economic Governance I contract's $79 million funding level seems to be mitigated by the Economic Governance II contract's $223.3 million funding level. Yet, by September 2004 when the new contract went into effect, the security environment had significantly deteriorated, the CPA expired, and fundamental changes occurred in Coalition and Iraqi relations that further undermined the success of FMIS. USAID's differences, however, extended beyond those it shared with Paul Bremer and the CPA.

USAID also traded complaints with Treasury OTA about which agency should have properly directed BearingPoint's activities: "In Iraq we were using BearingPoint. [Treasury] looks at it, even though they are our contractors, that they ought to be in charge," declared one dismayed USAID official.[36] A USAID contractor traced OTA's resentment of USAID to American economic development efforts in Europe: "OTA was very, very angry that they did not get the technical piece in Kosovo for the fiscal and financial sector, and I think they were not going to let that happen again [in Iraq], and they were like a bulldozer. They brought a team of people in, but they do not have a programmatic way of moving the ball forward."[37] Treasury officials, in turn, expressed their own concerns about USAID's management of the BearingPoint contract and its dependence on USAID's private-sector contractors. "The Treasury Department does not have the authority to tell the BearingPoint contractor what to do, even though we are responsible for the policy," one senior Treasury official observed. "They report to USAID, and it makes for additional difficulty in aligning policy objectives and actual implementation. [We experienced] an all-day effort from the moment we walked in working on Iraq budget issues because [USAID] tried to step out on their own and take control over policy of what Iraq's budget should look like. By coffee time, we had more or less reined that agency back. It's still a full time job, sorting out what the size of the budget should be, it is something we work on and effectively control from the U.S. advisory side."[38] USAID clearly intended that BearingPoint only report to USAID, and, according to Treasury staff, refused, for example, to share BearingPoint monthly progress reports with Treasury. Noted another Treasury official, "There are things about that reporting relationship that make it difficult, frankly frustrating, to coordinate policy and systems of implementation. There are many instances for Treasury to say it ... but if you are

[35] Interview with USAID official, October 30, 2006.
[36] Interview with USAID official, October 24, 2006.
[37] Interview with BearingPoint official, June 30, 2006.
[38] Interview with Treasury Department official, February 23, 2009.

interested actually in implementation and the consecutiveness between policy
and implementation, you have to try to get private sector implementers on the
same page as government officials who are responsible for policy. I found it was
sometimes difficult to do that, and it was frustrating, partly because the task is
really difficult."[39] Thus, the management of the BearingPoint contract both
created and highlighted tensions between CPA leadership and USAID.
Problems with interagency coordination remained a hallmark of the Iraqi reconstruction effort.

Finally, further complicating the management of the contract, USAID suffered from the Coalition's endemic lack of personnel, which hampered the
agency's oversight of BearingPoint. USAID normally relied on an oversight
system in which Cognizant Technical Officers (CTO) with relevant technical
expertise conducted the oversight of contractors. According to a senior USAID
officer, the USAID management contingent consisted of 103 Americans, 102
Iraqi staff, and some federal employees detailed from other federal agencies on a
temporary duty assignment basis. Of the 103, no more than sixteen were regular
Foreign Service Officers, some of whom acted as CTOs. The remainder consisted
of contractors from the firm International Resources Group (IRG). The overextended CTOs came to rely on the contractors to oversee the BearingPoint
contractors, a violation of standard operating oversight procedure. "So,"
recalled the USAID officer, "we had a situation where we had a contract with
IRG to provide us with people, and those people were sitting there in our offices.
They were essentially performing the jobs of government employees. ... then we
had a direct hire [regular USAID employee] who was the CTO, who was a
foreign service officer, but we also had IRG people who were under the CTO
who were responsible for providing oversight and managing the BearingPoint
effort on a day-to-day basis."[40]

2. The FreeBalance Decision: The second explanation for the failure of FMIS
stemmed from BearingPoint's decision to employ FreeBalance eFinancial's
"off-the-shelf" software programs in the system. The contract called for the
automation of Iraqi budgeting and accounting in a new financial management
information system, in place of the existing manual pencil and paper procedures.
The software programs BearingPoint selected to create this automated FMIS

[39] Interview with Treasury Department official, March 7, 2008.
[40] Interview with USAID employee, May 1, 2008. On problems with contractors overseeing other
contractors, see U.S. Government Accountability Office, "Contingency Contracting:
Improvements Needed in Management of Contractors Supporting Contract and Grant
Administration in Iraq and Afghanistan," GAO-10-357, Washington, DC, April 2010.
Speaking more broadly about proper contractor oversight, Jeffrey Zients, Deputy Director of
the U.S. Office of Management and Budget and the federal government's Chief Performance
Officer, stated: "In some situations it's hard to distinguish, actually, between contractors and
federal employees. And believe it or not, there are still cases where we have contractors managing
other contractors – clearly unacceptable loss of control and oversight." Michelle Jamrisko, "Big
Contractors May Lose Out as Federal Agencies Cut Back," *Washington Post*, July 18, 2011, A11.

came from the FreeBalance firm, whose primary clients in 2003 were governmental units in Canada and the United States. Critics of BearingPoint claim that in the selection of these programs the firm neglected to conduct an effective needs analysis that considered the Iraqis' capacity to absorb this complicated new system, the contractors failed to communicate effectively with the Iraqis to determine what their information management needs might be, they ignored the lack of infrastructure required to implement the system, and BearingPoint failed to take into account the hostile physical and resource conditions under which the system would be introduced. "At that time [when BearingPoint selected FreeBalance], BearingPoint had a number of advisors who worked in Kosovo with a FreeBalance application, and they were willing to come to Iraq," a BearingPoint team leader recalled. "So then FreeBalance became the application. But what happened during all of the post-occupation enthusiasm there was not really a lot of coordination. Not a whole lot of energy was spent trying to find out did the Iraqi budget work. Turned out that it really was a more complex animal than was assumed. So while in Kosovo, the Ministry of Finance had all of its operations in one small office in one building, in Iraq what they found was that a lot of the government's financial management was significantly [physically] decentralized."[41] "The FreeBalance system," a senior IMF official involved in monitoring the success of the project noted, "was chosen to play the role of the system to connect all the users and connect the Ministry of Finance to be the system, to be the FMIS for Iraq. But unfortunately, the client requirements, from the Iraqi side, were never really outlined. They were never really based on what the Iraqis wanted to see. This whole thing never really became what we all wanted to see, a system to replace the existing legacy system, and to provide automatic data collection and generation for public records."[42] A more biting evaluation of BearingPoint's performance came from a U.S. OMB officer who assessed the firm's activities: "I thought they were horrible.... they were useless. I don't think they had a very good plan. They misunderstood the basic capacity of the Ministry of Finance even to understand working with computers. The IT infrastructure wasn't there. BearingPoint did not spend enough time with the Ministry in the beginning. They designed an FMIS system based on generally agreed principles of what an FMIS should be, not within the local context. That would mean things like power outages."[43]

BearingPoint justified the FreeBalance selection by claiming they were under the pressures of the moment to choose an automated system, and that the obstacles experienced during the installation of FreeBalance would be faced during the installation of any modern system. "The decision to select the FreeBalance application," a March 2005 BearingPoint report stated, "was one taken in a difficult and exigent environment. The unique circumstances in

[41] Interview with BearingPoint official, December 19, 2007.
[42] Interview with IMF official, January 22, 2008.
[43] Interview with U.S. Office of Management and Budget official, August 5, 2009.

postwar Iraq meant the normal project management steps of conceptual design, functional analysis, tendering process and implementation were telescoped into a brief selection process followed by a detailed implementation program."

The report acknowledged the various difficulties that hitherto prevented FMIS's activation, including problems with security, reliable power supplies, dependable transportation, lack of communication, infrastructure deficiencies, the safe delivery of equipment, the "negligible IT skills within the government service," and a reluctant Ministry of Finance. Despite these obstacles, the BearingPoint report declared that "currently, we are more than two-thirds of the way towards completing the original goal."[44]

The Coalition teams working with the Iraqis quickly discovered the challenge of establishing the FreeBalance system immediately after the invasion. "There was a real lack of knowledge about modern computer technology," a USAID officer noted. "In 1982, time stopped in Iraq. These people were using FoxPro databases, some real antiquated types of computer technology."[45] Computer programs commonly used in the development of public budgets, such as Windows and Excel, were unknown to the Iraqis. Coalition authorities and the BearingPoint team in Iraq realized that a broad program of computer training would be necessary to activate FMIS, and the training element served as a fundamental component of the contract. Also, by July 2003, the signing date of the contract, the Coalition and BearingPoint recognized that extensive repairs and rebuilding were needed at the looted Finance Ministry and other government buildings.

If a new computer system were to be introduced to replace the existing manual record keeping, however, more than simple physical restoration was required. What the Coalition and BearingPoint were not prepared for when selecting FreeBalance was the challenge of wiring together the ministries or linking them with Internet capabilities that would support the system. BearingPoint first needed to survey the ministries, locate their buildings, which were located throughout Baghdad, determine what equipment required purchasing, install that equipment in the ministries, and provide initial servicing and maintenance. All of this took time. Yet even when it was installed, the BearingPoint group confronted the seemingly endless limitations that operating in Iraq presented in maintaining this system. "You will always hear they need computers. Okay, now automation has its point," a BearingPoint team leader acknowledged. "But if you are looking at an integrated, enterprise financial management system, which USAID was proposing, there are two things those systems like. They like electricity and they like a robust telecommunications infrastructure. What are the two things that Iraq did not have? Electricity and robust telecommunications."[46] BearingPoint's monthly reports to USAID in

[44] BearingPoint, "The Iraq FMIS: Myths and Realities," Baghdad, Iraq, March 22, 2005, p. 9.
[45] Interview with USAID official, January 10, 2007.
[46] Interview with BearingPoint official, December 19, 2007.

2005 and 2006, for example, regularly identified problems with Internet connectivity and electrical shortages.[47] The FMIS computers consumed huge amounts of power to operate and to propel air conditioning systems to keep the computers cool in the blazing Iraqi heat. Air conditioning systems were sometimes poorly maintained, electrical blackouts required backup generators, and when these failed, additional redundant generators needed to be installed under often difficult security conditions.

3. **Security:** The third explanation for BearingPoint's limited success in installing FMIS stemmed from Iraq's chronic security problems. "[The] number one reason [we are experiencing difficulties] is security, both in terms of training and getting access to the ministries in Baghdad," reported a BearingPoint project leader in 2007. "I think there are three ministries completely off limits. They are situated in areas in Baghdad that when you are driving to them they are difficult to get in and out of, which makes them susceptible to attack."[48] The firm required access to the Finance Ministry's facilities and personnel in order to fulfill its contract. During the early months of the contract the BearingPoint team traveled relatively freely to the Finance Ministry four to five times a week. By the fall of 2004, as the violence spread from Fallujah to Baghdad, the security situation deteriorated rapidly, causing BearingPoint to begin housing its personnel within the Green Zone, keeping its teams there sometimes for weeks at a time. Where BearingPoint planned to spend $900,000 on security, actual security expenses cost some $37 million during the first year of its contract. Coalition and BearingPoint convoys were subject to attacks as they traveled to the Finance Ministry. "Driving to the Ministry of Finance," said a USAID officer "is one of the most dangerous things you can do in the world. It's like a gauntlet, that route."[49] As a BearingPoint trainer observed, "The only way that you can do this properly . . . is if you work and sit with the Iraqis day-to-day. You can't be in the palace, and then in their ministry, and think you are going to effect change. You need to work with them as partners, side-by-side. . . . But the time we had to work in the ministries was cut short by the security situation. . . . The Ministry of Finance is in Sadr City. It was the most dangerous ministry of all the ministries."[50] The BearingPoint monthly report to USAID for January 2005, for example, ruefully noted that one of its personnel, Tracy Huslin, who managed the firm's administrative operations in Iraq, had been killed. "BearingPoint advisor activity involving counterparts was slowed in the month of January, with only 11 trips into the red zone. Sadly and most notably, BearingPoint and

---

[47] For example, both the November 2005 and February 2006 reports noted "internet connectivity and electricity shortages." BearingPoint, "USAID-Funded Economic Governance II Project, Monthly Report, Period Covered: November 1–30, 2005," Baghdad, Iraq, p. 18, and "USAID-Funded Economic Governance II Project, Monthly Report, Period Covered: February 1–28, 2006," Baghdad, Iraq, p. 14.

[48] Interview with BearingPoint official, December 19, 2007.

[49] Interview with USAID official, March 25, 2008.

[50] Interview with BearingPoint official, December 19, 2007.

its security provider Kroll Intl. were fatally struck by a VBIED [Vehicle-Borne Improvised Explosive Device] returning from Baghdad International Airport on January 3. BearingPoint therefore stopped all traffic entering the country, which also contributed to the low number of counterpart contact hours this month."[51]

The security event that essentially brought the FMIS project to a halt and effectively ended BearingPoint's continuity of effort with the Finance Ministry occurred on May 29, 2007. An estimated forty Iraqis dressed in national police uniforms kidnapped a British BearingPoint contractor and his four private security guards employed by the firm GardaWorld in front of the Ministry. According to one report, "It was one of the most brazen, coordinated assaults on Western civilians at an Iraqi government building since the war started, and the ease of the attack amplified concerns that elements of Iraq's government may be playing a more active role in targeting Westerners – or at least allowing attacks to occur."[52] At the same time, tension between the Finance Ministry and the Coalition increased as four ministry personnel were killed and two wounded, including three women, as U.S. Army troops fired on the bus they occupied in Baghdad in November 2007.[53] In December 2009, Britain's longest hostage scenario since the 1980s came to an end when Peter Moore, the BearingPoint consultant, gained release from his captors. Iraqi authorities discovered the bodies of three of Moore's guards in June 2009, leaving the fourth bodyguard presumed dead.[54] The abduction of the contractor and his bodyguards clearly appeared to be the work of insiders who knew the working schedule. As a result of this event, USAID suspended the contract, causing BearingPoint's work on FMIS to be terminated for more than a year.

The area surrounding the Finance Ministry's buildings remained dangerous, as waves of violence accompanied the June 2007 bombing of the Golden Mosque in Samarra. A senior Treasury OTA official related that the finance minister himself rarely visited the Ministry's headquarters building, and that he was informed that the Iraqis could not guarantee his safety when traveling to or entering the Ministry. Iraqi officials and workers at the Ministry were themselves killed, injured, or kidnapped. On August 19, 2009, bribed checkpoint guards enabled insurgents to set off truck bombs that exploded outside of the Ministry of Foreign Affairs and Ministry of Finance headquarters buildings, as shown in Illustration 5.1. This tragedy, quickly labeled "Bloody Wednesday," resulted in

[51] Ellen McCarthy, "BearingPoint Thinks Global," *Washington Post*, October 3, 2005, D. 1. BearingPoint, "USAID-Funded Economic Governance II Project, Monthly Report, February," January 31, 2005, Baghdad, Iraq, p. 21.
[52] Damien Cave, "5 British Civilians Abducted from Iraqi Finance Ministry," *New York Times*, May 29, 2007. http://www.nytimes.com/2007/05/29/world/africa/29iht-Iraq.4.5915937.html?scp=3%26sq=5%20british%20civilians%20abducted%20in%20iraq%26st=cse/.
[53] "Six Finance Ministry Personnel Killed, Wounded by U.S. Fire in Baghdad," Voices of Iraq, November 27, 2007. http://www.iraqupdates.com/scr/preview.php?article=24400/.
[54] "UK Hostage Tells of 'Execution,'" BBC News, January 26, 2010. http://news.bbc.co.uk/2/hi/uk_news/8482114.stm/.

ILLUSTRATION 5.1. Bombing of the Ministry of Finance, August 19, 2009
Photo: AP/Hadi Mizban

ILLUSTRATION 5.2. Bombing of the Ministry of Finance, December 8, 2009
Photo: AP/Khalid Mohammed

the killing of 82 and the wounding of 1,203 Iraqis. On December 8, 2009, another series of explosions leveled the street in front of the Rafidain Bank that housed the Finance Ministry's makeshift offices that staff occupied following the October bombings that rendered their headquarters unusable, as shown in Illustration 5.2. The explosions killed and wounded Ministry employees and destroyed files, thereby severely disrupting ministerial activities related to budget execution, including the processing of payments for civil servant salaries, procurement of payment authorizations to contractors, and the generation of budgetary data used in the calculation of Iraq's budget execution figures. These blasts, intended to disrupt forthcoming parliamentary elections, also targeted the Ministry of Labor and other government facilities, leaving at least 127 people dead and some 450 wounded on "Bloody Tuesday."

4. **Iraqi Resistance to FMIS:** The most important barrier to BearingPoint's access to the Finance Ministry and success of FMIS came from Iraqi refusal to take ownership of the program. The resistance to buy into FMIS came from both lower and mid-level Iraqis working in the Ministry, and, most important, from the Ministry's top leadership. Rank-and-file Iraqis in the Ministry resisted FMIS because they were comfortable with the existing paper and pencil procedures that protected them during the Saddam regime. Change threatened the established order, required learning new and relatively complex systems, and produced no immediate organizational or personal rewards. A senior Treasury

official concurred and evaluated FMIS by saying, "The problem with FMIS is that it was *the* wrong system, and shame on them [USAID and BearingPoint].... The IFMIS system was so wrong for Iraq.... [The Iraqis] had a system, and when it got bombed out [in the 1991 Gulf War] they cobbled together what they had with a FoxPro data base. The point is they had a way of doing things, and they are terribly resistant to change. Especially change brought in by somebody who just invaded them. So they fought IFMIS, because IFMIS required them to change processes. If you go back to the Saddam era, the way to stay alive was to never make a decision and follow the administrative processes. I've never seen guys like these. I've seen things for $10,000 that had to be signed off by the Minister of Finance. They just don't want to take initiative.... So to give them a system that required all new processes, it was going to be discordant from the beginning."[55] A BearingPoint contractor recalled discussing FMIS's merits with an Iraqi official opposed to the system: "It was as if the COI [Ministry of Finance Chief of Information] said to me, 'What you are selling me has absolutely nothing to do with the problems I face.' The solutions that were being proposed were totally, totally removed from the reality of being useful to Iraq.... So why are you bothering these people, why do you expect them to be excited about adopting something that does not work?"[56] Another Treasury OTA officer agreed, saying, "They need to recognize the legal status of an electronic document. They had their paper documents, someone signs it, and attests that it's real, and it goes on up. The Ministry of Finance, at least the late Director General of Accounting, had absolutely no interest in bringing in an automated system, because he needs the paper documents because the paper documents are the legal documents. So does an electronic document, a scanned document, have the same legal authority as a paper document?"[57]

Regardless of how the regular Iraqi staff working in the Ministry regarded BearingPoint and FMIS, they received their cues on how to respond to BearingPoint's efforts from the Ministry's top officials. If FMIS were to be installed, activated, and employed in a meaningful manner, the system required a champion in the finance minister and the Ministry's leadership. "If you don't have a champion in that minister," said a frustrated BearingPoint employee, "then the next level misses meetings, they don't schedule things, they never do what they agreed to, and there are no repercussions or consequences, and it goes very slowly, or we do all the work, which is really not the point. You don't get any learning out of that, and the system shuts down."[58] To make FMIS come into being, the finance minister needed to signal formally to his bureaucracy that he actively valued the system, because negative or simply passive aggressive

[55] Interview with Treasury Department official, February 23, 2009.
[56] Interview with BearingPoint official, December 19, 2007.
[57] Interview with Treasury Department official, December 19, 2007.
[58] Interview with BearingPoint official, October 30, 2006.

behavior sent a sufficient signal throughout the Ministry that FMIS was unwanted.

Dating from the March 2003 invasion through 2010, six individuals served as acting finance minister or finance minister. Hashim Obeid (Acting Finance Minister from April 2003 to September 2003), appointed by the CPA; Kamil Mubdir al-Gailani (Finance Minister from September 2003 to June 2004), appointed by the Interim Iraq Governing Council; Adel Abdul-Mahdi (June 2004–May 2005), served in the Interim Iraqi Government; Ali Abdul-Amir Allawi (May 2005–May 2006), served in the Transitional Iraqi Government; and Baqir Jabr al-Zubeidi (May 2006–December 2010), served in the government of Prime Minister Nouri al-Maliki. Of these six ministers, Obeid and al-Gailani served during the period of CPA rule when the Coalition directed the policies of Iraq's government, including the drafting of the 2003 and 2004 Iraqi budgets. CPA rule meant that Coalition personnel gained regular access to the Ministry and its staff, especially in 2003 when security issues were largely under control. Working during this period of CPA dominance, BearingPoint found Minister al-Gailani to be understandably receptive to FMIS. The subsequent ministers proved to be significantly less welcoming following the grant of sovereignty to Iraq in June 2004.

Granting sovereignty proved to be a critical juncture in Coalition relations with Iraq that reached down to the question of whether the Iraqis would permit the installation of FMIS. Iraqi ministers needed to demonstrate that they were independent of the Coalition, and especially the American Embassy, for domestic political reasons, but they also did so because they truly were nationalists. Al-Gailani, for example, was followed by Adel Abdul-Mahdi. Although he worked with the Coalition, and especially the Treasury Department, in managing the Paris Club agreements to reduce Iraq debt, Finance Minister Abdul-Mahdi was not perceived to be strongly supportive of American interests or values. "Al-Mahdi did not like the Americans," recalled Ali Allawi. "He was an Iraqi French Socialist. He was not willing. He was not a friend of the Americans."[59] A BearingPoint team leader concurred, saying, "He was a state planner. He was a French Socialist. I only spoke to him in French; he did not speak English very well. He wasn't totally convinced of market principles."[60] Though the firm identified a number of accomplishments with FMIS during this period, BearingPoint found its efforts meeting with either a mixed response or overt hostility during Abdul-Mahdi's regime as finance minister.

Coalition officials welcomed Ali Allawi's appointment as finance minister in May 2005. The Coalition viewed the MIT- and Harvard-educated Allawi as a progressive reformer who would be sympathetic to rebuilding the Ministry in a manner consistent with international best practices, particularly when compared to the French-educated, pro-statist al-Mahdi. On May 18, BearingPoint

[59] Interview with Ali Allawi, May 15, 2007.
[60] Interview with BearingPoint official, December 19, 2007.

presented Allawi with its Economic Governance II plan for Iraq's economy, including the continuation of the FMIS project. Despite a significant increase in violence in 2005, BearingPoint reported to Allawi its success in building up the Finance Ministry's Data Center with new computers, translating FMIS instructions into Arabic, training various ministry staff in FMIS, surveying the computer needs of other ministries and governmental units, and providing selected ministries with FMIS hardware. The plan called for more of this, but it significantly emphasized the need for the Ministry "to increase involvement and ownership" of FMIS by, among other things, requiring that staff "must fully participate" in training and "formally establishing" steering and interdirectorate working committees for purposes of coordinating and empowering the project in the Finance Ministry.[61] For Allawi, in spite of these plans, BearingPoint's accomplishments in the end proved to be quite limited, a view shared by other Middle Eastern leaders who regarded the firm as simply a group of profit seekers.[62] "If I was going to grade it, I would give it a D–, if you judge these things by their results," said Allawi. "A huge amount of money was wasted, spent on consultants, and we still don't have a functioning FMIS."[63] Allawi himself turned out to be a mixed blessing for FMIS. On the one hand, he appeared to be more accepting of FMIS and to granting greater access to BearingPoint, but, on the other hand, he failed to raise FMIS as a priority and the system was never completed during his administration. Comparing the Iraqi Transitional Government and Allawi to its successor and its finance minister, Baqir Jabr al-Zubeidi, a USAID official observed, "Currently in the Ministry of Finance there are some weaknesses with regard to the push from the top down to make things happen. I think during the transitional government there was still a

---

[61] BearingPoint, "USAID/Economic Governance II Project, Presentation to the Minister of Finance," May 18, 2005, p. 8.

[62] Consider these observations by Ashraf Ghani, Afghanistan's former Minister of Finance: "USAID has no competence in preparing budgets. All it is, is an outsource contract manager. What it does is it hires BearingPoint, and BearingPoint has no competence.... The largest unit [in USAID] is the contract writing department, not research, not development, not operations, not implementation. Then [the contractors] create a parallel hierarchy that is responsible to USAID or to themselves. If you get people from those that are seconded to you in the government, their accountability or loyalty is not to the government, but to the firm that has hired them.... I fired close to sixty people from BearingPoint because they were incompetent, but USAID will not cancel their contract.... I asked in my last month as minister of finance that their contract not be renewed. Soon as I left the Ministry of Finance I think they were given another contract for $215 million.... BearingPoint developed a software type of treasury [for Afghanistan]. Their software wouldn't talk to budgeting, it wouldn't talk to accounting, it wouldn't talk to other ministries.... This is a money making enterprise; it is not a capacity building enterprise." Ghani compared the British Department for International Development's form of capacity-building assistance to USAID's, finding that unlike USAID, the DIFID contracting "system is not precooked in terms of a monopoly on all the major contracts." Ghani did describe the U.S. Treasury OTA as "Excellent, superb. The U.S. Treasury is really competent. A remarkable group of individuals, because they come from the heart of functioning system." Interview, September 16, 2008.

[63] Interview with Ali Allawi, May 15, 2007.

fair amount of access, and there were also people in the transitional government who the Americans knew from Coalition days. For example, Allawi was minister of finance. Allawi was well-known to the CPA, and well-known to many of the people working on reconstruction programs. So access to Minister Allawi was very reasonable. After the new government took place ... the view of the Iraqi people in terms of the American occupation, as they call it, and the American presence, has impacted accessibility to certain ministers."[64] Other assessments of Allawi's support for FMIS were less favorable. "Allawi could have done it, and he chose not to," said a BearingPoint contractor who worked on FMIS. "[Finance Minister Baqir] Jabr [al-Zubeidi], who is like the spawn of Satan to some people, has actually been more supportive and taken action to support implementation of an automated system, much more than Allawi, who had much more access to the BearingPoint advisors."[65]

Coalition officials viewed al-Zubeidi's appointment as finance minister in May 2006 with great apprehension. Al-Zubeidi previously served rather notoriously as Minister of Interior, a ministry associated with rampant corruption and Sadrist sectarian affiliations.[66] More important, in terms of the fate of FMIS, al-Zubeidi brought with him Aziz Jaffar Hassam to run the Ministry's day-to-day affairs. The consummate bureaucratic survivor, Aziz served at the Finance Ministry under Saddam as a director-general, was dismissed, and then was recruited to the Ministry immediately after the 2003 invasion by Treasury OTA, who appreciated his technical skills and English-speaking ability. He served as a senior advisor under Finance Minister Abdul-Mahdi and led the drafting of the 2005 Iraqi budget, was removed by Allawi, and then returned to the Ministry under al-Zubeidi, who needed his expertise to manage the Ministry. Aziz firmly opposed FMIS. "There was a lot of resistance to it before I came," recalled Allawi. "For nearly a year and a half, especially by Aziz, because he really ran the ministry. He basically sidelined the BearingPoint people. All the old guard thought the budget making process was adequate and should not be tinkered with, and that the system that the BearingPoint people were trying to impose or implement was too sophisticated for their capacity. At some point they were right. It would have required much more IT literacy than we had. The program was well-intentioned, but resisted, and was not really designed to take into account the under capacity of the Iraqi ministries."[67] An American Treasury

---

[64] Interview with USAID official, February 12, 2008

[65] Interview with BearingPoint official, December 19, 2007.

[66] Ken Silverstein, "The Minister of Civil War: Bayan Jabr, Paul Bremer, and the Rise of the Iraqi Death Squads," *Harper's Magazine*, August 2006, 67–73.

[67] Interview with Ali Allawi, May 15, 2007. Allawi added these other observations about Aziz: "The key people included Aziz Jaffar, who had been sidelined, he was a director-general under the old MOF, sidelined under the last years of the regime ... The Finance Ministry during this period was really run by the deputy finance minister, a man called Aziz Jaffar. Mahdi did not really avail himself of the day-to-day management. He maybe did not go to the ministry more than ten times during his administration.... When I came to the ministry, this fellow Aziz Jaffar, who was

attaché elaborated on Aziz's influence: "Aziz is a double-edged sword. In a system which is very ritualistic, he knows how the rituals are played out. If you want to get things done, you really need Aziz to get them done, because he really knows how to make the building work, because he has been there so long. The people in the building are very mistrustful of who is there and how long they are going to be there. But Aziz has been there forever, and they are trustful of that. But on the other hand, he is just mired in the past. He wants to implement nothing new, and he is just locked into the late 80s. So you will get no progress under Aziz. If IFMIS comes out, it will be because we threw money and effort in until it became a *fait accompli*."[68] Aziz's command of the bureaucracy, his unique, practical value to Coalition officials, and the respect, loyalty, and even fear he engendered in Ministry personnel, enabled him to block BearingPoint. Aziz, for example, exercised sufficient authority to determine when FMIS training would occur and which ministry personnel would attend and to decide

developing a mini-empire, had an entirely different perspective on how to run [it], so we had a short altercation and I asked him to leave. He left. But then he was then taken up by Mahdi, who had become vice president. So he just sat in the vice president's office while I was minister of finance . . . he was brought back [by Jabr] and basically runs the ministry. . . . He is basically of the old school. He is an accountant. He was pushed into the 'free zone' at the Ministry of Finance, and had little to do. When the Americans came in, he presented himself. . . . He speaks English quite well, and could speak to the CPA." As Allawi states, Aziz was brought into the Finance Ministry by Treasury OTA officials soon after the invasion because he knew the Ministry and could speak English. Allawi removed him from the Ministry while he served as finance minister, but Finance Minister Jabr brought Aziz back once again

[68] Interview with Treasury Department official, February 23, 2009. "Aziz is not deputy finance minister. He is senior economic advisor to Vice President Adil Abdul-Mahdi, who is over Jabr. When Jabr was appointed Finance Minister when he was Interior minister, he went to Abdul-Mahdi and said he needed Aziz's help. Jabr gives Aziz vast power to run the building." Said another Treasury attaché: "He was a constant presence at the Ministry. He lived in Iraq through Saddam. Technocrat trained as an accountant. A detail guy. When Americans thought there was no Iraqi government, there were people he could call and get answers. He was only deputy finance minister during the interim government. When he came back with Jabr, his title is senior advisor. He's treated by the Iraqis as one step below the minister. In that capacity he exercised tight control over the budget process. He had a couple of key directors-general work for him, one on the budget formulation side, one on the budget execution side. It was very clear that they worked for him, and did not do things without approval from him." Interview with Treasury Department official, April 7, 2009. Also, Ambassador Reis observed: "The main power in that ministry is a guy named Aziz. He basically moved the paper when the paper was going to be moved. One of the problems was that Aziz's deputy, the director general for accounts, had been assassinated in the middle of 07. It was really a big blow at the center of a very antiquated ministry of finance, which still operated on the basis of paper records and treasury accounts, which were very centrally controlled. So Aziz was very hostile to IFMIS. He didn't like IFMIS at all, he thought the system was wrong, it was a single treasury account system that didn't allow for multiple accounts of the kind that they had. It had been designed by U.S. contractors for Afghanistan, he was insulted. He never liked it. He didn't like the BearingPoint people, and of course we had the kidnapping." Interview with Charles Ries, Minister for Economic Affairs and Coordinator for Economic Transition in Iraq, February 2, 2010.

whether to share the data needed to make FMIS work with Coalition and BearingPoint officials.

Despite tension with the Coalition, al-Zubeidi signed a directive in February 2007 ordering the implementation of FMIS, and during the spring of 2007 the Finance Ministry finally formed the FMIS steering committee that BearingPoint had called for since 2004, with Treasury and USAID advisors added to the committee. This order appeared to signal real progress, yet an internal April 2007 briefing to Ambassador Tim Carney solely on the topic of FMIS noted an unwillingness by the Finance Ministry to share data generated by the system, and that "to bring public financial management throughout Iraq will require significant capacity development, training, and mentoring.... Many ministries retain internal procedures and systems that are either inefficient or yield data that must be manually entered into IFMIS. This has contributed to a lack of timely reports and data, which frustrates GOI managers and USG [United States government] advisors who monitor GOI budget execution."[69]

Then to make matters worse, the BearingPoint contractors were kidnapped in front of the Finance Ministry in May. An evaluation of the effects of the kidnapping on FMIS and the Ministry provided to the Ambassador on July 3 pointed to the Iraqis' continuing reluctance to accept FMIS. "It has never been embraced by current Minister of Finance, Baqir Jabr [al-Zubeidi]. This became clear when, after the abduction of the five British USAID contractors on May 29, the system went down. Now, a month later, we know of no ministry or other spending unit complaints over the loss. In fact, most first learned of the situation in recent meetings with the Treasury Attaché."[70] The kidnapping caused the contract to be suspended until January 2008, when al-Zubeidi signed a memorandum of understanding with USAID to restart the FMIS implementation process. As the American Embassy announcement of the agreement stated, "A financial management system is essential for a functional national government to create, execute and monitor a national budget in an efficient and transparent manner. Restarting IFMIS helps the GOI meet a benchmark under the IMF's 2008 Stand-by Agreement and its commitments under the International Compact with Iraq."[71]

What eventually moved the Ministry's leadership to accept FMIS were not the years of entreaties by Coalition officials and BearingPoint contractors. The Finance Ministry finally succumbed to the pressure of meeting the demands of

---

[69] U.S. Treasury, "The Iraqi Financial Management Information System, Briefing to Ambassador Tim Carney, April 11, 2007, p. 2.

[70] U.S. Treasury, "Action Memorandum to the Ambassador, 'Suspension of USAID Project Support for the Iraqi Financial Management Information System (FMIS) and Conditions for Resumption of Project,'" July 3, 2007, p. 1.

[71] U.S. Embassy Baghdad, "Minister of Finance Signs MOU to Restart Implementation of the Iraqi Financial Management Information System (IFMIS)," January 16, 2008. Also see David F. Biggs, "Iraq," in Robert P. Beschel Jr. and Mark Ahern (eds.), *Public Financial Management Reform in the Middle East and North Africa*, Washington, DC: The World Bank, 2012, 101–112.

international donors to upgrade its budgetary and fiscal operations to bring them up to a level of acceptable best practices. For example, referring to al-Zubeidi's highly influential senior advisor who managed the Ministry's daily operations, a Treasury OTA official assessed his very reluctant acceptance of FMIS. "Dr. Aziz, who is Minister Jabr's advisor, the man is a serious nationalist, and Aziz is not interested in adopting FMIS or any other reforms more than the extent that it takes for them to qualify for debt reduction relief."[72] Whatever their disputes and disagreements, where Iraqi political leadership, especially the leadership of the Finance Ministry, and the Coalition stood in firm agreement was in the desperate urgency of reducing Iraq's international debt obligations. To the extent that FMIS helped fulfill that ambition, al-Zubeidi's memorandum suggested the Iraqis were willing to comply with activating the system. Nevertheless, a year after al-Zubeidi signed the memorandum of understanding, another USAID independent review of FMIS released in January 2009 concluded, "It is the opinion of the assessment team that while there appears to be increased political will within the GOI to implement this system, until such time as all GOI stakeholders see IFMIS as a priority and are willing to take ownership of it, it will likely never be fully implemented, the MOU [Memorandum of Understanding] between USAID and the MOF [Ministry of Finance] notwithstanding."[73]

CONCLUSION

The Coalition's experience with USAID's Economic Governance contract pointed to the challenges of imposing "international best practices" on a reluctant beneficiary, as well as the inappropriateness of assuming that such practices are always desirable. The attempt to implement the contact also reflected the CPA's lack of a cohesive reconstruction strategy and command structure, the challenges of relying on contractors to conduct assistance work, and the difficulties of gaining buy-in from aid beneficiaries. USAID's management of BearingPoint suffered from disputes with the CPA's leadership as well as with Treasury OTA staff. USAID's own understaffing hampered its ability to monitor BearingPoint's activities, and, despite several years of the firm's inability to install FMIS, USAID made little effort to revise, reconsider, or terminate the contract given the firm's lack of success. USAID continued to entrust BearingPoint with large and costly development and governance contracts, even though the firm's overall operations suffered from significant mismanagement and accounting problems. The firm's difficulties included being spun off from its parent company, the international accounting firm KPMG, in addition to BearingPoint losing $516 million in 2004, $721 million in 2005, and

---

[72] Interview with Treasury Department official, December 19, 2007.
[73] USAID, "Iraq Financial Management Information System Situation Assessment, Executive Summary," Baghdad, Iraq, January 20, 2009, p. 13.

$231 million in 2006.[74] BearingPoint's financial problems prompted the Securities and Exchange Commission to investigate its activities in 2005, leading the firm to cease trading its shares on the New York Stock Exchange. In 2009, the firm sought bankruptcy protection and began selling off its various divisions to other companies, with its government consulting units sold to the global consulting firm Deloitte.[75] According to USAID, the end date for the five-year Economic Governance II contract came on September 2, 2009, without a completed FMIS in place. A review by the USAID Inspector General concluded that "Some key contract deliverables were not completed, and the Government of Iraq employees were not fully satisfied with the training provided. As a result, users cannot perform their work using the new system, and the Ministry of Finance has not accepted the Iraq Financial Management Information System as their system of record."[76] At the contract's end, the Canadian firm FreeBalance attempted to work directly with the Ministry of Finance to resuscitate FMIS. Yet by the end of 2011, a FreeBalance official acknowledged that the Iraqis had yet to use FMIS for accounting, internal budget controls, or budget formulation.[77]

Despite the Coalition's authority as an armed occupational power aided by the influence of financial donors, the Iraqis succeeded in preventing the Coalition's agent BearingPoint from installing FMIS. The FMIS system imposed on the Ministry of Finance threatened its standard operating procedures without offering clear incentives and immediate benefits.[78] In hindsight, as a senior Treasury official acknowledged, the position taken by Aziz Jaffar, the official who led the Finance Ministry opposition position on FMIS, was the correct one: "He was right on in terms of some aspects of Financial Public Management Information System. He was one of the early critics, saying that the system that was being proposed, more than proposed, installed, was more complicated, more expensive, bigger, than was needed. An approach that took into account

---

[74] Kathleen Day, "BearingPoint Getting Close to Timely," *Washington Post*, July 9, 2007, D2.

[75] Alejandro Lazo, "BearingPoint Seeks Bankruptcy Protection," *Washington Post*, February 19, 2009, D1; Galen Moore, "Keane Plans BearingPoint Buyout," *Mass High Tech Business News*, July 9, 2009. http://www.masshightech.com/stories/2009/07/06/daily45-Keane-plans-BearingPoint-buyout.html/; Jonathan Starkey, "BearingPoint Nears End of Difficult Run," *Washington Post*, September 25, 2009, A14.

[76] USAID Office of Inspector General, "Audit of USAID/IRAQ'S Implementation of the Iraq Financial Management Information System," Audit Report No. E-267-10-002-P, Baghdad, July 19, 2010, 7.

[77] Interview with FreeBalance official, October 15, 2011. The World Bank agreed with this evaluation of BearingPoint's working with the Iraqis. "Most notable perhaps was the absence of a conceptual design document, which international experience shows to be a key requirement.... This would have helped define the high-level functional requirements with participation from major stakeholders." Robert P. Beschel Jr. and Mark Ahern, *Public Financial Management Reform in the Middle East and North Africa*, Washington, DC: The World Bank, 2012, 105.

[78] On incentives for aid beneficiaries, see Clark C. Gibson, Krister Andersson, Elinor Ostrom, and Sujai Shivakumar, *The Samaritan's Dilemma: The Political Economy of Development Aid*, New York: Oxford University Press, 2005.

better Iraq's needs, its absorptive capacity, its ability to make use of such a system, was needed."[79]

"The FMIS project was simply not a success," U.S. Ambassador to Iraq Ryan Crocker concluded. "It was more sophisticated than the Iraqis wanted or needed. It never really had their buy-in. It was unfortunate, but at some point you've got to stop beating a dead horse."[80] The Iraqis refused to take ownership of FMIS. They successfully employed a form of passive resistance to foil Coalition and international donor agency demands that they install FMIS. The Iraqis agreed to the formal requirements of aid conditionality, but at the same time they limited BearingPoint's physical access to Finance Ministry facilities and obstructed the training of Ministry personnel. The Coalition continued to face the challenge of gaining buy-in as it attempted through other capacity development programs to build Iraqi budget execution.

[79] Interview with Treasury Department Official, January 30, 2009.
[80] Interview with Ambassador Ryan Crocker, September 24, 2010.

6

The 17th Benchmark and the Challenge of Iraqi Budget Execution

In response to the increasing violence and the deteriorating security situation that engulfed Iraq in 2005 and 2006, the Bush administration released its "New Way Forward" strategy in February 2007, which ordered the surge in U.S. troop levels, promoted counterinsurgency efforts, and renewed efforts to bring "essential services" to the Iraqi people.[1] The Iraqi government would never gain the people's confidence and successfully deter violence, American officials reasoned, unless the government delivered on its promises to rebuild the country's infrastructure and provide basic services, such as electricity and water. Providing these services meant spending more money, not just Coalition and donor funds, but a focused target of spending more Iraqi money.

Encouraging and assisting the Iraqis to spend their money became part of American law. As part of the 2007 appropriations that helped fund the new strategy, the legislation established eighteen benchmarks that evaluated American progress in Iraq. The 17th Benchmark measured Iraqi success in "allocating and spending $10 billion in Iraqi revenues for reconstruction projects, including delivery of essential services on an equitable basis." The two key words in the benchmark are "allocating" and "spending."[2] Allocating refers to the processes of budget formulation and adoption by designated political authorities. Spending refers to budget execution and the actual expenditure of funds.[3] By 2007, with the guidance of CPA Order 95, the Financial Management

[1] Office of the Press Secretary, "Fact Sheet: The New Way Forward," Washington, DC: The White House, January 10, 2007. http://georgewbush-whitehouse.archives.gov/news/releases/2007/01/20070110-3.html.

[2] H.R. 2206, "U.S. Troop Readiness, Veterans' Care, Katrina Recovery, and Iraq Accountability Appropriations Act, 2007," Public Law 110–28, Statue 112, enacted May 25, 2007. See Section 1314 (b)(1)(A)(xvii) for the listing of benchmarks.

[3] On budget execution, see Robert N. Anthony and David W. Young, *Management Control in Nonprofit Organizations*, Boston: Irwin, 1994; Robert L. Bland and Irene S. Rubin, *Budgeting: A Guide for Local Governments*, Washington, DC: International City/County Management

Law, the Iraqis could reasonably draft a budget, eventually get it adopted through the political process, and spend its operational budget, which essentially paid government salaries and pensions. What the Iraqis could not do very well was spend their investment budget for capital projects. By the end of 2006, Coalition reconstruction, civil service training, and ministerial and provincial assistance efforts focused on helping the Iraqis execute the capital budget. Thus, the 17th Benchmark and the spending of the capital budget became a significant measure of the success of Coalition and Iraqi governance. This chapter examines the pressures on the Coalition to encourage Iraqi spending, the origins of the 17th Benchmark, its strengths and limitations as a metric, and the role budget execution served in promoting Coalition budgetary state building in Iraq.

SPENDING MONEY IN IRAQ

The Iraqi FY 2003 and FY 2004 budgets drafted by David Oliver and the CPA focused on operating or recurrent expenditures, with the CPA using much of the Development Fund for Iraq funds to pay these expenses. More than any other budgetary matter, the CPA urgently needed to pay civil service salaries and pensions to get bureaucrats back to work at the ministries, maintain civil order, reduce unemployment, and assist as many Iraqis as possible in their ability to purchase essential goods and services. Budget execution issues, particularly problems with transparency and accountability plagued this effort. Paying civil servants and pensioners proved to be "a complex task," Paul Bremer noted, "because Iraq's ministries had very limited budgeting capacity and in effect there was no banking system to distribute funds."[4] To make these payments in a cash-based economy, the CPA, and especially Treasury's OTA, worked with the Iraqis to reformulate the government's civil servant classifications and pay scales, identify the various beneficiaries, withdraw billions of DFI dollars deposited in the Federal Reserve Bank in New York, distribute cash throughout Iraq, arrange pay dates, and establish centers where Iraqis could pick up their cash payments. Making these payments proved to be highly controversial, due to the CPA's lack of budgetary accountability and transparency and Iraq's dubious civil servant and pension lists. Between April 2003 and June 2004, the CPA obtained $11.9 billion in Iraqi funds held at the Federal Reserve primarily to pay operating expenditures, but by the end of its administration the CPA was unable to ensure that $8.8 billion of these funds were used as intended and that proper accounting occurred.[5]

Association, 1997; Robert D. Lee, Jr. and Ronald W. Johnson, *Public Budgeting Systems*, Gaithersburg, MD: Aspen Publishers, 1998; Jerry L. McCaffery and L. R. Jones, *Budgeting and Financial Management in the Federal Government*, Greenwich, CT: Information Age Publishing, 2001; and David C. Nice, *Public Budgeting*, Stamford, CT: Wadsworth, 2002.
[4] L. Paul Bremer III, *My Year in Iraq*, New York: Threshold Editions, 2006, 67.
[5] Office of the Special Inspector General for Iraq Reconstruction, "Audit Report: Oversight of Funds Provided to Iraqi Ministries through the National Budget Process," Report No. 05-004, Arlington,

Compared to operational costs, the amount allocated for capital programs and investments remained a relatively small portion of total expenditures in the Iraqi budget until FY 2005. The FY 2003 and FY 2004 budgets provided just 4 and 10 percent of their respective total expenditures for capital investment. The CPA set such low levels of Iraqi investment spending because the massive amounts of capital spending included in the IRRF and donor funding flowing into Iraq offset the urgency of including capital funding in the Iraqi budgets. Aside from addressing the Iraqis' ability to spend the operating budget, the CPA became overwhelmingly preoccupied with the challenges it faced managing and spending the IRRF and donor funds as quickly as possible. The Coalition experienced its own problems spending money promptly, effectively, and in an accountable fashion. Although by September 2006, 74 percent of the $20.9 billion IRRF funds appropriated in 2004 were disbursed, two years later a quarter of IRRF money still remained unspent, with the last amounts of IRRF money still flowing as late as January 2009.

In addition to relying on its own funding resources, another reason the Coalition paid relatively little attention to Iraqi capital budgeting during the early years after the invasion is because of Iraq's search for some sort of political stability. Iraq went through three governments in less than three years following the transfer of power. This meant working with three different finance ministers, which disrupted cohesive and comprehensive budgeting of any kind. In this shifting political environment, the Iraqis were responsible for developing, adopting, and executing a budget for the first time without Saddam Hussein's direction since he became president in 1979. Following the Interim Government's eleven months in office from June 2004 to May 2005, and then the Transitional Government's year in power from May 2005 to May 2006, Prime Minister Nouri al-Maliki and the new Iraqi National Assembly finally took office on May 20, 2006.[6] As shown in Figure 6.1, the buildup in the investment provisions in the Iraqi budgets began with the Interim Government's FY 2005 budget and the Transitional Government's FY 2006 budget, where, at the Coalition's urging, the Iraqis allocated 24 and 18 percent of these respective budgets for investment purposes. Thereafter, the amount included in the budgets for investments reached at least 20 percent of the total allocation. Despite the formal inclusion of capital spending in their budgets, Iraq's ministries during this transitional period simply lacked the capacity to plan, formulate, and execute meaningful and effective capital budgets. The ministries still struggled to recover from the damage inflicted on their infrastructure by the waves of looting that followed the 2003 invasion. They lacked trained personnel who could perform basic capital planning and the fundamental requirements of budget execution, such as writing contracts and making procurements. Sectarian differences undermined their

---

VA, January 30, 2005; Donald L. Barlett and James B. Steele, "Billions over Baghdad," *Vanity Fair*, October 2007, 336–380.

[6] On the 2005 election, see Kenneth Ktazman, "Iraq: Post-Saddam National Elections," RS21968, Washington, DC: Congressional Research Service, March 11, 2005.

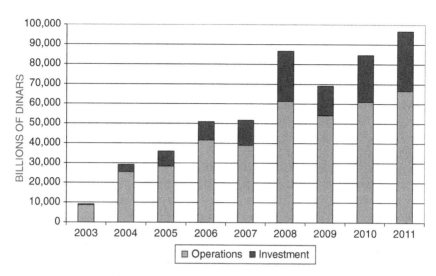

FIGURE 6.1. Iraqi Budgets, 2003–2011
Source: Iraq Ministry of Finance

ability to work together. While sectarian divisions and ministerial competition separated the leadership of the ministries of Finance and Planning, little or no communication existed between the Finance Ministry and the Central Bank of Iraq. The ministerial staffs were still coming to grips with learning and implementing the new budgetary process created by CPA Order 95. Meanwhile, provincial governments never effectively existed during Saddam's reign, and they lacked any meaningful experience in budgeting. The transfer of power forced the Iraqis to take command of the budgetary process, but they were unprepared to formulate and execute large-scale reconstruction and investment programs.

THE CRISIS OF IRAQI BUDGET EXECUTION

Beginning in July 2005, as required by law, the Department of Defense began issuing quarterly reports to Congress, titled "Measuring Stability and Security in Iraq." These reports reflect Iraq's growing security crisis and the rising concern for Iraqi budget execution. The initial volumes of the report offered a somewhat optimistic view of the security situation. The October report, for example, noted that although the quarter registered an increase in the number of attacks on infrastructure, which significantly "impacted the generation of oil revenue," the rate of conflict actually declined since 2004.[7] Moreover, the report declared that

---

[7] U.S. Department of Defense, "Measuring Stability and Security in Iraq," Washington, DC, October 2005, 23. According to a Defense Department official responsible for coordinating this report, the document is generated by the Office of the Secretary of Defense–Under Secretary for

the Iraqi government took steps to promote the 2006 budget's "transparency and credibility," in line with the International Monetary Fund's Stand-by Arrangement and Paris Club debt reduction agreement.[8] While the February 2006 report described an expansion in violence and causalities associated with the attack on the Golden Temple, it favorably observed that "the capability of the Ministry of Finance to execute a sound budget process is helping the Government of Iraq to determine priorities for rebuilding and reinvigorating its economy."[9] The Finance Ministry, the report observed, worked to create a new chart of accounts that would enable the Iraqis to organize their various programs and spending items into systematic categories and continue the expansion of the Financial Management Information System. The report raised the warning, however, that "under-spending of the capital budget threatens to slow the pace of reconstruction and limit investment in oil infrastructure."[10]

The August 2006 report provided greater insight into the problems plaguing Iraqi budgeting, as the security situation rapidly deteriorated. "The Government of Iraq's continued inability to execute its budget places delivery of basic services, as well as future economic expansion, at risk.... Budgets are not effectively delegated from the Ministry of Finance (MOF) to other ministries and provinces. The procedures to enable contracts through the MOF are proving too cumbersome, and officials are not willing to risk applying perceived 'incorrect procedures,' as several officials have been detained with investigations pending into possible breaches of regulations. Communications between the CBI [Central Bank of Iraq] and the MOF have all but stopped; several employees at the CBI have been intimidated and have therefore failed to show up for work."[11]

Corruption permeated the Iraqi government. "Experienced or talented employees are often purged and replaced with party elements/cronies as a result of a spoils system. Many of Iraq's political factions tend to view government ministries and their associated budgets as sources of power, patronage, and funding for their parties."[12]

Defense Policy–Deputy Assistant Secretary for the Middle East, International Security Affairs. The "budget section comes from Multi-Forces Iraq, which is under Centcom and then is sent to an interagency Treasury, State review. It goes through three major drafts over month and half. The original draft comes from military, but in close working with Treasury, State in the Embassy." Interview with Defense Department official, November 14, 2008. For a critical view of these reports, see Anthony H. Cordsman, "The Quarterly Report on 'Measuring Stability and Security in Iraq:' Fact, Fallacy, and an Overall Grade of 'F,'" Washington, DC: Center for Strategic and International Studies, June 5, 2006.

[8] *Ibid.*, 10.
[9] U.S. Department of Defense, "Measuring Stability and Security in Iraq," Washington, DC, February 2006, 13.
[10] *Ibid.*, 19.
[11] U.S. Department of Defense, "Measuring Stability and Security in Iraq," Washington, DC, August 2006, 15.
[12] *Ibid.*, 13.

By June 2007, the subject of budget execution received its own permanent heading in the quarterly Stability and Security reports. That month's report offered a blistering analysis of Iraqi budgeting capacity. Though the Iraqi government executed its FY 2006 operating budget reasonably well, it spent only 22 percent of its $6.2 billion capital budget, a figure the Government Accountability Office later reduced to 19 percent. The Iraqis executed just $90 million of the vital Ministry of Oil's investment budget of $3.5 billion. "Because [the Ministry of Oil] is not subject to market pressures to stay in business," the report explained, "it has little incentive to invest its full capital budget."[13] Shoring up Iraq's oil industry, which provided 95 percent of the government's revenues, was an obvious reconstruction priority. A report issued by the Iraqi Ministry of Oil's Inspector General in 2006 indicated that Iraq lost an estimated $24.7 billion in revenue between 2004 and 2006 due to attacks on the pipeline system, a drop in oil production, and the failure to reconstruct and develop the oil industry.[14] Nonetheless, the Iraqis allocated a mere $2.38 billion for the Oil Ministry's investment budget for 2007, but even in this case, "Given past experience, [the Oil Ministry] will likely be challenged to execute the lower amount."[15] According to the Defense Department's reports, these budgetary problems obstructed political progress, even as complaints about budget execution came from military commanders in the field who desperately attempted to quell Iraq's wave of escalating violence and the growing number of casualties taking place throughout Iraq and especially in Baghdad. The U.S. government soon made remedying Iraq's budget execution problems a top priority.

THE LOGIC OF THE 17TH BENCHMARK

In his January 9, 2007, address to the nation, President Bush outlined his "New Way Forward" strategy. "To show that it is committed to delivering a better life," the president declared, "the Iraqi government will spend $10 billion of its own money on reconstruction and infrastructure projects that will create new jobs."[16] The Congress then embedded this goal into law by passing HR 1591,

[13] U.S. Department of Defense, "Measuring Stability and Security in Iraq," Washington, DC, June 2007, 11. The GAO reduced the 22 percent figure to 19 percent in 2008. See U.S. Government Accountability Office, "Securing, Stabilizing, and Rebuilding Iraq: Progress Report: Some Gains Made, Updated Strategy Needed," GAO-08-837, Washington, DC: June 2008, table 3, 45.
[14] This report also claimed that $290 million, not $90 million as noted later in the June 2007 "Measuring Stability and Security in Iraq report," of the $3.5 billion allocation was spent in 2006. Moreover, "The report said many of the so-called 'strategic projects' aimed at increasing production, exports and refining capacity haven't been implemented, citing a lack of participation from international companies and contracts because of security issues and a delay in the release of money by the Ministry of Finance." Hassan Hafidh, "Iraq Lost $24.7 Billion 04–06 on Sabotage, Lack of Investment-Study," Dow Jones Newswires, November 13, 2006.
[15] *Ibid.*, 12.
[16] White House, Office of the Press Secretary, "President's Address to the Nation," Washington, DC, January 10, 2007. http://georgewbush-whitehouse.archives.gov/news/releases/2007/01/20070110-7.html.

the U.S. Troop Readiness, Veterans' Care, Katrina Recovery, and Iraq
Accountability Appropriations Act of 2007. The legislation required the White
House to make "determinations of Iraqi government success," including the
"allocation of Iraqi revenues for reconstruction projects." The bill also threatened to withhold 50 percent of American appropriations for economic assistance for Iraq, unless, together with other conditions, the Iraqis had "allocated
and begun expenditure of $10,000,000,000 in Iraqi revenues for reconstruction
projects, including delivery of essential services, on an equitable basis." Bush
vetoed this bill, in no small part because of this withholding provision.[17] Then in
May, Congress passed another version of the bill, HR 2206 that Bush signed,
which left out the withholding provision but, as shown in Table 6.1, delineated
eighteen benchmarks for measuring the Iraqi government's "record of performance." Of these eighteen benchmarks, only the 17th addressed the purpose and
operation of Iraq's public administration. The 1st Benchmark referred to the
creation of a constitutional review committee, benchmarks 2 through 7 called
for the Iraqis to pass various types of legislation, benchmarks 8 through 15, and
the 18th concerned security issues, and the 16th Benchmark declared that Iraq
should respect the rights of minority parties. The bill further required that Bush
submit two reports to Congress evaluating Iraqi success with the eighteen benchmarks, including "Allocating and spending $10 billion in Iraqi revenues for
reconstruction projects, including delivery of essential services, on an equitable
basis."[18]

The White House's July and September 2007 "Benchmark Assessment
Reports" offered candid evaluations of existing Iraqi budgeting capacity. On
the positive side, the Iraqis "allocated," or approved, a detailed FY 2007 capital
budget by February 2007. Although this was a month after the beginning of the
fiscal year, the pace of obtaining political approval for the budget was faster than
in the preceding year, and the technical quality of the budget reflected a more
sophisticated document than the less professional FY 2006 capital budget. The
September report also highlighted the role of the provincial governments in the

[17] H.R. 2206 was actually a milder version of an earlier bill, H.R. 1591, which threatened to
withhold 50 percent of American economic support appropriations for Iraq, unless, together
with other conditions, the Iraqis had "allocated and begun expenditure of $10,000,000,000 in
Iraqi revenues for reconstruction projects, including delivery of essential services, on an equitable
basis." This bill demanded that "The President shall make and transmit to Congress the following
determinations of Iraqi Government success" in a number of areas, including the "allocation of
Iraqi revenues for reconstruction projects." The bill also included a troop withdrawal time
schedule. President Bush vetoed this bill. "H.R. 1591, U.S. Troop Readiness, Veterans' Care,
Katrina Recovery, and Iraq Accountability Appropriations Act, 2007, (Enrolled as Agreed to or
Passed by Both House and Senate)," Section 1904(f) and Section 1904(a), pp. 30–31. March 29,
2007.
[18] H.R. 2206, "U.S. Troop Readiness, Veterans' Care, Katrina Recovery, and Iraq Accountability
Appropriations Act, 2007," Public Law 110-28, Statue 112, enacted May 25, 2007. See
Section 1314 (b)(1)(A)(xvii) for the listing of benchmarks, and Section 1314 (b)(1)(B) for the
reporting requirements.

TABLE 6.1. *2007 Benchmarks for Assessing Progress in Iraq*

1. Forming a Constitutional Review Committee and then completing the constitutional review.
2. Enacting and implementing legislation on de-Ba'athification.
3. Enacting and implementing legislation to ensure the equitable distribution of hydrocarbon resources of the people of Iraq without regard to the sect or ethnicity of recipients, and enacting and implementing legislation to ensure that the energy resources of Iraq benefit Sunni Arabs, Shia Arabs, Kurds, and other Iraqi citizens in an equitable manner.
4. Enacting and implementing legislation on procedures to form semiautonomous regions.
5. Enacting and implementing legislation establishing an Independent High Electoral Commission, provincial election law, provincial council authorities, and a date for provincial elections.
6. Enacting and implementing legislation addressing amnesty.
7. Enacting and implanting legislation establishing a strong militia disarmament program to ensure that such security forces are accountable only to the central government and loyal to the Constitution of Iraq.
8. Establishing supporting political, media, economic, and services committees in support of the Baghdad security plan.
9. Providing three trained and ready Iraqi brigades to support Baghdad operations.
10. Providing Iraqi commanders with all authorities to execute this plan and to make tactical and operational decisions, in consultation with U.S. commanders, without political intervention, to include the authority to pursue all extremists, including Sunni insurgents and Shiite militias.
11. Ensuring that the Iraqi Security Forces are providing even-handed enforcement of the law.
12. Ensuring that, according to President Bush, Prime Minister Maliki said "the Baghdad security plan will not provide a safe haven for any outlaws, regardless of [their] sectarian or political affiliation."
13. Reducing the level of sectarian violence in Iraq and eliminating militia control of local security.
14. Establishing all of the planned joint security stations in neighborhoods across Baghdad.
15. Increasing the number of Iraqi security forces units capable of operating independency.
16. Ensuring that the rights of minority political parties in the Iraqi legislature are protected.
17. Allocating and spending $10 billion in Iraqi revenues for reconstruction projects, including delivery of essential services, on an equitable basis.
18. Ensuring that Iraq's political authorities are not undermining or making false accusations against members of the Iraqi security services.

Iraqi budgeting process. In 2006, the Iraqi provincial governments gained the power to submit investment budget requests to the central government for funding. So, as the report quite justifiably declared, "The 2007 Iraqi budget represents the first time in modern Iraqi history that provincial governments have been able to formulate and implement their own capital budgets."[19] Despite these advances in Iraqi capacity, the September assessment reported that the level of capital spending thus far taking place in FY 2007 was "on par with last year's level" when the government executed only 22 percent of its FY 2006 capital budget, and as a consequence the Iraqi people continued to suffer from a lack of basic services and infrastructure. The Bush administration found Iraq's overall progress with the 17th benchmark to be "satisfactory."

The GAO's September report to Congress, though more gloomy about Iraqi progress, largely concurred with the two White House assessments of the allocating and spending benchmark. The GAO employed a three-level classification of performance in evaluating the benchmark. GAO declared that if the $10 billion had been allocated and spent by the end of 2007, then the benchmark would be "met." If the funds were allocated but not spent by the end of the year, then the benchmark would be considered "partially met." If the funds were neither allocated nor spent, then the benchmark would be "not met." For this benchmark, GAO awarded it a grade of partially met. This evaluation placed Iraqi budget allocation and spending among the success stories of the Iraqi occupation, as the GAO found just three of the eighteen benchmarks met, four partially met, and eleven unmet. The accomplishments identified by the White House and GAO rested on the ability of the Iraqis to formulate a capital budget and to gain approval for those proposals through the Iraqi political system. This gained the Iraqis half-credit for the benchmark, but the other half, the actual spending of the capital budget remained unfulfilled. Though the Iraqis passed their budgets in a relatively timely manner and they were expected to increase their capital spending over FY 2006, a "large portion" of the targeted $10 billion investment budget "will likely go unspent."[20] Where the White House praised the provincial governments' new engagement in the capital budget process, the GAO remained more cautious about the implications of devolving capital budgeting down to the provinces. The provincial capability to develop and execute a capital budget was in its infancy, and that meant the investment funds allocated and entrusted to these local governments, approximately 20 percent of the total $10 billion, would most likely remain unspent if not uncommitted. The White House and the GAO, therefore, respectively graded the 17th Benchmark as "satisfactory" and "partially met."

[19] White House, National Security Council, "Benchmark Assessment Report," Washington, DC, September 14, 2007.

[20] U.S. Government Accountability Office, "Securing, Stabilizing, and Rebuilding Iraq: Iraqi Government Has Not Met Most Legislative, Security, and Economic Benchmarks," GAO-07–1195, Washington, DC, September 2007, 64.

Spending the Iraqi capital budget did make sense as a metric for grading American progress in Iraq on several levels. There was a deeper logic to the benchmark than simply getting the Iraqis to rebuild infrastructure and provide basic services. First, for the Coalition, the success of the Iraqi government was at stake. "The critical battle is going to be over services," observed a State Department official responsible for overseeing the Iraqi economy. "If they can't move that money out the door effectively, to build a power plant, the sewage treatment facilities, the electrical distribution and generation, if they can't get that done, they are going to go down. Nothing else is going to matter. They are going to go down."[21] American military commanders firmly embraced the idea that making progress in reconstruction and service provision added to the government's legitimacy, strengthened popular support, and reduced Iraqi security threats as part of an overall counterinsurgency strategy. "The Iraqi government has to be able to deliver consistent services," declared General Raymond T. Odierno, the commanding general of U.S. military forces in Iraq. "Electricity is probably the most important. They're working towards this, but if they don't do this the citizens over time will potentially start to move against the government if they have to wait too much longer for services."[22] The very act of making a credible capital budget and seeing it put into effect encouraged Iraqi ownership and participation in provincial and municipal governments. Remarking on U.S. Marine Corps efforts in Al-Anbar province, Major General W. E. Gaskin, the Multi-National Forces–West Commanding General, related that "In discussing this with [Sunni] tribal leadership, they are talking past security. They are believing that we eliminated Al-Qaida and they want to be involved in economic development.... getting involved in the political process, getting involved in city councils, municipal assemblies, involved in the budgets – the things that will bring them the things they need, in terms of electricity, sewage, water, rubble removal in the case of Ramadi. But that political involvement, that connection with the national government, they realize is the future."[23] For the military, an effective Iraqi budgetary process and budget execution contributed to making the Iraqis invested stakeholders in the success of their central and local governments.

Second, aside from these political, security, and economic benefits, the 17th Benchmark reflected the Coalition's attempt to shift the cost of the war's reconstruction from the United States to the Iraqis, while preparing them for the withdrawal of Coalition financial support. The Americans recognized that by 2008 the IRRF funds would nearly be fully spent and Congress showed little interest in providing another $20 billion for Iraqi reconstruction. Iraq appeared

[21] Interview with State Department official, January 22, 2008.
[22] Jim Michaels, "Gen. Odierno: Iraqi Government Must Improve Services," *USA Today*, September 29, 2008. http://www.usatoday.com/news/world/iraq/2008-09-29-odierno_N.htm/.
[23] Major General W. E. Gaskin, Multi-National Forces–West Commanding General, Televised Pentagon Briefing from Iraq, July 20, 2007. Televised on C-Span.

more than capable of finding the revenues for this effort, as GAO predicted Iraq's cumulative budget surplus for the years 2005 through 2008 could range from $67 billion to $79 billion, though the final size of the surplus remained contingent on oil prices and the Iraqis spending their $22.3 billion 2008 supplemental budget.[24] Projections of these huge Iraqi budget surpluses created by spikes in oil prices generated bipartisan political opposition to spending additional American funds for Iraqi reconstruction. In April, Senators Ben Nelson and Susan Collins introduced legislation requiring that U.S. funds for Iraq take the form of loans rather than grants. "I think the American people are growing weary not only of the war," noted Senator Nelson, "but they are looking at why Baghdad can't pay more of these costs. And the answer is they can." Collins agreed, saying, "It's really difficult for Americans who are struggling with the high cost of energy to see us paying for fuel costs in a country that has the second largest oil reserves."[25] In hearings held by the U.S. House Budget Committee during September 2008, Chairman John Spratt declared that Iraq should finance its own reconstruction, even as he quoted Deputy Defense Secretary Paul Wolfowitz's 2003 claim that "We're dealing with a country that can really finance its own reconstruction, and relatively soon."[26] Shifting the cost of the

[24] On the spending of IRRF and supplementary U.S. funds ending: "U.S. capacity development efforts have shifted from long-term institution-building projects to an immediate effort to help Iraqi ministries overcome their inability to spend their capital investment budgets. As U.S. funding for Iraq reconstruction totaling $45 billion is almost 90 percent obligated ($40 billion) and about 70 percent disbursed ($31 billion) as of April 2008, the need for Iraq to spend its own resources becomes increasingly critical to economic development." U.S. Government Accountability Office, "Securing, Stabilizing, and Rebuilding Iraq: Progress Report: Some Gains Made, Updated Strategy Needed," GAO-08–837, Washington, DC, June 2008, 44. On the surplus, Associated Press, "Iraq's Free Budget Ride Coming to an End?" *Charlottesville Daily Progress*, April 15, 2008, A7. Also see Office of the Special Inspector General for Iraq Reconstruction, *Hard Lessons: The Iraq Reconstruction Experience*, Washington, DC: U.S. Government Printing Office, 2009, 267: "Improving the ability of the Iraqi government to spend its own revenue became the keystone in a new arc of capacity-development activities. It was all part of a shift in the reconstruction program to supporting Iraqi priorities with Iraqi resources."
[25] Associated Press, "Congress Might Slash Iraq Funds: Iraq's Financial Free Ride May Be Over," *USA Today*, April 14, 2008. http://www.usatoday.com/news/world/iraq/2008-04-14-iraq-payment_N.htm/. Also, Representative Dana Rohrabacher introduced legislation that would prevent the United States from entering into a "status of forces" agreement with Iraq, unless Iraq paid for "all of the costs of the services of the American Armed Forces." "Blood Money," *Los Angeles Times*, April 11, 2008, http://articles.latimes.com/2008/apr/11/opinion/ed-iraq11/.
[26] The Wolfowitz quote is from his March 27, 2003, testimony before the House Defense Appropriations Subcommittee. For Spratt's hearing, see U.S. House of Representatives Committee on the Budget, "Iraq's Budget Surplus: Hearing Before the Committee on the Budget, House of Representatives," Serial 110–40, Washington, DC: U.S. Government Printing Office, September 16, 2008. The GAO reported in August 2008 that the Iraqi budget surplus could range between $38.2 billion and $50.3 billion for Iraq's FY 2008 budget, but then in September revised that figure to between $67 billion and $79 billion, as oil prices rose. Despite the Iraqis' projecting annual budget deficits for the years 2005 through 2008, the failure to spend their capital accounts contributed to the accumulation of surpluses. U.S. Government Accountability

war also emerged as a significant political issue during that year's presidential election, as candidate Barack Obama announced in a campaign address, "The second thing we learned this week was that the Iraqi government now has a $79 billion budget surplus thanks to their windfall oil profits. And while this Iraqi money sits in American banks, American taxpayers continue to spend $10 billion a month to defend and rebuild Iraq. That's right. America faces a huge budget deficit. Iraq has a surplus."[27] During his September presidential debate with Senator John McCain, Obama twice pressed this issue. "We are currently spending $10 billion a month in Iraq when they have a $79 billion surplus," Obama said. "It seems to me that if we're going to be strong at home as well as strong abroad, that we have to look at bringing that war to a close."[28] Political forces in America determined that IRRF and other sources of U.S. reconstruction assistance funding would soon run dry, and the Iraqis needed to increase petroleum exploration and production, broaden to the extent possible their internal revenue sources and their tax collection capacity, seek new and additional private-sector external investment, and continue to obtain new donor support.

Third, some Coalition officials feared the Iraqis had succumbed to a donor-dependent mentality, whereby the Iraqis withheld their own resources while they instead relied on external financing to fund their reconstruction. The Iraqis are "slow in investing in their police, army, and infrastructure," a senior SIGIR official reflected. "Do you blame them when the international community is dumping $50 billion on their heads? The absorptive capacity of that exceeds the capability of the country. If the other guy is going to spend his money, why should you spend your money? So you let the international community pay for your infrastructure.... But part of that is their own financial brinkmanship, where they knew if they didn't spend the money, the Americans ... would come running in with a bunch of money and pay for their logistics, arms, building more police stations, and they totally understand how that game is played, and they are playing it."[29] A Treasury attaché responsible for monitoring the Iraqi economy concurred, adding, "When I first arrived, and there probably still is, this donor-dependency syndrome, because Iraqis are very clever people. From their own self-interest, it is better to use somebody else's money ... rather than use your own money."[30]

Office, "Stabilizing and Rebuilding Iraq: Iraqi Revenues, Expenditures, and Surplus," GAO-08–1031, Washington, DC, August, 2008, and U.S. Government Accountability Office, "Stabilizing and Rebuilding Iraq: Iraqi Revenues, Expenditure, and Surplus," GAO-08–1144T, Washington, DC, September 16, 2008.

[27] Barack Obama, "Obama: Iraq Budget Surplus Highlights Need for Change in Washington – Delivers the Weekly Democratic Radio Address," August 9, 2008.
[28] *New York Times*, "The First Presidential Debate," September 26, 2008, A12.
[29] Interview with SIGIR official, October 6, 2009.
[30] Interview with Treasury Department official, February 23, 2009.

This concern for Iraq's donor-dependency coincided with the widely held view that the Iraqi bureaucracy lacked initiative and the ability to delegate authority, including those decisions required to spend the budget. "The phenomenon of Iraqis preferring to sit back and have the donors come in and spend is true," agreed Ambassador Charles P. Ries, who served as the Minister for Economic Affairs and Coordinator for Economic Transition in Iraq in 2007 and 2008, "but it's not because of either an economic or a calculation that they would get more resources by having the foreigners do it. It was more a characteristic of Iraqi political culture."[31] This culture reflected the fear of working under a dictatorship, the reluctance to make decisions, particularly in the absence of written orders, the reliance on ministers to make even trivial decisions, and the fear of being accused of corruption. "So it was easier to get the foreigners to actually build things that they could take credit for," said Ries. "They had no risk that way. They had no risk of making the wrong decisions; they had no risk of being accused as corrupt. Now, there is a lot of corruption. That's why they feared getting accused of it, because it is almost impossible to spend a million dollars in Iraq without lots of corruption. So the best thing if you are interested in your long-term longevity in the job is not to spend the million dollars and get the Americans to spend a million dollars, and that's the safest for you."[32] So whether the underlying motivation for the lack of capital spending lay with a donor mentality or bureaucratic culture, the Coalition needed a credible commitment from the Iraqis to build their own revenue base and spend their own money. The 17th Benchmark would encourage them to make that commitment, reduce the Iraqis' fiscal dependency, and place limits on the Iraqis' ability to play the donor game.

THE LIMITS OF THE 17TH BENCHMARK

Despite its advantages, there were limits to the practicality of the 17th Benchmark's emphasis on capital spending as a standard of government effectiveness. First, the complex nature of the Iraqi security situation and its state of political and economic development constrained what could actually be accomplished by external agents to boost capital spending. "The whole concept of benchmarks; it works in the U.S. [but] Iraq is a very different complex environment," Ambassador Ryan Crocker observed. "You could get all the benchmarks and fail in Iraq, or you could get few of them and actually get success. These are too precise and discreet of measures to really capture the enormous magnitude of a nation finding its feet or not."[33] "Capital spending is a dastardly difficult thing to accomplish," noted Larry McDonald, Deputy Assistant Treasury Secretary

---

[31] Interview with Charles Ries, Minister for Economic Affairs and Coordinator for Economic Transition in Iraq, February 2, 2010.
[32] *Ibid.*
[33] Interview with Ryan Crocker, Ambassador to Iraq, September 24, 2010.

for Technical Assistance Policy, "even in countries that are not burdened by ethnic strife, political divisions, and a difficult security environment. Countries that are not burdened by those things, throughout the world, still find it difficult to execute a capital budget effectively.... So, if you are talking about this latest phase of helping the Iraqis in their efforts to spend their oil money on capital projects, it's an important thing, but a difficult thing to grade the U.S. engagement on."[34] Effective capital and investment spending, particularly in the face of urgent need when prompt action is required, is more typically the hallmark of politically advanced governments. Yet when evaluated by the same standard, the Coalition proved to be unable to spend IRRF money for investment and infrastructure in a timely fashion.[35] Meanwhile, the benchmark notably failed to consider Iraq's progress spending its recurrent budget for salaries and pensions. "Iraq was very good at executing its recurrent budget, almost all of which was salaries," a Treasury attaché observed, "and this should not be underestimated."[36] There is, therefore, a sense that capital spending inappropriately, if not unfairly, measured both the Iraqis and the external assistance provided to them, given the many challenges facing the Iraqi government at that stage of its development.

A second limitation with focusing on capital spending amounts and rates is that it measured success essentially by what proportion of the capital budget was spent, not whether these funds were spent effectively, efficiently, and in a manner that encouraged budgetary accountability. "The benchmark acts as an incentive to bypass the review system for assessing projects and encourages the Ministry of Finance to spend the money regardless of the accountability. The criterion is how fast is the money being spent, the incentive is for spending," observed a GAO

---

[34] Interview with Larry McDonald, Deputy Assistant Treasury Secretary for Technical Assistance Policy, January 30, 2009.

[35] On IRRF spending, see, for example, Robert Looney, "A Return to Baathist Economics? Escaping Vicious Circles in Iraq," *Strategic Insight*, 3, July 2004, 7, 6; Anne Ellen Henderson, "The Coalition Provisional Authority's Experience with Economic Reconstruction in Iraq: Lessons Identified," *Special Report*, No. 138, United States Institute of Peace, April 2005. The United States government has experienced its own problems in budget execution, as in the spending of the stimulus funds provided by the American Recovery and Reinvestment Act of 2009. For example, the Division A, Discretionary Appropriations spend-out of "The American Recovery and Reinvestment Act of 2009" of $308.3 billion in outlays was scheduled to take place over the fiscal years 2009–2019, with the great majority of spending occurring in FY 2010–2012. Douglas Elmendorf, Director, Congressional Budget Office, Letter to Honorable Nancy Pelosi, Speaker of the House of Representatives, table 1: Summary of Estimated Cost of the Conference Agreement for H.R. 1, The American Recovery and Reinvestment Act of 2009, as Posted on the Web Site of the House Committee on Rules," February 13, 2009. On concerns with the speed of the spend-out, see, for example, Cecilia Kang, "Obama Approves $795 Million to Expand Broadband," *Washington Post*, July 3, 2010, A14. This amount "is less than half of the $7.2 billion set aside in the stimulus." By September 2011, the Department of Energy had yet to spend $879 million of its $2.5 billion grant program. Ed O'Keefe, "Energy Dept. Stimulus Program Lags Behind Goals, Audit Says," *Washington Post*, September 8, 2011, A17.

[36] Interview with Treasury Department official, April 7, 2009.

official who helped analyze the status of the benchmark."[37] Expressing a similar
view, Ambassador Ries concluded that "An exclusive focus on budget execution
... sort of says, well we just want them to waste money, and if they waste money
but spend all their money, it would be a good thing. Like all indicators, if you
have an exclusive focus on one indicator, it leaves you to distort what you do. In
particular, we did not want to see wasted money."[38] Corruption in Iraqi contracting and the execution of the budget at the ministerial and provincial levels
often overwhelmed oversight efforts by units like the Supreme Board of Audit,
the Commission on Public Integrity, and ministry inspector generals. In this way,
the benchmark produced incentives that ran counter to the institutional development of credible fiscal oversight systems that are necessary to promote accountability, encourage transparency, and fight corruption.

Third, competing measures complicate the calculation and evaluation of Iraqi
capital spending rates. In the American budgetary process the budget provides
budget authority. Budget authority is the authority for federal agencies to incur
obligations, where obligations consist of contracts or other binding commitments an agency may incur that require immediate or future expenditures. The
actual expenditures for a given fiscal year are called outlays. Where budget
authority for operational expenses, particularly obligations for salaries, are
expended in a single year, in the case of capital projects, appropriations law
permits obligations and outlays derived from budget authority, depending on
the particular appropriations account, to be spent over multiple years. So, for
example, contractual obligations and their subsequent outlays expended to
build a bridge, highway, or hospital may cover several years.

Iraqi capital budgeting, by comparison, reflects a simpler but at the same time
more complex spending process. Budgeting for a capital project is a single-year
affair. There is no Iraqi equivalent to budget authority or multiyear budgeting.
Nor is there carry-over spending from one year to the next. If a project is not fully
paid for during the current fiscal year, the leftover funds revert to the Ministry of
Finance. If a project is to be continued or completed, it must be included and then
gain new approval in the next budget.

Furthermore, Iraq relies on "commitments" to outline the financial relationship between the government and contractors, rather than firm contractual
obligations. Commitments represent what passes in Iraq as an obligation, a
type of contractual agreement to, say, build infrastructure, and to spend
money to pay for that commitment. Yet these commitments are often nonbind-
ing, flexible, and renegotiable. There is some difference of opinion about
whether a commitment of funds means the same thing as the actual spending
of funds that are derived from commitments, which can create confusion about
the level of capital spending taking place. The rates reported by the Ministry of

---

[37] Interview with GAO official, September 18, 2007.
[38] Interview with Charles Ries, Minister for Economic Affairs and Coordinator for Economic
    Transition in Iraq, February 2, 2010.

Planning and Development Cooperation represent commitments to spend, while the rates reported by the Ministry of Finance reflect actual cash payments.[39] So, for the Planning Ministry, a commitment can be considered 100 percent spent and executed if the commitment is agreed to between a governmental unit and a contractor. The Ministry of Finance only reports the actual cash payments on this commitment, which may produce far smaller execution amounts and rates.[40]

Within the time between issuing a contract and spending to fulfill that contract there exists the possibility for nonperformance, nonpayment, and malfeasance. "This gets to an overarching issue, which is how they define spending," Stuart Bowen, the Special Inspector General for Iraq Reconstruction, observed. "The specter of corruption hovers over all of this. So I have become dubious about published numbers from ministries. . . . The money gets committed. Where it goes after commitment is fuzzy, and that's at the ministry level. That does not even cover what's going on at the provinces. You go from weak national oversight to nonexistent oversight at the provincial level."[41]

Relying on provincial budget execution figures, as Bowen claimed, may be even more problematic than central government numbers. The data the Ministry of Finance provided to the State and Treasury Departments came only as aggregate figures, which were compiled from data generated by the ministries and provinces. As the Defense Department noted, difficulties with these data included counting the Kurdistan Regional Government's spending rates: "The KRG does not provide any budgetary performance to the central government. The [Ministry of Finance] therefore considers any funds transferred to the KRG as expended."[42] The Coalition depended on U.S. Provincial Reconstruction Teams (PRT) to collect and disaggregate budgetary information by province.

[39] According to a Grant Thornton contractor who assisted the Ministry of Planning and Development Cooperation with its budget execution, "It depends if you are talking to the Minister of Planning or the Minister of Finance. To the Ministry of Planning, it means you have allocated or contracted to do something. If you are talking to the Ministry of Finance, the money has actually been executed and spent, because whatever you have contracted for has been delivered, and you are now paying for those goods or services. When you look at budget execution, if you are looking at Planning, the numbers are obviously going to be very different than if you look at Finance." Interview with Grant Thornton official, November 11, 2009. The Ministry of Planning figures also included data based on letters of credit, which are particularly employed in international purchases. In these cases, banks issue letters of credit that guarantee a buyer's payment to a seller will be made or the bank will make that payment. The bank also guarantees to a buyer that payments will not be made until the purchased item is shipped. The data thus reported by the Ministry of Planning reflects the anticipation that the shipment and payment will take place, rather than that cash has actually changed hands.
[40] "They also don't have a uniform definition of commitments," concluded a staff member of the GAO who assisted in writing the agency's benchmark report. "Depending upon who you talk to you get a different definition." Interview with GAO official, September 18, 2007.
[41] Interview with Stuart Bowen, Special Inspector General for Iraq Reconstruction, July 15, 2009.
[42] U.S. Department of Defense, "Measuring Stability and Security in Iraq," Washington, DC, September 2008, 10.

Discrepancies emerged between the rate of commitments and the rate of expenditures in these provincial numbers. A GAO report submitted to Congress on Iraqi budgetary statistics assessed the value of provincial commitment data submitted to it by the Bush administration saying, "The extent to which committed funds indicates actual spending is unknown. Given the capacity and security challenges currently facing Iraq, many committed contracts may not be executed and would not result in actual expenditures."[43] Through October of the 2007 fiscal year, the PRTs reported that 96 percent of Iraq capital and reconstruction funds distributed to the provinces had been committed and 77 percent spent. Yet, as the GAO noted, "our field work raised questions about their reliability."[44]

The reliability issued stem, in part, from the PRTs' dependence on provincial authorities for their budgetary data, which were then passed on to the State and Treasury Departments. The senior State Department official responsible for assessing these data described the problems inherent in their credibility and the potential for creativity in the calculation of provincial data:

Those [data] come from the PRT foreign service officer, PRT team leader, sitting across from the governor or provincial council chairman, or the head of the PRDC [Provincial Reconstruction and Development Committee], and saying, "How are you doing, what does it look like these days?" Then that Iraqi official sliding over a piece of paper that says, "We're doing really good." We got better over time checking that claim, asking the military to send out a civil affairs team to look at some of the claimed projects that they had accomplished with last year's budget. But that fact checking is the exception and not the rule. I really wonder about some of those numbers, and I am frankly skeptical about the linear arc [of progress]. I don't think they have a healthy enough skepticism of the leadership in the provinces to check them.... Very few teams have the wherewithal to really call out the provincial leadership on some of those numbers. There is a little bit of a conflict of interest. This became the way we measure PRT success.... I am really skeptical of the numbers. I am really skeptical of the quality of projects that were claimed to have been completed. I think a lot of that money leaked out along the way. I think a lot of it has been handed out to cronies, friends, contractors, the usual holes in the system.[45]

Despite the questionable quality of these data, some Coalition officials and contractors working at the provincial level favored the use of commitment data, as did the Ministry of Planning. According to a State Department PRT team leader in Kirkuk, USAID contractors there encouraged and trained provincial officials to employ commitment data. When the province entered into a commitment to build infrastructure, this created a budget execution rate of 100 percent on that project. This reflected well on the Ministry of Planning that managed the investment budget, on the provincial government that agreed to the

[43] U.S. Government Accountability Office, "Iraq Reconstruction: Better Data Needed to Assess Iraq's Budget Execution," GAO-08–153, Washington, DC, January 2008, 10.
[44] *Ibid.*, p. 12.
[45] Interview with State Department official, June 9, 2010.

commitment, and on the contractors who worked with the provincial government's officials.[46]

Yet some PRTs recognized the serious gap that existed between commitments and the actual spending of cash on the construction of capital projects. Sometimes the problem rested with the failure of the Finance Ministry and the Ministry of Planning to distribute funds from the budget to the provincial governments, which led to the province lacking the funds needed to pay contractors after commitments were made. Sometimes the problem rested with the lack of provincial capacity to manage capital projects. A PRT in Babil province reported to Baghdad, "Pressure to increase the rate of spending is not likely to produce results as commitments are already running ahead of the availability of funds.... The continued focus on budget execution rates, combined with steadily increasing funding levels, is stretching provincial resources to the limit.... The multiplying projects and tenders exceed the implementation capacity of provincial procurement and management staff, as well as the absorptive capacity of the construction industry.... resulting in more projects of substandard quality and financial and monitoring vulnerability."[47]

These various conflicts in the collection and reporting of data are significant, because an air of uncertainty rests over the validity of the figures used to identify the success of Iraqi budget execution. The U.S. Treasury Department, which experienced closer relations with the Finance Ministry, relied on and reported

[46] U.S. officials and USAID contractors working in the provinces often promoted the use of commitment data. RTI contractors noted that "There are significant differences in accounting for expended funds.... Funds are considered expenditures only after receipts are presented and funds paid out. Based on these accounting methods, capital investment expenditures lag considerably behind current operating expenses and substantially behind expenditures for government employee salaries." Ronald W. Johnson and Ricardo Silva-Morales, "Budgeting Under Resource Abundance and Hesitant Steps to Decentralized Investment Planning and Budgeting in Iraq," in Charles E. Menifield (ed.), *Comparative Budgeting: A Global Perspective*, Sudbury: Jones & Bartlett Learning, 2011, 209. A State Department official serving as a team leader with a PRT in Kirkuk offered a similar justification for using commitment figures: "This is going to be a function of how RTI set up budget execution metrics, versus other provinces or Baghdad. We reported budget execution on an accrual basis. Baghdad was looking at a cash basis. That's messed up. You're not seeing the whole picture. Because if you've got a two or three year project, and you've got a third of it done in the first year, then it seems like in that particular project, you are only 33 percent budgeted. We said that if you are obligated, we have contracts obligated, that's 100 percent executed. If we don't have cash to pay for them, that's because Baghdad didn't send the money. But from the standpoint of executing the budget, that's 100 percent." Interview with State Department Official, October 3, 2012.

[47] U.S. State Department Regional Embassy Office Hillah, Michael Chiaventone to U.S. Embassy, "Babil's Budget Execution Rate High but Needs Improved Allocation from Central Government," Baghdad, September 19, 2008. The report noted that in addition to providing training to provincial officials, "The most significant remaining barrier to improving budget execution rates is the time it takes MOF and MOPDC to release capital investment funds to the Province.... Since the inception of the ARDP fund, provincial allocations have consistently been released by the MOPDC and MOF in a slow and unpredictable manner."

that ministry's spending data to determine national budget execution rates. Various Coalition agencies and contractors relied on and reported Ministry of Planning and provincial commitment data when it served their purposes. Despite these differing interpretations, the Coalition employed these different measures of investment spending and budget execution as a primary metric of successful state building. Therefore, although the notion of commitments somewhat corresponds to the American understanding of obligations, a problem with using commitments as the measure of budget execution is that simply because a contract is entered into to build a project, this does not mean the project is actually under construction. Actual spending is the better measure of the rate of investment activity and budget execution.

IRAQI INVESTMENT BUDGET EXECUTION RATES, 2005–2011

The 17th Benchmark raised Iraqi capital spending as a significant measure of evaluating the success of the Iraqis and their Coalition advisors in providing essential services to the Iraqi people and laying the foundation for economic reconstruction and political stability. The Benchmark's specific spending element required the Iraqis to spend their 2007 12.6 trillion ID ($10 billion) investment budget. Assessing Iraqi compliance is complicated by the shifting and sometimes incompatible accounting methodologies employed by both the Iraqis and the Coalition to determine the level and rate of spending, as well as by the dubious and tardy data supplied by both ministries and provincial governments.[48] Relying on Ministry of Finance data, the Coalition determined that the

[48] Three further reasons help account for the difficulty in interpreting Iraqi budgetary data. First, Coalition assessments of the early Iraqi budgets tend to inflate the amount of the total capital investment allocation and spending. The early budgets make a distinction between "investment projects" and "operating capital." The budget laws for 2005 and 2006 clearly identify investment projects as the capital reconstruction element, whereas "operating capital" is those expenditures "which are necessary for keeping up the work of a Ministry. These expenditures do not represent a capitalist project or investment; the expenditure allocated for purchasing new vehicles is listed under this article." See, for example, Ministry of Finance Budget Directorate, "Government General Budget for Year 2005," Baghdad, September 2004, 20. The exact same language is used in the 2006 budget document to describe operating capital. It appears, however, that the U.S. Government Accountability Office included operating capital in calculating the total investment allocation and expenditure levels in determining the level of budget execution. Consequently, the size of both the allocation and level of spending may be inflated. For example, in its June 2008 report, the GAO stated the 2006 investment allocation was $8.312 billion (12.5 trillion ID); whereas the Iraqi budget document allocated $6.2 billion (9.3 trillion ID). At least 2.1 trillion ID of the difference may be accounted for by the budget's operating capital allocation. Note that GAO's capital spending rate for 2006 changes between October 2007, where the spending rate in Figure 6.2 is 22 percent, and June 2008, where the rate that can be calculated in Table 3 is 19 percent. See U.S. Government Accountability Office, "Stabilizing and Rebuilding Iraq: US Ministry Capacity Development Efforts Need an Overall Integrated Strategy to Guide Efforts and Manage Risk," GAO-08-117, Washington, DC, October 2007, figure 3, 21; U.S. Government Accountability Office, "Securing, Stabilizing, and Rebuilding Iraq: Progress

Iraqis spent 2.8 trillion ID ($3.4 billion) of the budget allocation, or 28 percent, far less than the targeted amount. The Iraqis, however, improved their level of investment spending over the 2005 level of 2.5 trillion ID ($1.7 billion), a rate of 34 percent, and 2.1 trillion ID ($1.4 billion) in 2006, a rate of 22 percent of the investment budget. Although the benchmark focused on a single year, the drive to raise the level of Iraqi investment spending remained a Coalition priority, especially as the price of oil surged in 2008 and the GAO predicted Iraq's cumulative budget surplus would reach $79 billion. As shown in Figure 6.2, in 2008 the Iraqis succeeded both in increasing the size of their investment allocation and raising their investment spending amount and rate to 10.1 trillion ID ($8.4 billion) and 40 percent.[49] Good data for 2009 are particularly difficult to obtain, as the bombings of the Finance Ministry in August and November 2009

Report: Some Gains Made, Updated Strategy Needed," GAO-08-837, Washington, DC, June 2008, table 3, 45. Second, the 2005 and 2006 data are not fully compatible with the budgets that follow. Beginning in 2007, Iraq complied with its IMF stand-by agreement by employing the IMF's chart of accounts that reorganized Iraqi accounting. This chart of accounts introduced new categories that reorganized the budget's reporting data and make the post-2007 data somewhat incompatible with the data from prior years. In these new accounts, "non-financial assets" represents ministerial investment spending, and a category labeled "grants" reflects provincial investment spending. According to the IMF's chart of accounts categorization scheme, grants may include transfers for capital spending. The uncertainty over what may be included in a grant, however, suggests that counting all "grants" as a capital transfer inflates the level of investment spending. Moreover, the non-financial assets category incorporated the Iraqis' "operating capital" category, which includes the purchasing of vehicles, thus also inflates the budget's capital investment allocation and spending levels. The chart of accounts is outlined in the IMF's *General Government Statistics Manual*, 2001. Third, the credibility of provincial expenditure data, especially their extraordinarily high rates of budget execution, remains an issue. As an internal Treasury memo noted, "The concern with the provinces in that their expenditure is so good when compared to ministries, that it brings into question what the funds were actually distributed for. This makes it appear that the provinces can utilize the procurement process including contracting, and can manage projects better than ministries.... But is it possible that provinces could have executed the budget almost three times better than ministries did? Provinces are commonly believed to have a lack of capacity in the procurement, contracting, and project management processes. The data seems to indicate there is no lack of capacity at all. The question is what the disbursed funds actually produced." "EXSUM MoP/MoF Comparison of Investment Projects Budget Execution," Undated 2010 memo.

[49] On 2008 budget execution, "Iraq significantly improved its budget execution in 2008.... Of the overall spending, roughly $9 billion was spent on capital investment projects in 2008, compared to just $3.4 billion in 2007." U.S. Department of Defense, "Measuring Stability and Security in Iraq," Washington, DC, September 2009, 12. One source of comparison between 2007 and 2008 rates of budget execution lies with the performance of provincial governments that poorly executed their budgets: "Provincial governments spent or committed $870 million of their $2.3 billion adjusted capital budget allocation through December 2007. This low rate of execution is partly due to last year's requirement for High Contracts Committee (HCC) approval for projects of more than $5 million. In addition, contracting regulations required local contractor solicitations before broadening the scope of advertisement nationwide." In 2008 the approval level was raised to $10 million and the Central Contracts Committee replaced the HCC to speed approvals. These changes helped raise provincial commitments in 2008. U.S. Department of Defense, "Measuring Stability and Security in Iraq," Washington, DC, September 2008, 9–10.

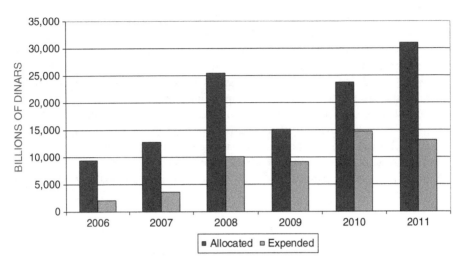

FIGURE 6.2. Iraqi Investment Budget Execution, 2005–2011
Source: Iraq Ministry of Finance

compromised the agency's data collection and processing efforts. What is known about Iraq's 2009 budget is that the ministerial and provincial governments were restricted in their ability to spend their investment allocations for the first four months of the year because of the budget's late approval in March and its official release in April. Furthermore, due to the dramatic fall in oil prices, reduced revenues, and a shift in the budget's fiscal balance from surplus to deficits, the budgeted allocation for investment spending fell significantly below the FY 2008 level. The budget allocation, as a result, simply funded existing projects approved in 2008, which actually enabled the government to improve its level of spending to 9 trillion ID ($7.7 billion), a rate of 61 percent. As the Defense Department's September 2009 "Measuring Stability and Security in Iraq" report noted, "Few new projects for 2009 will be funded with the reduced budget, and lack of rollover funds and the on-going 2008 projects will be funded with the 2009 budgetary monies."[50]

In spite of the decline in investment spending recorded for 2009, the Iraqis reported that a significant rebound occurred in 2010 to as much as 14.7 trillion ID ($12.6 billion), a budget execution rate of 62 percent. The March 2010

[50] U.S. Department of Defense, "Measuring Stability and Security in Iraq," Washington, DC, September 2009, 12. Large disparities appeared in the 2009 data, as reported by the Ministries of Planning and Finance. Through November 2009, the Planning Ministry reported a capital budget execution rate of 77 percent, almost $10 billion, whereas the Finance Ministry reported $6 billion executed, a rate of 47 percent. Some of this difference may be accounted for by the Planning Ministry's inclusion of $4 billion in letters of credit that funded operational rather than investment spending. U.S. Department of Defense, "Measuring Stability and Security in Iraq," Washington, DC, June 2010, 13.

Stability and Security report indicated that "budget execution, particularly for the capital investment budget, has been a challenge for the GOI since 2005, but national ministries and provincial governments have substantially improved their ability to execute capital budgets.... Despite progress, impediments to spending across ministries and provinces remain, including bureaucratic bottle-necks, unclear rules and regulations, technical capacity, security, and absorption capacity."[51] A SIGIR official declared that the growth in spending, not the annual percent spent should be considered the critical measure for evaluating the Iraqis. "Don't look at percent of the budget spent," said the official. "Just look at the sheer amounts of dollars that they have been able to execute, and you consider the absorptive capacity of a government that was completely destroyed, and that had to rebuild itself, and get functioning as a central government. You forget the percentage of what they budgeted, look at what they've managed to execute, over time it has been fairly steady and increasing, percentage wise, very steadily across the years. They are able to execute more and more money."[52] Capital spending more than doubled from 2007 to 2008, and then more than tripled the 2007 rate in 2010 after the fall in spending in 2009.

"Has budget execution improved? Yes," said Stuart Bowen, still wary of Iraqi-generated budgetary statistics, particularly of those emanating from the provinces that reported an astonishing budget execution rate of 105 percent for 2009 and 89 percent for 2010. "At least that is what the Iraqis report."[53] These budget figures, as Bowen observed, do not account for whether the Iraqis used their investment funds effectively or how much budgetary leakage occurred due to corruption.

THE ONGOING CHALLENGE OF BUDGET EXECUTION

Despite the sometimes optimistic increase in budget execution figures for 2010, both the budget execution rate and amount of investment spending fell in 2011. The rate fell from 62 to 42 percent and the amount of spending fell from 14.7 trillion ID to 13.1 trillion ID. Some of this decline may be explained by the Iraqis' failure to adopt a budget in a timely manner, but ineffective budget execution continues to plague Iraq despite massive increases in all forms of government spending, including allocations for capital investments. This ongoing difficulty with budget execution contributes greatly to the public's despair over the government's poor provision of public services, especially water and power. In June 2010, in a foretaste of larger events occurring the following year, Prime Minister Maliki dismissed Karim al-Wahid, the minister of electricity, in response to protests in Basra and Nasiriyah. Wahid decried the public's "impatience" after Iraqis demonstrated against the government's failure to meet its promises to

---

[51] U.S. Department of Defense, "Measuring Stability and Security in Iraq," Washington, DC, March 2010, 13.

[52] Interview with SIGIR official, October 6, 2009.

[53] Interview with Stuart Bowen, Special Inspector General for Iraq Reconstruction, July 15, 2009.

provide two hours of electricity out of every six hours.[54] General Kendall Cox, commander of U.S. Central Command engineering, estimated that Iraq would not be able to meet electrical demand until 2013 or 2014. Demand for electricity was estimated at 12,000 to 14,000 megawatts, with the supply at 6,000 megawatts.[55] The next year, after mass demonstrations took place throughout Iraq, including a bloody "Day of Rage," and the resignation of a third provincial governor, Maliki demanded that his Cabinet ministers significantly boost the provision and quality of public services, reduce unemployment, and combat corruption. Maliki promised to evaluate his ministers' performance after one hundred days. For those failing the test, Maliki declared on February 26, "changes will be made on the assessments."[56]

Delays in Budgetary Approval

Some of these budget execution problems stemmed from the budget process itself. The Iraqis' perpetual inability to approve their budget by the beginning of the fiscal year stalled the funding of capital projects. CPA Order 95 called for the Council of Ministers to present their proposed budget to the Parliament by October 10. With the exception of the 2010 budget, which was presented on October 13, the Council typically submitted the budget one to two months late, sometimes leaving less than a week before the start of the fiscal year on January 1. This delay greatly limited the Parliament's ability to review the budget and make its own proposals in a timely fashion, resulting in the Parliament passing the budget a month or more into the fiscal year. Then the Presidency Council, consisting of the president and two vice presidents, commonly gave its approval a week or more following the Parliament's vote on the budget. Consequently, the ministries and the provincial governments were delayed in their initiation of the contracting, procurement, and construction cycles associated with building capital projects. "On large dollar procurements, you are already behind the curve," noted an American contractor working with the Ministry of Planning who assessed the effect of these delays on executing investment projects. "Then in Iraq, you get into summertime, when everything slows down. Then you get into Ramadan, where everything pretty much comes to a stop. October, November, December, are torrid months for spending." The contractor then described the consequences of Iraq's annual budget process, where capital projects required yearly inclusion in the budget and political approval. "They don't like to cross fiscal years with projects. You start from zero again. So you

[54] "Outrage Continues Even as Iraqi Electricity Minister Resigns," *Christian Science Monitor*, June 24, 2010, http://www.iraqupdates.com/scr/preview.php?article=74497/.

[55] "Iraq Unable to Meet Current Power Demand Until 2013: US," AFP, September 7, 2010, http://news.yahoo.com/s/afp/20100907/wl_mideast_afт/iraqelectricityus/.

[56] Ammar Karim, "Iraq PM Gives Cabinet 100-Day Warning after Demos," AFP, February 27, 2011, http://news.yahoo.com/s/aft/20110227/wl_mideast_afт/iraqpoliticsunrest.

might have a project that went for three months, and then stopped while the new budget was approved. Then you start up again. This really introduced a lot of chaos to the system."[57] CPA Order 95 anticipated such delays by empowering the finance minister in Section 7–4 to release on a monthly basis up to one-twelfth the value of the preceding year's budget, but these funds could not be used to finance new capital investment projects.

Other aspects of Iraq's economic and administrative practices contributed to the government's budget execution problems.[58] Iraq's dependence on oil as the sole significant source of revenue, for example, delayed the budget's formulation and approval. Great fluctuations in oil prices forced several revisions in the drafting of the 2009 budget and played a critical role in delaying that budget's final approval by the Presidency Council to April 2, 2010. When the Finance and Planning ministries finally agreed on a projected price when developing revenue estimates, they could conservatively price oil so far below actual market values to limit budget deficits that the government might be forced to produce a supplemental budget, as in 2008, given unexpected revenues. Or an overestimate of oil prices might indeed eventually require the government to produce smaller revised budgets, as in 2009.[59]

Coalition Asset Transfers to Iraq

The issue of investment asset transfer also affected Iraqi budget execution and the delivery of essential public services. Following the transfer of power, the Coalition pressed the Iraqis to take ownership, finance, complete, maintain, and provide security for capital projects initiated by the CPA. These projects included those created through the U.S. military's Commanders Emergency Response Program (CERP), in which projects could be initiated and funded without official Iraqi participation. The Iraqis often resented these projects, viewing them as the product of occupation, constructed without their desire or cooperation, passed off sometimes in incomplete stages of construction, and imposed without regard to the Iraqi budget's investment priorities.[60] The Special

[57] Interview with Grant Thornton official, November 11, 2009.
[58] Misconi provides a useful overview of budget execution problems, and Herring's challenge to neoliberalism and the lack of attention to human capital formation in Iraq also point to problems in budget execution. Human Misconi, "Iraq's Capital Budget and Regional Development Fund: Review and Comments on Execution Capacity and Implications," *International Journal of Contemporary Iraqi Studies*, 2 (2008) 2, 271–292; Eric Herring, "Variegated Neo-Liberalization, Human Development and Resistance: Iraq in Global Context," *International Journal of Contemporary Iraqi Studies*, 5 (2011) 3, 337–355.
[59] Ali Merza, "Oil Revenues, Public Expenditures and Saving/Stabilization Fund in Iraq," *International Journal of Contemporary Iraqi Studies*, 5 (2011) 1, 47–80.
[60] On Iraqi resentment, particularly regarding unfinished Coalition projects, see Timothy Williams, "A Search for Blame in Reconstruction After War," *New York Times*, November 21–22, 2009, 4; Ernesto Londono, "Barren Iraqi Parks Attests to U.S. Program Flaws," *Washington Post*, January

Inspector General for Iraq Reconstruction outlined the dilemma: "By the middle of 2006, 579 IRRF projects, valued at $765 million, had been officially transferred to the Iraqi Ministry of Finance. However, this was only 18 percent of the total number of completed IRRF projects. Still more projects would come from the other reconstruction funds, including CERP and the ISFF [Iraq Security Forces Fund]. The cost of maintaining IRRF projects alone was estimated in 2006 at approximately $1.2 billion annually."[61] SIGIR identified numerous examples of such projects. One four-year contract valued at $722 million awarded to the firm KBR, a Halliburton subsidiary, funded by both IRRF and DFI money, was intended to help rebuild Iraq's oil production facilities. SIGIR found the contracted projects "took longer than planned; were frequently modified, scaled back, and/or terminated; and increased over time." Moreover, the Iraqi government "may not be properly maintaining the rebuilt facilities and equipment that cost hundreds of millions of dollars," and it "does not appear to be committed to completing and using some projects."[62]

The key issue, said Stuart Bowen, was getting Iraqi "buy-in as an essential element to a project's long-term success," but the Coalition often initiated projects without obtaining Iraqi commitment to maintain this infrastructure. Bowen cited numerous examples of such projects, including the building of a $35 million economic zone at the Baghdad airport and $13.4 million spent on the construction of classrooms and an office complex. Another smaller example of an asset transfer issue came when the SIGIR recommended that $26 million in funding be halted for the construction of an academy for senior Iraqi security officers, because, said Bowen, "At this point, it is unclear if the GOI will budget for the operations and maintenance of the Iraq International Academy upon completion."[63] To incorporate these legacy projects into their own infrastructure system, the Iraqis would be required to finish incomplete and poorly constructed projects and maintain the completed ones. The asset transfer issue, therefore, placed a direct fiscal burden on the government's investment budget, which limited the Iraqis' ability to fund capital projects of their own choosing. The transfers also placed a burden on the operational budget, as these projects,

3, 2010, A1; and Timothy Williams, "U.S. Fails to Complete, or Cuts Back, Iraqi Projects, *New York Times*, July 5, 2010, 5.

[61] Office of the Special Inspector General for Iraq Reconstruction, *Hard Lessons: The Iraq Reconstruction Experience*, Washington, DC: U.S. Government Printing Office, 2009, 269. SIGIR also faults American agencies for failing to provide the Iraqis with appropriately coordinated and detailed asset transfer information. "One of the flaws of the asset transfer approach as it was structured in 2006 was that each U.S. agency working in Iraq had different procedures, levels of detail, and due diligence requirements for transferring projects." *Ibid.*, 270.

[62] Walter Pincus, "Report Details Iraq Contract Failures," *Washington Post*, January 14, 2009, A14. Both equipment and facilities left behind could be looted if not properly secured, including military equipment. Ernesto Londono, "Millions Worth of Gear Left In Iraq," *Washington Post*, December 7, 2009, A1.

[63] Walter Pincus, "US Office Urges Halt in Funds for Iraq Security Institute," *Washington Post*, January 26, 2011, A4.

including hospitals and sewage treatment plants, required staffing with a sufficient number of trained personnel; otherwise they would operate at diminished
capacities or be essentially useless.

The Challenge of Project Maintenance

The funding of maintenance costs, whether for indigenous Iraqi projects or those
transferred from the Coalition, raised an important *caveat* regarding the interpretation of Iraqi budget execution figures and the sustainability of capital
projects. The Iraqi budget tended to underemphasize and underfund maintenance costs, a practice encouraged by the CPA's emphasis on spending for new
facilities and equipment rather than maintenance.[64] The lack of sufficient and
proper maintenance sapped the effectiveness of the Iraqi government's daily
operations, including its security activities, and diminished the long-term sustainability of Iraq's capital investments. The government's operating budgets
primarily funded salaries, and its investment budgets funded both capital construction costs and most maintenance expenses. The Planning Ministry favored
new capital construction in developing the investment budget to the detriment of
maintaining existing projects. "So a perfect example is the Mosul Dam," suggested an American contractor working with the Planning Ministry. "It needs to
be dredged and is not holding up, and they have to drill pylons into the dam to

[64] Andrew Alderson, the director of the CPA's Economic Planning and Development Department,
who managed the CPA budget for Basra province in 2004, commented on the CPA's spending
tendencies: "The great irony for me was that what we were being asked to do was to perform like
any old-style command economy. The United States of America, the great champion of free-
market economics, was telling us to focus on how much we spent rather than how well it was
spent. So, for example, we spent several million dollars on provision of a small fleet of shiny new
fire engines for a petrochemical factory in the south, yet there was no allocation for maintenance
of the fleet. The Iraqis in the ministry responsible certainly had no budget available and we were
rapidly using up all our money. The result? As far as I know the fire engines were run into the
ground for lack of money in the kitty to keep them running properly.... The problem became
progressively worse as the months rolled on and more and more projects came on line. Instead of
maintaining the equipment we were promoting a culture of obsolescence." Andrew Alderson,
*Bankrolling Basra: The Incredible Story of a Part-Time Soldier, $1 Billion, and the Collapse of
Iraq*, London: Robinson, 2007, 144–145. The problem of maintenance extended to Iraq's security
forces. "Even when Iraqi Army units have the necessary equipment, faulty maintenance of that
equipment can be a critical weakness. U.S. commanders and soldiers in the field repeatedly
informed the Commission that the Iraqis in general fail to maintain equipment. Iraqis are
unfamiliar with many of the new systems and platforms they have purchased in the past few
years. When a vehicle becomes non-operational, there are no backup or reserve vehicles to replace
it. Preventive maintenance is an alien concept to Iraqis, an attitude that exacerbates the lack of
spare or backup vehicles. When maintenance teams do exist and Iraqi commanders do make
upkeep of equipment a priority, they face the further hurdle of acquiring spare parts from Taji
National Depot, which appears unable to keep up with requirements." General James L. Jones,
The Report of the Independent Commission on the Security Forces of Iraq, Washington, DC,
September 6, 2007, 69.

stabilize it. It really is a maintenance issue. There isn't something in their operating budget for this; it all comes out of the capital budget. So every year they have to determine, do they do something new or take a piece of the capital budget and maintain the dam? Their mentality is not to maintain, it is to build something and let it deteriorate, and when it goes away we will build a new one, or buy a new one."[65] A calculation about budget execution that assumes the investment budget supported only building new capital projects and infrastructure thus would be questionable.

CONCLUSION

The 17th Benchmark ushered in a new chapter in Coalition state building in Iraq. The Coalition had reached a point familiar in foreign assistance, peace-keeping, and postconflict operations when donors prefer to develop on-budget capacity rather than rely on off-budget donor funding. During the early years of the occupation the Coalition relied on its own off-budget sources, donor funds, and control over the Development Fund for Iraq to finance the reconstruction of Iraqi infrastructure. The Iraqis, meanwhile, proved to be able to fund their operational expenses through their own on-budget processes. By 2007, the Coalition found this arrangement unsatisfactory. Providing humanitarian relief, de-Ba'athifying Saddam loyalists, overseeing credible elections, and even training security forces, no longer constituted sufficient intervention in Iraqi affairs. To help counter the escalating insurgency the Coalition demanded that the Iraqi government substantially boost its provision of essential services and build urgently needed infrastructure. As attested to by the World Bank, the IMF, and various donors, Iraq indeed suffered from a vast infrastructure deficit, and even critics who favored increased funding for social services acknowledged the need to build Iraqi budget execution.[66] As Iraqi oil revenues grew, the United States sought to limit its financial commitment for Iraqi reconstruction and reduce Iraq's dependence on donor funding.

The Benchmark, furthermore, reflected Coalition strategy since the beginning of the occupation that the reconstruction of Iraq demanded large-scale investment spending. Whether the spending flowed through American IRRF appropriations or through the DFI allocations determined by the CPA's Program Review Board, billions of dollars and dinars financed massive infrastructure projects throughout Iraq. Ironically, although critics of the Iraq war often point to a neoliberal agenda guiding the occupation, CPA leadership openly turned to Keynesian spending and American New Deal public works programs as inspiration for rebuilding the Iraqi economy. The 17th Benchmark reaffirmed that

[65] Interview with Grant Thornton official, November 12, 2009.
[66] See, for example, Eric Herring, "Variegated Neo-Liberalization, Human Development and Resistance: Iraq in Global Context," *International Journal of Contemporary Iraqi Studies*, 5 (2011) 3, 337–355.

approach. Beginning with the 2007 budget and through the remainder of the Coalition's presence, there would never be sufficient Iraqi spending. For many of the Coalition's state-building efforts, success would henceforth be formally measured by the rate of spending of Iraq's investment budgets. The Benchmark consequently offered some direction and coherence to the Coalition's often uncoordinated assistance program. This focus on the investment "burn-rate," however, created its own perverse incentive of exaggerating and distorting the rate's calculation to make the various interested parties appear effective in their duties. At the same time, the Coalition placed less emphasis on building budgetary oversight and accountability. Iraqis simply lacked the complementary oversight institutions necessary to ensure that their budgets were effectively and honestly spent.

Fulfilling the Benchmark's investment spending target nevertheless demanded a deeper engagement on the part of the Coalition in the formation of the Iraqi state. To meet the Benchmark's spending goals the Iraqis needed to develop their on-budget capabilities. Iraqi budget execution certainly suffered from a host of problems, including delays in budget formulation, delays in the Parliament's approval of the budget, delays in the allocation of investment funds to the provincial governments, the reliance on an inefficient annual capital budgeting process, great fluctuations in oil prices that undermined the calculation of revenues, and the insufficient maintenance of existing infrastructure. Yet the lack of administrative capacity acted as the great impediment to the budget's successful execution. Executing capital budgets "downstream" in the budget process required different technical skills sets and procedures from the "upstream" activities associated with budget formulation and spending operational accounts.[67] To address these limitations, the Coalition initiated a number of ministerial and provincial capacity development programs to train Iraq's bureaucracy in the international best practices of budget execution. As the next chapter indicates, the response to these efforts exposed the frailties of creating institutional change and state building in Iraq.

---

[67] On the challenges of strengthening "downstream" budget execution versus "upstream" budget formulation, see Matt Andrews, "Which Organizational Attributes Are Amenable to External Reform? An Empirical Study of African Public Financial Management," *International Public Management Journal*, 12 (2011) 2, 131–156.

7

Building Iraqi Budgetary Capacity

The 17th Benchmark's focus on budget execution expanded Coalition budgetary state building beyond the ministries of Finance and Planning to much of the Iraqi government. Whereas the responsibility for formulating the budget resided primarily in these two financial ministries, the task of spending the investment budget involved virtually the entire administrative apparatus. Successful investment budget execution required planning, contracting, procurement, and capital project management skills throughout the bureaucracy, particularly in those ministries with large capital budgets. After de-Ba'athification, sectarian purging of ministries, years of violence, and the exodus of much of the civil service from Iraq, the government simply lacked the necessary personnel to engage in the dramatic turnabout in capital spending demanded by the Benchmark. To build this administrative capacity the Coalition and several key donors initiated broadly based and targeted capacity development programs to train the Iraqi civil service at the ministerial and provincial levels. Over time, the Coalition extended its budgetary technical assistance to Iraq's Parliament, the Council of Representatives. These training programs encountered the challenges familiar to capacity-building efforts, including the struggle to develop cohesive technical assistance that reflected shared goals, coordinate training efforts among participants, overcome resistance and gain beneficiary buy-in and ownership, and measure and evaluate the effectiveness of this assistance. These attempts to layer new institutions and administrative practices reflect the difficulties of achieving institutional change in Iraq. This chapter examines these Coalition efforts at building budgetary capacity throughout the Iraqi government.

IRAQ'S ADMINISTRATIVE DEFICIT

The Coalition initiated a broad set of assistance programs and projects aimed at improving the administrative capacity of Iraq's various ministries virtually from the beginning of the occupation. While the Department of Defense and its allied contractors focused their assistance on the Iraqi ministries of Defense and Interior, other U.S. agencies, contractors, and Coalition partner agencies assisted many of the remaining Iraqi ministries and the provincial governments. These efforts included the Department of Agriculture conducting capacity-building efforts with the Iraqi Ministry of Agriculture, the Department of Education working with the Ministry of Education, and the Department of Justice training the Iraqi police. These agency-ministry assignments date from the prewar planning phase when American agencies were paired with Iraqi ministries during General Jay Garner's February 2003 "rock-drill" meeting. Then the CPA created its system of shadow ministries that advised the Iraqi ministries.

These early assistance activities were often characterized by limited planning and coordination, the lack of a strategic approach for building up the Iraqi bureaucracy, and the absence of a shared understanding of what exactly constituted ministerial capacity development. Assessing Coalition ministry capacity building through mid-2007, the GAO reported: "From their inception in 2003, U.S. efforts evolved without a plan for capacity development or the designation of a lead entity. Instead, U.S. agencies individually provided assistance to four successive governments [the CPA, interim government, transitional government, and constitutional government] in response to immediate needs, according to former CPA officials and senior advisors. In 2003, for example, the first programs at the ministries were initiated by the CPA's senior advisors, who ran the ministries using U.S. funds and made personnel and budgetary decisions. According to State and former CPA officials, each senior advisor operated their ministries without an overall plan or overarching guidance; efforts to create an overall plan in late 2003 were dropped after the United States decided to transfer control of the ministries to a sovereign Iraq by mid-2004."[1] The separate shadow ministries and agency advisors practiced capacity building in their own ways, often with minimal coordination, shared programmatic objectives, or harmonized training doctrine existing either between themselves or with the Iraqi ministries. "There were many unrelated training efforts going on all different levels of government," a senior SIGIR official concluded. "So USAID was doing some of it, the Department of Defense had advisors inserted into the ministries, the State Department had all of these temporary hires and they were working at all the ministries, and everybody was doing a different thing. There wasn't a focus. . . . everybody was trying to help their ministry do what it was better."[2] One such example of an ineffective capacity development project was the USAID's failure through its BearingPoint contract to introduce an operational financial management information system into the bureaucracy.

[1] U.S. Government Accountability Office, "Stabilizing and Rebuilding Iraq: U.S. Ministry Capacity Development Efforts Need an Overall Integrated Strategy to Guide Efforts and Manage Risk," GAO-07-903, Washington, DC, September 2007, 13.
[2] Interview with SIGIR official, October 6, 2009.

These ministerial development efforts proved to be disjointed in their intent and often ineffective in building the ministries' core administrative capabilities.

The presence of these capacity-building programs failed to prevent the accelerating deterioration and general administrative breakdown of the Iraqi ministries that followed the June 2004 transfer of power. Prior to the 2003 invasion, Iraq did possess a sufficient number of skilled bureaucrats to conduct the basic functions of government under Saddam, but these individuals tended to be located in the ministries' senior ranks, many of whom were educated abroad before the Gulf War. To address its staff training requirements, the Iraqis in the 1970s established the National Center for Consultation and Management Development (NCCMD), which reported to the Minister of Planning. Yet the National Center offered an outdated curricula and training on increasingly antiquated computers. After the 2003 invasion, Coalition advisors commonly observed that the Iraqi bureaucracy lacked modern administrative skills and techniques, its leadership lacked initiative, its procedures proved to be rigid and paper-driven, and it suffered from dated office equipment and supplies, especially in its use of computers and information technology systems. Nonetheless, "You had a technocratic class from the 1970s that was well-trained," a Treasury OTA officer noted, but following the Gulf War Saddam curtailed these training opportunities, and the technocrats' skill in contemporary administrative techniques faded. "In 2003, you did have senior people there who are now in their 50s and 60s.... When we went in, the people in the higher ranks, our interlocutors, were very capable, but they hadn't trained anyone behind them ... there wasn't the training of the class under them."[3] "It's like the world stopped in 1978," reported a Grant Thornton contractor who worked with Ministry of Planning personnel. "It's hard for them to move forward, and to realize that for 30 years they were out of touch."[4]

This administrative deficit among the middle and lower ranks of the bureaucracy rapidly accelerated during the years following the invasion. De-Ba'athification, assassinations, violence, sectarian purges, and patronage appointments thinned all levels of the bureaucracy, thus reducing its technical competency. As violence escalated in 2005 and 2006, several million Iraqis fled the country. This migration proved particularly damaging to the government's ministries, as they lost many of their most educated and competent civil servants who used their skills to find employment outside of Iraq. One estimate by the United Nations' High Commissioner for Refugees claimed that by June 2007 Iraq lost 40 percent of its professional class.[5] This loss of talent "was compounded when either the people who worked for us were assassinated, like the [Ministry of Finance's] director-general of accounting [killed in a roadside

[3] Interview with Treasury Department official, October 28, 2008.
[4] Interview with Grant Thornton official, November 12, 2009.
[5] Carolyn Lochhead, "Conflict in Iraq: Iraq Refugee Crisis Exploding," *San Francisco Chronicle*, January 16, 2007, A1.

explosion] was, or the Ba'ath Party folks and rich Sunnis fled to Jordan, and then the Christians started leaving – those bureaucratic class Christian Iraqis," said the Treasury OTA officer. "Further after the sectarian violence, you also, as the ministries rotated with the new governments, you saw a lot of polarization, getting rid of the Ministry of Finance technocrats."[6]

BUILDING MINISTERIAL AND PROVINCIAL ADMINISTRATIVE CAPACITY

The growing attention paid to building Iraq's budget execution capabilities eventually produced some direction and cohesion in the Coalition's capacity development and training activities. In the absence of a clearly defined mission, budget execution offered clarity and measurement of purpose. "The most savvy amongst us," recalled a State Department official who worked with Provincial Reconstruction Teams, "quickly realized that one thing we could get our hooks into was this budget process, enabling provincial governments to plan, prioritize, and execute this new money that they had. It was also a time when we were groping for metrics.... Budget execution was like a godsend to that question, because it gave us some measure, some hard statistics, which were very useful at the Embassy and Washington, in terms of justifying fielding such a significant State Department and agency presence outside of Baghdad."[7] As a SIGIR official noted, "There was a fundamental shift because prior to the focus on budget execution, the U.S. capacity building program was lacking focus."[8] By 2006, "budget execution" became the mantra throughout Coalition and donor agencies in their assistance efforts in Iraq.

---

[6] Interview with Treasury Department official, October 28, 2008. Also, in testimony before the House Budget Committee, Joseph Christoff, the GAO's team leader on Iraq, commented, "We are also looking at Iraqi refugees, for example, and in meeting a lot of the Iraqi refugees in Syria and Jordan over the past month, I encountered a lot of the civil servants they need who have technical expertise in budgeting and accounting and procurement that have left the country. So some of the concerns, and some of their problems, are the result of brain drain that among the 2 million Iraqis that have left the country, many of them were the Sunni technocrats that had the kinds of skills and capabilities." U.S. House of Representatives Committee on the Budget, "Iraq's Budget Surplus: Hearing Before the Committee on the Budget, House of Representatives," Serial 110–40, Washington, DC: U.S. Government Printing Office, September 16, 2008, 21. On the rotation of ministries, in April 2007, for example, political differences over the timetable of the withdrawal of U.S. troops between Prime Minister al-Maliki and Moqtada al-Sadr resulted in the Sadrist faction's six ministers boycotting the government. Several weeks later, six ministers of the Sunni bloc party Iraqi Consensus Front walked out of the government. The loss of leadership, even for a few months, undermined the command structure and the ability of these ministries to function. ABC News, "Sadr Group to Boycott Iraq Government," April 16, 2007, http://www.abc.net.ua/news/newsitems/200704/s189787802.html/. Tina Susman and Saif Hameed, "Sunni Bloc Quits Iraqi Cabinet," *Los Angeles Times*, June 30, 2007, A6.

[7] Interview with State Department official, June 9, 2010.

[8] Interview with SIRIG official, October 28, 2008.

Beginning in 2006, and then especially in 2007, the Coalition and donor agencies intensified their technical and training assistance to Iraq's ministries, provincial governments, and eventually to its Parliament. All aspects of budgeting were covered in these training and advisory sessions, including budget formulation, execution, and oversight. The following sections examine the primary U.S. assistance programs that attempted to build budgeting skills in the ministerial and provincial governments, including USAID's *Tatweer* program, the Defense Department's Task Force on Business and Stability Operations, the Provincial Reconstruction Teams operating under the direction of the State Department, and assistance offered by international donor organizations.

1. USAID's *Tatweer*

In July 2006, USAID initiated the Iraq National Capacity Development Program, known in Arabic as *Tatweer*.[9] Funded at $209 million, *Tatweer* aimed at providing specialized ministerial training in basic public administration and management skills. "The initial mission of *Tatweer*," said an official with Management Systems International (MSI), USAID's prime contractor for the program, "was to train a critical mass of civil servants to do their jobs. Then that critical mass will hit the tipping point, and then the ministries will start to function."[10] The eleven ministries picked for inclusion in *Tatweer's* Phase I shared the commonality of providing "essential services" and managing capital budgets: Agriculture, Electricity, Finance, Health, Justice, Municipalities and Public Works, Oil, Planning, Water Resources. In addition to working with these ministries, MSI aimed to develop a presence at the provincial level in Mosul, Basra, and Erbil. During *Tatweer's* Phase I, which lasted approximately one year, MSI attempted to develop working relationships with targeted ministries and educate a core group of 150 Iraqis in the Training of Trainers (TOTS) program, who later would play a key role in Phase II. MSI needed to gain the approval of Iraq's NCCMD before offering these courses. During Phase I, each ministry produced a Capacity Development Plan (CDP) as part of its participation in *Tatweer*. These CDPs served as the broad roadmap for the ministries' efforts to build their administrative capacities. The ministries drafted statements with the assistance of MSI that outlined their existing mission tasks and goals,

---

[9] On *Tatweer*, see USAID/Iraq, "USAID/*Tatweer* Project: Developing National Capacity in Public Management, Annual Report, Year 1, September 2006–September 2007," Washington, DC: MSI, December 19, 2007; USAID/Iraq, "USAID/*Tatweer* Program: Developing National Capacity in Public Management, Quarterly Progress Report, 11, January–March 2009," Washington, DC: MSI, April 30, 2009; USAID/Iraq, "USAID/*Tatweer* Program: Developing National Capacity in Public Administration, Annual Report, Year 3, October 2008–September 2009" Washington, DC: MSI, October 30, 2009; and USAID/Iraq, "Fact Sheet: National Capacity Development," Washington, DC: USAID, April 2008.
[10] Interview with MSI official, April 1, 2008.

their policies and procedures, and their organizational strengths and deficiencies. Following approval by the NCCMD, each ministry produced an Organizational Self-Assessment Transformation Program that provided a more detailed plan for the actual training of ministry personnel in Phase II. During this second phase, approximately half of the TOTS would become trainers in their own right. TOTS worked with MSI contractors to teach tens of thousands of Iraqi civil servants in training sessions lasting four to six days in classes on topics including leadership and communications, information technology, and human resources.

Tatweer paid special attention to building budget execution capabilities through strategic planning, project management, cash management, and procurement courses offered to a thousand ministerial and four provincial government trainees in Phase I. In some ministries, such as Electricity and Oil, new budget execution units were created to speed the procurement and contracting phases of budget execution. The Ministry of Planning and several other ministries, particularly Agriculture and Health, proved to be relatively receptive to *Tatweer*'s mission. "The Ministry of Planning was actually engaged in the design of our project from the very beginning," recounted an MSI program officer. "It was a partner with USAID in putting together the shape of *Tatweer*, so that buy-in came pretty early on, and gained a lot of confidence that we weren't trying to impose ourselves on, for instance, what goes into their plans."[11] The Planning Ministry's participation was critical, because arguably its dysfunctional management of Iraqi investment spending acted as "one of the weak links in the chain," said the MSI officer, and created greater problems for budget execution than Finance or the other ministries. As the American contractors discovered, the Planning Ministry failed to educate the line ministries and the provincial governments in the capital projects' proposal process and in the submission of appropriate project plans and specifications. The forms and procedures employed by the line ministries varied greatly, as did the ministries' skill levels and competencies in developing and preparing these proposals and conducting these projects through their project contracting, procurement, and implementation phases. *Tatweer* aimed at overcoming some of these limitations by aiding the Planning Ministry in developing harmonized forms and procedures, training ministerial personnel in the basics of capital planning and execution, and organizing meetings between ministries to break down organizational barriers, all in an effort to address these and other administrative deficiencies in the Iraqi bureaucracy.

Making *Tatweer* a success proved to be difficult. According to SIGIR, "Implementation of the *Tatweer* program was slow. By December 2006, MSI had positioned advisors only in the Ministries of Oil and Electricity . . . . The lack

[11] Interview with MSI official, April 22, 2008.

of MSI advisors ... seriously compromised the overall effort."[12] Furthermore, MSI's actions to build up the Planning Ministry's NCCMD where much of the training would take place confronted a resistant Iraqi bureaucracy. "By December 2006," SIGIR continued, "USAID reported that the center's ability to host and expand on MSI training programs was limited. Two subsequent audits found that implementers were having difficulty finding Iraqis who were willing to participate in the training programs, and that the center prohibited foreign advisors from visiting its premises because their presence would draw attention to the compound and create security risk to Iraqi attendees."[13] Gaining the Iraqis' confidence took time before the ministries willingly sent their personnel to attend *Tatweer* classes. There existed a range of ministry engagement in the program. "You can start at one extreme with the Ministry of Finance," recalled an MSI program director. "We really were not able to gain much traction. On the other extreme, probably the ministries of Health, Agriculture, and Planning being the most progressive so far in reacting to us."[14]

Perhaps the most significant obstacle to *Tatweer*'s success in budget execution training came after the Ministry of Finance refused to draft its CDP and then pulled out of *Tatweer* altogether. As it barred access to BearingPoint and objected to USAID's attempt to install and activate the Financial Management Information System, the Finance Ministry also barred access to MSI and refused to participate in USAID's *Tatweer* program. A senior program officer for MSI assessed the Finance Ministry's decision this way: "I think that we look for buy-in from the minister and from the senior leadership of a ministry for the things we would like to undertake, and the minister of Finance never really committed to that with us. In the early days of our project, the first two years or so, we could never really get the level of support we thought it necessary to proceed, so we backed off. I think they were reticent to let too many people into their operations. They felt that this was material that should be closely guarded and held as financial data for the country. They were a little leery of foreigners poking around so much."[15] Another explanation for this opting out of *Tatweer* was that the Finance Ministry's leadership simply did not want to lose control over their personnel. According to Ambassador Ries, "*Tatweer* was mainly training programs that were operated out of a center in Kut, and they were essentially tools courses offered by MSI at this compound for mid-level bureaucrats. The Ministry of Finance had very few of those, and [Senior Advisor to the Finance Minister Jaafar Hassar] Aziz did not want to let them out of his sight ... and we didn't force him. The idea behind *Tatweer* was this had to be something the ministry welcomed.... we did not have the clout to impose training, and we did

[12] Office of the Special Inspector General for Iraq Reconstruction, *Hard Lessons: The Iraq Reconstruction Experience*, Washington, DC: U.S. Government Printing Office, 2009, 266.
[13] *Ibid.*, 266.
[14] Interview with MSI official, April 22, 2008.
[15] *Ibid.*

not think it would be particularly useful to do so. The Ministry of Finance was pretty immune to our capacity development efforts, by and large, both of the *Tatweer*-type and the software-development type."[16]

The long-standing division that existed between the leadership of the Finance and Planning ministries complicated the relationship between the Finance Ministry and MSI. *Tatweer* operated out of the Planning Ministry's NCCMD, and the Finance Ministry had little desire to cooperate with its rival ministry. Sectarian differences, in part, accounted for the tension between the Minister of Planning, Ali Baban, an ethnic Kurd allied with a Sunni party, and the Minister of Finance, Baqir al-Zubeidi, who was also known as Bayan Jabr, a Shiite. "Thus, if you are a Sunni from the Ministry of Planning," warned a Treasury OTA official, "you're not even going to think about setting foot in that ministry [of Finance], as a matter of self-preservation."[17] Reflecting on this mutual lack of good will between the two ministries, Stuart Bowen, the Special Inspector General for Iraq Reconstruction, recalled a conversation with Ali Baban: "Baban is not a fan of Bayan Jabr [al-Zubeidi]. When I interviewed him last November [2008], he spent most of the interview complaining that the Ministry of Finance was not funding his plans, which if they did, Iraq would recover. There's a clear gap between what the Ministry of Planning wants to do and what the Ministry of Finance will permit it to do."[18] Evaluating the tension in the relationship between the two ministries, Ambassador Ries recalled,

[The two ministries] had this arrangement where if a project came in, both the Ministry of Finance and the Ministry of Planning had to say that the project was appropriate for the budget line that it is being proposed for, from a ministry or a province. Then both the Ministry of Planning and the Ministry of Finance had to approve each disbursement.... Jabr thought it was silly to have the Planning Ministry in that loop, and every time we would complain about budget execution or the implementation of a particular project, he would blame it all on the Planning Ministry.... The long and short of it is the relationship wasn't that good. Baban didn't have the powerbase, certainly not of the kind that Jabr had.[19]

Referring to this project approval process where both the Finance and Planning ministries signed off on project funding, a senior MSI contractor noted, "There was a huge bottleneck at the Ministry of Planning, because the units they had in charge of project approval were very small, very poorly staffed, and very inconsistent. They would receive a sheet of paper with somebody's writing on it, saying 'This is the project we would like to do for $2 million in Dialya.' On the other hand, someone would present them with a 40-page document with

[16] Interview with Charles Ries, Minister for Economic Affairs and Coordinator for Economic Transition in Iraq, February 2, 2010.
[17] Interview with Treasury Department official, February 23, 2009.
[18] Interview with Stuart Bowen, Special Inspector General for Iraq Reconstruction, July 15, 2009.
[19] Interview with Charles Ries, Minister for Economic Affairs and Coordinator for Economic Transition in Iraq, February 2, 2010.

facts and figures they couldn't decipher. It was all over the map. They would get overwhelmed and let them pile up, and projects wouldn't get approved."[20] The rivalry and lack of cooperation between the Finance and Planning ministries stemmed from their sectarian differences, leadership conflicts, and their institutional roles in the Iraqi budgetary process that dated from the Soviet-inspired Iraqi budget laws of the 1970s and 1980s. All of this spilled over into the Finance Ministry's willingness to participate in *Tatweer* and compromised the government's ability to execute its capital budget.

Assessing *Tatweer*'s contribution to promoting Iraqi budget execution is difficult for a number of reasons. First, according to the USAID Inspector General, "the Program did not have outcome indicators to measure the achievement of the stated overall goal of the Program to build the capacity of key Iraqi ministries to deliver core services.... we found the program/strategic goal for effective delivery of services is not being measured at any level. With no results indicators reflecting the overall goal of the Program, there is no way to determine if the desired impact is being achieved."[21] By the end of the contract in 2011, with a cumulative *Tatweer* budget of $339 million, MSI trained approximately 1,200 TOTS and offered hundreds of courses taught primarily by TOTS and expatriates to some 106,000 Iraqis selected by the ministries. These things could be measured. Yet, these students were rarely tested to determine exactly how they improved their skills by taking these classes. MSI avoided testing Iraqis in order to not embarrass them and drive them and their colleagues away from taking additional classes. "Never underestimate 'save face' in Iraq," said an MSI program officer. "Because no matter how good your content [of training material] is, you always have to put 'save face' number one. So you have to consider that in implementation if you truly want to have success, and it's hard.... Students are not graded. They either complete the course or they don't."[22]

Whatever testing did take place examined comprehension of course material, not actual on-the-job administrative activity. So, until 2008, USAID and MSI did not test whether the students mastered, retained, and transferred the materials presumably learned in the classroom back into the various ministries, thus actually contributing to the change of ministerial procedures and practices. MSI instead principally relied on after-training interviews to assess whether its classes benefited the trainees and their ministries. As a senior MSI officer noted, "We can teach them how to do things, but we can't force them to execute [the

[20] Interview with MSI official, April 22, 2008.
[21] USAID Office of Inspector General, "Iraq," "Audit of USAID/Iraq's National Capacity Development Program, E-267-09-001-P, Washington, DC: Office of the Inspector General, USAID, November 25, 2008, 8.
[22] Interview with MSI official, April 1, 2008. On the significance of shame in Arab societies, see David Pryce-Jones, *The Closed Circle: An Interpretation of the Arabs*, Chicago: Ivan R. Dee, 2009, chapter 2.

budget] in a particular way."²³ USAID's evaluation of *Tatweer*'s effectiveness after three years in operation concluded:

> While Iraq's ability to spend its overall budget has improved each year, capital expenditures remain under-budgeted and under-spent. With USAID/*Tatweer* assistance the [government of Iraq] has been able to spend more of its capital budget, but these vital investments still represent a small percentage of the total. USAID/*Tatweer* has helped build the foundation for excellent budget execution through a combination of [Iraqi] staff capacity, enhanced requisition systems, and bolstering the institutions in which this improvement is taking place. These activities will continue in 2010 in order to reach the goal of [an Iraqi] budget execution process that is productive as well as sustainable.²⁴

A third-party evaluation of *Tatweer* concluded that MSI achieved all planned goals, however, as "there are no direct quantitative indicators for the improvement of administrative systems"; success would be measured by the budget execution rates of the ten ministries participating in the program. All ten ministries achieved high rates of budget execution, though there are questions about the validity of these figures.²⁵ As USAID claimed credit for Iraqi budget execution through *Tatweer*, so too would other agencies and groups engaged in Coalition efforts to boost Iraqi investment spending. USAID's National Capacity Development *Tatweer* project expired on January 31, 2011.

2. DOD's Task Force on Business and Stability Operations

The Department of Defense took a different and separate approach to building Iraq's budget execution capabilities. In 2006, the same year as USAID initiated *Tatweer*, Defense established a Task Force on Business and Stability Operations. The Task Force, under the direction of Deputy Under Secretary Paul Brinkley, emerged from a broader effort to promote Defense's general contacting operations in Iraq to one that encouraged economic reconstruction, in order to "ensure alignment to theater commanders' goals for reconstruction and economic development … to fully leverage economic development as a strategic and operational tool."²⁶ Staffed by 200 military personnel and contractors

---

²³ Interview with MSI official, April 22, 2008.

²⁴ USAID/Iraq, "*Tatweer* Program: Developing National Capacity in Public Administration, Annual Report, Year 3, October 2008–September 2009" Washington, DC: MSI, October 30, 2009, 18.

²⁵ USAID/Iraq, "*Tatweer* National Capacity Development Program Final Evaluation," Washington, DC: QED Group, April 2011, 14. The budget execution figures may exaggerate the rate of spending. This evaluation relies on Ministry of Planning data, which report significantly higher budget execution figures than the Ministry of Finance, as the Planning data appear to include letters of credit. See footnote 126 on this point. The USAID Inspector General is reportedly conducting its final review of the *Tatweer* program, with its release scheduled in 2011 or 2012. Also see MSI's final report, USAID/Iraq, "USAID/*Tatweer*, Final Report," October 31, 2011.

²⁶ Task Force on Business and Stability Operations, "About TFBSO." http://tfbso.defense.gov/www/about.aspx/. Also see Paul Brinkley, "A Cause for Hope: Economic Revitalization in Iraq," *Military Review*, July–August 2007, 64–73. Brinkley's view of working with state-owned enterprises set him

with a budget that grew to some $135 million in 2008 and 2009, the Task Force facilitated private-sector opportunities for American businesses seeking to do business with Defense. These efforts expanded to include encouraging foreign direct investment in Iraq, working with the U.S. Treasury to develop electronic banking, reforming and restarting state-owned enterprises, and directing contracts from U.S. firms toward Iraqi businesses. Many of these projects depended on the Iraqis running a credible and effective contracting and procurement operation. Finding problems with the Iraqis' ability to manage and execute contracts, Brinkley contracted with the firm Grant Thornton in February 2007 to work with the Ministry of Planning and the ministerial and provincial contracting offices to develop their procurement system.

Arriving in Iraq in May 2007, Grant Thornton found the Planning Ministry's procurement capability flawed throughout the entire project planning, capital budgeting formulation, and contracting process. Problems emerged beginning in the earliest stages of the planning process, the creation of project feasibility studies. "In Iraq, it's all about the feasibility studies, the engineering studies, getting the land right, even back into budgeting and planning," observed Grant Thornton's project chief. "The ministries had their wish list, but they needed to be more realistic about what their capacity was to execute the types of projects they were picking out.... What we found out on the back end was almost nonexistent, in terms of contract administration."[27] Unlike *Tatweer*'s MSI, whose solution to the problem of budget execution relied on mass training of civil servants, Grant Thornton approached this problem by working inside the ministries directly with the contracting officials on selected transactions involving, for example, the large-scale purchase of jet aircraft and 4,000 trucks for the Iraqi Ministry of Defense. Commenting on the *Tatweer* approach, the Grant Thornton project chief declared, "You trained thousands, supposedly, of procurement professionals? We can't find them all, and what's the impact? Once the budget is published, supposedly the ministries are able to write a contract. Then the contract is written, you still have to execute a letter of credit. The Trade Bank of Iraq, which is doing most of these letters of credit, is not really motivated to

at odds with the State Department and other U.S. agencies. "In the end, the embassy could not stop Brinkley. He had the support of the senior Pentagon officials and top military commanders in Iraq. But the embassy is not bending over backward to help him, the [embassy] economic officer said." Rajiv Chandrasekaran, "Agencies Tangle on Efforts to Help Iraq," *Washington Post*, March 11, 2007, A1. Also Rajiv Chandrasekaran, "Defense Skirts State in Reviving Iraqi Industry," *Washington Post*, May 14, 2007, A1. Commenting on relations between his unit and the State Department, Brinkley said, "We tend not to deal with them very often. We have our own mission, and we do our own thing." For a critique that questions TFBSO's contribution to reducing Iraqi unemployment, see Joshua Foust, "Cutting through Pentagon Spin about Businesses in Iraq," *The Atlantic*, August 2011, http://www.theatlantic.com/international/archive/2011/08/cutting-through-pentagon-spin-about-business-in-iraq/243773/.

[27] Interview with Grant Thornton official, November 11, 2009.

move those things real fast, because they are getting a lot of interest off the money.... For each of those things, you almost have to have a person assigned to get it through."[28] The capability to write a modern contract that, for instance, built in warranty and maintenance clauses, could not be assumed. The sanctions against Saddam stemming from the Gulf War limited Iraq's ability to make purchases in the world market, and as a result the Iraqis often were forced to make cash purchases for second-tier, often used products, such as buying aircraft and equipment for their dilapidated oil industry. To address these problems, such as managing letters of credit that are a critical element in purchasing overseas goods, Grant Thornton focused on helping the Iraqis shepherd targeted big projects through the project development funding life cycle. Contracts for large capital purchases required Grant Thornton's personal attention working with Iraqi program officers, with the hope that Iraqis would learn from these selected experiences in building up the process of budget execution.

The Grant Thornton team discovered that creating a working relationship with the Iraqis required time and patience. Like MSI, Grant Thornton learned it would not be working with the Ministry of Finance. Grant Thornton avoided that ministry following the kidnapping of the BearingPoint contractors in 2007. "The Ministry of Finance," said one of Grant Thornton's contractors "is an area to stay away from."[29] "We had a lot of access into the Ministry of Planning," the firm's project director acknowledged. "The Ministry of Finance scares me."[30] Also, understanding how the Iraqis functioned and what they valued did not come immediately. The team initially attempted to work with the Planning Ministry's Office of Government Contract and Procurement Policy that provided much of the contracting authority for the Ministry. Anticipating how they would approach the Office, the Grant Thornton project manager recalled what they actually experienced: "We went there thinking that speed will be of the essence. So we were going to build this high speed help desk. When we got there, not knowing the culture, what we found was that for the Iraqis speed wasn't of the essence. The crimping, the stamp, the right format, that is what they cared about. They wanted a piece of paper in the file. We wanted to answer the phone [to answer procurement questions]. No way!"[31] Facing resistance from ministerial personnel, the contractors concluded the Iraqis would better respond to other Iraqis. Grant Thornton then located three Iraqis who acted as contractors to the State Department, and financially staked them into building their own firm of 105 Iraqis, including some former Iraqi directors-general, who would then work directly with the ministries. "The Iraqis wanted to see Iraqis helping them out," said the firm's project manager. "They wanted Western consultants, but they didn't want them out front and center.... Within this company, we could

[28] *Ibid.*
[29] Interview with Grant Thornton official, November 12, 2009.
[30] Interview with Grant Thornton official, November 11, 2009.
[31] *Ibid.*

employ Iraqis, not expats, but guys who stayed throughout the entire time, and they have a lot of legitimacy."[32]

Much of Grant Thornton's energy went to establishing and staffing Procurement Assistance Centers (PAC) throughout Iraq. These PACs supported contract and procurement operations at twenty ministries, while Provincial Procurement Assistance Teams operated in fifteen of the eighteen provinces, with approximately forty contractors located at the provincial capitals. As measures of success, the Task Force claimed that in 2008 the PACs played an advisory role in 78 percent of the execution of all 5,049 provincial investment projects, "resulting in a 168% increase in Provincial capital budget execution ($0.6B in 2007 to $1.6B in 2008)."[33] The PACs conducted forty-eight workshops on developing capital project proposals, procurement practices, processing letters of credit, and financial management for more than thirteen hundred Iraqis. In a conclusion that apparently attributed virtually all the gain in Iraq's improvement in budget execution to the PACs, an assessment of the Task Force's accomplishments conducted by the Center for Strategic and International Studies declared, "Aside from these input measures and assistance efforts, the Iraqi government has improved its budget execution abilities at all levels (national and provincial) during the past three years.... Overall, Iraqi capital budget execution has increased from 18 percent to 38 percent."[34] Grant Thornton's contract with the Defense Department expired on March 29, 2010.

3. Provincial Spending, USAID's RTI, and State's Provincial Reconstruction Teams

In 2007, Iraq's Deputy Prime Minister Barham Salih declared, "This central bureaucracy is broken. The national ministries have proven incapable of spending their budgets."[35] In agreement with Salih, the central government's fiscal constipation led the Coalition to build the spending capacity of Iraq's provincial and municipal governments. Prior to the invasion, Iraqi local government and popular participation in the political process existed in name only. Decisions emanated from the center to the periphery, with public administration, including the spending of public funds, exercised by central ministerial authorities in the form of regional directors-general stationed in the governorates. Central government funds were allocated to ministerial accounts in government banks located in the provinces. Ministry of Finance treasurers assigned to the provinces then

---

[32] *Ibid.*

[33] Task Force on Business and Stability Operations, "Procurement Assistance," http://tfbso.defense. gov/pac.aspx, as of April 12, 2010.

[34] Center for Strategic and International Studies, "Task Force for Business and Stability Operations: Lessons Learned Final Project, Final Report on Lessons Learned," Washington, DC: Center for Strategic and International Studies, November 6, 2009, 44.

[35] James Glanz, "Provincial Ways Find Favor in Rebuilding Iraq," *International Herald Tribune*, October 2, 2007, 4.

authorized the release of funds to the provincially based ministerial directors-general. Provincial and local budgets essentially consisted of the compilation of the funds allocated to these directors-general.

RTI'S LOCAL GOVERNANCE PROGRAM

Although preoccupied with the administration of Iraq's central ministries, the occupation introduced meaningful local government to Iraq. To its credit, USAID planned before the war for this long-term developmental undertaking when the attention of other U.S. agencies focused almost exclusively on humanitarian relief and the occupation of the central government. Together with the military, USAID assumed much of the responsibility for promoting local Iraqi self-governance. In April 2003, USAID contracted with the giant consulting firm Research Triangle Institute International (RTI) to manage the "Local Governance Program" to promote Iraqi local governance and administrative competence.[36] The North Carolina–based firm functioned, as one senior RTI vice president noted, as "an autonomous contractor operating independently" in working with the Iraqis.[37] With its own security force, offices in seventeen of the eighteen provinces, two offices in Baghdad, and a staff that numbered as many as twenty-five hundred people, RTI acted as one of the largest American contractors in Iraq. USAID and the firm's earliest efforts were directed at organizing local political participation through the development of neighborhood advisory councils, encouraging Iraqis to run for public office, and holding elections. The Coalition's efforts culminated in the famous "purple finger" national elections of January 2005 that provided for the National Assembly, eighteen provincial assemblies, and a Kurdistan regional assembly.

The long-term development challenge of building local public administration, however, proved to be much more difficult than holding elections. Once provincial governments and municipal councils were elected, RTI attempted to provide training in rudimentary political and administrative skills to the newly elected council officials and their administrative staffs. Except for the holdovers from

[36] Naomi Klein, "Iraq: RTI Designing Government for Baghdad," *The Nation*, February 23, 2004. http://www.corpwatch.org/article.php?id=11151&printsafe=1.

[37] On the Local Governance Program, see, for example, USAID, "Iraq Local Governance Program (LGP) 2007 Annual Report, October 1, 2006–December 31, 2007," Research Park, NC: RTI International, January 15, 2008, esp. 13. This report is prepared by RTI for USAID. On the Local Government Program from the view of an RTI contractor and the CPA's lack of support for USAID decentralization programs, see Derick W. Brinkerhoff and James B. Mayfield, "Democratic Governance in Iraq? Progress and Peril in Reforming State-Society Relations," *Public Administration and Development*, 25 (2005) 1, 59–73, esp. 66, and Derick W. Brinkerhoff, "Building Local Governance in Iraq," in Louis A. Picard, Robert Groelsema, and Terry F. Buss (eds.), *Foreign Aid and Foreign Policy: Lessons for the Next Half-Century*, New York: M.E. Sharpe, 2008, 109–128. On the ethical responsibility of leaving Iraq with a functioning electoral system, see Noah Feldman, *What We Owe Iraq: War and the Ethics of Nation Building*, Princeton: Princeton University Press, 2004.

the local ministerial offices, as RTI's contractors learned, these provincial and local governmental units needed to be trained from the ground up. A senior RTI officer charged with teaching budgeting to the Iraqis observed that when it came to local budgeting, the central government's allocations to the directors-general were "the only way the term 'provincial budget' would mean anything to the Iraqis, and that I had not expected. They had no administrative systems by which they even pooled their common resources, or even looked at something as a budget for Babel province."[38] The reluctance of locally based ministerial officials to accept these newcomers to the budget process added to the difficulty of training completely inexperienced Iraqis in budget formulation and public finance. "Resistance at the local level tended to come from ministry officials, the DGs (directors-general) and some of their staff," the RTI officer recalled. "Because, after all, their system existed before, with no resistance from councils, because the councils were brand new. Obviously, one of the big questions for us is as soon as you hand it back to the Iraqis, are the councils disbanded? This is not an Iraqi institution."[39] The Coalition invented this institutional system of provincial and local governments, and its rules also applied to local public finance.

The legal framework governing Iraq handed down by the Coalition complicated efforts to build provincial budgetary capacity. CPA Order 95, the Financial Management Law and Public Debt Law, and CPA Order 71, Local Government Powers, authorized the governorates, or provinces, to establish governorate councils, the provincial governorates to establish local districts (*qada'as*) and subdistricts (*nahiyas*), and the central government to provide the provinces with funds from the national budget. The governorate councils received the authority to set provincial priorities and pass their local budgets, incur debt with the permission of the Ministry of Finance, and raise their own revenues and fees. These orders did not, however, alter the ministries' responsibilities for the provision of public services in the provinces or provide for the coordination of ministerial and provincial reconstruction efforts. Despite the authorization of provincial governments and the granting to them of some budgetary authority, the budgetary allocations to the governorates, the bureaucratic apparatus for selecting projects for funding, and control over revenues effectively remained under the direction of the central government. The Ministry of Finance, which operated Iraq's tax collection services, for example, strenuously opposed provincial efforts at raising revenues despite their authority to do so. As the USAID's "Republic of Iraq District Government Field Manual" noted, "The Ministry of Finance (MOF) has consistently opposed the raising of revenues by the governorate councils, despite the fact that Order 71 explicitly authorizes it.... The decentralization principle embodied in Order 71 has not won favor at the center, and indeed, decentralization in general has been overtly

---

[38] Interview with RTI official, April 16, 2008.
[39] Interview with RTI official, July 15, 2008.

resisted by the Ministry of Finance (MOF) and the Ministry of Planning and Cooperative Development (MOPCD)."⁴⁰

Under these conditions, RTI's ability to train local Iraqis in budgeting in the years immediately following the invasion proved to be limited in scope and effectiveness. As part of the Local Governance Program, RTI contractors conducted training conferences and workshops in Iraqi budgeting, and employed training modules that broadly covered the operations of local public administration. "So we set up training modules for all of the kinds of skills you would expect to see in a municipal government," reported an RTI officer, including "financial planning and resource development."⁴¹ The provincial and local governing councils, nevertheless, had little stake in budgeting, as they neither controlled the selection of projects nor received investment funds from the center. The provision of public services and reconstruction remained in the domain of the central ministries. So rather than provide training in provincial budget preparation and formulation RTI focused its efforts on educating provincial authorities and ministerial directors-general in how to comply with central government directives and processes stemming from CPA Order 95. "In that system," said an RTI official, "all you could do is work with the DGs in improving their ability to influence their managers in Baghdad in the budget that comes down, to influence the budget allocations within the ministry."⁴²

In 2009, the USAID Office of Inspector General audited the Local Governance Program's training of local elected officials and administrators. The audit found the provincial councils benefited from the courses offered, including those on financial management and budgeting, and that all eighteen councils completed work on provincial development plans. Budget execution reached a collective 60 percent in the provincial governments for early 2008, which suggested some degree of success, although this figure relied on dubious Ministry of Planning data. Nonetheless, in only three of the eighteen councils did the members demonstrate core competencies in basic management capabilities, and though the RTI offered courses to some 26,600 local officials, "the success or short-term impact of that significant amount of training on improving local governance was not

---

⁴⁰ USAID, "Republic of Iraq District Government Field Manual, Volume 1," Research Park, NC: RTI International, July 2007, 12. Also see USAID, "Writing the Future: Provincial Development Strategies in Iraq," Research Park, NC: RTI International, November 2007, and Michael Knights and Eamon McCarthy, "Provincial Politics in Iraq: Fragmentation or New Awakening?" *Policy Focus* 81, Washington, DC: The Washington Institute for Near East Policy, April 2008, 15. "Federal resistance to fiscal decentralization has been evident ever since orders 71 and 95 were passed. ... As a result, the provinces experienced serious ongoing frustration throughout the first years of Iraqi self-rule. The MOF [Ministry of Finance] and Ministry of Municipalities and Public Works continued to dominate district and local service delivery while federal ministries could still effectively ignore the demands of provincial councils due to the lack of a formal needs-assessment framework."

⁴¹ Interview with RTI official, April 16, 2008.

⁴² Interview with RTI official, July 15, 2008. See also Brinkerhoff and Mayfield, *ibid.*, 70, on the lack of local budgetary authority.

measured."[43] USAID neglected to identify which officials and administrators should receive instruction or what type of instruction they should receive, which lessened the impact of the training regime. USAID needed to exercise greater oversight over the actual course content, as the relationship of these classes to "the mission's goals was not clear because the mission largely relied upon the implementing partner to determine which training courses to offer." RTI determined the content and scope of these classes, but their substance left the Inspector General to observe that they "may not produce the most benefits for the mission or for Iraqi governmental officials in the long term."[44] Finally, some of the raw numbers of trainees may have been inflated due to officials and administrators repeating courses.

PRTS AND PROVINCIAL BUDGETING

In 2005, a significant change came in the manner in which the Coalition provided budgetary training and other forms of assistance to the provinces. U.S. Ambassador to Iraq Zalmay Khalilzad recommended that the Provincial Reconstruction Team concept be introduced in Iraq. First used in Afghanistan in 2002, where Khalilzad served prior to Iraq, PRTs evolved from small groups of Americans military civilian affairs officers who were organized into Coalition Humanitarian Liaison Cells that were created to evaluate Afghan humanitarian needs, assist in the development of small-scale reconstruction projects, and work with the UN Assistance Mission in Afghanistan.[45] Secretary of State Condoleezza Rice approved Khalilzad's recommendation, which led to the first PRTs in Iraq being stationed in Mosul, Hilla, and Kirkuk in November 2005. PRTs in Iraq varied in size, organizational membership, and mission. Initially, Provincial Support Teams (PST) were led by a State Department regional coordinator and a military deputy officer and were staffed by some six to eight persons drawn primarily from the U.S. Army, USAID, and the Coalition's Iraqi Reconstruction Management Office. The PSTs worked with the State Department's newly created Provincial Reconstruction and Development Committees (PRDC) that funded

[43] USAID Office of Inspector General, "Audit of USAID/IRAQ's Local Governance Program II Activities," Audit Report No. E-267-09-003-P, Baghdad, May 31, 2009, 6.
[44] *Ibid.*, 1.
[45] On the evolution of the PRTs, see John D. Drolet, "Provincial Reconstruction Teams: Afghanistan vs. Iraq: Should We Have a Standard Model?" Carlisle, PA: U.S. Army War College, May 2006; Sean C. McLay, "Provincial Reconstruction Teams (PRTs): A Panacea for What Ails Iraq?," Montgomery, AL: Air Command and Staff College, April 2007; Robert M. Perito, "Provincial Reconstruction Teams in Iraq," *Special Report*, 185, Washington, DC: United States Institute for Peace, March 2007; Michelle Parker, "The Role of the Defense Department in Provincial Reconstruction Teams," Santa Monica: Rand, September 2007; and Nima Abbaszadeh, Mark Crow, Marianne El-Khoury, Jonathan Gandomi, David Kuwayama, Christopher MacPherson, Meghan Nutting, Nealin Parker, and Taya Weiss, "Provincial Reconstruction Teams: Lessons and Recommendations," Princeton, NJ: Woodrow Wilson School, January 2008.

small-scale reconstruction projects. State established the PRDCs to give provincial governors some authority and experience in developing investment priorities and selecting capital projects that would be built with Coalition money. PRDC committees usually consisted of thirty to forty members, including U.S. officials, the provincial governor, and the central ministries' regional directors-general who represented the key service-providing ministries, such as Electricity, Housing, and Municipalities and Public Works. In May 2005, General George W. Casey, the commanding general of Multi-National Forces–Iraq, directed that $80 million from the Commanders Emergency Response Program be distributed to the PSTs to fund projects selected by eight PRDC provincial committees and approved by the U.S. Embassy. Although only three months remained in the U.S. 2005 fiscal year to select the projects and spend the money, one informal evaluation of this effort indicated that the Iraqis were able "to expend the majority of the funds provided."[46] In April 2005, Ambassador Khalilzad's review of the PSTs led to their being renamed Provincial Reconstruction Teams, with the size and missions of the individual teams greatly expanded to "assist Iraq's provincial governments with developing a transparent and sustained capacity to govern, promoting increased security and rule of law, promoting political and economic development, and providing provincial administration necessary to meet the basic needs of the population."[47]

Thirteen months later, President Bush ordered a civilian surge as part of the New Way Forward strategy to complement the military surge taking place under the command of General David H. Petraeus. This additional surge included doubling the number of PRTs from ten to twenty, and by August 2008, eleven regular PRTs operated in provincial capitals, with an additional thirteen embedded provincial reconstruction teams (ePRT) deployed with U.S. brigade combat teams. These teams ranged in size from approximately ten to forty-five persons,

---

[46] John D. Drolet, "Provincial Reconstruction Teams: Afghanistan vs. Iraq: Should We Have a Standard Model?" Carlisle, PA: U.S. Army War College, May 2006, 9. On the CERP program, see Ernesto Londono, "US 'Money Weapon' Yields Mixed Results," *Washington Post*, July 27, 2009, A1; Mark S. Martins, "The Commander's Emergency Response Program," *Joint Forces Quarterly*, 37, April 2005, 46–52; Mark S. Martins, "No Small Change of Soldiering: The Commander's Emergency Response Program (CERP) in Iraq and Afghanistan," *The Army Lawyer*, February 2004, 1–20; United States Joint Forces Command, "Military Support to Stabilization, Security, Transition, and Reconstruction Operations Joint Operations Concept, Version 2.0, Arlington, VA: Department of Defense, December 2006, 44, 52; Office of the Special Inspector General for Iraq Reconstruction, "Commander's Emergency Response Program in Iraq Funds Many Large-Scale Projects," SIGIR-08-006, Arlington, VA, January 25, 2008; Donald P. Wright and Timothy R. Reese, *On Point II: Transition to the New Campaign: The United States Army in Operation Iraqi Freedom, May 2003–January 2005*, Ft. Leavenworth, KS: United States Army Combat Studies Institute, 2008, chapter 9; and Peter R. Mansoor, *Baghdad at Sunrise: A Brigade Commander's War in Iraq*, New Haven: Yale University Press, 2008, 135–137.

[47] Robert M. Perito, "Provincial Reconstruction Teams in Iraq," *Special Report*, 185, Washington, DC: United States Institute for Peace, March 2007, 3.

for a total of 450 personnel. They were led by a State Department regional coordinator and a military deputy officer and were heavily staffed and supported by military personnel, various federal agency officers, such as the Departments of Agriculture and Justice, some Coalition partner personnel including staff seconded from the United Kingdom's Department for International Development, and USAID contractors.[48] RTI's contractors were incorporated into teams, and though the firm no longer acted in a relatively independent fashion, its contractors still bore the much of the responsibility for training and developing the Iraqis' administrative and budgetary skills. The PRTs attempted to provide training and act as an intermediary between the central government's ministries and provincial government officials. The need for a liaison stemmed, for example, from the Planning Ministry's failure to inform and work with the provincial governments on how to prepare and submit capital projects for funding by the central government. Finally, in addition to advising the governorate councils in the development of provincial budgets, each PRT gained access to several sources of U.S. funding, including $10 million in CERP funds, Quick Response Funds, USAID Economic Support Funds, and IRRF money, to promote the delivery of essential services and fund reconstruction projects.

The Coalition's growing demands for improved Iraqi budget execution and a dramatic change in center-periphery relations that occurred in 2006 raised the need to build provincial budgeting capacity. Following the election of the National Assembly that brought regional voices to the political process and Coalition pressure to increase Iraqi spending, in addition to funding provincial operating expenses, the 2006 Iraqi budget allocated $2 billion in the form of budget transfers to the governorates to fund provincial development projects. This meant that, as an RTI officer stated, "there now needs to be real budgetary training in the provinces to manage these funds. Real money on the table, with real provincial governors. Money goes through the ministries, but now there is interaction between the DGs with the governors, who is the real connection.... Budgeting becomes much more of 'what do we need in the provinces?'"[49] The infusion of these funds raised the stakes for provincial political actors to learn about budgeting. These local political authorities now had an incentive to increase the number of their administrative staff who engaged in budgeting, to encourage them to learn how to prepare budgets, draft project proposals for ministerial review, and execute budgets in a timely and effective manner. Furthermore, in what would be Iraq's first effort in decentralized planning, with the encouragement of USAID, RTI, and DFID, each governorate began producing a Provincial Development Strategy (PDS) that would serve as a five-year plan for the provision of public services and economic development projects.

[48] U.S. Government Accountability Office, "Provincial Reconstruction Teams in Afghanistan and Iraq," GAO-08-905RSU, Washington, DC, October 1, 2008, 12–14.
[49] Interview with RTI official, July 15, 2008.

EVALUATING PRT EFFECTIVENESS

Several evaluations of the effectiveness of PRTs highlight the difficulties the teams faced through 2008 and the challenges of operating with the drawdown of U.S. military forces beginning in 2009. The PRT program experienced numerous obstacles during the first several years of its existence. In a report issued in 2006, SIGIR found that a year into the program the State and Defense departments had yet to reach a working arrangement for the provision of adequate security for PRT units and Iraqis alike and that "because of security concerns, face-to-face meetings between provincial government officials and PRT personnel are often limited and, in some cases, do not occur."[50] State Department personnel operated under State's diplomatic security standards, "which were very restrictive," a State Department PRT team leader recalled, and "meant we were in most cases stuck on the base."[51] Not until the summer of 2007 did State and Defense agree to a memorandum of understanding that allowed PRTs to operate under military security standards, thus for the first time giving them real mobility to move about in the provinces and work in anything approaching a sustained basis with the Iraqis.

Other assessments of the PRTs identified the ongoing challenge of finding personnel to fill out the civilian surge, including the staffing of PRTs by State Department and other agency personnel who were willing to serve in Iraq, and the difficulty of sufficiently training team members to fulfill their responsibilities. In the case of RTI, for example, because its contract with USAID required the firm to provide three full-time expatriates for each PRT, most RTI contractors were either Iraqi expatriates or recruited from surrounding Arab countries. Nonetheless, according to SIGIR, only 29 of the 610 personnel assigned to the PRTs possessed knowledge of Arabic or a background in Iraqi culture or traditions.[52] The backgrounds, experiences, and effectiveness of American and non-American contractors alike varied greatly. This meant that one PRT budget expert might be a former American city manager and another team's budget expert might be a Jordanian who served in a ministry of finance revenue

---

[50] Office of the Special Inspector General for Iraq Reconstruction, "Status of the Provincial Reconstruction Team Program in Iraq," SIGIR-06-034, Arlington, VA, October 29, 2006, ii.

[51] Interview with State Department Official, June 9, 2010.

[52] Staffing for PRTs was particularly difficult early in the program. As of September 2006, only 60 percent of civilian PRT billets were filled, with no teams staffed by more than nine civilians. Office of the Special Inspector General for Iraq Reconstruction, "Status of the Provincial Reconstruction Team Program in Iraq," SIGIR-06-2006, Arlington, VA, October 29, 2006, 16. Also see Nima Abbaszadeh, Mark Crow, Marianne El-Khoury, Jonathan Gandomi, David Kuwayama, Christopher MacPherson, Meghan Nutting, Nealin Parker, and Taya Weiss, "Provincial Reconstruction Teams: Lessons and Recommendations," Princeton, NJ: Woodrow Wilson School, January 2008. Media reports suggest State Department personnel were noticeably reluctant to volunteer to serve in Iraq. On SIGIR's assessment of the number of PRT personnel with Arabic capabilities, see James Glanz, "Congress Told of Problems in Rebuilding Provinces," *Washington* Post, September 6, 2007, A8.

collection office. These contractors who were to be inserted into Iraq needed to be taught RTI's approach to working with the Iraqis and educated in the vagaries of Iraqi politics, administrative processes, and budgeting and contracting rules that stemmed from various CPA orders. The urgency of staffing the PRTs reduced the time available to RTI to train its contractors for service in the field. "We have very little time," an RTI officer candidly noted, "because with the PRTs we are under pressure to move people on. Most of their orientation happens once they get to Baghdad. So we just walk them through the program." Personnel churn within the PRTs, including their leadership cadres, threatened long-term progress. "There is just no continuity," said the RTI official, who expressed concern about the turnover in State and Defense department PRT leadership. "There's hardly anything that holds over. When you replace the PRT leadership structure in a province, the PRT team leader, the deputy team leaders, then those people rotate out, somebody else comes in, and everything changes. But then that person leaves, somebody else comes in and says 'I don't care what you did before, this is how I am going to do it.'"[53]

For their part, State Department PRT team leaders did not always find RTI contractors to be effective team members. Reported one team leader, "When I moved up to Wasit province, a couple months into my time I got three RTI people. One was American, two were African. They were not effective at all.... It was a struggle at the beginning to have them understand that they were actually part of the PRT, had any responsibility to coordinate with the PRT, to report to the PRT. Once we got that ironed out, they just did not have the expertise, or the kind of aggressive attitude that you need in that environment to succeed."[54] A PRT team leader for another province identified similar problems with RTI, saying, "When I showed up in Al-Muthanna province, it took me a year to understand what RTI was doing in Muthanna in terms of technical assistance in budgeting and other areas of governance. It really came to light over the course of the year that they weren't doing anything. They were filling out the sheets and saying 'we were doing training,' and offering PowerPoint briefs to the council, and sending that up to Baghdad and calling it a day."[55] A United States Institute of Peace report suggests these observations made by PRT personnel about RTI were not uncommon: "Many PRT staff expressed frustration that they have little idea of what RTI does – whom it trains, what the training consists of, etc. – despite the fact that RTI expatriate staff are located on the PRT. RTI cites security concerns as the reason for not being forthcoming

[53] Interview with RTI official, July 15, 2008.
[54] Interview with State Department Official, June 9, 2010.
[55] Interview with State Department Official, June 9, 2010. Added the official: "All these traveling guys, the RTI, the Brinkley group, I never saw them [on any sustained basis] .... The Brinkley group did an overnight with me, looked at two state-owned industry sites they were going to refurbish, never heard from them again, never saw them again. In terms of training out in the far-reaching provinces, never saw it."

about its activities. However justified these concerns might be, this extreme 'stove-piping' is counterproductive."[56] A USAID Inspector General investigation in 2008 reported similar findings, indicating that "Another theme that emerged during interviews with PRT and Brigade Combat Team officials was the lack of coordination between USAID and the PRT/Brigade Combat Team."[57] At the same time, some anecdotal references do point to the variability in PRT experiences, where PTR team leaders viewed RTI contractors more favorably. One State Department PRT team leader who served in Kirkuk province expressed his admiration for the two former American city managers in his group. Another PRT leader declared that the Tunisian public finance expert hired by RTI "was a goldmine," who diligently and patiently worked with three provincial councils. Yet, that State Department official conceded, "Our personnel and recruitment processes are not great. You get some superstars and you get some duds."[58]

Particularly during their early introduction to Iraq, from 2005 through mid-2007, PRTs confronted ongoing coordination problems, suffered from a lack of defined objectives, and struggled to create lasting institutional change in the face of Iraq's shifting political and security environment. In 2007, the USAID Inspector General reported a lack of coordination, communication, and direction from USAID headquarters in Baghdad to its staff assigned to PRTs in the field, stating that "The reason for the lack of coordination was the failure of USAID/Iraq to adopt and implement procedures to ensure coordination from the beginning."[59] A review conducted by the U.S. House of Representatives' Committee on Armed Services released in April 2008 indicated that neither the departments of State or Defense had established nor measured clearly defined PRT goals and metrics for success.[60] An evaluation of the PRTs released by the United States Institute of Peace late in 2008 found that "even where the PRTs have successfully improved capacity – in terms of government coordination,

[56] Rusty Barber and Sam Parker, "Evaluating Iraq's Provincial Reconstruction Teams While Drawdown Looms: A USIP Trip Report," Washington, DC: United States Institute for Peace, December 2008, p. 8.
[57] USAID Office of the Inspector General, "Audit of USAID/Iraq's Community Stabilization Program," E-267-08-001-P, Washington, DC, March 18, 2008, 8.
[58] Interview with State Department Official, June 9, 2010.
[59] USAID Office of the Inspector General, "Audit of USAID/Iraq's Participation in Provincial Reconstruction Teams in Iraq," Audit Report No. E-267-07-008-P, Washington, DC, September 27, 2007, p. 7.
[60] U.S. House of Representatives Committee on Armed Services, "Agency Stovepipes vs. Strategic Agility: Lessons We Need to Learn from Provincial Reconstruction Teams in Iraq and Afghanistan," House Armed Services Committee: Washington, DC, April 2008. According to Rep. Vic Snyder (D-Ark.) who chaired the subcommittee responsible for the report, "If the current [PRT] structure was working well, we should have a smooth operation now. But we don't." Said the ranking member, Rep. Todd Akin (R-Mo.), "The organizational structure is a little goofy, [it has been] put together with glue and baling wire." Karen DeYoung, "US Effort to Rebuild from War Criticized," *Washington Post*, April 18, 2008, A18.

project implementation and budget execution – it is difficult to argue that they are engaged in long-term institution building. Rather, they primarily build relationships and facilitate interactions between various Iraqi officials for short-term progress. What will happen when these individuals leave office – for example, through elections? Many PRT members opined that, in such circumstances, PRTs will essentially start from scratch."[61] The January 2010 provincial elections did in fact result in a significant change in local leadership, with the result that "the PRTs took years to develop capacity and competency among Iraq's provincial leadership. But much of that leadership has been voted out of office … and the incoming leadership will not be familiar with Iraq's arcane budgetary and governing process."[62] The 2008 U.S.-Iraq Status of Forces Agreement, which called for American troops to leave Iraq by the end of 2011, further challenged the PRTs' long-term effectiveness. The high point of PRT presence in Iraq came in late 2007 and 2008, when the Coalition deployed twenty-nine teams in Baghdad and throughout the provinces. Four ePRTs were disbanded or absorbed into other teams in 2009 because of the redeployment of several Army brigades out of Iraq, with all ePRTs scheduled for demobilization by the end of 2010. The State Department directed that the total number of PRTs would be reduced to six by December 2011, with the effectiveness of these remaining teams and their ability to engage the Iraqis still dependent on the security environment in which they attempt to operate.[63] USAID's Local Governance Program expired on June 30, 2011.

USAID'S LEGISLATIVE STRENGTHENING PROGRAM

In 2008, USAID extended capacity building beyond the ministries and provincial government to the Iraqi Parliament through its Legislative Strengthening Program (LSP). Iraq's Council of Representatives established a committee system in 2006 that included the Financial and Economic, Investment, and Reconstruction committees, whose tasks included reviewing the proposed budgets submitted by the Ministry of Finance. As part of their constitutional obligations and consistent with the Financial Management Law, these legislators would analyze the proposed budget, ask pertinent questions of ministerial officials, and make fiscal recommendations to the speaker and to the Council. To support the Council's legislative effectiveness and build budgetary oversight capacity, in October 2008 USAID awarded a $24 million contract to the firm

[61] Rusty Barber and Sam Parker, "Evaluating Iraq's Provincial Reconstruction Teams While Drawdown Looms: A USIP Trip Report," Washington, DC: United States Institute for Peace, December 2008, p. 6.
[62] Spencer Ackerman, "As Troops Withdraw, Iraq Provincial Reconstruction Teams to Change," *Washington Independent*, March 11, 2009. http://washingtonindependent.com/33361/iraq-diplomacy-program-to-change/.
[63] U.S. Department of Defense, "Measuring Stability and Security in Iraq," Washington, DC, July 23, 2009, 5.

AECOM to manage the LSP. The program focused on strengthening the Council's management, information technology, communications, and budgetary oversight capabilities, and gaining the Council's support for creating an Iraq Center for Parliamentary Development. AECOM assessed the Council's abilities to engage in budgetary deliberations and analyze the government's proposed 2009 budget and found them generally insufficient. Most Council members expressed little interest in the budget or the budgetary process, and any analytic capability largely rested with the Finance Committee. Meanwhile, budgets submitted by the Ministry of Finance to the Council contained a variety of defects, including inconsistent, missing, and irreconcilable data.[64]

The LSP attempted to build the Council's institutional capacity by offering a variety of training classes and manuals to educate members and committee staff on how the budgetary process worked, how to read and analyze the budget, and how to question ministry officials about their budgets and programs. The firm encouraged the use of open public hearings, the release of more transparent budgetary and programmatic information from the ministries, and the development of budgetary reviews by all committees, not just the Finance committee. LSP also gained approval for establishing a Budget Research Office of four staffers within the Council's Research Directorate who would monitor budgetary matters and provide budget analysis to the members.[65] "Our training was good," recalled an Iraqi AECOM instructor, "and they learned a lot from us.... We brought the capacity of the [members of Parliament] to conduct their oversight on their own ministries. We had lots of roundtables with the committees. We showed them the basics, how to read the budget, how to find the weak points in the budgets – 'Why did number 8 go someplace? Why did number 8 cost so much?' Most of their questions were addressed to the ministers. The MPs had prepared those questions [from] what they had been taught by LSP in those roundtable sessions."[66]

Nonetheless, at the conclusion of the LSP contract in December 2011, the program's aspirations confronted the challenge of arriving at a condition of shared interests, the realities of Iraqi politics, and Iraqi resistance at buying fully into the Coalition's institutional reconstruction. Individual Council members did seek out analytical advice and information, best practices were shared with committees and their staffs, and some committees did conduct open hearings.

---

[64] Robert J. Viernum, "Understanding and Understandability: Post-Budget Review of the Iraqi Council of Representatives Involvement in the FY 2009 Federal Budget Process," USAID Iraq Legislative Strengthening Program, Baghdad, March 2009.

[65] For a review of LSP activities, see the program's quarterly and annual reports, such as USAID/Iraq, "Legislative Strengthening Program, *Quarterly Report*, January–March 2010," Arlington: AECOM, March 31, 2010, which describes the training of the Budget Research Office, 35–45. The USAID Inspector General reportedly will be conducting a review of LSP at the conclusion of the contract in December 2011. USAID, however, may extend the contract through March 2014, for a total cost of $73,189,750.

[66] Interview with AECOM official, November 23, 2011.

The Council, moreover, became increasingly assertive with the ministries through the budget and the budgetary process. Still, despite the creation of the Budget Research Office and the training of its staff, their analytical capabilities remained, said another Iraqi trainer, "on a basic level," and the selection of the staff depended strictly on their bloc membership, not their technical expertise.[67] "When we met with MPs and the Budget Research Office, they had no skills. Now they can read budget, now they can analyze budget, they can locate and point to anything wrong with the budget, but they can't change anything, because it's about politics." "We were aiming to enable every single committee to establish its own report on the draft budget, to focus on their specific ministry . . . but they did not cooperate, and instead they said they were too busy. Pressure from higher up." "The Council denied the LSP from achieving one of the biggest objectives, an investment budget. We tried our best [for] two years. Talked to the Council people, talked to the Council leadership, tried to convince them. We provided them with manuals and booklets on how to establish an investment budget, but the result wasn't good." The LSP goal of establishing a Center for Parliamentary Development, noted an AECOM team leader, "is one of the obstacles that has stalled. The politics are a constant obstacle. The added political dynamic is that the Sadrist party [led by Muqtada al-Sadr] holds the balance of power, not only within the Parliament, but within the government. And they have been very clear in lacking interest in working with US funded projects."[68] Thus, like MSI, Grant Thornton, and RTI, ACEOM experienced pushback from Iraqis when the attempt to induce institutional change and layer new institutions on existing practices failed to coincide with Iraqi interests.

CORRUPTION AND BUDGETARY TRANSPARENCY

The focus of Coalition capacity-building efforts on helping the Iraqis execute their budgets points to the issue of the trade-offs involved in the sequencing of budgetary state building. From the beginning of the occupation, in the sequence of institution building, the Coalition concentrated its attention and resources on those budgetary institutions that engaged in spending, while relatively minor attention was paid to those institutions engaged in financial accountability. The strategy underlying the 17th Benchmark reasoned that spending money, providing essential services, and building infrastructure would beat back the insurgency. The 17th Benchmark said nothing about accounting, effective cash management, transparency, and fighting corruption. As a result of this

---

[67] Interview with AECOM official, November 23, 2011. According to Kamal al-Field, a former deputy finance minister who lectured to the Council on Representatives on the budgetary process at the request of USAID, "These are people who are very weak. We train them from time to time. They are not specialists at all, they are there because they belong to different parties. They don't have expertise." Interview with Kamal al-Field, August 4, 2011.

[68] Interview with AECOM official, November 23, 2011.

trade-off, in terms of institutional layering, the Coalition generally failed to provide Iraq with the formative institutions that could provide a credibly transparent and accountable system of financial management, leaving the Iraqis largely on their own to fight corruption.

The Coalition did take steps to help the Iraqis control corruption. The CPA issued orders that created new Iraqi agencies, established rules for contracting and procurement, and promoted financial reporting requirements.[69] The CPA "reestablished" the Supreme Board of Audit, an institution created during the British Mandate, and authorized the creation of three new institutions, the Iraq Inspector Generals (IIG), the Commission on Public Integrity (CPI), and the Central Criminal Court of Iraq to try cases of corruption. Yet, during the early critical years of occupation, Coalition support for these new institutions generally lacked direction, coordination, and funding. Although the Coalition professed its desire to reign in corruption, the State Department observed that "The expenditure of U.S. government funds on anticorruption has been *ad hoc* and modest ... under $65 million" through 2006. "Despite the fact that attacking corruption is among the top U.S. priorities in Iraq, this amount represents less than .003 percent of total IRRF funding to date. Non-U.S. donor funding has been even more modest."[70]

Reacting to criticism that its assistance programs were fragmented and ineffective, the Coalition established the Office of Accountability and Transparency (OAT) in 2006 to provide guidance to the Board of Supreme Audit, the CPI, and the IIG. A series of congressional hearings held in 2007 and 2008, however, resulted in testimony indicating that the Coalition still lacked a coherent plan for aiding the Iraqis, OAT's leadership and staff suffered from frequent turnover, and OAT meetings were infrequent and poorly attended.[71] According to Judge Arthur Brennan, an OAT director, "no" coordinated strategy existed to help the

---

[69] These orders include CPA Order 55 "Delegation of Authority Regarding the Iraq Commission on Public Integrity," January 27, 2004; CPA Order 57 "Iraqi Inspector Generals," February 5, 2004; and CPA Order 77 "Board of Supreme Audit," April 18, 2004.

[70] U.S. Department of State and the Broadcasting Board of Governors, Office of Inspector General, "Report of Inspection: Survey of Anticorruption Programs, Embassy Baghdad, Iraq," Report No. ISP-IQO-06-50, August 2006, 10.

[71] Many of these congressional hearings were initiated after the Democrats won control of the Congress in the 2006 election. They include: U.S. Senate Democratic Policy Committee, "An Oversight Hearing on Waste, Fraud and Abuse in US Government Contracting in Iraq," February 14, 2005; U.S. House of Representatives Committee on Oversight and Government Reform, "Hearings on Waste, Fraud, and Abuse of Taxpayer Dollars," February 6–9, 2007; U.S. House of Representatives Committee on Oversight and Government Reform, "Assessing the State of Iraqi Corruption," October 4, 2007; U.S. Senate Appropriations Committee, "Senate Appropriations Committee Examines Waste, Fraud and Abuse of American Tax Dollars in Iraq," March 11, 2008; U.S. House of Representatives Committee on Oversight and Government Reform, "Accountability Lapses in Multiple Funds for Iraq," May 22, 2008; and U.S. Senate Democratic Policy Committee, "An Inside View of the 'Second Insurgency': How Corruption and Waste Are Undermining the US Mission in Iraq," September 22, 2008.

Iraqis fight corruption. "I think Ambassador Crocker was serious about going forward on this, but I don't think everybody is serious about it, and if they are serious, then somebody else should have been doing their job."[72] SIGIR offered a similar view in 2007, noting that "these figures point to a rising tide of corruption in Iraq, and its anticorruption institutions are not well poised to stem it.... [There exists] a continued lack of high-level support for Iraq's anticorruption efforts" at the U.S. Embassy.[73]

Corruption, in any case, engulfed Iraq, and the deeply flawed, ineffective oversight of Coalition and Iraqi spending contributed to that corruption. "Corruption is widespread in Iraq," concluded a 2006 State Department report on the topic. "All objective indicators support this judgment."[74] In 2007, a State Department official described corruption in Iraq as "real, endemic, and pernicious" as another State Department assessment found that "Currently, Iraq is not capable of even rudimentary enforcement of anticorruption laws."[75] Numerous official reports, media stories, and participant observations described corruption valued in the tens of billions of dollars emerging in every financial aspect of Coalition and Iraqi reconstruction efforts. The flow of funds through the Coalition and the Iraqi budgets served as the conduit for that corruption, fiscal malfeasance, and flawed budget execution. The Coalition's management and spending of American appropriations also created opportunities for corrupt activity.[76] Corruption emerged in the Coalition's management and spending of

[72] On the OAT and its operations, see U.S. House of Representatives Committee on Oversight and Government Reform, "Memorandum: Additional Information on Iraqi Corruption and U.S. Efforts," October 4, 2007, 4.

[73] Stuart Bowen, "Testimony of Stuart W. Bowen, Jr., Special Inspector General for Iraq Reconstruction, 'Assessing the State of Iraqi Corruption,'" U.S. House of Representatives Committee on Oversight and Government Reform, October 4, 2007, 3, 8. Also, Office of the Special Inspector General for Iraq Reconstruction, "Transferring Reconstruction Projects to the Government of Iraq: Some Progress Made but Further Improvements Needed to Avoid Waste," SIGIR-08-017, Arlington, VA, April 28, 2008; and James Glanz, "As US Rebuilds, Iraq Won't Act on Finished Work," *New York Times*, July 28, 2007, http://www.nytimes.com/2007/07/28/world/middleeast/28reconstruct.html?scp=1/.

[74] U.S. Department of State and the Broadcasting Board of Governors, Office of Inspector General, "Report of Inspection: Survey of Anticorruption Programs," Embassy Baghdad, Iraq, Report No. ISP-IQO-06-50, August 2006, 3. That year, for example, five senior Finance Ministry officials, including the chief assistant to the director general for accounting, were sentenced to three years in prison for spending unauthorized funds. United Press International, "Iraqi Finance Staff Jailed for Corruption," December 20, 2006, http://www.politicalgateway.com/news/read/54031/.

[75] Karen DeYoung and Walter Pincus, "Corruption in Iraq 'Pernicious,' State Dept. Official Says," *Washington Post*, October 16, 2007, A13; U.S. Department of State, Untitled Report with heading of "Sensitive but Unclassified: Not for Distribution to Personnel Outside the US Embassy in Baghdad, Iraq," 2007, 2. On this report, see "Draft Report: Iraq Government 'Not Capable' of Fighting Corruption," CNN.Com, September 27, 2007, http://articles.cnn.com/2007-09-27/world/iraq.draft.report_1_anti-corruption-iraq-s-commission-iraqi-government?_s=PM:WORLD/.

[76] There are numerous reports on the failure of the Coalition civilian and military authorities to create proper internal financial controls on the spending of U.S. and Iraqi funds. In addition to

Iraqi DFI money.[77] Corruption emerged in the Iraqis' management and spending of the Iraqi budget.[78] Corruption occurred in the transmission and cash management of funds, in awarding contracts, in procurement, in the failure to maintain records required to track missing funds, in the overspending and padding of contracts, in underperformed and uncompleted projects, in the lack of credible and systematic auditing of Coalition and Iraqi money. Looking specifically at the Iraqi budget, the International Budget Partnership "Open Budget Survey 2010," a measure of transparency, accessibility, and oversight, all of which contributed to controlling corruption, ranked Iraq's budget 91st of 94 countries.[79] The survey generously noted that the budget document did indeed outline the allocation of funds and where they would be directed, but the government rarely produced timely or credible information on how those funds were spent.

The Iraqi institutions created by the CPA to control the "explosion" of corruption taking place in the ministries and throughout Iraq lacked administrative capacity and the political backing of their government.[80] Prime Minister al-Maliki designated 2008 a "Year of Reconstruction and Anticorruption." That year, Salam Adhoob, former chief CPI investigator, informed the U.S. Senate that the cost of corruption and waste reached some $18 billion, half of which came from the misuse of IRRF money. Moreover, "there are powerful people in Iraq who do not want this story to be told. I investigated corruption in Iraq for three years, but eventually had to flee the country because of numerous

SIGIR reports, there are studies of financial controls conducted by the Department of Defense's audit units. For example, see Mary L. Ugone, Deputy Inspector General, "Accountability Over Several Funds to Support the Iraq War, Including the Iraq Security Forces Fund, the Commander's Emergency Response Program, and the Seized and Vested Assets for the Iraqi People," offered in testimony before the Committee on Oversight and Government Reform, U.S. House of Representatives, May 28, 2008, and U.S. Department of Defense, Inspector General, "Internal Controls over Payments Made in Iraq, Kuwait, and Egypt," Report No. D-2008-098, May 28, 2008. On the failure to maintain proper controls over contracting, see, for example, Commission on Wartime Contracting in Iraq and Afghanistan, "At What Cost? Contingency Contracting in Iraq and Afghanistan, Interim Report to Congress," Washington, DC, June 2009.

[77] See, for example, Office of the Special Inspector General for Iraq Reconstruction, "Development Fund for Iraq: Department of Defense Needs to Improve Financial and Management Controls," SIGIR-10-020, Arlington, VA, July 27, 2010. SIRIG's audit found that the Defense Department failed to create bank accounts and provide oversight of $8.7 billion of DFI money. Ernesto Londono, "Pentagon Faulted on Control of Fund," *Washington Post*, July 27, 2010, A15.

[78] See, for example, Ali A. Allawi, *The Occupation of Iraq: Winning the War, Losing the Peace, op. cit.*, chapter 20, on massive corruption in the Iraqi Ministry of Defense budget.

[79] International Budget Partnership, "Open Budget Survey 2010," October 19, 2010, http://internationalbudget.org/files/2010_Full_Report-English.pdf/. This ranking might actually be seen as a mark of progress. Iraq was unranked in both the 2006 survey that ranked 59 countries, and the 2008 survey that ranked 85 countries. The budget survey considered Iraq to be deficient in, among other things, making various budget documents and reports accessible. The Ministry of Finance, unlike the Ministry of Planning, for example, lacked a Web site until 2009, which limited public access to and scrutiny of government budgets and records.

[80] Ali A. Allawi, *The Occupation of Iraq: Winning the War, Losing the Peace, op. cit.*, 353.

death threats against me and my family.... Thirty-one of my co-workers were murdered in retaliation against our efforts."[81] In testimony before the U.S. House of Representatives, Rahdi al-Radhi, the former director of the CPI, asserted that his office identified some $11 billion in fraud and bribery taking place in the ministerial system. "Most ministries are involved. Some officials, such as the minister of defense, have been dismissed, but we have about $4 billion in corruption cases [and] $2 billion in cases involving the Interior Ministry."[82]

The minister of the Interior referred to by al-Radhi was Baqir al-Zubeidi, who Maliki appointed finance minister in 2007. The State Department reported that as Interior minister al-Zubeidi employed anticorruption rules more as a form of internal organizational control than to police corruption, as "he developed a reputation for ruthlessness in applying the anticorruption laws to control his staff. CPI is powerless to prevent this type of abuse."[83] In 2008, al-Zubeidi called for the CPI's abolition, claiming its investigations impeded budget execution. "The Commission has intimidated the ministers who are not opting for avoiding involvement in large-scale projects," said al-Zubeidi, "so that they might not end up accused of corruption charges."[84]

Both Adhoob and al-Radhi asserted that the Maliki government obstructed the CPI. "Prime Minister al-Maliki routinely blocked corruption investigations and directed government officials not to cooperate with our efforts," said Adhoob. "Ministers and other top government officials routinely blocked investigative efforts and threatened CPI employees."[85] Al-Radhi produced documents showing that al-Maliki's chief of staff interfered with CPI activities, saying, "We received different secret orders blocking [the] prosecution of former and current ministers."[86] By the end of 2009, just 397 Iraqis had been convicted

[81] Salam Adhoob, "An Inside View of the 'Second Insurgency': How Corruption and Waste Are Undermining the U.S Mission in Iraq," U.S. Senate Democratic Policy Committee Hearing, September 22, 2008.
[82] Corey Flintoff, "Iraqi Watchdog Official Alleges High-Level Corruption," NPR, September 29, 2008. http://www.npr.org/templates/story/story.php?storyId=14245376&sc=emaf/. Also see James Glanz and Riyadh Mohammed, "Premier of Iraq Is Quietly Firing Fraud Monitors," *New York Times*, November 18, 2008, http://www.nytimes.com/2008/11/18/world/middleeast/18maliki.html?/.
[83] U.S. Department of State, Untitled Report with heading of "Sensitive but Unclassified: Not for Distribution to Personnel Outside the US Embassy in Baghdad, Iraq," 2007, 8.
[84] "Iraq's Finance Minister Demands Abolition of Public Integrity Commission," Voices of Iraq, Memri Economic Blog, "January 21, 2008, http://memrieconomicblog.org/bin/content.cgi?news=798/.
[85] Salam Adhoob, "An Inside View of the 'Second Insurgency': How Corruption and Waste Are Undermining the U.S Mission in Iraq," U.S. Senate Democratic Policy Committee Hearing, September 22, 2008.
[86] Corey Flintoff, "Iraqi Watchdog Official Alleges High-Level Corruption," NPR, September 29, 2008. http://www.npr.org/templates/story/story.php?storyId=14245376&sc=emaf/.

of corruption charges by the CPI since its founding in 2004.[87] In 2010, Transparency International's "Corruption Perception Index" ranked Iraq 175 of 178 countries on its measures of corruption, the worst in the Middle East and North African regions.[88] Finally, in a positive development, perhaps in response to the February and March demonstrations taking place throughout Iraq, the Parliament on April 18, 2011, struck Article 136B from the Iraqi Criminal Code. The Article permitted ministers and other top officials to stop investigations of their own ministries by the Board of Supreme Audit, CPI, and IIG. Ministers employed Article 136B 54 times in 2009 and 95 times in 2010. At the same time, however, the Parliament rescinded this law on two other occasions, only to resurrect it, apparently to accommodate Iraq's leadership.[89]

COORDINATION OF COALITION ASSISTANCE PROGRAMS

As challenging as Iraqi resistance proved to be to the success of the Coalition's various capacity-building programs, the lack of a unified and coherent strategy and ongoing coordination problems undermined the Coalition's efforts to build Iraqi budget execution. The absence of a unified approach for building capital budget execution during the CPA stemmed from its preoccupation with other budgetary issues, including the crafting of the FY 2003 and FY 2004 budgets, drafting budget-related CPA orders, negotiating with international donors to reduce Iraq's sovereign debt, and paying government wages and pensions through the operating budget. Spending the Iraqi capital budget did not take center stage until after the CPA disbanded. Following the CPA's departure, Treasury downgraded its presence in Iraq to a single attaché. The attaché cobbled together a small staff of some ten non-agency personnel to fill the agency's liaison role with the Ministry of Finance and the Central Bank of Iraq. To analyze budgetary issues, the attaché relied on two or three seconded staff who rotated through the unit from the Iraq Reconstruction Management Office.[90] Treasury left the details of the budget to the Iraqis. "The U.S.

---

[87] Mark Santora, "Pervasive Corruption Rattles Iraq's Fragile State," *New York Times*, October 29, 2009. http://www.nytimes.com/2009/10/29/world/middleeast/29corrupt.html/.

[88] Transparency International, "Corruptions Perceptions Index 2010 Results," 2010, http://www.transparency.org/policy_research/surveys_indices/cpi/2010/results/.

[89] "Iraq's Parliament Repeals Article Used to Block Corruption Investigations," Musings on Iraq, April 26, 2011, http://musingsoniraq.blogspot.com/2011/04/iraqs-parliament-repeals-article-used.html/.

[90] The attaché also served as the director of the Iraq Reconstruction Management Office, Office for Financial and Fiscal Affairs. Other than the attaché, only one or two of the Treasury office staff in Baghdad consisted of regular Treasury professionals. The attaché, using his initiative, filled out the staff from State Department contractors and temporary Iraq Reconstruction Management Office 3161 excepted service employees. Kevin Taecker, "Treasury/IRMO-FFA Staffing and Resources for Continuity of Coverage," U.S. Treasury Department Financial Attaché, Baghdad, January 3, 2006. On 3161s, see U.S. Code 3161 – Title 5: Government Organization and Employees, January 2004. Also see Jeremiah S. Pam, "The Treasury Approach to State-Building and Institution Strengthening Assistance: Experience in Iraq and Broader

government wasn't approving [the] budget on a line-by-line basis," said an attaché. "We were concerned about some big top-line issues, like the amount allocated for security forces, and direct provincial budget allocations.... Budget formulation was in some ways the easier part of Iraqi budget matters, because the budgets were being formulated at a time of rising oil prices and expanding budgets, and significantly, across-the-board under execution of budgets."[91] Budget execution grew in importance, however, and to create some type of interagency cooperation, in 2006 the attaché established the Budget Execution Group to try to improve communication and doctrine among Coalition partners and contractors.

As Iraqi budget execution emerged as a high Coalition priority, State, Defense, USAID and other agencies separately expanded their ministerial capacity-building efforts. The coordination problem identified by Treasury was that each of these agencies and their contractors approached budget execution in their own way, with each effort starting anew as personnel rotated in and out of Iraq. "When we started," an attaché remarked, "everyone was all over the map. The general dynamic was that this was a problem that plagued Iraq from the very beginning, you have the tyranny of turnover, and you have new people coming in and not having any baseline knowledge."[92]

The absence of shared doctrine, the lack of communication, the constant turnover in personnel, and the inherent organizational biases and modes of operating, all contributed to a history of independent decision making and action. "USAID hired from the beginning on a lot of contracts and was off and running for years now," a Treasury OTA staffer observed, "whether it's RTI governance with the provinces or issues they were doing even before PRTs. Then before we had *Tatweer*, we had the CPA with their advisors. Treasury OTA is used to doing its own work with Ministries of Finance."[93] Although it was an important attempt to build coordination, without firm authority over these other stakeholders the Budget Execution Group served principally as a discussion group rather than as a policy-making or agenda-setting body. A GAO report noted the absence of such a force in setting policy, declaring that "The implementation of U.S. efforts to help build the capacity of Iraqi national government over the past four years has been characterized by multiple U.S. agencies leading individual efforts, without overarching direction from a lead entity or strategic

Implications," *Special Report*, 216, Washington, DC: United States Institute of Peace, October 2008, 9.

[91] Interview with Treasury Department official, April 7, 2009.

[92] *Ibid.*

[93] Interview with Treasury Department official, October 28, 2008. Coordination problems with RTI apparently began with ORHA. "Without coordinating with ORHA, the CPA, and the MSCs [major subordinate commands], RTI began its mission in late April [2003] when it started work in Basra." Celeste J. Ward, "The Coalition Provisional Authority's Experience with Governance in Iraq: Lessons Identified," *Special Report*, 139, Washington, DC: United States Institute of Peace, May 2005, 4.

approach that integrates their efforts."[94] By itself, an understaffed Treasury unit with its *ad hoc* Budget Execution Group could not counter the centrifugal force of agencies and contractors conducting capacity building in their own way. The Coalition clearly required additional centralizing authority to lend programmatic coherence to their efforts.

In 2007, following the release of the New Way Forward strategy and the 17th Benchmark, the Embassy and the Treasury mounted new efforts to strengthen interagency coordination. In February, Ambassador Crocker created the position of Minister for Economic Affairs and Coordinator for Economic Transition in Iraq, first held on a temporary basis by Tim Carney. Charles Ries arrived in Iraq in July to assume authority over the key U.S. civilian agencies principally engaged in economic reconstruction and development activities, including budget execution. "What I did," explained Ries, "was, I made all of the eight or nine agencies that worked for me sit down a couple of times a week with me, and then twice a week with Ambassador Crocker and the military, and we made sure we were on the same wavelength, and that our projects were complementary and reinforcing."[95] Ries's position enabled him to force the agencies to meet and attempt to work out their differences, with the aim of producing a more harmonized set of programs and tactics for boosting Iraqi capital spending. Also in 2007, the Treasury stepped up its presence in Iraq with a "surge" of twelve extra OTA staff, including several who worked on budget issues, and it attempted to enhance its efforts at interagency coordination. With ambassadorial support, in June 2008 the attaché formed a new coordinating committee called the Public Finance Management Action Group (PFMAG), which, like the Budget Execution Group, provided a place for stakeholders to discuss budget execution techniques and policy. At these meetings, an attaché described, "people would showcase what they were doing, and other people could see how they fit into the puzzle. When there were new budget regulations, we would brief them and distribute them, so these guys would be on top of stuff."[96] Not until late 2007

---

[94] U.S. Government Accountability Office, "Stabilizing and Rebuilding Iraq: U.S. Ministry Capacity Development Efforts Need an Overall Integrated Strategy to Guide Efforts and Manage Risk," GAO-08-117, Washington, DC, October 2007, 8.

[95] Interview with Charles Ries, Minister for Economic Affairs and Coordinator for Economic Transition in Iraq, February 2, 2010.

[96] Interview with Treasury Department official, February 23, 2009. Many observers comment that PFMAG did not coalesce as a group until 2009. Said a contractor in 2009: "What gets in your way, you put thirty people around the Budget Execution Group or the PFMAG table, and they all want to be the hero that saved Iraq. It's so hard to coordinate all of those people." Because the Iraqi budget statistics varied so greatly, "Nobody had the same set of numbers, and that makes it really hard in a meeting to say what budget execution is like. 'We say it's 20 percent,' 'We say it's 30 percent.' Depending upon your power base, 'The ministries are better.' 'No, the provinces are better.' It's hard to corral all of those people." Said a Treasury official in 2008: "The coordination of all these things together was something, and there are a lot of battles and personalities. AID versus State versus Treasury, and then Defense coming in. The idea of the PFMAG was to try and overcome all of these and bring people together, and it is still getting its legs here."

into 2008 and then 2009 did the presence of someone serving at the Embassy with ministerial rank to coordinate economic reconstruction activities, the existence of PFMAG, and the charge to the Embassy's Iraq Transition Assistance Office (ITAO) to manage capacity development programs, did there slowly emerge some centralized institutional coordination for the various agencies and contractors engaged in building Iraqi budget execution.[97] Nonetheless, said an attaché, "these coordination problems are deep and profound, and extraordinarily frustrating," as turf battles, organizational barriers, and informational stovepipes between and among agencies, contractors, and the Iraqis continued to plague Coalition assistance programs.[98]

The endemic nature of the coordination problem may be seen in the presumably simple effort of developing a harmonized set of training material to teach Iraqis how to understand their budgetary system and execute their budget. Because of their proprietary interests, however, communications among agencies and contractors often proved to be limited, and the coordination and sharing of training materials rare. "This business, I will be real frank with you," said a Grant Thornton program officer employed by the Defense Department, "it's kind of cutthroat. Even the USAID guys looked at us as encroaching on their space. We were identified with DOD, and so obviously we didn't understand capacity building. We did not fit their mold of a group of PhDs who had studied capacity building. We were business guys.... They really did not want us in that space."[99] On four occasions, the contractor reported, he hired private security services to visit RTI to share training material, but "every time we went, they did not share their syllabus with us." When asked if his training materials corresponded with those of other firms, an MSI senior official replied that he had not reviewed the materials used by other firms, saying, "I don't know to what extent our materials overlap with theirs."[100] An RTI official responsible for overseeing his firm's budget execution efforts observed that "I am not familiar with the MSI materials."[101] Added another RTI officer, who compared RTI to MSI, but neglected to note that MSI operated in four provinces, "we have different clients. They work at the central level, we work at the

---

[97] On the condition of coordinating and measuring capacity development in 2007, see Office of the Inspector General for Iraqi Reconstruction, "Status of Ministerial Capacity Development in Iraq," SIGIR-06-045, Arlington, VA, January 30, 2007, iv: "As reported, multiple organizations and offices, have engaged the Iraqi ministries in numerous capacity-development activities. However, during the course of this review, we determined that U.S. government organizations introduced many of their activities without articulating clear achievable goals, especially the basis for measuring progress.... And, most important, no single U.S. government office or official is responsible or accountable for measuring and reporting on overall U.S. ministerial capacity-development progress."

[98] Interview with Treasury Department official, April 7, 2009.
[99] Interview with Grant Thornton official, November 11, 2009.
[100] Interview with MSI official, April 22, 2008.
[101] Interview with RTI official, July 15, 2008.

provincial and local level.... I don't think there is a seamless linkage between what they do and we do."[102] Meanwhile, State Department PRT team leaders exercised limited authority over RTI contractors, whose greater sense of obligation rested with USAID. "RTI is a USAID contract," declared a State official responsible for overseeing PRTs. "The division between USAID and the PRTs and the State Department generally is one of the glaring shortcomings of our involvement in Iraq."[103] Commenting on his difficulty of working with USAID, an exasperated Treasury attaché explained, "The whole contracting structure is designed to create stovepipes. So, an AID contractor is set up to talk only to AID program officers. Even when I was doing things that were directly related to an area of expertise and focus of an AID contractor ... RTI contractors, who were the American authorities on Iraqi provincial budget execution issues. It was very, very difficult for me to get my staff to be able to work directly, side-by-side, with the RTI people."[104] Part of the coordination problem may be intrinsically tied to relying on contractors to provide developmental assistance, suggested Ambassador Ries: "When you use contractors to deliver assistance, the contractors don't want to cooperate with each other, unless they are forced to by the donor, because they have the feeling they might be training for the guy who's going to bid the next RFP [request for proposal] that comes around, you're going to give experience to the other contractor, who might be a better competitor. That's very much of a downside for a contractor based system."[105] Summing up the firewalls that separate the contractors and agencies, a SIGIR official concluded in 2009, "There is no coordination. Every contractor, every agency, does pretty much what it is going to do."[106]

CONCLUSION

As shown in Chapter 6, the Coalition adopted the 17th Benchmark to induce and measure Iraqi budget execution. If the data are correct and a tripling of capital spending really occurred, which suggests a significant improvement taking place in Iraqi administrative capacity, it is nearly impossible to identify what efforts the Coalition made that contributed to this outcome. Although sponsoring agencies and their contractors separately claimed credit for the rise in spending, according to the oversight reports of the USAID Inspector General and SIRIG none of the major agencies, State, USAID, or Defense, created credible measures that demonstrated the link between MSI, Grant Thornton, and RTI's ministerial capacity-building efforts and Iraqi budget execution. When asked

---

[102] Interview with RTI official, April 16, 2008.
[103] Interview with State Department official, June 9, 2010.
[104] Interview with Treasury Department official, April 7, 2009.
[105] Interview with Charles Ries, Minister for Economic Affairs and Coordinator for Economic Transition in Iraq, February 2, 2010.
[106] Interview with SIGIR official, October 6, 2009.

whether USAID would attempt to assess the separate and interactive effects of these programs, an agency official responded:

What is the aggregation of all these streams of input? ... With so many vectors going into improving the performance of the Iraqi public sector in the last four years, what vector, what input really worked? ... The indispensable party to improving budget execution is the partner and the decision maker in the Iraqi bureaucracy. So it's going to be very difficult to disaggregate and to find out which point of entry worked.... We are not going to commission a *post hoc* retrospective that tries to disaggregate, well, the Brinkley Group was also involved in this ministry [together with a USAID contractor], and RTI kind of touched it down at the provincial level.... I doubt that the data quality is going to allow the running of that type of regression analysis and be able to factor that out.[107]

Further complicating any assessment of an organization's contribution is that their separate histories vary in terms of when they began their capacity-building activities or how long it took for them to develop an effective working relationship with the Iraqis. For example, a SIGIR report stated that MSI's "implementation of the *Tatweer* program was slow" and did not have a sizable presence in Iraq until 2007, and the movements of the PRTs with their RTI consultants were greatly restricted until mid-2007 when a security agreement could be reached between State and Defense.[108] Although they worked with a number of important ministries, neither MSI nor Grant Thornton gained access to the Ministry of Finance, an obviously vital agency for building Iraqi ministerial capacity and budget execution competencies. Given these experiences, it is fair to say that meaningful budget execution capacity building by MSI and Grant Thornton did not begin at the ministerial level until mid-2007, with their intervention beginning to peak in late 2008. RTI's activities in the provinces date from the earliest stages of the occupation, with their attention on budget execution becoming more focused in 2006, as that year the provinces were granted the right to submit reconstruction project requests to the ministries. The Grant Thornton contract expired in March 2010, the MSI Tatweer contract expired in January 2011, and the RTI Local Governance Program expired in June 2011. In the absence of clear metrics and evidence for success, however, each agency and contractor pointed to the overall increased spending as the result of its particular programs and training activities. Perhaps the best that can be said is that the cumulative effect of all the various capacity-development programs promoted the growth in investment spending.

Budget execution became the ubiquitous metric for evaluating success in Iraq, not only for Coalition agencies and contractors, but for also for donor organizations. The World Bank, for example, employed $18 million from the Iraq Trust Fund, of which $14 million was spent on contractors, to finance its Public

---

[107] Interview with USAID official, November 9, 2010.
[108] Office of the Special Inspector General for Iraq Reconstruction, *Hard Lessons: The Iraq Reconstruction Experience*, Washington, DC: U.S. Government Printing Office, 2009, 266.

Finance Management Project. The project aimed at building procurement, cash management, and financial control systems and producing a new accounting manual. When evaluating progress against indicators, the only category measuring more than 20 percent accomplished was budget execution. Because the Iraqis increased capital spending by 10 percent, budget execution received a score of 100 percent.[109] How the Bank's small project aided budget execution sufficiently to claim credit for billions of dollars in increased capital spending when its other project components measured 15 and 20 percent, or how the Bank's contribution differed from the various Coalition capacity-building exercises, or whether improved security conditions encouraged investment spending, went unexplained. Simply put, the World Bank, as did Coalition agencies and their contractors, claimed credit for the same outcome because budget execution served as the most accessible and convenient measure that could be used to point to their success in reconstructing Iraq's institutions.

Even if these agencies, donors, and contractors contributed to the rise in budget execution, the boost in spending ultimately depended on the Iraqis. "The majority of success should be credited to the Iraqis," concluded a senior State Department official who worked with the PRTs. "At the end of the day, we need to be very humble on the impact we have had on them.... A lot of the problems we faced were solved by Iraqi decisions or Iraqi trends, Iraqi events, and not by us. I believe that's true of budget execution."[110] Moreover, as the nature of the capacity development programs evolved from fundamental training, the Iraqis increasingly bore the full responsibility for building up their budget execution capabilities. "We've more or less completed our basic task of training and basic functions of budget execution," an MSI officer responsible for the *Tatweer* program observed. "I say that because not only we have trained a sufficient number of people [more than one hundred thousand], but we've got a sufficient number of Iraqi trainers from Iraqi ministries that they can carry on the training themselves. That part is pretty much done."[111] The success of Iraqi budgeting, and whether they would maintain and employ the Coalition's budgetary rules, thus rested with the Iraqis themselves.

[109] World Bank, "World Bank Iraq Trust Fund Public Finance Management (TF094552/TF094654-P110862), Project Summary Sheet," Washington, D.C, September 2010, 46.
[110] Interview with State Department official, June 9, 2010.
[111] Interview with MSI official, April 22, 2008.

8

Iraqi Budgeting

The Coalition's invasion and occupation left the Iraqis with new budgetary institutions, the mandate to boost investment spending, an effort to build budgeting capacity, and donor requirements to develop budgetary processes consistent with international best practices. The Coalition Provisional Authority imposed rudimentary budgetary templates in the form of the 2003 and 2004 budgets, followed by a set of CPA-issued orders that defined the budgetary process, empowered the Ministry of Finance, and provided an initial framework for the central government's fiscal relations with provincial and local governments. The Coalition layered these changes in budgetary rules and organizations on Saddam Hussein's institutional arrangements, which Saddam, in turn, had layered on British and Ottoman budgetary practices. Then the June 2004 transfer of power raised critical questions about the success of the Coalition's budgetary state-building efforts in Iraq. Would the Iraqis accept, take ownership, and invest in the CPA's budgetary institutions, or abandon them? Would these rules and procedures be sustainable and serve the Iraqis in their efforts to make budgetary decisions in politically and economically difficult times? What budgetary decisions would they make? What political and economic obstacles confronted the Iraqis in their efforts to budget effectively? The answers to these questions and the practical successes and long-term sustainability of these freshly imposed institutions would be tested in day-to-day budgeting. This chapter provides a detailed examination of how the Iraqis' buy-in, ownership, and investment in the budgetary process occurred as they faced harsh fiscal challenges, ongoing security threats, and political instability. In this way, Iraq's ownership and continued use of these new budgetary rules, procedures, and organizations served as important tests of the Coalition's capacity to transform Iraqi institutions.

IRAQI OWNERSHIP OF THE CPA BUDGETARY PROCESS

The Iraqi government conceivably could have discarded or significantly modified the CPA's budgetary institutions following the June 2004 transfer of power, considering them nothing more than the vestige of an unwanted occupation. The Iraqis, however, preserved and took ownership of that process, maintaining it at least through the formulation and approval of the 2012 budget. Iraqi buy-in occurred for a number of reasons, including the reality of the ongoing occupation, Iraq's reliance on donor assistance and the requirements of aid conditionality, the rise of new Iraqi stakeholders in the budgetary process, and the fact that the CPA layered their new rules on existing Iraqi institutions, thus making their acceptance more palatable. In the context of the fairly rapid transfer of power from the Coalition to the Iraqis, this layering of institutions meant that some CPA reform efforts, such as the transformation of Iraq's paper-based bureaucratic culture and the possible termination of organizations such as the Ministry of Planning largely went unrealized. Most important, the Iraqis found the CPA's process useful in managing their ongoing fiscal and political matters, including the prickly issues related to fiscal decentralization and the division of oil revenues. The value offered by these new budgetary institutions simply outweighed the cost of replacing them. At the same time, Iraq continued to suffer from extensive budget execution problems and fiscal corruption that severely undermined reconstruction efforts and encouraged popular discontent with the government.

THE REALITY OF OCCUPATION

The Iraqis retained the CPA budget process, first, because as a matter of *realpolitik* Iraq remained an occupied country. In a practical sense this ensured that under the Coalition's watchful gaze Iraq's new constitution resembled some form of an acceptable democratic-republican framework, rather than revert to an unacceptable Saddam-like autocratic system of governance. So too did the broad practices of Iraq's administrative apparatus, including its budgetary institutions, processes, and rules. Following the transfer of sovereignty the Iraqis immediately faced the challenge of developing the budgetary rules that would be incorporated into their new Constitution. The Constitution's Article 107 empowered Iraq's federal government with the authority to formulate the state's economic policies, including fiscal policy and the drafting of the national budget. Article 77 charged the President's Cabinet with drafting the budget, closing the accounts of the preceding year's budget, and developing the government's investment plans. Article 59 required the Council of Ministers to submit the draft budget and the closing account to the Council of Representatives, while specifying that the Council might transfer funds between budgetary accounts, reduce the size of the total budget, and propose increases in the size of the total budget. Article 117 directed that the national government allocate federal revenues to regional governments based on need and the region's share of the national population. To be sure, the Constitution left unresolved important questions regarding fiscal federalism, provincial government budget formulation, and the fundamental issue of the production, collection, and distribution of oil revenues. These broad Constitutional provisions, nevertheless, proved to be consistent with various CPA Orders, including Order 95, which outlined the formulation of the budget by the Ministries of Finance and Planning. This order directed the Ministry of Finance, in consultation with the Planning Ministry, to develop guidelines for the spending ministries in the preparation of their detailed budget proposals. Then the Finance Ministry, again in consultation with the Planning Ministry, would develop a draft budget for submission in September to the Council of Ministers for revisions and approval. The Council of Ministers would then send the draft budget to the Council of Representatives by October 10, with the goal of legislative approval and final approval by the Presidential Council by January 1, the beginning of the fiscal year.

THE CONSTRAINTS OF AID CONDITIONALITY

Second, the Iraqis' preservation of the CPA budgetary process reflected the pressures of aid conditionality. The International Monetary Fund and the World Bank's financial agreements required the Iraqis to adopt international best practices to reform their budgetary processes and financial controls. In the September 2004 IMF Emergency Post-Conflict Assistance agreement, for example, Iraq pledged to develop regulations that would strengthen the CPA budget laws to promote budget formulation.[1] The Iraqis also agreed to donor requirements that it adopt the IMF's chart of accounts to better categorize programs and track spending, as well as install the Financial Management Information System to track how these funds were allocated and managed. Although the Iraqis preserved the CPA's budgeting rules, the fulfillment of their promises to adopt the chart of accounts and FMIS came late, or not at all. In 2007, for example, the IMF Executive Board conducted a review of its $727 million 2005

---

[1] International Monetary Fund, "Use of Fund Resources: Request for Emergency Post-Conflict Assistance," Middle East and Central Asia Department, Washington, DC, September 24, 2004, 16. Also see International Monetary Fund, "Iraq: Letter of Intent, Memorandum of Economic and Financial Policies, and Technical Memorandum of Understanding," Baghdad, September 24, 2004, Point 38, 8. In addition, Iraqi promises to strengthen financial management may be found throughout various IMF staff evaluations of Iraqi compliance with various donor agreements beginning in 2004. So too is staff frustration with Iraqi progress, as, for example, the staff observation that "implementing the Financial Management Information System (FMIS) is proceeding slowly," in International Monetary Fund, "First and Second Reviews Under the Stand-By Arrangement, Financing Assurances Review, and Request for Waiver of Nonobservance and Applicability of Performance Criteria," Middle East and Central Asia Department, Washington, DC, July 17, 2006, 9.

Stand-By-Arrangement with Iraq. The Board agreed to grant a waiver to Iraq for its failure to audit ministerial accounts held by the Central Bank of Iraq and implement the chart of accounts due to the violence spreading throughout the country and because of the lack of ministerial capacity.[2]

In 2009, the World Bank and the Iraqis agreed to a capacity-building effort that among other projects aimed to enhance budget formulation, budget execution, and cash management capacities.[3] After a three-year effort the Iraqis finally instituted the IMF's chart of accounts, though the actual use of this new accounting system varied among the ministries. A report issued by the World Bank Iraq Trust Fund in 2009 found "there is still considerable variability in the extent to which the system is understood and applied by the staff of spending units. As a result, the Ministry of Finance is required to employ a mapping system to convert data supplied by spending units into a consistent format. Moreover, delays in reporting occur routinely, resulting in weak management control and supervision of spending both within the spending units and at the level of the central ministries."[4] To receive the IMF's $3.6 billion loan, in 2010 Iraqi leadership pledged that "Over the next two years, we intend to transform and modernize our public financial system (PFM) system. Late last year, in consultation with the IMF and the World Bank, we adopted a three-year action plan that identified priority measures in the areas of budget preparation, execution, and reporting; cash management; public procurement; and the accounting framework."[5] The Iraqis promised to standardize the administration of accounting rules throughout the government. Once again, the government committed "to undertake an assessment of the functionality" of the FMIS, despite its repeated failure to make that system come to fruition.[6] The Coalition simply failed to gain the Iraqis' acceptance of FMIS and move the bureaucracy in a significant way

---

[2] International Monetary Fund, "IMF Executive Board Completes Fifth Review of Financing Assurances Under Iraq's Stand-By Arrangement, and Approves Three-Month Extension of the Arrangement to December 2007," Press Release No. 07/175, Washington, DC, August 2, 2007.

[3] The World Bank initiated its broad-based economic capacity-building project in 2004, which included fiscal and financial management. On World Bank engagement in building Iraqi fiscal management, see, for example, World Bank, "Rebuilding Iraq: Economic Reform and Transition," Economic and Social Development Unit, Washington, DC, February 2006. Also see the World Bank's 2009 grant proposal, "Emergency Project Paper for a Proposed Grant in the Amount of US $18.0 Million from the World Bank Iraq Trust Fund to the Republic of Iraq for the Project Finance Management Project, June 27, 2009," Report No. 46861-IQ, Social and Economic Development Sector Unit, World Bank, Washington, DC, June 27, 2009.

[4] World Bank Iraq Trust Fund, "Update to IRFFI Donor Committee: Public Expenditure and Institutional Assessment, Key Issues in Public Financial Management," Washington, DC, February 18, 2009, 2.

[5] Baqir S. Jabr Al-Zubaydi and Sinan Al-Shabibi, "Letter of Intent and Iraq: Memorandum of Economic and Financial Policies for 2010–11," Baghdad, Ministry of Finance and Central Bank of Iraq, February 8, 2010, 7.

[6] *Ibid.*, 8.

from its paper-based culture. Nonetheless, the Iraqis' ongoing reliance on donor funds ensured they would be subjected to requirements calling for continued improvements and some degree of scrutiny by international organizations of Iraqi budget preparation, budget execution, and fiscal management.

THE PERSISTENCE OF IRAQI INSTITUTIONS

Third, the Iraqis accepted and took ownership of the budgetary process because in many ways the process at its deeper levels remained fundamentally Iraqi in design. The CPA rule structure did not completely replace the budgetary process that preceded the invasion, nor did CPA authorities intend to do so. The CPA team that drafted the 2003 and 2004 budgets intentionally drew on the existing relationship between ministries and budgetary procedures rather than fully imposing their own vision of proper budgeting. As David Oliver reflected, "What I was trying to do was use the Iraqi system so that the Iraqis could carry it out."[7] Iraqi procedures for both budget formulation and budget execution often remained intact. Even when American leaders viewed elements of the Iraqi ministerial system with disdain, they lacked either the time or the authority to carry out desired changes. Top Coalition officials, for instance, clearly viewed the Iraqi Ministry of Planning as a distasteful remnant of Saddam's system of Soviet central planning. "A ministry of planning is the hallmark of a centrally planned economy," U.S. Ambassador to Iraq Ryan Crocker concluded. "It didn't work well for them during the Saddam years, God knows, and I'm not sure it would ever work well for them. We certainly did not press for its formal abolishment, it would not have been appropriate to do so, and politically very difficult, but if it stays moribund, then no bad thing."[8] The transfer of power occurred before steps could be taken to eradicate that Ministry, and after the transfer the Coalition lacked the authority to impose this change, certainly by the time Crocker became ambassador in 2007. The Coalition then faced the paradox of being forced to build up an undesirable ministry. A contractor from the firm Grant Thornton charged with aiding the Planning Ministry described the situation: "It became apparent how broken the Ministry of Planning was. So we started working on their planning, their ability to do feasibility studies, oversight, and do contracting on the back end. I went to a [Coalition] budget execution meeting [at the U.S. Embassy].... They said they were not looking to go back to the days of Saddam and central planning. The American side was a little bit flummoxed. They really didn't like the Ministry of Planning. They really didn't want to make it have any power. And here I was helping the Ministry of Planning."[9] So despite Coalition discomfort, the Iraqis retained the Ministry of

[7] Interview with David Oliver, June 9, 2007.
[8] Interview with Ryan Crocker, September 24, 2010.
[9] Interview with Grant Thornton official, November 11, 2009.

Planning and Development Cooperation, though its budgetary and fiscal authority as outlined in CPA Order 95 remained secondary to that of the Ministry of Finance.[10]

THE RISE OF NEW BUDGETARY CLAIMANTS

Fourth, the maintenance of the CPA budgetary rules and process reflected the deepening integration of new budgetary claimants into that system. Budgeting served as a critical form of power sharing that leveraged broader political agreements in Iraq. As described by the political scientist Aaron Wildavsky, budgets reflect broad political forces that include the rise of new interest groups. These potential stakeholders seek political legitimacy and make claims on public resources through the budgetary process. Politically successful claimants gain a "fair share" of public expenditures, with this share then incorporated into the budget base, or the total budget that is the sum of all fair shares. Gaining entry into the base, for Wildavsky, "means more than just getting it in the budget for a particular year. It means establishing the expectation that the expenditure will continue, that it is accepted as part of what will be done. . . . 'Fair share' means not only the base an agency has established but also the expectation that it will receive some proportion of funds, if any, which are to be increased or decreased below the base of the various governmental agencies."[11] The implication of Wildavsky's thesis is that budgetary claimants, such as ministries, provincial governments, and other interests, come to expect their fair shares in the overall budget base. These claimants then become stakeholders and owners of the institutions and processes that produce these budgetary rewards. In Iraq, these new stakeholders not only sought fiscal benefits through the budget, but more importantly they sought to strengthen the institutions that constituted the budgetary process. They sought to formalize the Parliament's oversight responsibilities, build its technical capabilities to participate in the process, and press the prime minister and Council of Ministers for greater transparency, accountability, and compliance with the CPA budgetary process. One example of this legislative capacity building proved to be reminiscent of the 1920s, when the new Iraqi parliament created during King Faisal's rule established a number of

---

[10] Despite this Coalition displeasure with the Ministry of Planning, the Ministry at times acted to promote Coalition efforts, such as by adopting regulations to implement CPA Order 87 "Public Contracts" in the form of the "2007 Implementing Regulations for Government Contracts" and the "2008 Instructions for Government Contracts' Execution." The CPA order and these regulations largely reflected international best practices and were supported by international donor organizations. At the regulatory level, therefore, examples can be found of the Iraqis creating rules that promoted CPA orders related to the budgetary process. See OECD, "Improving Transparency within Government Procurement Procedures in Iraq: OECD Benchmark Report," Paris, March 5, 2010.

[11] Aaron Wildavsky, *The Politics of the Budgetary Process*, Boston: Little, Brown and Company, 1984, 17.

committees, including a Finance Committee, to coordinate their consideration of the budget. Iraq's contemporary Council of Representatives followed this course in 2006 when they established twenty-four standing committees, including the new Financial Committee charged with reviewing and developing counterproposals to the Council of Minister's budget.

THE PRESSURES OF POLITICAL AND ECONOMIC UNCERTAINTY

Fifth, the exigencies surrounding the formulation and adoption of each new budget deepened the Iraqis' reliance on the existing framework and limited their options in developing alternative systems. The budgetary process served as a coordinating mechanism for developing government priorities, allocating resources, setting economic plans and oil prices, selecting capital projects, planning for oil production efforts, engaging the provincial governments, resolving disputes between stakeholders, and responding to donor demands. Furthermore, as will be shown throughout the rest of this chapter, the process offered procedural continuity and regularity in policy making in the face of security threats and violence, the rapid overall growth in operational and investment programs, extreme swings in oil prices, rising budget deficits, and the long uncertainty stemming from Iraq's 2010 electoral stalemate.

THE IRAQI BUDGET PROCESS AT WORK, 2005–2011

The following examination of the seven budgets the Iraqi government enacted from 2005 to 2011 suggests a process of institutional layering. The Iraqis built their budgets on the foundation of the one preceding it, with CPA Order 95 serving as the architecture for the overall budgetary process. This institutional layering is reflected in the emerging Iraqi ownership of the budgetary process, the rise of new budgetary participants and claimants, and the growing Parliamentary institutionalization of the budget. The great test of the Iraqis' acceptance and outright ownership of the CPA budgetary process came from their actual and continued use of that process under trying circumstances. During these years the Iraqis experienced several transitions in government, the rapid turnover of finance ministers, Coalition pressures to engage in massive spending for complex large-scale capital projects, a roller-coaster ride of rapidly fluctuating oil revenues and projected budget deficits, and then a nine-month absence of parliamentary government in the midst of political conflict over who would govern Iraq.

Each fiscal year challenged the Iraqis in different ways. In 2004, the Iraqis began drafting their 2005 budget while the CPA still remained in existence, and the exigencies of the moment left the new Iraq government with little choice other than to employ the CPA's budgetary process and largely follow the format of the CPA's 2004 budget. In 2005, under a new aggressive finance minister the Iraqis openly proclaimed their ownership of the budgetary process and the formulation of its 2006 fiscal priorities. In 2007, the Coalition pressured the

Iraqis to boost their capital expenditures, making this the 17th Benchmark for measuring success in Iraq. A dramatic spike in oil prices led to a large 2008 budget, followed by a significant supplemental budget. An equally dramatic drop in oil prices curtailed this exuberant spending, created huge budget deficits, and produced deep reductions in the 2009 budget. Although the 2010 budget reflected the stabilization of oil prices, Iraqi politics severely tested the budget process, as the political deadlock over who should lead the government interrupted the deliberations and passage of the 2011 budget. Consideration of the 2011 budget also offered one more test of the fiscal relationship between Baghdad and the Kurdistan Regional Government.

What follows is a more detailed assessment of the 2005–2011 Iraqi budgetary process. Though the reader may wish to bypass this degree of technical budgetary information surrounding the formulations of these seven budgets, examining these sometimes seemingly separate events leads to a greater understanding of the incremental process of institutional layering. Budgeting is an annual process. Through annual repetition and adaptation to incremental challenges, these budgeting rules, practices, and procedures become increasingly institutionalized, legitimate, and layered. The obstacles faced and overcome during the formulation of each of these fiscal years resulted in the cumulative building of a budgetary system the Iraqis accepted as politically legitimate and administratively credible.

1. THE IRAQI 2005 TRANSITION BUDGET

A critical step in the layering of CPA institutional rules on the budgetary process was their actual use by the Iraqis. Despite the transition from the CPA and the Iraqi Governing Council to the Transition Government, as well as the transition in finance ministers that took place during the formulation process, the Iraqis succeeded in drafting and adopting a budget. Work began on Iraq's first budget in May 2004, a month before the transfer of power occurred. Finance Minister Kamil Mubdir al-Gailani initiated the 2005 budget process during the CPA's last month of existence. Appointed by the Iraqi Governing Council in September 2003, al-Gailani served primarily to execute David Oliver's 2003 and 2004 budgets. Following the June transfer of power, the Interim Iraqi Government appointed its own finance minister, Adil Abdul-Mahdi. Abdul-Mahdi, a member of the powerful Shi'a Supreme Islamic Iraqi Council party, served as finance minister for less than a year, from June 4, 2004, through April 6, 2005, when he became Iraq's first vice president under the Transitional Government. During this brief term Abdul-Mahdi faced the difficult task of overseeing the completion of the 2005 budget's formulation while reconciling the CPA's budgetary rules with the emergence of a new Iraqi government.[12]

---

[12] Though viewed by some as hostile, an American Treasury attaché described Abdul-Mahdi as "remarkably competent. No great finance experience, but good common sense. [He] relied

TABLE 8.1. *CPA-Drafted 2004 and Iraqi-Drafted 2005, 2006, and 2007 Budgets (all figures are in billions of Iraqi dinars)*

	2004	2005	2006	2007
Spending Allocations				
Operations	25,432.3	28,431	41,691	39,062
Investments	3,797.5	7,550	9,272	12,665
Total allocations	29,889.8	35,981	50,963	51,727
Revenues				
Oil	21,262.0	25,623	42,106	41,103
State-owned enterprises		2,250	181	
Reconstruction levy (import duties)	172.5	225	600	
Personal income tax	7.5	65	90	
Corporate income tax		25	1,422	
Civil service pension contribution	101.4	197	144	
Other Revenues	191.5	573	849	961
Total Revenues	21,729.1	28,958	45,392	42,064
Deficit/Surplus	−8,160.7	−7,023	−5,571	−9,663

Source: Coalition Provisional Authority, Iraq Ministry of Finance.

Building on the framework of line items and account structure set out in the CPA's 2004 budget, the 2005 budget first outlined the finance minister's strengthened position in the budgetary process outlined by CPA Order 95. The budget document asserted the finance minister's rights in a variety of financial transactions, including the authority to allocate reserve funds, authorize the use of advanced funds for capital projects, and review and approve the planning budgets of state-owned enterprises. The budget proposal called for reducing the budget deficit, increasing investment allocations, and diversifying Iraq's revenue base. Declaring that "the 2005 budget represents the minimum level required for government work to continue in the best possible way," the budget proclaimed the value of market-based economies and the failure of Saddam's Soviet-style version.[13] As shown in Table 8.1, the budget called for total spending of 35.9 trillion Iraqi dinars (ID) ($23 billion),

effectively on his support staff. Strong party affiliations, but non-sectarian in how he operated the ministry. [He] willingly took on the very tough job of re-Iraqizing the ministry. Of course the CPA had written the new budget law. It was not automatic that all aspects of that law would be implemented in all ways. So through trial and error it was Abdul-Mahdi's challenge to bring the operations of the MOF into conformity with the law, as well as with preexisting law.... There was a very tough transition period." Much of the continuity in formulating the budget between the Al-Gailani and Abdul-Mahdi administrations rested with Aziz Jaffar, who served as deputy minister under Al-Gailani and senior advisor to Abdul-Mahdi. Abdul-Mahdi relied on Aziz to develop the budget, while he spent much of his time on Paris Club debt management negotiations. Interview with Treasury Department official, April 7, 2009.

[13] Ministry of Finance, "Government General Budget for Year 2005," Baghdad, September 2004, 7, 4.

of which 28.4 trillion ID ($18 billion) would be spent on operational expenses, and 7.5 trillion ID ($5 billion) on investments. Though both operational and investment spending grew, with the investment allocation increasing by 48 percent over 2004, the projected increase in revenues enabled the government to run a deficit 41 percent lower than the preceding year. Oil provided 88 percent of projected revenues, with oil priced at $26 a barrel with an expected 1.8 million barrels of oil exported per day. The Parliament approved the budget in late January or early February, and as the last step in the approval process, the Presidency Council adopted the budget on February 16, a month and a half after the beginning of the fiscal year.

Summary

The formulation and adoption of the 2005 budget by the Iraqis, despite the challenges posed by a transfer in the position of minister of finance and the transition to a new government, proved to be a significant accomplishment. This budget, which primarily funded operational expenses, nonetheless benefited from the Coalition's technical assistance, even as the CPA came to an end. Iraq's first "ownership" budget came the following year, with the formulation of the 2006 budget.

2. THE 2006 OWNERSHIP BUDGET

Although the Iraqis might be granted credit for producing a credible 2005 budget given the tremendous obstacles faced by Abdul-Mahdi in preparing and gaining political approval for the budget, the budget's harshest critic proved to be the next finance minister, Ali Allawi. Allawi served as Minister of Trade and Minister of Defense under the Iraqi Governing Council and then replaced Abdul-Mehdi in May 2005.

Allawi's Declaration of Ownership

The drafting of the 2006 budget took place under Allawi's leadership, and this version served as the breakthrough ownership budget for Iraq. "The 2006 budget," he recalled, "was all generated internally by the Ministry of Finance, trying to use the budget as a resource allocation, rather than just as an accounting convention.... That was the first time that a budget of this kind was made. I basically had to do it myself with two other people who did the numbers.... On the macro side, on the allocation side, they did not have any idea where this money was supposed to go to. Their idea was to take last year's budget and divide it up again. So I tried to introduce resource allocation criteria and sectorial choices. All of these things were done unilaterally, because nobody else was prepared or able to discuss them in a meaningful way. Nobody in Iraq had been trained to think this way. Most of these decisions had been done by Saddam. The U.S. Treasury did not play much of a role, neither did the U.S. Embassy."[14] In the Ministry of Finance's draft 2006 budget, Allawi declared that "the Budget is the only mechanism through which the government's fiscal and investment program, and its priorities and policies, can be manifested in a direct way." Prior budgets proved to be "linear in their form, based on the budgets of previous periods with little in the way of policies for revenue-generation, limiting entitlement programs, investment and sectoral prioritization, and social welfare reform."[15]

Unlike earlier budgets, the 2006 version would be formulated on new assumptions that avoided the "myth of the flood of donor cash that was going to solve Iraq's reconstruction problems."[16] Donor money, particularly American IRRF funds, and non-oil revenues would fall, security expenses would rise, and entitlement subsidies would become unsustainable. The public needed to be weaned off of their food and petroleum product subsidies, for example, and the budget would cut those programs by 25 percent. Most critically, Iraq required a massive increase in oil production to meet the costs of its reconstruction programs while reducing its budget deficit. The budget's operational spending grew by 47 percent and the investment component increased 23 percent over 2005, with the Ministry of Oil's capital budget growing by 18 percent. Iraq required this inflow of investment outlays because although the budget assumed oil prices of $46.61 a barrel with an export production of 1.65 million barrels per day, Allawi projected a lower production rate for 2006 due to sabotage and smuggling. As shown in Table 8.1, the total budget called for spending of 50.9 trillion ID ($34 billion), with 41.7 trillion ID ($27.8 billion) used for operational expenses and 9.2 trillion ID ($6.2 billion) designated for investment expenses. The projected deficit would drop by 21 percent, from 7 trillion ID in 2005 to 5.6 trillion ID in 2006, and be financed by cash assets held overseas, without borrowing or printing money.

In what proved to be a significant shift in promoting Iraqi fiscal federalism, the budget transferred some 3 trillion ID in planning and construction grants to the provincial government through the Accelerated Reconstruction and Development Program (ARDP). The provincial governors and councils directly controlled these funds, which were allocated to the provinces on the basis of population.

---

[14] Interview with Ali Allawi, May 15, 2007. A senior Treasury official concurred, assessed Allawi's contribution to the Iraqi budgeting process, saying that he "was the first to bring an Iraqi vision to the Ministry of Finance.... In the 2006 budget he took face on some of the institutional management issues with Finance. He tried to modernize the financial management system. He wrote an extensive treatise for the 2006 budget. It was very unfortunate he became ill at an IMF meeting. He was physically incapacitated and unable to be in Baghdad during the last couple months of his tenure, really about January 2006 to May 2006." Interview with Treasury Department official, February 23, 2009.

[15] Ali A. Allawi, "Strategy and Policy for the 2006 Budget," Ministry of Finance, Baghdad, 2005, 1.

[16] *Ibid.*

The 2006 budget, therefore, proved to be a noteworthy improvement over its predecessors. Allawi's 2006 budget deserves credit for boosting investment spending at both the central government and provincial levels. Allawi also initiated the Finance Ministry's adoption of the IMF's chart of accounts system to better manage and track government funds. Furthermore, Allawi later proudly wrote about his efforts to engage the issues of revenue generation and subsidies, noting that "no government since April 2003 had been able to present a meaningful program to tackle these problems.... a crude amateurism prevailed.... for the first time in modern Iraq's history, a budget was developed on the basis of an underlying economic vision."[17] He nonetheless neglected to consider that the CPA's 2004 budget also addressed both the revenue and subsidy issues, as well as the need to expand the budget's coverage beyond Saddam's distinction of breaking Iraq into its Center and South components, rather than all eighteen provinces, which Allawi also elected to do. Like the 2006 budget, the 2004 budget projected that revenues would be generated from a variety of sources to indicate the need to diversify Iraq's revenue base, including corporate and personal income taxes and taxes on interest income, although these taxes proved to be virtually uncollectible. Still, Allawi complained that prior budgets were simply "linear in form, based on the budgets of previous periods."

Summary

Although the 2006 budget is a technical improvement over its predecessors in that it provides more details, like the CPA budgets it retains the Saddam-era on- and off-budget distinctions for regular state-funded activities, such as the ministerial budgets, and the off-budget category for presumably "self-financing" entities, such as state-owned enterprises. Many ministries experienced incremental changes in their spending levels, based on prior year allocations, and, perhaps because the Ministry of Finance had not yet developed the capacity, the budget provided revenue and expenditure projections only for the coming fiscal year, rather than making multiyear spending estimates. Nevertheless, despite the challenges that accompanied the transfer of power, the transitions in government, and the installation of three finance ministers within a two-year period, the Iraqi government successfully formulated and adopted the 2005 and 2006 budgets.

3. THE 2007 BUDGET: BUDGETING UNDER THE 17TH BENCHMARK

The 2007 budget is noteworthy for the government's commitment under Coalition pressure to boost investment spending and the reaffirmation of the central position of the Finance Ministry in the formulation and execution of the budget.

---

[17] Ali A. Allawi, *The Occupation of Iraq: Winning the War, Losing the Peace*, New Haven: Yale University Press, 2007, 429.

More important, in terms of institutional development, the debates over this budget reflected the growing participation by the Council of Representatives in the oversight and engagement in the budget's formulation and administration, and the rising participation by the provinces and other interests as claimants in the budgetary process.

Budget Formulation

The budget, as shown in Table 8.1, then the largest in Iraqi history, continued to escalate the government's spending plans. The budget provided for 51.7 trillion ID ($41 billion) in expenditures, 42 trillion ID ($34 billion) in estimated revenues, and a projected 9 trillion ID ($7.3 billion) deficit. The deficit would be financed from prior year surpluses accumulated from the unspent 2005 and 2006 allocations and a rise in projected oil prices. Planning Minister Ali Ghalib Baban noted that the projected deficit "is more a theoretical deficit than realistic because the State has some cash reserves in the Development Fund for Iraq."[18] The budget included 12.6 trillion ID ($10 billion) for investment spending, a figure that complied with the American 17th Benchmark target, an amount 37 percent greater than the 2006 allocation and nearly 70 percent larger than 2005. Commenting on the size of the investment allocations and Iraq's other budgetary needs, Prime Minister Nouri al-Maliki observed, "This year's budget does not meet all the government's ambitions. We hoped that the largest sums would be channeled into the field of investment, but it is a realistic budget that took into consideration Iraq's exceptional circumstances."[19]

Powers of the Ministry of Finance

Responsibility for drafting the 2007 budget fell to Baqir Jabr al-Zubeidi, Iraq's third finance minister in three years. Al-Zubeidi's appointment brought some stability to the Ministry, however, as he served in that position through the formulation of the 2011 budget. Much of the 2007 budget's text highlighted the Finance Ministry's central role in the country's public finances. The budget law stated that appropriations allocated in the budget must comply with spending plans approved by the Ministry. The law granted the Ministry the sole authority to disburse funds, the power to delegate to ministries and other units the right to transfer funds between units, the authority to disburse advance payments to non-ministry affiliated units, the power to determine projects and investment expenditures conducted by ministries in the governorates and regions, and the

[18] "Minister of Planning: The Budget Does Not Meet the Aspirations of Development," *Iraq Directory*, January 2, 2007, http://www.iraqupdates.com/scr/preview.php?article=13058/.
[19] Santa Michael, "Maliki Urges Parliament to Speed Up Approval of the Draft Budget," Voices of Iraq, January 15, 2007, http://www.iraqupdates.com/scr/preview.php?article=13471/.

right, in coordination with the Ministry of Planning, to transfer funds from projects if 25 percent of their appropriations were not "implemented" during the first half of the fiscal year. The Ministry of Finance's "Instructions for Executing the Federal Budget of 2007" declared that any ministerial expenditure exceeding 5 million dinars required the approval of both the Finance Ministry's minister and director-general for the budget. The Ministry, moreover, managed the financing of terminated government employees and the subsidies that paid their salaries in the private sector. When a ministry "transferred" an employee from the public to the private sector, the Finance Ministry through its own accounts would assume half of the employee's private-sector salary for two years, with the employee's home government entity funding the other half of the salary.[20]

Parliamentary Participation in the Budgetary Process

In a significant development in Iraqi democratic governance, the budgetary process offered members of the Council of Representatives a venue to voice their opinions about public priorities and conduct oversight of ministerial activities. To focus attention on Iraqi budget and economic policy, the Council's 2006 Rules of Procedure established twenty-four standing committees, including a new Financial Committee.[21] The Committee consisted of seven persons and was chaired by Dr. Iyad al-Samarr'i, a prominent Sunni who lead the Iraqi Accord Front parliamentary group. Al-Samarr'i would also be elected the Council's speaker in April 2009. The Committee derived its analytical budgetary support from four to eight staff members of the Council's research office. The Committee organized itself in February to review the Ministry of Finance's 2007 budget proposals and especially assess the budget's projected deficit. The deficit stood at 9 trillion ID, and, according to al-Samarr'i, "It will be financed from the surplus achieved in last year's budget because its allocations were not fully spent.... The surplus is either because the state was unable to spend the money on investment project and reconstruction, or due to the increase in global oil prices.... We depended upon the Iraqi dinar when drafting the 2007 budget, rather than the dollar. The exchange rate of the Iraqi currency has seen a clear improvement. The dollar is now exchanged for 1,260 dinars after it has been exchanged earlier for 1,500 dinars."[22] In this way the Iraqis ironically benefited from their inability

[20] "Instructions for Executing the Federal Budget of 2007," Ministry of Finance, Budget Directorate, Baghdad, 2006, 4–8.
[21] "Parliament to Form Financial and Economic Committee to Revise Iraq's Budget," *PortAl Iraq*, February 1, 2007, http://www.iraqupdates.com/scr/preview.php?article=14125/.
[22] "Iraq Budget Said 'Largest' Ever, Projecting Oil Output Rise," Also, the Ministry of Oil pledged to raise output to 1.7 million barrels of oil from 1.6 million, at $50 per barrel. *Al-Adalah*, February 15, 2007, http://www.iraqupdates.com/scr/preview.php?article=14585/.

to execute their budget. The rollover of unspent funds from one budget to another helped them finance their budget deficits. Indeed, according to the Finance Ministry, Iraq proved to be unable to spend most of its 2005 and 2006 investment budgets, thus providing $9 billion in prior year funds to finance the 2007 deficit.[23] Some members of the Committee also expressed concerns about the Ministry's decisions to withdraw funding from a governmental unit if it failed to complete its investments on time, saying it was inappropriate to punish a ministry or province due to the underperformance of a handful of projects.

Complaints also emerged regarding perceived corruption in the budget's administration, specifically about the actions of Finance Minister al-Zubeidi. Muhammad al-Dayni, a deputy for the National Dialogue Front, questioned whether the Finance Ministry's control over 2 trillion ID for transfer among the ministries was proper. "While the finance minister was presenting the budget to the Council of Representatives," said al-Dayni, "and after he mentioned the deficit, a number of deputies confronted him with statements he made earlier in which he said that there was a surplus in the 2006 budget, and not all of it was spent. He had estimated the surplus in those statements at between $14 billion and $15 billion. The amount was supposed to be transferred to the 2007 budget, which the minister said had a deficit of $7 billion. But everyone was surprised when the minister said he did not make such statements. When a number of deputies confronted him with evidence and gave dates, and when others said they kept a recording of the interview in which he talked about a surplus in the 2006 budget, the minister admitted that he said there was a surplus, but he denied that he said the figure was $15 billion, saying the surplus was only $8 billion." Al-Dayni also pointed to corruption in the number of employees reported in the budget. When the minister of Human Rights, Wujdan Salim, defended her budget before the Council, al-Dayni noted that she indicated that 350 employees worked in her ministry, but the budget identified 1,223. "If this is the case with a small ministry like the Ministry of Human Rights, how is the situation in big ministries like the ministries of defense, interior, transport, and health, where there are about one million employees?"[24] Despite al-Dayni's accusations, in a process where "legislators battled over every single paragraph in the budget and had to vote on each one of them separately," the Council of Representatives voted to approve the budget on February 12.[25]

[23] Salem Takleef, "Iraqi Ministries Failed to Spend Up to 50% of Allocations Last Year, Finance Minister Says," *Azzaman*, February 14, 2007, http://www.iraqupdates.com/scr/preview.php?article=14531/.

[24] "Iraqi MP Says 15bn Dollars Unaccounted for in 2006 Budget," Quds Press, January 29, 2007, http://www.iraqupdates.com/scr/preview.php?article=14001/.

[25] "Iraq Budget Set at USD 41bn budget, USD 1.5mn for Compensating Kuwait," Kuwait News Agency, February 12, 2007, http://www.iraqupdates.com/scr/preview.php?article=14437/.

Provincial Budgetary Claimants

The budget process, in addition, offered provincial representatives and officials the opportunity to make their claims on public resources. Although the 2006 budget process first allowed the provinces to develop their own investment projects for central government funding, and allocated 3 trillion ID for that purpose, the debates over the 2007 budget registered a significant number of provincial leaders calling for spending allocations to benefit their regions, even if such funding occurred at the expense of other provincial governments. Governor Aziz Kazem Alwan of Dhi Qar province, for instance, declared that three hundred villages in his province went without electricity and that the central government needed to fund more irrigation, road, and school construction projects. "All our farmers and sheikhs are waiting for these projects," the governor said.[26] Munadil al-Mayahi, head of Basra's municipal council's Economic Committee proclaimed that the forthcoming 2008 budget should address Basra's urgently pressing needs. "We look forward for the Iraqi central government and parliament to support the province of Basra by increasing its share from the 2008 budget, taking into consideration Basra's need for infrastructure services and its economic and demographic weight.... Why is it that the budget of Baghdad is five times that of Basra, Iraq's only port and oil artery, which has a population of over 3 million?"[27] In response to such demands, the budget included an additional 3 trillion ID that would be allocated to the governorates on the basis of population. These additional funds would support construction projects that would be developed and implemented by the provincial governors under the supervision of the Ministry of Finance.

Summary

The rise and participation of new budgetary claimants and the commitment to boost investment spending characterized the development of the 2007 budget. The Parliament followed up on its newly created Rules of Procedure with the establishment of new committees that marked the Council of Representatives' deeper engagement in the budgetary process. This engagement was reflected in calls for greater transparency in the release of more detailed budgetary figures by the Ministry of Finance and increased accountability in the use of government funds. Moreover, provincial and local officials became emboldened in their calls for funding for their respective governments. The government attempted to accommodate this demand for more funding, coupled with continuing

---

[26] "Even in the More Stable South, Iraq Rebuilds Slowly," Reuters, November 13, 2007, http://www.iraqupdates.com/scr/preview.php?article=23930/.

[27] "Basra Local Government Urges for More Budget Funds," Voices of Iraq, November 23, 2007, http://www.iraqupdates.com/scr/preview.php?article=24270/.

Coalition and donor demands for greater spending on capital infrastructure, in
the 2008 budget.

4. THE 2008 GOOD TIMES BUDGET

The 2008 budget presented Iraq with a new challenge. Beginning with the 2003
CPA budget and continuing into 2008, Iraq benefited from six consecutive years
of accelerating revenue growth. Starting with the formulation of the 2008
budget, however, Iraq experienced a dramatic three-year cycle of oil revenue
boom, bust, and rebound that produced volatile swings in the size of the budget's
spending allocations and deficits. This fiscal instability severely tested the government's ability to manage a fiscal crisis in the face of growing demands from
budgetary claimants for more resources. The government's reliance on the
budgetary process to manage this crisis further embedded and layered these
rules onto Iraq's political institutions.

Budget Formulation

Projections of oil revenues drove Iraqi budget planning and formulation. In
September 2007, Finance Minister al-Zubeidi released the revenue baseline for
the 2008 budget. The draft budget optimistically called for a production rate of 1.7
million barrels of oil per day, with the government reducing its dependence on oil
revenues from 97 percent of all revenues in 2006, to 93 percent in 2007, to 85
percent in 2008, with the remaining 15 percent derived from mobile phone and
other taxes.[28] In reaction to a drop in oil prices in 2006 and 2007 that helped drive
up the 2007 deficit, the Finance Ministry conservatively priced oil at $50 per barrel,
far lower than the market rate of $93. With this rate of production, even with these
modest prices, estimated revenues would grow by 20 percent, from 42 trillion ID to
50.7 trillion ID. As shown in Table 8.2, these new revenues enabled the government to propose a budget of 59.8 trillion ID ($49.9 billion), a 13 percent increase,
including allocations of 44.2 trillion ID ($36.8 billion) for operational expenses
and 15.7 trillion ID ($13 billion) in investment spending, an increase of 23 percent.
The 2008 deficit stood at 9 trillion ID ($7.6 billion), the same as in 2007. Just as the
Iraqis looked to unexecuted investment funds to finance the 2007 deficit, so too the
2008 deficit would be covered by rolling over unspent amounts from the 2007
budget. Very pleased with the big investment budget, Ambassador Ryan Crocker
declared, "Mr. Minister, the IMF may have a few problems with your budget, but I
can tell you that I don't, and I know the people of Iraq don't either."[29]

[28] "Finance Not to Rely on Oil Next Year," *Al-Sabaah*, Sept. 20, 2007, http://www.iraqupdates.
com/scr/preview.php?article=21945.
[29] "Iraq PM Proposes $48 bn Budget," *The Peninsula*-Qatar, November 26, 2007, http://www.
iraqupdates.com/scr/preview.php?article=24369/. Ryan Crocker also pointed out how the Iraq
budget directly benefited the United States. "Iraq's 2008 budget has allocated $13 billion for

TABLE 8.2. *The Surge, Decline, and Restoration Budgets, 2008–2011 (all figures are in billions of Iraqi dinars)*

	2008a	2008b	2009a	2009b	2009c	2010a	2011a	2011b
Spending Allocations								
Operations	44,191	61,282	71,013	62,104	54,148	60,981	64,022	66,596
Investments	15,671	25,335	23,016	16,930	15,017	23,676	28,957	30,066
Total allocation	59,862	86,617	94,029	79,034	69,165	84,657	92,980	96,663
Revenues	50,775	80,476	73,712	60,941	50,408	61,735	78,705	80,934
Deficit/Surplus	−9,086	−6,141	−20,317	−18,093	−18,757	−22,921	−14,275	−15,727

2008a: February Budget
2008b: Includes August Supplemental Budget
2009a: September Draft Budget
2009b: March Draft Budget
2009c: April Budget
2010a: February Budget
2011a: December Draft Budget
2011b: February Budget

Source: Iraq Ministry of Finance.

Parliamentary Participation in the Budgetary Process

The Council of Ministers approved the Finance Ministry's proposed budget on November 14, but debate and division in the Council of Representatives delayed final consideration of the budget until mid-February. Efforts by Council members seeking to defend the integrity of the budgetary process delayed its consideration. Some members asserted that consistent with the formal budgetary process, the budget should have been sent to the Parliament in October rather than November. Others, led by Finance Committee chair al-Samarra'i, called for more transparency and information in the budget. Mahdi al-Hafiz, a former minister of planning, claimed the lack of information on foreign grants in aid was "a significant gap," final accounts for the prior four years were not submitted in the draft budget, and that the $3.3 billion allocated to the provinces for investments did not identify specific projects.[30]

The debate over the Kurdistan Regional Government's 17 percent spending share also stalled final consideration of the budget. The Iraqi Constitution called for provincial budget allocations on the basis of population. Some members who questioned the distribution of funds to the KRG asserted that because census data were old and incomplete the KRG's real population was unknown. Planning Minister Baban stated that his data indicated the KRG's population to be 14.5 percent of all Iraqis, but "I expect the budget for the region will be 17 percent because normally we give more than the percentage of the population to secure provinces to encourage these provinces to implement projects."[31] Other members objected to the Kurds collecting their own import fees, while refusing to send these revenues or accounts of the revenues to Baghdad. Moreover, members also expressed displeasure with the KRG's reliance on central government funds to pay for its militia, the Peshmerga.[32] The Kurds, in turn, defended their allocation. Mahama Khalil, a KRG representative in Parliament, declared, "We consider the demands to lower our share of the budget below 17 percent are a political conspiracy against the Kurds and our rights."[33] "The share was determined by a law enacted during the former government under Iyad Allawi," announced Fouad Massoum, a Kurdish block leader, "and it needs

---

reconstruction, and a $5 billion supplemental budget this summer will invest export revenues in building the infrastructure and providing the services that Iraq so badly needs. This spending also benefits the United States – Iraq recently announced its decision to purchase 40 commercial aircraft from the U.S. at an estimated cost of $5 billion." "Testimony of Ambassador Ryan C. Crocker before the Senate Armed Services Committee," April 8, 2008, 8. http://www. defense.gov/pdf/Ambassador_Crocker_SFRC_Testimony.pdf/.

[30] "Mahdi Al Hafiz Criticizing the Iraqi Budget Figures," Iraq Directory, January 31, 2008, http://www.iraqdirectory.com/DisplayNews.aspx?id=5468/.

[31] Wisam Mohammed and Ahmed Rasheed, "Problems Seen for Iraq Budget Despite Compromise," Reuters, February 6, 2008. http://www.alertnet.org/thenews/newsdesk/L06867089.htm/.

[32] Alissa J. Rubin, "Kurd's Power Wanes as Arab Anger Rises, *New York Times*, February 1, 2008.

[33] Wisam Mohammed and Ahmed Rasheed, "Problems Seen for Iraq Budget Despite Compromise," Reuters, February 6, 2008. http://www.alertnet.org/thenews/newsdesk/L06867089.htm/.

another law to cancel this share."[34] Finally, in a deal that packaged together the budget, the Provincial Powers Act, and an amnesty for twenty-six thousand Sunnis detained by the government, the Council voted to approve the budget on February 13, 2008, after the Parliament's speaker, Mahmoud al-Mashhadani, threatened to disband the body, claiming the government lost more than 4 trillion ID in oil revenues because of the failure to pass the budget by the end of 2007, even as scores of legislators stormed out of Parliament in protest.

The Iraqi 2008 Supplementary Budget

Almost as quickly as the Council of Representatives passed the budget, the Finance Ministry began drafting a supplementary 2008 budget. Oil revenues skyrocketed, as the price per barrel reached $145 in July. Where the Iraqis based the primary budget on a price per barrel rate of $50, the supplemental rate was set at $91 dollars per barrel. This meant that total projected revenues for the fiscal year jumped by nearly 60 percent, from 50.7 trillion to more than 80 trillion dinars. The August supplemental budget raised the total 2008 budget to 86.6 trillion ID ($72.2 billion), with operational spending set at 71 trillion ID ($51 billion) and capital spending at 25.3 trillion ID ($21 billion). With this new spending, Prime Minister Maliki noted, "The money allocated for provinces increased by 90 percent for each one in the fiscal budget for the calendar year 2008." The provinces should therefore "speed up the completion of projects in order to allocate extra money through the complementary budget starting in the mid of this year."[35] The supplemental budget provided additional allocations of 118 billion ID to Basra, 118 billion ID to Mosul, and 178 billion ID to Baghdad.

The American Embassy strongly approved of the supplemental budget's huge increase for investments. Embassy officials clearly were conscious of the discussions taking place in Washington about how the Iraqis should bear costs of reconstruction given their growing budget surpluses. Simply put, more Iraqi spending meant less American spending, noted Ambassador Crocker. "I do think you're seeing a shift into more Iraqi spending," said Crocker, "which means less US spending.... Their supplemental is all about a surplus." At the same time, Crocker emphasized the need to execute this investment spending. "Because oil prices have increased, the finance ministry has announced a $5 billion supplemental for the summer, but to be able to tap into it, you have to demonstrate a certain rate of execution on your regular budget, both for the federal ministries and for the provinces. So it's a real incentive to, you know, to actually execute.....it hasn't been, in my judgment, lack of will to execute; it has been a lack of capacity. And, you know, the amount of progress you can make is

---

[34] "Political Aims Behind Delay in Approving 2008 Budget-MP," *Voices of Iraq*, February 8, 2008, http://www.iraqupdates.com/scr/preview.php?article=27083.

[35] "Al-Maliki Calls Governors to Accelerate Provincial Projects," *Voices of Iraq*, March 4, 2008, http://www.iraqupdates.com/scr/preview.php?article=28120.

finite on that. It takes time.....The [Planning] Ministry has now agreed that in developing project priorities for the provinces that are executed by the federal government through the directors general, they will take as their base document not a Baghdad-generated plan but provincial plans that the provinces will put together and send up to Baghdad. So that's also a first as of just this spring."[36] On Crocker's point, the Coalition certainly endorsed the Iraqis' supplemental budget given the discussion in Washington about Iraq running budget surpluses, but this extra stimulus led to both negative and positive fiscal outcomes. Ambassador Charles Reis recalled: "I regret that in 2008, when oil prices went through the roof, Washington went crazy. 'Why are we spending any money in Iraq when oil is $140 a barrel, and they are making $5 billion a month with their exports of oil?' We had enormous pressure from Washington to get them to spend more and do a supplemental budget. So, in January or December, the minister of finance told me, if oil keeps up as high as it is, we will do a supplemental budget.... They started that process, but they gave up on requiring essentially performance [by the ministries], and in the logrolling in the cabinet, in the Council of Ministers, in the Parliament, that particular supplemental budget got enormously big. It went from $4 to $5 billion, which is what they were talking about, to over $20 billion, with a huge pay increase for all the civil servants. Most of it was spent on operational money.... We were pushing them to spend all of this windfall currently. It was partially because we were in a hurry, partially because they were in a hurry.... We were actually saved by their difficulty in ramping up spending that fast. In 2009, the backlog of 2008 projects that hadn't been undertaken and finished kept the economy from crashing. Because you would have had a big stimulus, you'd double the reconstruction spending in one year, and then you'd cut it down by a quarter of the bigger number the next year. So, the inability of the Iraqis to program and spend money as fast as we sometimes wanted them to do is probably their savior."[37] The inability to execute the budget thus smoothed the rate of spending over a longer fiscal horizon and paradoxically aided the Iraqis in the management of their fiscal policy.

Summary

The 2007 and 2008 budgets demonstrated that Iraq could formulate budgets calling for big spending increases, thereby greatly pleasing both domestic claimants and Coalition officials. Iraq's reconstruction needs were indeed enormous, and paradoxically the government's inability to execute its prior budgets enabled it to manage its deficits with rolled-over funds. Nonetheless, as a

---

[36] U.S. Embassy in Iraq, "Roundtable Interview with Ambassador Ryan Crocker," April 11, 2008, http://iraq.usembassy.gov/remarks_04112008.html/.

[37] Interview with Charles Ries, Minister for Economic Affairs and Coordinator for Economic Transition in Iraq, February 2, 2010.

petroleum-dependent state, Iraq and its budget process had yet to be tested by a significant drop in oil prices that would dramatically upset its revenue calculations and induce painful budget cuts. The 2009 budget provided that test.

5. THE 2009 CRISIS BUDGET

Budgeting with growing resources is relatively easy. Expanding revenues enable a government to fund demanding budget claimants, reach political spending agreements, and thereby restrain political conflict. Contracting revenues creates dissatisfied claimants, promotes political conflict, and tests the resilience of budgetary institutions. Such a surge and decline in resources occurred in Iraq with the 2008 and 2009 budgets and tested the budgetary process's ability to overcome great fiscal adversity and political stress.

Budget Formulation

Building on the 2008 budget and flush with real and expected revenues, the Ministry of Finance announced in September that the forthcoming 2009 budget would grow to 94 trillion ID ($79 billion), with significant increases in operational and capital allocations. The planned budget projected oil prices at $100 per barrel with a production level of 2.38 million barrels per day, a substantial increase over the 1.7 million per day figure estimated for the preceding year. This higher production rate, of course, depended on effective capital budget execution to create the infrastructure required to generate this output.

Then the bottom dropped out of the oil market. By the end of October, oil prices fell to less than half of the peak price of $145.29 a barrel reached on July 3, 2008, which forced the Finance Ministry to revise the revenue base of the 2009 budget to a lower rate of $80 a barrel. Two weeks later on November 1, Oil Minister al-Shahristani announced the budget would assume a price of $62 per barrel. Three days later, Finance Minister al-Zubeidi stated the budget would be reduced from $80 billion to $67 billion. "Our budget dropped from $80 billion to $67 billion after our difficult discussions with the International Monetary Fund," al-Zubeidi acknowledged. "We are at a critical time. . . . The budget I submitted a month and a half ago to the Council of Ministers was examined in the cabinet and was in the process of voting until the collapse in oil prices occurred."[38] As oil prices continued to slide the Cabinet cut this revised October budget in November by more than $1 billion. By December, however, the price of oil continued to fall to an estimated $50 per barrel. The Council of Ministers approved one version of the 2009 budget on December 24. By mid-January, 2009, just days before major provincial elections, with oil falling to $40 a barrel, the Council decided to cut

---

[38] "The Ministry of Finance: Iraq's Budget for 2009 Will Be $67 Billion Instead of $80 Billion," *Iraq Directory*, November 4, 2008, http://www.iraqupdates.com/scr/preview.php?article=39259/.

spending by an additional 4.7 trillion ID ($4 billion), leaving the budget with a deficit of 22.5 trillion ID ($19 billion).

Cutting the Budget

On March 5, the Council of Ministers passed a 69 trillion ID budget ($58.9 billion), which the Presidential Council approved on April 3, more than three months into the fiscal year. The government's investment allocations fell to just below the 2008 level. The budget, however, assumed $50 per barrel of oil versus the current $38 market price, and a production level of 2 million barrels of oil per day, versus Iraq's actual 1.8 million per day production. The deficit, newly projected at 18 trillion ID ($15.2 billion), would be partially financed by drawing on unspent 2008 investment allocations, by soliciting new loans from the IMF, and by generating additional mobile phone license fees.[39] To meet this budget reduction, al-Zubeidi called for higher oil production. "Clearly we will face a great crisis in 2010. We started to make plans to face this, such as privatization, widened

---

[39] In May, at the peak of the fiscal crisis, the government turned to a number of sources to finance the deficit. First, the Central Bank fought off Finance Ministry efforts to withdraw funds from the Bank's $70 billion in cash balances and foreign currency reserves. The Bank refused, considering the Ministry's attempt to be a violation of the Bank's independence that was protected by CPA Order 56. "Attempts to take foreign currency directly from the central bank's reserves," said a Bank statement, "to cover various government expenses will weaken the ability of monetary policy to bring stability." "Iraq Cenbank Tells Govt Not to Spend FX Reserves," Reuters, May 26, 2009, http://www.iraqupdates.com/scr/preview.php?article=51868/. Also "(CBI) Declined Government's Request to Borrow from Reserved Funds," *Iraq Directory*, May 6, 2009, http://www.iraqupdates. com/scr/preview.php?article=50535/. Second, the Iraqis approached the IMF for a $7 billion loan. The IMF countered with a $5.5 billion proposal, with the condition that Iraq reduce its overall operational spending levels by making cuts in civil servant salaries. Negotiations with the IMF, and then with the World Bank for $500 million in Fiscal Sustainability Development Policy loans, extended through the rest of 2009 and into the spring of 2010. In June 2010, the IMF approved a $440 million loan to Iraq, the first installment of a $3.7 billion loan package, followed by a second installment of $741 million in October. The IMF reported that "Iraq has continued to make good progress in rebuilding key economic institutions and maintaining macroeconomic stability, under very difficult conditions." "IMF Says Iraq Has Made Good Progress with Its Economy," BBC News, October 4, 2010, http://www.iraqupdates.com/scr/preview.php?article=80090/. Third, the Ministry of Finance pressured the National Communications and Media Commission of Iraq (NCMCI) to generate $1.975 billion in license fees from mobile phone companies. The fees set by the NCMCI are the second largest source of government revenue after the revenues generated by the Ministry of Oil. By ministerial decree in 2007, all revenues derived from these fees were directed to the central treasury, with a ministerial committee headed by the Finance Ministry formed to supervise mobile phone and other communications licenses. In 2009, this committee's powers were transferred to the NCMCI. Iraq's three major mobile phone companies and other communications entities overseen by NCMCI owed the government $1.8 million, with each paying $4 million in annual fees, with a $625 million installment on the license, plus $45 million penalty for the delays in their payments. Sa'ad Salloum, "The Communications and Media Commission: We Provide the State with Billions of Dollars," *Niqash*, December 23, 2009, http://www.iraqupdates.com/scr/preview.php? article=64645/.

taxes, mobile licenses.... But the question is can we face these pressures in 2010 and 2011 through these measures? I say no. For that reason I say we need another way ... the fundamental element facing this crisis is increasing oil exports. If [oil prices rise] above $70, then we'll have no problems."[40] "The decrease in the budget is directly linked to the fall in oil prices," complained Khalid al-Attiya, the Parliament's deputy speaker. "The government knows this is not realistic."[41] Lamented Sinan al-Shibibi, governor of the Central Bank of Iraq, "Of course, this occurs at the wrong moment because of the fact that Iraq actually needs to embark on huge projects and it will affect that."[42]

These dramatic and unforeseen budget cuts led to programmatic reductions, diminished aspirations, and even fiscal panic. Interior Minister Jawad Bolani warned he would be forced to freeze the hiring of new security forces. Bolani's warning came despite the growth in security personnel from 250,000 in 2007 to more than 600,000 in 2009, at a cost of 35 percent of total budget expenditures. "We were aiming to recruit 66,000 people during 2009 and 2010," he said, "and that is now on hold."[43] Central government funding for the provinces also experienced deep cuts. Accelerated Reconstruction Development Program funds transferred from Baghdad to the provinces fell from 4 trillion ID in 2008 to 2.55 trillion ID in 2009. As shown in Table 8.3, Basra's allocation was slashed by 36 percent, and Babel's budget was cut by 48 percent. Meanwhile, provincial governments incurred deficits, as Karbala's deficit reached 164 billion dinars. As a result, Abbas Nasser Hassani, the provincial council head, explained, "The deficit hampers local government's plans in implementing 2009 projects. The deficit will cause a confusion in the local government's commitments towards contractors and companies which implements projects as there is no available cash for them."[44]

Iraqis feared the budget would be further cut in 2010. Ali Hussein Balo, chair of the Parliament's Oil and Gas Committee, predicted that "If the oil price remains the same, $50 per barrel, the Iraqi budget will be cut by about 50 percent next year."[45] Oil prices, however, never fell below $45 a barrel and then rebounded to $63 a barrel in May. The rise in prices even encouraged the Finance Ministry to develop a 535 billion ID supplementary budget to aid the provinces in 2010, which the Cabinet approved in July. "The rise in oil prices

---

[40] "Iraq Fears Budget Crisis, Urges Oil Export Boost," *The Guardian*, December 7, 2008, http://www.iraqupdates.com/scr/preview.php?article=41326.

[41] "Iraqi MPs Cut Billions Off 2009 Budget," AFP, March 6, 2009, http://www.iraqupdates.com/scr/preview.php?article=46565.

[42] "Iraq Parliament Cuts 09 Budget by 7 Percent," Reuters, March 6, 2009, http://www.iraqupdates.com/scr/preview.php?article=46566.

[43] Massoud A. Derhally, "Iraq Freezes 66,000 Police Hires as Oil Falls, Minister Says," Bloomberg, March 22, 2009, http://www.iraqupdates.com/scr/preview.php?article=47680.

[44] "ID 164 Billion Budget Deficit in Karbala," *Aswat Al Iraq*, July 22, 2009, http://www.iraqupdates.com/scr/preview.php?article=55407/.

[45] Qasim Khidhir Hamad, "Oil Dispute Threatens Iraqi Economy," *Niqash*, April 17, 2009, http://www.iraqupdates.com/scr/preview.php?article=49302.

TABLE 8.3. *Advanced Reconstruction Development Program Funds, 2008–2010*
(all figures are in millions of Iraqi dinars)

GOVERNORATE*	2008	2009	2010
Anbar	220,000	132,600	130,000
Babel	240,800	158,100	152,500
Baghdad	1,060,000	650,250	794,455
Basra	368,000	237,150	276,474
Dhi Kar	260,000	168,300	165,000
Diwaniya	160,000	102,000	131,000
Diyala	201,600	122,400	242,223
Karbala	136,000	91,800	90,000
Kirkuk	172,000	117,300	115,000
Maysan	144,000	94,350	198,000
Muthanna	100,000	66,300	65,000
Najaf	172,000	109,650	170,000
Ninewa	428,000	277,950	321,600
Salah ad Din	176,000	114,750	112,500
Wasit	161,600	107,100	102,500
Total	4,000,000	2,550,000	3,066,252

* Kurdistan Regional Government provinces of Erbil, Dohuk, and Sulaimaniyah not included in ARDP.

Source: U.S. Treasury, "2010 Provincial Budgets," April 15, 2010.

and production," said Prime Minister al-Maliki, "could allow us, God willing, to present a supplementary budget and add other funds to the provinces."[46]

Summary

The dramatic fall in oil prices forced the Iraqis to make painful cuts in the 2009 budget that upset aspirations, spending plans, and reconstruction efforts. Expectations that oil prices might continue to drop, coupled with projections of growing deficits, led Iraq to approach international donor agencies for additional funding, thus ensuring that Iraq would be called on to comply with donor aid conditionality requirements. Iraqi officials responsible for constructing the 2010 budget, therefore, successfully worked through the challenge of stabilizing the overall budget with a questionable revenue base while accommodating the Coalition's insistence that Iraq raise its investment spending.

[46] "Rising Oil Prices May Let Iraq Spend More: PM," AFP, June 9, 2009, http://www.iraqupdates.com/scr/preview.php?article=52755/.

6. THE 2010 STABILIZATION BUDGET

The Iraqi government retained and relied on the budgetary process to impose deep spending reductions on ministries and provincial governments. Yet, the tense politics surrounding the 2010 budget reflected the pressures of meeting the growing demands of budgetary claimants with constrained levels of spending.

Budget Formulation

On September 30, 2009, Deputy Finance Minister Fadhil Nabi outlined the draft 2010 budget. The budget called for 78 trillion ID ($66.7 billion) in overall spending, including 20 trillion ID for capital outlays; it assumed a price per barrel of $60, versus the market price of $74; and it estimated oil production at rate of 2.15 million barrels per day. Though the budget's total spending level would be higher than the final 2009 budget, both overall and investment spending would be less than in 2008 and the initial 2009 budget.

Pressure on the Iraqis to spend both more and less came from the Coalition and the international donor community. American military officials, for example, responded immediately and harshly to the budget's security spending levels. "The budget, no question, is a challenge," said Lt. General Frank Helmick, commander of the Multi-National Security Transition Command–Iraq. "This is a significant challenge for the security ministers as they try to secure weapons systems as well as ensure the flow of personnel."[47] "I think the budget is a problem for them to equip and outfit the military the way they want," said Major General John Johnson, the director of U.S. military planning in Iraq.[48] These officers claimed the government's budget constraints undermined military purchases and the construction of a supply chain necessary to provide material for the security services. Prime Minister Maliki, however, countered that security spending crowded out investment spending. "This is a dangerous phenomenon for the Iraqi economy," said Maliki. "Instead of allocating 74 percent of this year's budget to pay salaries, we think that a big part of our budget should go to construction."[49] Maliki's support for a larger investment allocation at the expense of security spending represented something of a change for the prime minister, who staked much of his and Iraq's future on reducing violence. As violence decreased, he reasoned, the demand for providing essential services

---

[47] "US Official: Security Risk in Iraq from Budget Shortfall," Associated Press, September 30, 2009, http://www.foxnews.com/printer_friendly_story/0,3566,557784,00.html/.
[48] "Budget of Iraqi Security Forces Strained, PM Says," Associated Press, October 10, 2009, http://www.iraqupdates.com/scr/preview.php?article=60121/.
[49] *Ibid.*

increased, and this demand needed to be met. At the same time, violence in Iraq
flared, as both the Ministries of Finance and Foreign Affairs were heavily
bombed in August, and then the Finance Ministry again in December.
Counterpressure to control spending came from the donor community that the
Iraqis turned to for assistance in financing the deficit. In reaction to this pressure,
Maliki announced that Iraq could not meet IMF demands for cuts in the operational budget to reduce the budget deficit in order to qualify for its $5.5 billion
loan request. "The IMF called on us to reduce Iraq salaries," said Maliki. "We
cannot in fact cut salaries."[50] On October 14, the Council of Ministers approved
the proposed budget, sending it to the Council of Representatives for its
consideration.

Parliamentary Participation in the Budgetary Process

The Council of Representatives' Finance Committee began its review in
December, taking testimony from a variety of budgetary claimants and interests.
Abdulrazeq al-Zuheiri, head of the Iraqi Chamber of Commerce, called on the
Parliament to speed its review of the budget. "The delay in passing the 2009
budget disturbed the economic process," he said. "The delay in passing this
year's budget will increase unemployment and the suffering of low-income
families.... Iraqi traders have suffered a lot throughout this year because of
the lack of a clear picture of the nature of the Iraqi economy and its duality –
capitalism and socialism. The non-circulation of the 2009 budget has affected
Iraqi traders."[51] The Interior Ministry also complained that Parliament's failure
to pass the 2010 budget in a timely manner damaged budget execution. Halim
al-Duleimy, Interior Ministry Under Secretary for Financial Affairs, declared,
"In previous years the budget was endorsed in the third month [after the Finance
Ministry submitted it to the Council of Ministers in September], but now it needs
three more months to be spent in the sixth month [June], underscoring that the
ministry's contracts need to be announced and duly endorsed, where the delay
will postpone the conducting of necessary contracts."[52] The Finance Committee
approved the budget on January 13 but recommended cuts in the Judicial
Council budget by 2.3 trillion ID ($2 billion) and increased the Council of
Representatives' budget by 9.4 trillion ID ($8 billion) to accommodate an
increase in the number of parliamentary members. The Committee then waited
for the Council of Ministers' approval of these revisions. "The modified budget

[50] "Iraq PM Says Cannot Cut Public Pay to Suit IMF," Reuters, October 8, 2009, http://www.
iraqupdates.com/scr/preview.php?article=60076/; "Iraq Not to Tap Hard Cash Reserves Despite
Fall in Oil Prices," *Azzaman*, April 28, 2009, http://www.iraqupdates.com/scr/preview.php?
article=50058/.
[51] "Head of Chambers of Commerce Asks to Speed Up Budget Passage," *Aswat Al Iraq*, December
16, 2009, http://www.iraqupdates.com/scr/preview.php?article=63986/.
[52] "Interior Ministry Warns Consequences of Delaying Budget Law 2010," Eye Media Company,
December 31, 2009, http://www.iraqupdates.com/scr/preview.php?article=64827/.

we have received will be endorsed by the committee only after the cabinet approves it," said Sami al-Atroushi, a member of the Committee. "Hopefully, it would be okayed by the cabinet by mid–next week so that the budget, after modifications, exceeded 84.6 trillion dinars, which upped the deficit by more than 22.9 trillion ID, and this should be covered by an increase in the oil prices among other resources."[53]

The Council of Ministers approved these revisions on January 20, but differences with the Parliament delayed the budget's final approval. Various blocs within the Council attempted to tie the budget's passing to other issues, such as the setting of election rules, customs duties, consumer protection laws, and efforts to cut salaries for legislators. Budgetary claimants, however, grew restless with the posturing over the process. Samira al-Moussawi, chair of the Woman and Childhood Committee, expressed concerns for the two hundred thousand widows who received social security benefits, declaring, "Some political blocs bargained approving the law with approving other laws. These blocs forgot that the government's institutions are waiting for the budget to be approved."[54] The budget process also allowed for publicly active claims for funding by provincial governments. In January, for example, the governor of Kirkuk registered his displeasure with his province's budget allocation. "We have received the budget allocated to Kirkuk (115 billion ID) in 2010," said Governor Abdulrahman Mustapha, "and we officially objected to it in a letter sent to the Planning Ministry. The budget is not enough and does not suit the province and its needs. We hope that the Ministry would reconsider this budget to help us reconstruct the destroyed infrastructure."[55] Nouzhad Hadi, the governor of Erbil province, made similar claims. "Erbil needs 540 billion ID as a budget to develop the province in 2010," Hadi said, though he also acknowledged that "Most of Iraq's provinces were not able to spend their budget allocated for them in 2009, as the percentage of implementing projects in some provinces range between 15 and 20 percent."[56] On January 27, the Council approved the 84 trillion ID ($72.4 billion) budget, with 61 trillion ID ($52 billion) allocated for operational spending and 23.7 trillion ID ($20.3 billion) allocated for investments. Total revenues were estimated at 61.7 trillion ID ($52.7 billion), leaving a 22.9 trillion ID ($19.6 billion) deficit to be financed by unspent funds from prior fiscal years. The Presidential Council gave its approval to the budget on February 11.

[53] "MP Says Budget Won't Be Endorsed Before Cabinet OKs It," *Aswat Al Iraq*, January 17, 2010, http://www.iraqupdates.com/scr/preview.php?article=65704/.
[54] "Woman, Childhood Committee Stresses Importance of Approving 2010 Budget," *Aswat Al Iraq*, January 22, 2010, http://www.iraqupdates.com/scr/preview.php?article=66040/.
[55] "Kirkuk Officially Objects to 2010 Budget," *Aswat Al Iraq*, January 7, 2010, http://www.iraqupdates.com/scr/preview.php?article=65161/.
[56] "Arbil Needs ID 540 Billion to Implement Projects in 2010 – Governor," *Aswat Al Iraq*, January 9, 2010, http://www.iraqupdates.com/scr/preview.php?article=65289/.

Summary

The 2010 budget represented the stabilization of government spending after rapid and dramatic increases in operational and investment funding allocations for 2006, 2007, and 2008, followed by the startling cuts in the 2009 budget. Even with this apparent bottoming out of the oil crisis, capital spending for 2010 fell below the 2008 level, thus undermining Iraqi reconstruction efforts. Iraqi budgeting became even more complicated, however, as the political standoff of the 2010 elections delayed the formulation and Parliamentary consideration of the 2011 budget.

7. THE 2011 BUDGET: ELECTORAL UNCERTAINTY AND PUBLIC UNREST

The political instability created by Iraq's tempestuous 2010 elections for the Council of Representatives tested Iraq's ability to adopt a budget under conditions far more trying than those stemming from the three-year roller-coaster ride in oil revenues. During the ensuing seven-month absence of parliamentary government, the budgetary process provided Iraq with a vital source of institutional stability.

Budget Formulation

In September 2010, Deputy Finance Minister Fathel Nabi announced that the government's initial spending proposals placed the total size of the budget at 102 trillion ID ($86.4 billion), based on a price of $70 per barrel of oil, with 2.4 million barrels of oil exported per day, leaving a deficit of 22 trillion ID ($18.6 billion). "The minister has the budget," said Nabi. "He will present it to the cabinet next week."[57] Despite the Finance Ministry's alacrity in drafting the budget, Iraq's electoral stalemate stalled the entire process. Earlier in the year, on March 7, 2010, Iraq conducted Parliamentary elections that resulted in a seven-month political standoff between Prime Minister Maliki's State of Law Coalition and Iyad Allawi's Al-Iraqiya Alliance. The contest over who became prime minister prohibited the Finance Ministry from advancing the new budget, which could not be considered by Parliament until a new government was formed. As Mohsen Saadoun, a member of Parliament observed, "Only when the concerned committees in the Parliament are set up can the budget be discussed and ratified."[58] Between the March election and when it resumed its discussions on the budget on October 27, the Parliament gathered for only one

---

[57] Hevidar Ahmad, "Iraq's 2011 Budget Will Be Sent to Govt," *AK News*, September 20, 2010, http://www.iraqupdates.com/scr/preview.php?article=79344/.

[58] "The Iraqi Government for the First Time Reveals: Unemployment in Iraq, 27 Percent and Foreign Debt 125 Billion Dollars?" *Dinar Trade*, September 13, 2010, http://www.iraqupdates.com/scr/preview.php?article=78792/.

session, on June 15, 2011. Complicating matters further, the Council of Ministers delayed the budget's first reading due to competing oil price estimates. Where the Finance Ministry projected the per barrel price at $70, the Oil Ministry set the price at a more conservative $65, versus the January estimate of $62.50, per barrel. Finally, on November 11, the new Iraqi President Jalal Talabani, a Kurdish leader, asked al-Maliki to form a new government, requesting that the budget be forwarded to Parliament as quickly as possible for review. Eventually, Muqtada al-Sadr's Supreme Islamic Council joined with the State of Law bloc to form the Iraqi National Alliance as the dominant coalition in the Parliament, and a power-sharing agreement was reached with Allawi. The agreement created a Supreme Council for Strategic Policies and divided up the ministries among the blocs.

The Council of Ministers' December Budget and Parliamentary Participation in the Budgetary Process

The Council of Ministers' first reading of the budget occurred on November 23 after the Finance and Oil ministries agreed to set the price of oil at $73 per barrel with exports of 2.3 million barrels per day. The Council approved the budget on December 1, but reduced the budget total to 93 trillion ID ($79.5 billion), allocating 29 trillion ID for investment spending and 64 trillion ID for operational expenses, while reducing the estimated deficit to 14 trillion ID ($12 billion). Again, the deficit would be financed by relying on unspent 2010 investment funds and through regional and international loans.

The Council presented the budget to Parliament, but Parliament was unable to consider the budget because it had yet to appointment members to the Finance Committee. In its place the Parliament instead discussed forming three temporary financial, economic, and legal committees to study the budget, followed by the first reading of the budget on December 18. The following day the Parliament voted to form a fifteen-member legal committee to review the budget.[59] Members of Parliament immediately complained that the budget's reading violated the budget process. Bayazid Hassan, a Kurdish member, declared that "Parliament cannot do the first reading for the draft budget until the Finance Committee prepares and presents its report about it, which has not yet been done."[60] Othman al-Juhayshi, a deputy for the Iraqiya Alliance, concurred, saying "The budget of next year should have been approved one month before now, but the delay in the parliamentary sessions and the crisis of forming the government prevented this. As we all know, approving the budget requires enough study by the Financial Committee to amend, add, and delete, and then it

---

[59] "Ninewa Does Not Receive Complete Budget – Member," *Aswat Al Iraq*, November 9, 2010, http://www.iraqupdates.com/scr/preview.php?article=82081/.

[60] Aiyob Mawloodi, "Kurds Oppose 2011 Draft Budget," *Kurdish Globe*, December 26, 2010, http://www.iraqupdates.com/scr/preview.php?article=84534/.

should be subjected for the first and second readings at the Council of Representatives before a vote takes place."[61] Parliament eventually conducted its first reading of the budget on December 26, its eighteenth session of the year. The Kurdistan Alliance walked out of the meeting in protest of the reduction of funds it would receive in the budget, because of the lack of clarification over federal funding for the Peshmerga militia, and because of the government's assumption that 150,000 barrels of oil from the province would be counted as revenues in the absence of a revenue agreement with the central government. The budget included provisions requiring the Kurdish Regional Government to commit to that level of oil exports or be denied its 17 percent share of the budget's funding. In return, Baghdad would pay foreign firms based on the profit-sharing provisions set by Kurdistan contracts with these oil companies operating in the province.

Meanwhile, on December 20, more than nine months after the March 7 election, Prime Minister al-Maliki presented members of his new cabinet to Parliament, including Rafe al-Essawi, a highly respected Sunni political leader, an orthopedic surgeon, and the outgoing deputy prime minister as the incoming finance minister. Al-Essawi's appointment served as part of Maliki's building of the new coalition government. A member of Iyad Allawi's Iraqiya Alliance bloc, Allawi appointed al-Essawi in March to lead the Alliance in negotiations with Maliki's State of Law Alliance over the creation of a coalition government.

Higher Oil Prices, the February Budget, and Lower Deficits

In January 2011, world oil prices rose to more than $100 a barrel, prompting reports that Iraq would run a budget surplus, not a deficit for its 2011 budget, as the Oil Ministry declared Iraq would boost production to 3 million barrels per day by the end of the year, compared to the current rate of 2.1 million barrels.[62] During a visit to the Kurdistan Regional Government to resolve the KRG's budget disputes with Baghdad, Finance Minister al-Essawi announced the budget would assume higher oil prices at $76.50 a barrel. This new price increased revenues and reduced the deficit, which the Central Bank stated could be financed by borrowing from its cash reserves.[63] Finally, on January 16 the Parliament completed its first reading of the budget and returned it to the

[61] *Ibid.*
[62] "Iraq Vows to Boost Oil Production to 3 Million Barrels Per Day," German Press Agency, January 13, 2011, http://www.iraqupdates.com/scr/preview.php?article=85398/.
[63] Motheher Mohammed Saleh, a Central Bank advisor noted that "the Iraqi Central Bank granted the right to the Iraqi government to borrow 10 trillion Iraqi dinars from its available deposits in government banks through the Finance Ministry. The value of deposits of the government departments and public sector banks is 32 trillion dinars, but are scattered among the banks because of the difficulty of coordination." Saman Dazaee, "Iraq Seeks Recover 2011 Deficit," AK News, January 31, 2011, http://www.iraqupdates.com/scr/preview.php?article=86317/. The Central Bank also warned that the continued delay in approving the budget undermined Iraqi

Council of Ministers for modifications based on the concerns expressed by the Kurdish and other parliamentary blocs. On February 7, the Council of Ministers sent its revised proposal to Parliament for its second reading of the budget. The new budget increased spending to 96.6 trillion ID ($81.9 billion), with 66.6 trillion ID set aside for operational spending and 30 trillion ID for investment purposes. The budget assumed revenues of 80.9 trillion ID, with oil prices at $76.50 per barrel of oil with projected exports of 2.2 million barrels of oil per day, including 100,000 barrels per day from the KRG, and a deficit of 15.7 trillion ID ($13.3 billion), which would be financed by a $4.5 billion loan the Finance Ministry would seek from the IMF and $2 billion from the World Bank.

Al-Maliki's Oil Deal with the KRG

In a significant move to end the government's budget dispute with the KRG and move the budget forward to final approval, Prime Minister al-Maliki pledged to honor the Kurds' two contracts with foreign oil firms on two oil fields. This issue of whether the central government would honor these contracts served as one of the major sources of contention between Baghdad and the KRG. Al-Maliki's decision ran counter to the centrist oil policies fostered by Oil Minister Shahristani. Shahristani, who al-Maliki later appointed as Deputy Prime Minister for Energy Affairs to oversee the Oil and Electricity ministries, sought service fee–based deals created when the Iraqi government paid firms a fixed sum for each additional barrel of extracted oil. By comparison, the Kurds preferred an arrangement whereby the regional governments paid oil companies on a shared profit basis. Al-Maliki set the precedent for other provinces to make their own deals by honoring the KRG system. Maliki justified his decision "because the nature of the extraction in Kurdistan is different from Basra." As Ruba Husari, the editor of the IraqOilForum.com Web site, concluded, "Even though Maliki was talking about the two contracts covering fields that are in production, he is still creating a precedent by legitimizing production-sharing contracts awarded by one region of Iraq."[64] Even with al-Maliki's Kurdish concession and the Kurd's subsequent willingness to embrace this oil deal, the Parliament delayed its second reading of the budget. Then an explosion of public discontent forced the government to make immediate budgetary accommodations to popular demands and approve the budget.

---

reconstruction. "The economic impact is not on the operational part of the 2011 budget," said Saleh, "but affects the investment part of the budget." Saman Dazzayi, "Concerns over Iraqi 2011 Budget Delay," February 6, 2011, AK News, http://www.iraqupdates.com/scr/preview.php?article=86702/.

[64] "Prashant Rao, "Iraq PM's Oil Deal Has Long-Term Impact: Experts," AFP, February 7, 2011, http://www.iraqupdates.com/scr/preview.php?article=86689/.

Iraqi Protests, a "Day of Rage," and Approval of the 2011 Budget

Following mass protests in Egypt and Tunisia in February that resulted in the fall of Egyptian leader Hosni Mubarak, tens of thousands of Iraqis protested throughout the country against the poor provision of public services and an unemployment rate estimated at more than 20 percent. In one demonstration, for example, two thousand Iraqis attacked government officials and burned public buildings in the city of Kut in Wasit province. On February 25, twenty-three Iraqis died in marches held throughout the country in a "Day of Rage." The Iraqi Parliament employed the budget to express its support with demonstrators and displeasure with the government's inability to provide the services demanded by the public. The Ahrar bloc in the Council reacted to this discontent by proposing that 15 percent of the budget be distributed directly to the public. With Iraqis marching in the streets, Maliki's government accepted a version of this proposal and proclaimed that each Iraqi would receive 15,000 dinars ($12.70) with their regular food rations. Funding for these payments came from the diversion of $900 million included in the budget for the purchase of F-16 jets from the United States, the first installment on a $3.3 billion contract. In response to public outrage over the lack of electricity, acting Electricity Minister Shahristani announced a subsidy of a free first one-thousand-kilowatt-hour of electrical use. The budget also included a popular 10 percent reduction in the salaries of senior government officials, beginning with those holding the rank of director-general.

In an aggressive assertion of legislative authority, the Council employed the budget to discipline ministries that failed to execute their budget allocations. Article 11 directed the Ministry of Finance in coordination with the Planning Ministry to redirect project funds away from any ministry or provincial government that did not execute 25 percent of its allocation within six months. The Finance Ministry would then provide a report to the Council explaining why this failure occurred. Finally, the budget law authorized the Council to withdraw its "confidence from the minister or head of the entity" in case that governmental unit failed "to execute 75 percent of the investment allocations assigned to his ministry or department from the federal public budget." The Council then resumed consideration of the budget, unanimously giving it final approval on February 21, though not before Speaker Osama al-Nujafi declared the Parliament would no longer accept a late budget submission or late budget accounts from the ministries. "The accounts should be submitted early because the ratification of the budget requires integrated financial audit accounts with reports from the fiscal supervising committee to determine the year's spending. We need to develop future strategies for the growing economy to serve national interests."[65]

[65] Khuloud al-Zayyadi, "Parliament Speaker Insists on Timely Submission of Federal Budget in Future," AK News, February 20, 2011, http://www.iraqupdates.com/scr/preview.php?article=87467/.

Summary

The bitter political divisions separating Prime Minister al-Maliki's State of Law bloc and Iyad Allawi's Al-Iraqiya bloc presented yet another challenge to Iraq's budgetary process. The seven-month delay in the creation of the governing coalition prevented the Parliament from considering the budget in any organized fashion, and the division of the ministries under the power-sharing agreement compromised the effective administration of the government's programs and budgets. The CPA 95 budget law allowed for such an event as the government's failure to approve the budget in a timely manner by permitting the continued funding of the operating budget based on the prior year's level. Yet, without Parliament's approval of a new budget, the government would still be unable to make its critical investment allocations. The Council of Representatives' inability to approve its budget through two months of the fiscal year contributed to the decline in government investment budget execution rate for 2011, from 62 percent in 2010 to 42 percent in 2011. The government's deficient provision of public services, as reflected in its weak rates of budget execution, exacerbated the public's anger, which led to violent demonstrations, protests, and demands for reform.

At the same time, throughout this period, the Iraqis employed the budget process to help manage their disputes and to keep the government functioning. The budgetary process and the allocation of the budget provided the one consistent institution that could bring the various blocs and sects together. As shown in Table 8.4, Iraq's budgets grew dramatically between 2005 and 2011, as the total budget expanded by 234 percent, with allocations for operational activities rising by 134 percent and investments by 298 percent. More remarkable, the difference in total budget allocations between the triaged 2003 CPA budget and the 2011 budget stood at 957 percent, with a 7,709 percent increase in allocations for investments. Nevertheless, the ongoing challenge of fiscal decentralization, particularly as it affected relations between Baghdad and the Kurdistan Regional Government, also characterized Iraqi budgeting, which reflected the government's limited ability to provide essential services to the Iraqi people.

BUDGETING IN THE KURDISTAN REGIONAL GOVERNMENT

Although each of Iraq's provinces experiences a unique relationship with Baghdad, the fiscal relationship between Iraq's central government and the Kurdistan Regional Government particularly complicates Iraqi budgeting and budget execution. The KRG operates its own extensive ministerial system, numbering as many as forty in 2008, reduced to nineteen by 2011, with a Ministry of Finance and Economy and a Ministry of Planning. Based on a somewhat dated census, the KRG receives a 17 percent proportional share of the central government's budget. The 2011 Kurdish budget of 13.9 trillion ID ($11.7B) allocated 9.7 trillion ID for operations with the balance for investments. Although investments constituted "only" 30 percent of the budget, this

TABLE 8.4. *Final Iraqi Budgets, 2003–2011 (all figures are in billions of Iraqi dinars)*

	2003*	2004	2005	2006	2007	2008	2009	2010	2011
Spending Allocations									
Operations	8,763	25,432	28,431	41,691	39,062	61,282	54,148	60,981	66,596
Investments	385	3,797	7,550	9,272	12,665	25,335	15,017	23,676	30,066
Total Allocation	9,148	29,889	35,981	50,963	51,727	86,617	69,165	84,657	96,663
Revenues	5,830	21,729	28,958	45,392	42,064	80,476	50,408	61,735	80,934
Deficit/Surplus	-3,318	-8,160	-7,023	-5,571	-9,663	-6,141	-18,757	-22,921	-15,727

* July–December.
Source: Iraq Ministry of Finance.

represented some growth in funding from the 10 to 15 percent allocated for capital projects in the 2006 and 2007 budgets.[66] Even with this growth, however, the KRG suffers from its own politics and investment budget execution problems.

The KRG's current budgetary institutional framework dates from elections the Kurds held in 1992, six months after gaining freedom as a consequence of the Gulf War. As a result of the politics surrounding the election, the Kurdistan Democratic Party (KDP) and the Patriotic Union of Kurdistan (PUK) party divided parliamentary seats on a 50–50 basis. Hostilities between the parties led to a civil war and the creation of two Kurdish governments, with the KDP government located in Erbil and the PUK capital based in Sulaimaniyah. Each government operated its own ministry of finance and budget. Following an election held in 2005, the KRG functioned with a unified government that ended the dual ministerial system. Because of distrust between the two parties, however, the KRG retained separate ministries for the Peshmerga military force, and for the ministries of interior and finance, with budgetary resources divided on a 60–40 basis between the KDP and the PUK. Not until 2012 did the parties agree to unify the KRG's Ministry of Interior and Ministry of Finance and Economy, retaining divided control over the Peshmerga.

Dependent on revenues from the central government, the Kurds frequently express displeasure with Baghdad's budgetary procedures while acknowledging their own limitations in budget execution. In 2010, for example, Rasheed Tahir, the Deputy Minister of Finance, explained how delays in Baghdad challenged the Kurds' efforts at capital budgeting. "Central Government sets budget without KRG officials knowing, they just send number on paper to Kurdistan, although there is a law which declares that KRG representative has to participate and coordinate to set budget, but they don't implement that in Baghdad, it is unknown that how many oil barrels have been estimated and how much cost for each barrel is estimated."[67]

The KRG planning process consisted of three steps.[68] The first step called for the line ministries to submit their proposed projects and their cost to the

---

[66] The "only" comment came from the Kurdistan Ministry of Planning, "The Investment Budget Preparation Process," January 12, 2011, http://www.mop-krg.org/detailsArticls_english.php?AID=ZID=2&CID=34&lang=3; "KRG Budget Not Spent Entirely for the Last Three Years," *Hawlati*, January 19, 2009, http://www.iraqupdates.com/scr/preview.php?article=43562/.

[67] Kurdistan Ministry of Planning, "Holding First Budget Debate," September 72, 2010, http://www.mof-krg.org/english/details.php?section=news&id=70/. The Kurds frequently blamed the central government for delays in budgeting. "The central government is not frank with the KRG and the Kurdish people," said Dier Shawes, head of the Parliament's Economic and Finance Committee, about the central government's often delayed 2007 budget. Alyob Mawloddi, "Kurdistan's 2007 Budget Approved, *Kurdish Globe*, July 27, 2007, http://www.iraqupdates.com/scr/preview.php?article=19961/.

[68] For a critical review of KRG's planning and budgeting capacity, see United Nations Development Programme, *Budget Execution Support in the Kurdistan Regional Government*, April 2009.

Planning Ministry. This occurred before the Planning Ministry entered into its negotiations with the Finance Ministry to determine the total size of the investment budget. Second, the line ministries provided data on Excel spreadsheets of existing projects, their costs, and stage of completion. Third, the line ministries supplied similar data for new projects, their costs, and expected dates of completion. Beginning in 2010, these ministries were to provide feasibility studies for each project before it could be approved. "Templates for feasibility study were provided by the central government," acknowledged the Planning Ministry in 2011, "and are supposed to be filled in by each Line Ministry in order to provide the Ministry of Planning with a project plan. However, the problem is that no staff is properly trained to fill in these templates and projects are still not supported with consistent analysis. Moreover, it has to be mentioned that, in general, each Ministry sends a long list of new projects willing to be financed and those are not sufficiently assessed and prioritized."[69] Delays in the budgetary process and bureaucratic capacity issues contributed to the KRG's budget execution problems, but so too did other aspects of the KRG's politics and government.

Criticisms of KRG budgeting focus on charges of patronage, the lack of transparency, corruption, and the government's poor provision of public services. Critics claimed the budget served to provide patronage and benefits for the KDP and the PUK, with the process of dividing funds between the two impeding budgetary transparency. Referring to this division, Ari Harsin, editor of the Kurdish newspaper *Awne*, commented, "There is no transparency. They are dividing the budget of the Kurdish Regional Government between the PUK and the KDP, 52 percent for the KDP, 48 percent for the PUK. It is a very strange model of democracy."[70] "We are waiting for the parties' political bureaus to give us their projects for the budget and approve it," said one member of the Kurdish legislature. "Parliament can't make any changes in the draft budget they receive except for linguistic changes."[71] Faysal Ali, president of the Economists Union of Kurdistan, complained about process and budget execution, saying that "there is a lack of transparency in Kurdistan's budget spending by KDP and PUK. In fiscal years 2006, 2007, and 2008, a total of 40 percent, 26 percent, and 25 percent have not been spent."[72] Noting the corruption in the awarding of

[69] Kurdistan Ministry of Planning, "KRG Investment Budget Preparation Process," January 12, 2011, http://www.mop-krg.org/detailsArticls_english.php?AID=-1&ZID=2&CID=34&lang=3.

[70] Kate Clark, "Corruption in Iraqi Kurdistan," BBC News, January 11, 2008, http://www.iraqupdates.com/scr/preview.php?article=26032/. For more on Kurdish political parties, see Gareth Stansfield, "Governing Kurdistan: The Strengths of Division," in Brendan O'Leary, John McGarry, and Khaled Salih, *The Future of Kurdistan in Iraq*, Philadelphia: University of Pennsylvania Press, 2005, 195–218.

[71] Alyob Mawloodi, "2008 Budget," *Kurdish Globe*, March 14, 2009, http://www.iraqupdates.com/scr/preview.php?article=28543/.

[72] Kate Clark, "Corruption in Iraqi Kurdistan," BBC News, January 11, 2008, http://www.iraqupdates.com/scr/preview.php?article=26032/.

contracts, a civil servant in the Planning Ministry related that investment contracts were awarded to friends, regardless of whether they really could execute the contract. "Ministers or officials try to give contracts to their own company of their friends' companies to get a bite of the pie."[73] Said Ari Harsin, "I see some of the officials who, twenty years ago, were with us in the mountains. They used to be purists, partisans. Now they are driving land cruisers with dark windows and a lot of body guards. They see how ordinary people are living. They have no shame."[74] American officials tolerated these payments made to party officials in the awarding of contracts. Said one senior U.S. Embassy official, these payments are "not necessarily done to steal the money. It is to spend and invest. We might qualify this as corruption or conflict of interest, but in an emerging economy, corruption is just unofficial fees and taxes."[75] Public protests against corruption in 2011 spread to the KRG, where police fired on demonstrators in Sulaimaniyah, who for several months daily protested for better provision of public services and a halt to corruption.[76] In the wake of these protests, Barham Salih resigned his position as prime minister of the KRG.

CONCLUSION

"The first principle of development and perhaps the most important is ownership," Andrew Natsios, USAID's former director, declared. "It holds that a country must drive its own development needs and priorities. The role of donor organizations is to support and assist this process as partners toward a common objective. It is essential that the country's people view development as belonging to them and not to the donor community; development initiatives must meet the country's needs and its people's problems as they perceive them, not as distant policy makers imagine them."[77] Through CPA Order 95 the Coalition layered a reasonably effective, sustainable set of budgetary rules onto existing Iraqi budgetary institutions. These newly imposed rules did make some dramatic changes. They raised the Ministry of Finance to the dominant position it held in the budgetary process during the period of the British Mandate. The rules included a particularly prescient provision that authorized the Finance Ministry to allocate on a monthly basis a twelfth of the previous year's budget in the event the Parliament did not approve the proposed budget

[73] *Ibid.*
[74] *Ibid.*
[75] Sudarsan Raghavan, "Iraq's Kurds Find Prosperity Breeds Distrust," *Washington Post*, March 21, 2009, A8.
[76] "Iraqi Police Said to Open Fire on a Protest, Striking 7," *New York Times*, April 18, 2011, http://www.nytimes.com/2011/04/18/world/middleeast/18iraq.html?emc=eta1/; Shwan Mohammed, "81 Hurt in Iraq Clashes with Protesters," AFP, April 18, 2011; http://news.yahoo.com/s/afp/20110418/wl_mideast_afp/iraqunrestprotests/.
[77] Andrew S. Natsios, "The Nine Principles of Reconstruction and Development," *Parameters*, 35, 2005, 3, 7.

for the current fiscal year. In this way the Iraqis could maintain the basic operations of government while avoiding the threats of shutting down the government or relying on continuing resolutions as in the United States when Congress fails to pass the budget. The rules broke ground in establishing the first operational system of fiscal federalism in Iraqi history.

The Iraqis took ownership of this process by adding the broad outlines of Order 95 to their constitution and gave it further legitimacy through their day-to-day use of these rules in the development of their budgets. In this way, these rules were layered onto Iraq's existing institutions. Exogenous forces in the form of the occupation and donor aid conditionality encouraged this ownership, but what made these rules stick is that the budgetary process serves endogenous domestic purposes. The Iraqi budgetary process serves the fiscal interests of ministries, regional and local governments, political parties, and coalitions. Budgeting, in other words, serves as a critical form of power sharing that leveraged broader political agreements in Iraq. The process serves the policy-making interests of parliamentarians, who found it offered a stable venue for deliberating on fiscal and economic policy matters in the face of volatile swings in oil prices, electoral uncertainty, and popular unrest. The process serves the procedural interests of parliamentarians, who added their own institutions in the form of new oversight and policy committees to promote budgetary transparency and accountability. The process serves the interests of new budgetary claimants who discovered they could participate in the decisions that allocated Iraq's economic resources. Most important, the process serves Iraq by providing it with a reasonable institutional budgetary framework for allocating and managing the massive revenues generated by the world's fourth largest oil reserves.[78]

The Iraqis demonstrated a notable ability to formulate and gain political approval for their budgets following the 2004 transfer of sovereignty. Between 2005 and 2011, they overcame repeated transitions in government, turnover in ministerial leadership, violence, rapid fluctuations in oil prices, disputes over fiscal federalism, limited administrative and governmental capacity, and bitter sectarian differences. These seven budgets may be characterized by the Iraqis' overt declaration of ownership of the process; dependency on oil prices to set the size of total budget allocations; the rise of new budgetary claimants at the parliamentary, provincial, and interest group levels; and the continued influence of donor institutions.

---

[78] Iraq is a petro state, and despite its vast wealth beneath ground the government remains vulnerable to volatile shifts in world oil prices. On this point, see World Bank, *Republic of Iraq: Public Expenditure Review*, Report No. 68682-IQ, Washington, DC, June 2012, 14–17; Terry Lynn Karl, *The Paradox of Plenty: Oil Booms and Petro-States*, Berkeley: University of California Press, 1997; Kiren Aziz Chaudhry, *The Price of Wealth: Economies and Institutions in the Middle East*, Ithaca, NY: Cornell University Press, 1997; and Miriam R. Lowi, *Oil Wealth and the Poverty of Politics: Algeria Compared*, New York: Cambridge University Press, 2009.

9

Successful State Building in Iraq?

Lessons from the Reconstruction of Iraqi Budgeting

This book examines the challenge of making of institutional change under highly adverse circumstances, specifically the attempt by the American-led Coalition to change indigenous government institutions following its invasion and subsequent nine-year conflict-ridden occupation of Iraq. This project focuses on one aspect of the Coalition's state-building and counterinsurgency efforts, the stabilization and reconstruction of the Iraqi government's vital budgeting system. The importance of budgeting, as various literatures on state building, failed states, and postconflict peacekeeping indicate, is that sustainable, effective, and responsible public budgeting systems contribute to state legitimacy, bureaucratic capacity, transparent and accountable public finance, and the efficient provision of public goods, services, and infrastructure. The analysis provided here indicates that through invasion, occupation, and aid conditionality, the Coalition achieved some success in imposing a new budgetary framework on the government of Iraq. The Iraqis, in turn, became invested in that process, and they continue to employ it to budget their expanding oil revenues. Building sustainable budgetary institutions stands as a highlight of the occupation. Evaluating the condition of Iraq's budgeting, U.S. Ambassador James Jeffrey remarked after the withdrawal of American troops in 2012, "This is a serious, serious, functioning part of Iraq. Many things about Iraq still don't function, but the budgeting process, the pledge to the IMF, the budget discipline on the ministries.... It's a miracle. It's something we had a great deal to do with earlier; we have only a limited amount to do with it now, because it's sort of on autopilot.... This is one of the first things they [the Iraqis] got right, with a lot of help from us. So it's a success story."[1]

---

[1] Douglass C. North, *Institutions, Institutional Change and Economic Performance*, New York: Cambridge University Press, 1990, 89.

Yet it is also the case that Coalition and donor efforts aimed at reconstructing how Iraq's ministries conducted their day-to-day activities to meet the budget execution demands of the 17th Benchmark often met with resistance, push-back, and obstruction. The Coalition proved to be unable to help the Iraqis overcome their sectarian and regional differences that delayed the budget's approval, beat back the country's endemic corruption, or provide the basic services and infrastructure demanded by the Iraqi people. The Coalition left the country with the Iraqis having yet to learn how to budget over the long term, to avoid the political and economic ramifications of the government's oil dependency that can bring with it deep budget reductions as well as large spending increases. The Coalition's experience in Iraq, therefore, demonstrates the limits of exogenously induced institutional change, the incremental nature of change, and the critical, if not decisive, role that indigenous buy-in, stakeholding, and ownership play in determining the course of change.

MAKING INSTITUTIONAL CHANGE

Coalition efforts at making institutional changes in Iraq's budgetary system occurred at several levels. First, the Coalition abruptly displaced Iraq's overarching budgetary legal framework, a framework historically rooted in the Ottoman Empire, the British Mandate, and the Ba'athist regime. The Coalition Provisional Authority imposed change by taking command of the budgetary process through its shadow ministries and formulating Iraq's 2003 and 2004 budgets. Next, the CPA issued orders to the Iraqi government mandating new budgeting and fiscal rules. These rules empowered the Ministry of Finance, dictated budget formulation, outlined principles of financial management, and established the foundations of fiscal federalism between the central and provincial governments. In 2007, as demanded by the Coalition, the Iraqi government substantially increased its investment budget allocations. The United States government viewed capital spending to be so important to its capacity-building and counterinsurgency efforts that it set these allocations and spending targets into American law as the 17th Benchmark for evaluating progress in Iraq. This abrupt and dramatic intervention in Iraq's existing rule structure and fiscal priorities is consistent with what Douglass North described as "discontinuous institutional change ... a rapid change in rules," what James Mahoney and Kathleen Thelen called a "radical shift" in institutions.[2]

These new processes and procedures, especially those addressing the functions and responsibilities of the Ministry of Finance, appear to have some degree of longevity or "stickiness" to them. The Iraqis employed these rules to administer their 2005 through 2011 budgets despite the extreme challenges, to name

---

[2] James Mahoney and Kathleen Thelen, "A Theory of Gradual Institutional Change," in James Mahoney and Kathleen Thelen (eds.), *Explaining Institutional Change: Ambiguity, Agency, and Power*, New York: Cambridge University Press, 2009, 16.

only a few, posed by the frequent replacement of governments and their ministerial leadership, regional and sectarian divisions in the Parliament, spikes in insurgent and sectarian violence, wild fluctuations in oil prices, rampant corruption, and the demands of implementing a new system of fiscal federalism.

Despite these obstacles, the Iraqis continued to rely on the timetable and processes set by the CPA budget law, as suggested by the formulation of the 2012 budget. Budget formulation began in September 2011, with the Ministry of Finance presenting an initial budget to the Cabinet in November. Taking into account the World Bank and IMF positions that investment spending should be increased and the deficit constrained, the Finance Ministry proposed a budget of 133.6 trillion ID ($112 billion) and a deficit of 23.9 trillion ID ($20 billion). Finding even this draft budget and its deficit to be excessive, the Council of Ministers approved a revised version on December 7 that called for 117 trillion ID ($98.4 billion) in spending, a 20 percent increase over 2011, and a deficit of 14 trillion ID ($12 billion). The Council set the investment allocation at 37 trillion ID, 35 percent of total spending, compared to 29 percent in the 2011 budget. In addition, the Council reduced the expected price of a barrel of oil in the Ministry of Finance's draft from $90 to a more conservative $85. The Parliament's Financial Committee and Economy and Investment Committee initiated their reviews of the Cabinet's proposals before the Council of Representatives began its readings of the budget. The committees urged that the price of oil be revalued and raised to the global price of more than $100 per barrel, and, in an attempt to promote greater transparency, they called for the Ministry of Finance to provide final accounts for the 2011 budget. Meanwhile, provincial governments and other claimants demanded, complained, and argued for increased funding for their fair shares of the budget.

In December, a dramatic escalation of sectarian conflict between Shia and Sunnis potentially threatened to disrupt the Parliament's consideration of the new budget. On December 19, Prime Minister Nouri al-Maliki ordered the arrest of his Sunni vice president, Tariq al-Hashimi, and in January 2012, an attempt was made to assassinate Rafe al-Essawi, the Sunni minister of finance, leaving Muqtada al-Sadr to call for new elections. Within days of the assassination attempt, however, Amin Hadi, a member of the Finance Committee, announced that Parliament would indeed move forward and act on the budget. "The adoption of the budget will not require political consensus, and this issue is far from the disputes and outstanding issues, and it is settled between the political parties," said Hadi. Moreover, "the Finance Minister Rafe al-Essawi called the House of Representatives to speed up the approving the budget in 2012. There are no objections from the Iraqiya List, in this regard."[3] On February 23 the Parliament approved the budget despite the deep divisions

---

[3] SHAFAAQ.com, "Finance Committee Confirms that the Political Crisis Has No Impact on Passing the 2012 Budget," January 4, 2012, http://www.iraqupdates.com/p_articles.php/refid/E2F-04-01-2012/article/105831/.

that separated the blocs. Thus, although there remains continued uncertainty over how the sectarian divisions that trouble Iraq will be resolved, the budgetary process offered one source of political and institutional stability.

The Iraqis have taken ownership of the CPA's process. They employ it to formulate their budgetary policies and debate their programmatic priorities. The Ministry of Finance coordinates the budget's formulation and management. The Parliament, through its committee system, attempts to oversee the budget, engage the Council of Ministers on budgetary priorities, and make more transparent the government's still too-opaque budgetary documents and data. Provincial and local governments act as stakeholders in the budgetary process. They demand their fair shares of the budget, develop local budgets, and submit investment proposals to the central ministries for funding. Political bickering and the assertion of claims for more resources occur frequently, as is to be expected in representative institutions. Thus, not surprisingly, Iraqi budgeting suffers from delays occurring in the formulation of budgets by the Finance Ministry; delays occurring in the Council of Minister's approval of the budgets that are submitted to Parliament; and delays occurring in Parliament's approval of the government's budgets due to sectarian strife and regional differences. These delays, to be sure, undermine administrative efficiency and effective budget execution. Yet it is worth noting that even as Iraq's leadership struggled in 2011 to reach a power-sharing agreement and assemble a working majority in the Council of Representatives, during its first six months the new government's most notable achievement was the formulation and adoption of a national budget.[4] The process, at least for the foreseeable future, with all of its deficiencies, operates in an institutionalized and routinized fashion that resembles an internationally acceptable budgetary system.

Prewar Planning

There are several factors that contributed to whatever success the Coalition experienced in budgetary state building. First, in a path-dependent fashion, where early choices and preconditions affected later outcomes, the political standing of agencies within the U.S. government hierarchy and prewar planning contributed greatly to the Coalition's early accomplishments in budgetary and economic matters. This certainly proved to be the case with the Treasury Department. The special relationship Treasury's leadership enjoyed with Secretaries Rumsfeld and Rice prior to the invasion, its standing as a cabinet-level agency, its prewar planning that considered the findings of the State

---

[4] Jack Healy, "Iraqi Lawmakers Take On a Quixotic Quest," *International Herald Tribune*, May 13, 2011, 7. "In the six months since competing factions quilted together a partnership government, Parliament has passed about 10 laws, none of them highly controversial. They have passed a budget, canceled some Saddam Hussein–era measures and moved to cut their own salaries and increase some public aid in response to calls for government reform."

Department's Iraq project, its ability to field an experienced group of Office of Technical Assistance personnel, and the agency's unique expertise in the relatively arcane topic of budgeting, all contributed to Treasury's ability to accomplish a number of significant tasks early in the occupation. Although overall planning for the Phase IV occupation proved to be short-sighted and fragmented, Treasury's political standing enabled it to receive direct presidential approval for its plans to convert Iraq's currency, to work with the Iraqi government to pay salaries and pensions, to initiate efforts to manage and reduce Iraq's international debt obligations, and to contribute to the CPA's formulation and monitoring of Iraqi budgets.

USAID also engaged in prewar planning. Whereas Treasury could focus effectively on the immediate task of stabilizing budgetary and economic affairs at the ministerial level, USAID planned for awarding a broad range of short- and long-term contracts aimed at all aspects of reconstructing Iraq. Whereas Treasury relied on a relatively small team of OTA personnel, USAID depended on contractors to implement large costly reconstruction and capacity-building contracts. Some of these contracts overlapped with Treasury's activities. In particular, USAID's Economic Governance contracts placed BearingPoint at the center of budgetary and economic policy making in occupied Iraq. USAID, however, lacked the formal authority and the political influence to overrule the CPA's leadership, with the result that BearingPoint played a negligible role in reconstructing the Ministry of Finance or setting economic policy.

Highly Visible Rules

Second, the Coalition achieved more institutional change when the rules involved were highly visible, salient, and enforceable than when change was directed at comparatively minor rules, processes, and procedures. The CPA's public finance orders, the 2004 and 2005 budgets, and the 17th Benchmark were, for example, all visible and high-priority concerns. The CPA's public finance orders constituted prime directives issued by Ambassador Bremer that specified identifiable budgetary procedures and processes. Because these rules focused on process and new duties assigned to the Ministry of Finance, even the small contingent of CPA and Treasury officials could monitor these aspects of Iraqi budgeting. The 17th Benchmark received the direct attention and support of President Bush, the Coalition leadership, and the donor community. This directed attention resulted in larger Iraqi budgetary allocations for investment spending.

Gaining Iraqi Ownership

Third, the Coalition gained Iraqi buy-in and ownership of the CPA budgeting process because it coincided with Iraqi interests. The Coalition replaced Saddam's compartmentalized, opaque, hierarchical, and authoritarian budgetary process with one that allowed debate, participation, representation, and democratic decision making. The new process allowed existing and new budgetary claimants to articulate their demands for fair shares of government resources. The Iraqis added their own modifying institutional layer to strengthen the process by establishing an oversight committee system reminiscent of one created during the British mandate. Although the politics of the Iraqi budgetary process could be highly contentious, the Iraqis accepted the system as a reasonable resource allocation and dispute resolution mechanism. The Iraqi case, in this regard, verifies a common assumption made about the decisive role that ownership plays in effective state building.

OBSTACLES TO INSTITUTIONAL CHANGE

The Coalition confronted numerous obstacles to its attempt to reconstruct Iraq's budgetary system. The challenge of building up the budgetary process, of course, was magnified by the host of overarching problems the Coalition experienced in Iraq cited by so many observers, including poor prewar planning, the failure to anticipate the insurgency, a dysfunctional Iraqi bureaucracy, endemic corruption, and the vast underestimation of the time, treasure, and blood required to invade and occupy Iraq. In the midst of this chaos and violence, the Coalition and the donor community initiated numerous capacity-building programs to promote budget execution, downstream spending, and financial accountability. The ability of the Coalition to make these programs work as desired was offset by the Coalition's own deficiencies in management and personnel practices, the difficulty of obtaining Iraqi ownership, the 2004 transfer of sovereignty from the CPA to the Iraqis, and the limited effectiveness of aid conditionality as a compliance tool.

Gaining Iraqi Ownership

First, the Coalition struggled and only partially succeeded in gaining Iraqi buy-in for its bureaucratic reforms, as the Iraqis not infrequently responded by way of passive resistance, pushback, and obstruction. As the Coalition discovered, formulating the budget and setting programmatic priorities proved to be much easier than building administrative capacity within the ministries and provinces to execute and spend the budget's investment allocations. These efforts often involved the CPA layering their bureaucratic reforms "on top of or alongside old ones," sometimes in ways that threatened existing or reemerging bureaucratic practices and political arrangements.[5] The Ministry of Finance blocked USAID's contractor BearingPoint from installing and activating the firm's financial management information system. The Ministry also refused to participate in

---

[5] Mahoney and Thelen, *ibid.*, 16.

USAID's *Tatweer* program run by the contractor MSI. The FMIS threatened both the Ministry's leadership that was unfamiliar with the new computer technology and the Ministry's rank-and-file that relied on the existing pencil and paper processes to protect themselves from superiors. As one deputy finance minister recalled of his colleagues, "Their school is old style. Their training is old training. For example, they never used a computer in their life."[6] The Council of Representatives accepted some components of USAID's Legislative Strengthening Program but rejected the contractor AECOM's proposed Center for Parliamentary Development and hindered AECOM's efforts at standing up the Council's analytical capacity to oversee the budgetary process. Both the Center and the small Budget Research Office threatened political blocs within the Parliament. "There was a political current that did not support the Center," an AECOM contractor candidly stated, "because they thought it would dilute their own power base.[7] In these cases, indigenous pushback limited the ability of the Coalition to layer their institutions on to those of the Iraqis.

Command, Coordination, and Control

Second, problems of command, control, coordination, and adequate staffing also troubled the Coalition's reconstruction programs. Command and coordination issues undermined the coherence of USAID's budgetary training programs. Primarily for proprietary reasons, contractors rarely shared training materials; what might be taught at the ministerial level might not coincide with training at the provincial level or even among ministries. As noted by the USAID Inspector General, the agency failed to provide sufficient oversight of its contractors. Coordination problems also affected the activities of the Provincial Reconstruction Teams. The Treasury Department attempted to instill some coordination through the Public Financial Management Action Group, but attendance and active participation were voluntary. In addition, the constant churn of personnel undermined the consistency needed to sustain capacity-building efforts at all levels of government. Quick rotations typified the time in Iraq spent by U.S. government employees and contractors alike. Contact, and thus the building of trust, between Iraqis and trainers proved to be intermittent. The CPA, agency, and contracting firms experienced understaffing both in terms of numbers of personnel and their levels of technical skills. Particularly as the level of violence increased, U.S. government personnel served in Iraq with great reluctance. In practical terms, this meant that the CPA's shadow finance ministry relied on *ad hoc* staffing, while at times the Coalition lacked the ability to conduct anything but the broadest of assessments of the Iraqi budget's effectiveness.

---

[6] Interview with Iraqi official, August 4, 2011.
[7] Interview with AECOM official, November 23, 2011.

Transfer of Sovereignty

Third, the 2004 transfer of sovereignty from the CPA to the Iraqis proved to be a critical juncture in the history of the occupation for many reasons, but particularly so in terms of how it limited the Coalition's capacity-building activities. Prior to the transfer, CPA personnel visited the ministries as needed. Following the transfer, the Iraqi leadership decided who gained access to the ministries. Although federal employees, especially OTA staff, generally maintained reasonably effective contact with the ministries, this was not always the case with contractors who conducted the great majority of capacity-building programs. As one contractor involved in budgetary training observed, "Physically they let you into the ministry, or not. You get into the part of the ministry they want to let you in, they determine who goes to the training sessions, not you who determines who goes to the training sessions. That juncture in time influences our approach and how we work with them."[8] Even Treasury's OTA, which normally embeds its personnel with ministries of finance as part of its assistance efforts, was unable to follow this practice in Iraq despite its relatively good relations with the Ministry of Finance.

The transfer of sovereignty also ended any Coalition consideration of eliminating the Ministry of Planning and Development Cooperation. This legacy of Saddam's regime not only survived the occupation, but contractors from the Defense Department and USAID endeavored to build the agency's planning capacity. In 2010, with the assistance of *Tatweer* contractors, the Planning Ministry issued a five-year National Development Plan. The incentive for the plan, declared Minister of Planning Ali Baban, was Iraq's "inability to manage the annual budget" and "allocate investments," as a result of "budgets being approved late in the year and the release of money thereafter."[9] In addition to offering a broad range of strategic proposals calling for some twenty-seven hundred investment projects valued at 218 trillion ID ($186 billion) that cut across all aspects of the economy, the plan recommended reforms for Iraqi financial management that included enhancing the Planning Ministry's role in the budgetary process. In support of the plan, Prime Minister al-Maliki announced that "When we want to develop a country suffering from sabotage, we have to have stable plans and budgets."[10] Nonetheless, one USAID evaluation indicated that although the government formally adopted the plan, the "national leadership has not translated that strategy into a coherent set of national programs."[11] Whether the plan will truly guide national priorities

[8] Interview with BearingPoint official, December 19, 2007.
[9] Ministry of Planning, "Foreword by the Minister of Planning," *National Development Plan for the Years 2010–2014*, Baghdad, 2010, 3.
[10] Iraq Business News, "Iraq Launches Five-Year Plan for Economic Development," July 6, 2010. http://www.iraq-businessnews.com/2010/07/06/iraq-launches-five-year-plan-for-economic-development/.
[11] Walter Pincus, "US Targets Reform of Iraq's Civil Service," *Washington Post*, October 5, 2010, A13.

depends on the inclusion of the Planning Ministry's priorities in future Iraqi budgets.

Effectiveness of Aid Conditionality

A fourth challenge faced by the Coalition and the donor community was the limited success of using aid conditionality to gain Iraqi compliance.[12] The Coalition, the World Bank, and the International Monetary Fund frequently employed aid conditionality to pressure the Iraqis into complying with their standards of international best practices in public finance. Effective aid conditionality requires clearly proscribed behavior, monitoring capabilities, coercive power, and the willingness to impose sanctions. Monitoring, however, is dependent on credible and consistent data, and good data, such as reliable figures on budget execution, proved to be in short supply in Iraq. Simply knowing that noncompliance exists, however, is insufficient. Even the threat of sanctions is inadequate if the coerced party recognizes that the degree of mutual dependence between the donor and the beneficiary undermines the reality of the application of meaningful penalties. Consequently, the Iraqis could passively resist international demands that they install a financial management information system because meaningful sanctions simply were not forthcoming. Meanwhile, though these international demands reached some level of visibility, such that they were included in various formal aid agreements with the Iraqis, Iraqi pushback and obstruction succeeded because the actual implementation of the FMIS was quiet, invisible, and bureaucratic. Some incremental change nonetheless occurred, as the Iraqis eventually complied with international community demands that the Ministry of Finance adopt the IMF's chart of accounts, years after they agreed to do so.

Evaluating Agency and Contractor Effectiveness

Fifth, the inability to evaluate the claims offered by Coalition agencies and their contractors that their various capacity-building programs promoted budget execution contributed to the Coalition's inability to learn what would be the best strategies and practices for it to pursue in Iraq. There is a basis for agencies and contractors to make such claims. Though prevented from working with the Finance Ministry, USAID's *Tatweer* program and the Defense Department's Task Force on Business and Stability Operations offered training sessions, consultation, and assistance in capital budgeting and contract and procurement

[12] For criticisms of the effectiveness of aid conditionality, see Paul Collier, *The Bottom Billion: Why the Poorest Countries Are Failing and What Can Be Done About It*, New York: Oxford University Press, 2007, 67, 108–109; and Daron Acemoglu and James A. Robinson, *Why Nations Fail: The Origins of Power, Prosperity, and Poverty*, New York: Crown Publishers, 2012, 450–455.

management to at least ten other ministries and thousands of Iraqi civil servants. Meanwhile, USAID's Local Governance Program worked at building the budgetary skills of newly empowered provincial and local government officials. This was dangerous work, conducted under often violent circumstances; contractors were killed, kidnapped, or injured. Nonetheless, the contribution these programs made, individually and collectively, to Iraqi budget execution remains unclear due to the U.S. government's failure to develop meaningful metrics of performance. In the absence of systematically targeted metrics, Coalition agencies, contractors, and donors all pointed to anecdotal examples of successful interventions and increases in budget execution rates as the standard for measuring their individual accomplishments. Although budget execution rates did indeed rise after 2007, as illustrated in Figure 6.2, the rate also dipped in 2009 before rising again in 2010, and then falling once more in 2011. Determining the source of these variations is complicated by a host of events occurring during those years, including a reduction in violence due to the 2007 surge, which may have influenced execution rates. Meanwhile, evaluations of these training and advisory programs by the Special Inspector General for Iraq Reconstruction and especially by the USAID Office of Inspector General point to problems of coordination, oversight, and lack of programmatic substance.

Summary

The institutional changes that occurred in Iraq most likely took place, on the one hand, where the exogenous demands for change were highly visible, salient, and subject to a system of monitoring and sanctioning by external actors, and, on the other hand, where the outcomes of change were the least threatening and most beneficial to their presumed beneficiaries. Institutional change, in other words, most likely occurred when there was a coincidence of interests. Finally, although a list of lessons may be assembled on budgetary reconstruction and making institutional change, what remains to be seen is how the U.S. government reacted to its experience in Iraq and whether these lessons are in any way incorporated into doctrine and practice.

THE AMERICAN REACTION TO IRAQ

The U.S. government's reaction to Iraq included changing agency doctrine to highlight the significance of a working public financial management system for successful stabilization and reconstruction efforts. These doctrinal changes took place as the government initiated broader reforms to strengthen interagency coordination for stabilization, reconstruction, and development operations. Some of these Bush-era reforms proved to be significant failures, leaving the Obama administration to replace them with new rules for coordinating interagency relations. The most important reaction to Iraq, however, would be the redirection in American foreign policy away from interventions and commitments that might require lengthy state-building and reconstruction projects.

NSPD-44 and S/CRS

On December 7, 2005, President Bush issued National Security Presidential Directive-44 (NSPD-44) to strengthen the coordination, planning, and implementation of U.S. stabilization and reconstruction activities. The directive, a reaction to the Defense Department's leadership in the prewar planning, coordination, and administration of the occupation through the CPA, authorized the Secretary of State to take the lead role in such efforts. In this "Whole of Government" approach, the secretary serves as the overarching coordinator for all aspects of reconstruction and stabilization, including interagency planning, policy, and program development as well as relations with foreign governments and nongovernmental organizations. The directive resulted in the creation of the Office of the Coordinator for Reconstruction and Stabilization (S/CRS), whose director also chaired a new Policy Coordination Committee and an Interagency Management System. American stabilization and reconstruction programs would be aided by a new Civilian Response Corps (CRC). The CRC's State, seconded agency, and civilian participants would provide immediate expertise to support designated in-country activities. These CRC personnel could, for instance, presumably supplement efforts by Treasury's OTA and USAID to reconstruct a targeted government's budgeting and public financial management system.[13]

Agency Public Financial Management Doctrine

Due to its experiences in Iraq, the Department of Defense recognized the need to build effective public finances as part of a reconstruction and counterinsurgency strategy. On November 28, 2005, the Defense Department released Directive 3000.05 *Military Support to Stabilization, Security, Transition, and Reconstruction Operating Concept*. The directive, reissued in 2009, declared that a "critical component" of stabilization and reconstruction operations is reconstituting essential ministries and supporting both short- and long-term economic development "to assist in the early recovery of local and national economic growth."[14] The directive called for "operations of civil-military teams and related efforts aimed at unity of effort in rebuilding basic infrastructure;

[13] White House, National Security Council, "National Security Presidential Directive/NSPD 44," Washington, DC, December 7, 2005. On the whole of government approach, see Matthew Cordova, "A Whole of Government Approach to Stability," DIPNOTE, U.S. Department of State Official Blog, June 10, 2009, http://blogs.state.gov/index.php/entries/government_approach_stability/.

[14] U.S. Department of Defense, *Military Support to Stabilization, Security, Transition, and Reconstruction Operations, Joint Operating Concept, Version 2.0*, Washington, DC, December 2006, 44.

developing local governance structures; fostering security, economic stability, and development; and building indigenous capacity for such tasks." These operations include using military funds to supplement indigenous budgeting. In more detailed fashion, the U.S. Army's *Stability Operations FM3-07*, "Essential Stability Tasks," issued in 2008, identified the need to "support national treasury operations."[15] These operations included standing up failed ministries of finance to ensure the payment of salaries and pensions, provide for essential public services, and finance capital reconstruction.

In 2009, the United States Institute of Peace and the U.S. Army Peacekeeping and Stability Operations Institute published their *Guiding Principles for Stabilization and Reconstruction. Principles* offers a comprehensive set of over-arching normative rules for reconstruction, including several pages devoted to fiscal management and budgeting. These rules call for establishing a fiscal authority that includes a budget bureau, a treasury, and tax and customs revenue-generating departments. To promote fiscal transparency, accountability, and predictability and to limit corruption, *Principles* states that budgetary reconstruction should provide for an auditing capacity, a code of fiscal conduct, and standardized procurement rules. Budget execution should be encouraged by aligning the national budget with citizens' interests, offering ministerial administrative and technical capacity development programs, establishing realistic project management goals, and keeping credible financial records. Central to all of these recommendations is the creation of a "public expenditure management" system: "Before preparing a budget, the government needs a mechanism by which to execute the budget – a treasury system and spending information management system that allows the state to monitor all expenditures."[16]

End of S/CRS and the QDDR's Reforms

By 2008, the Office of the Coordinator for Reconstruction and Stabilization, the interagency reconstruction coordinating unit created by the Bush administration, clearly failed in its mission. "If you look at NSPD-44, it had a fundamental flaw," observed Ambassador Robert Loftis, the State Department's Acting Coordinator for Reconstruction and Stabilization, "which was you would create an office within the State Department that would be responsible for having oversight over other federal agencies. That was just beyond reality. The only entity in the federal government that has the authority to do that is the National Security Council staff.... It also doesn't help if you don't give the office more

---

[15] U.S. Army, *Stability Operations FM3-07*, October 2008, 3–16. Also see Department of Defense Instruction, "Subject: Stability Operations," Number 3000.05, Office of the Under Secretary of Defense for Policy, November 16, 2009, 3.

[16] United States Institute of Peace and the U.S. Army Peacekeeping and Stability Operations Institute, *Guiding Principles for Stabilization and Reconstruction*, Washington, DC, 2009, 9–141.

than 20 people. Who are you kidding?"[17] Ambassador Patricia Haslach, who served as the State Department's Coordinator for Iraq Transition, concurred, saying, "It was never resourced. They were never allowed by the regional bureaus to take lead in engagements that mattered. They didn't work on Haiti. They didn't feel they had the capacity to work on Iraq. They were invited into Afghanistan very late. It was a model that didn't work. Why didn't it work? Because the power is with the regional bureaus. The power is with our ambassadors and our regional bureaus."[18] Not only was there pushback to this coordination scheme from within State, other agencies like USAID reacted harshly to the Interagency Management System, with the result that it never became operational.[19] Moreover, the Congress specifically denied funding for the State's Civilian Response Corps' civilian component established by NSPD-44. By 2011, the CRC had fielded just 235 personnel during its three years of existence, only one of whom possessed any knowledge of public budgeting and financial management.[20]

Then in 2010, Secretary of State Hillary Rodham Clinton and the State Department issued the strategic planning document *Leading Through Civilian Power: The First Quadrennial Diplomacy and Development Review* (QDDR). The QDDR attempted to provide some relief for the endemic coordination problems that were to be addressed by NSPD-44 and the S/CRS. The QDDR reaffirmed that the overarching authority for coordinating U.S. policy in-country rested with an embassy's chief of mission – the ambassador – and each chief of mission supported by the regional bureaus would establish the appropriate organizational arrangement for managing interagency responsibilities. The QDDR outlined State's relationship with USAID, particularly in terms of which agency would take the lead in foreign assistance operations. The Secretary would determine what type of condition existed, and then State would lead in operations where there existed political and security conflicts while AID would lead in humanitarian crises. Thus, the locus of interagency coordination rested with the NSC in conjunction with the Secretary of State, with the chief of mission determining the coordination structure of a given embassy, and the arrangements of the different agencies and their personnel required to fulfill designated tasks. Although the chief of mission formally would oversee the activities of agencies in-country, it should be noted that this control remains incomplete as long as the separate agencies involved maintain their relative autonomy, funded

[17] Interview with Ambassador Robert G. Loftis, December 9, 2011.

[18] Interview with Ambassador Patricia M. Haslach, October 5, 2012.

[19] Renanah Miles, "The State Department, USAID, and the Flawed Mandate for Stabilization and Reconstruction," *Prism*, 3, December 2011, 1, 37–46.

[20] U.S. Department of State, *Civilian Response*, Washington, DC, Summer 2011, 14, 22. Interview with Ambassador John H. Mongan, director of the Civilian Response Corps, December 19, 2011. For the single CRC member with a budget background, see U.S. Department of State, "Civilian Response Corps Member Profile: 'Ged Smith,'" *Civilian Response*, Washington, DC, Spring 2010, 10, 6.

as they are by separate appropriations bills funded by different congressional appropriations subcommittees.

The QDDR proposed a number of organizational and administrative reforms to address problems that emerged in Iraq and improve the performance of the State Department and USAID, including reducing USAID's reliance on contractors and the need to evaluate agency performance on measures other than rates of spending. The QDDR called on the Congress to provide sufficient appropriations to hire new Foreign Service Officers and triple USAID's mid-level staffing to enable the agencies to rebuild their depleted ranks.[21] Hiring additional staff would be only part of the solution required to repair USAID's organizational and performance deficiencies, a discussion that long consumed the agency's supporters and critics.[22] The QDDR pointedly declared that State and USAID would "fundamentally change our management approach by turning to the expertise of other federal agencies where appropriate – *before* engaging private contractors. This will help all federal agencies build lasting relationships with foreign counterparts and reduce our reliance on contractors."[23] USAID's contracting oversight, procurement, and budgeting capacities would be strengthened. The QDDR also called for refocusing the evaluation of agency performance from budgetary spending rates to other measures of effectiveness. Both State and USAID would adjust their evaluations of programs on real outcomes, rather than rely on indirect measures such as the burn rate of dollars expended, "on dollars spent rather than the results delivered."[24] Finally, by establishing a new "knowledge and learning center," USAID would analyze and learn from its experiences to boost future performance. The learning center identified in the QDDR to create these new evaluation measures has yet to prove itself, and there remains resistance to measurement of any kind among USAID's defenders.[25]

---

[21] Renanah Miles points out that much of the QDDR looks to the lack of resources, not organizational culture, as the primary problem in Miles, *op. cit.*, 37–46.

[22] Mary Beth Sheridan, "Leadership Vacancy Raises Fears About USAID's Future," *Washington Post*, August 5, 2009, A1; Walter Pincus, "USAID Leader Outlines His Change in Strategy," *Washington Post*, January 25, 2011, A17; J. Brian Atwood, M. Peter McPherson, and Andrew Natsios, "Arrested Development: Making Foreign Aid a More Effective Tool," *Foreign Affairs*, November–December 2008, 87, 6, 123–132; and Jeffrey D. Sachs, "Reforming US Foreign Assistance for a New Era," Senate Foreign Relations Committee Hearings on the Case for Reform: Foreign Aid and Development in a New Era," July 22, 2009.

[23] United States Department of State, *Leading Through Civilian Power: The First Quadrennial Diplomacy and Development Review, Executive Summary*, Washington, DC, 2010, 6. In support of the call for hiring more foreign service officers, see American Academy of Diplomacy, "A Foreign Affairs Budget for the Future: Fixing the Crisis in Diplomatic Readiness," Washington, DC, 2008.

[24] *Ibid.*, 16.

[25] Andrew Natsios, "The Clash of the Counter-Bureaucracy and Development," Center for Global Development, Washington, DC, July 2010.

Implementing the QDDR's reforms is an ongoing project whose success remains to be seen. For example, building appropriate metrics and getting USAID to employ them, as Ambassador Loftis acknowledged, is difficult. "It's a real work in progress, because you are trying to figure out the impact of what your money is going for is a lot harder than looking at how much money is spent. Unfortunately, there is a disconnect ... what are we getting for our money? When you are finally getting down to the contract execution, that qualitative evaluation is somehow swept aside for that quantitative evaluation. How much money have you spent, how many people have you trained, how many meeting have you held? All of those things, I have trained 50 people, but are they doing their jobs?"[26] Furthermore, budgetary politics in the United States that are aimed at deficit reduction produces hiring freezes and reductions, not increases, in the federal government's foreign assistance and related agency budgets and programs. Without new funding to hire additional personnel, USAID fundamentally remains a contract management agency that lacks adequate staffing to manage and oversee its contracts. Currently, the Treasury Department stands as the only agency with the capacity to deploy its own personnel with technical budgetary expertise overseas. The State Department, however, more closely aligned politically and administratively with USAID, relies on that agency and its contractors to address any short-term stabilization and longer-term development needs. Thus, regardless of the QDDR, the administrative apparatus that managed and achieved very mixed results from its budgetary capacity-building programs in Iraq remains intact.

Future American State Building?

The war and occupation of Iraq left the United States suffering from state-building and reconstruction exhaustion, and as a consequence the government's foreign policy seeks to avoid such wars and large-scale state-building projects. Nonetheless, only time will tell whether future U.S. foreign interventions will resemble the quick, relatively inexpensive overthrow of Muammar Gaddafi in Libya, or the long, exorbitantly expensive overthrow of Saddam Hussein in Iraq. Even in the case of Libya, however, the policy question remains whether a dysfunctional, perhaps failing, state should be permitted to emerge in the aftermath of regime change, particularly when the United States actively deposed that country's leadership. President Obama responded to that question by declaring, "Even if Gaddafi does leave power, forty years of tyranny has left Libya fractured and without strong civil institutions. The transition to a legitimate government that is responsive to the Libyan people will be a difficult task. And while the United States will do our part to help, it will be a task for the international

---

[26] Interview with Ambassador Robert G. Loftis, December 9, 2011.

community, and – more important – a task for the Libyan people themselves."[27] Thus, the Obama administration's position is that the United States would participate in the building of state institutions with the international community and domestic actors playing the more active, leading role in a state-building effort.

This position is reflected in the QDDR's assertion that Iraq, as well as Afghanistan, is essentially a one-time experience. As the QDDR stated, "Afghanistan and Iraq are not the primary models for building our civilian capacity to respond to crises and conflicts."[28] In this vein, State replaced the Office of the Coordinator for Reconstruction and Stabilization in 2011 with the Bureau of Conflict and Stabilization Operations. This new unit neither "coordinates" nor directs "reconstruction," because American foreign policy presumably will successfully avoid placing the United States in a position where it would be engaged in reconstruction efforts reminiscent of Iraq or Afghanistan. The Defense Department reportedly is engaged in "a remarkable shift" of setting aside the "large-footprint counterinsurgency and nation-building" strategies employed in Iraq and Afghanistan in favor of targeted, quick, and relatively inexpensive military engagements.[29]

Avoiding costly wars and state-building projects is, of course, a highly laudable foreign policy goal and a valuable lesson learned from Iraq. Yet, perhaps the greatest obstacle to learning from Iraq is the U.S. government's desire to put that experience behind it, in the past as an unpleasant memory. The danger lies in the bureaucratic tendency to revert to what is comfortable and familiar. For to accommodate even the Obama administration's more restrained state-building aspirations, the government must change its own institutional practices and remedy the state-building disappointments and failures experienced during the Iraq war. This learning is necessary, because if the United States elects to engage in another Libya- or even Iraq-like scenario, the success of such a foreign intervention may entail leaving behind a functional state with a functional budgetary process.

[27] United States Department of State, *Leading Through Civilian Power: The First Quadrennial Diplomacy and Development Review*, Washington, DC, 2010, 125.

[28] Peter Juul, "U.S. Military Strategy Shifts Focus," Center for American Progress, December 20, 2011. Intentional institutional forgetting occurred after Vietnam. Following that unpopular war, for example, the U.S. government, and particularly the military, quickly set aside the hard-won lessons of that conflict, only to have to rediscover and relearn counterinsurgency strategies in Iraq. http://www.americanprogress.org/issues/2011/12/us_military_strategy.html/.

[29] "Obama's Remarks on Libya," *New York Times*, March 28, 2011. http://www.nytimes.com/2011/03/29/us/politics/29prexy-text.html?pagewanted=all/.

Bibliography

Abbaszadeh, Nima, Mark Crow, Marianne El-Khoury, Jonathan Gandomi, David Kuwayama, Christopher MacPherson, Meghan Nutting, Nealin Parker, and Taya Weiss. "Provincial Reconstruction Teams: Lessons and Recommendations." Princeton, NJ: Woodrow Wilson School, January 2008.

ABC News. "Sadr Group to Boycott Iraq Government." April 16, 2007. http://www.abc.net.ua/news/newsitems/200704/s189787802.html/.

Acemoglu, Daron and James A. Robinson. *Why Nations Fail.* New York: Crown Publishers, 2012.

Ackerman, Spencer. "As Troops Withdraw, Iraq Provincial Reconstruction Teams to Change." *Washington Independent*, March 11, 2009. http://washingtonindependent.com/33361/iraq-diplomacy-program-to-change/.

Addison, Tony and Alan Roe. "Introduction," in Tony Addison and Alan Roe (eds.), *Fiscal Policy for Development.* New York: Palgrave Macmillian, 2004, 1–23.

Adhoob, Salam. "An Inside View of the 'Second Insurgency': How Corruption and Waste Are Undermining the U.S. Mission in Iraq." US Senate Democratic Policy Committee Hearing, September 22, 2008.

Agresto, John. *Mugged by Reality: The Liberation of Iraq and the Failure of Good Intentions.* New York: Encounter Books, 2007.

Alderson, Andrew. *Bankrolling Basra: The Incredible Story of a Part-Time Soldier, $1 Billion, and the Collapse of Iraq.* London: Robinson, 2007.

Allawi, Ali A. *The Occupation of Iraq: Winning the War, Losing the Peace.* New Haven: Yale University Press, 2007.

Allen, Richard. "The Challenge of Reforming Budgetary Institutions in Developing Countries." WP/09/96, Washington, DC: International Monetary Fund, May 2009.

al-Shabibi, Sinan. "The Iraqi Economy: Some Thoughts on a Recovery and Growth Programme," in Kamil A. Mahdi (ed.), *Iraq's Economic Predicament*, Reading, UK: Garnet Publishing Ltd., 2002, 349–371.

al-Zubaydi, Baqir S. Jabr, and Sinan Al-Shabibi. "Letter of Intent and Iraq: Memorandum of Economic and Financial Policies for 2010–11." Baghdad: Ministry of Finance and Central Bank of Iraq, February 8, 2010.

American Academy of Diplomacy. "A Foreign Affairs Budget for the Future: Fixing the Crisis in Diplomatic Readiness." Washington, DC, 2008.

Andrews, Matt. "Which Organizational Attributes Are Amenable to External Reform? An Empirical Study of African Public Financial Management." *International Public Management Journal*, 14 (2011) 2, 131–156.

Anthony, Robert N. and David W. Young. *Management Control in Nonprofit Organizations*. Boston: Irwin, 1994.

Associated Press. "Iraq's Free Budget Ride Coming to an End?" *Charlottesville Daily Progress*, April 15, 2008, A7.

Associated Press. "Congress Might Slash Iraq Funds: Iraq's Financial Free Ride May Be Over." *USA Today*, April 14, 2008. http://www.usatoday.com/news/world/iraq/2008-04-14-iraq-payment_N.htm/.

Atwood, J.Brian, M.Peter McPherson, and Andrew Natsios. "Arrested Development: Making Foreign Aid a More Effective Tool." *Foreign Affairs*, November–December 87 (2008), 6, 123–132.

Bahry, Donna. *Outside Moscow: Power, Politics, and Budgetary Politics in the Soviet Republics*. New York: Columbia University Press, 1987.

Baker, James A. III and Lee H. Hamilton. *The Iraq Study Group Report*. New York: Vintage Books, 2006.

Baram, Amatzia. *Building Toward Crisis: Saddam Husayn's Strategy for Survival*. Washington, DC: Washington Institute for Near East Policy, Paper 47, 1998.

Barber, Rusty and Sam Parker. *"Evaluating Iraq's Provincial Reconstruction Teams While Drawdown Looms: A USIP Trip Report,"* Washington, DC: United States Institute for Peace, December 2008.

Barlett, Donald L. and James B. Steele. "Billions over Baghdad." *Vanity Fair*, October 2007, 336–380.

BearingPoint. "The Iraq FMIS: Myths and Realities." Baghdad, March 22, 2005.

BearingPoint. "USAID/Economic Governance II Project, Presentation to the Minister of Finance." May 18, 2005.

Bensahel, Nora, Olga Oliker, Keith Crane, Richard R. Brennan, Jr., Heather S. Gregg, Thomas Sullivan, and Andrew Rathmell. *After Saddam: Prewar Planning and the Occupation of Iraq*. Santa Monica: Rand, 2008.

Bergson, Abram. *The Economics of Soviet Planning*. New Haven: Yale University Press, 1964.

Biggs, David F. "Iraq," in Robert P. Beschel Jr. and Mark Ahern (eds.), *Public Financial Management Reform in the Middle East and North Africa*. Washington, DC: The World Bank, 2012, 101–112.

Blaisdell, Donald C. *European Financial Control in the Ottoman Empire*. New York: Columbia University Press, 1929.

Bland, Robert L. and Irene S. Rubin. *Budgeting: A Guide for Local Governments*. Washington, DC: International City/County Management Association, 1997.

Blimes, Linda J. and Joseph E. Stiglitz. *The Three Trillion Dollar War: The True Cost of the Iraq Conflict*. New York: W.W. Norton & Company, 2008.

Bowen, Stuart. "Testimony of Stuart W. Bowen, Jr., Special Inspector General for Iraq Reconstruction, 'Assessing the State of Iraqi Corruption.'" U.S. House of Representatives Committee on Oversight and Government Reform, October 4, 2007.

Boxell, James and Jennifer Thompson. "Total Chief Faces Court Grilling Over Iraq Oil-for-Food Corruption Claims." *Financial Times*, August 3, 2011, 1.

Boyce, James K. and Madalene O'Donnell. "Peace and the Public Purse: An Introduction," in James K. Boyce and Madalene O'Donnell (eds.), *Peace and the Public Purse: Economic Policies for Postwar Statebuilding*. Boulder, CO: Lynne Rienner, 2007, 1–14.

Boyle, Peter. *Strategy and Impact of the Iraq Transition Initiative, OTI in Iraq (2003–2006), Final Evaluation*. Washington, DC: Social Impact, Inc., and USAID, September 30, 2006.

Bremer, L.Paul III. *My Year in Iraq: The Struggle to Build a Future of Hope*. New York: Threshold Editions, 2006.

Bremer, L.Paul III. "Where Was the Plan?" *New York Times*, March 16, 2008.

Brewer, John. *The Sinews of Power: War, Money, and the English State, 1688–1783*. Cambridge: Harvard University Press, 1990.

Brinkerhoff, Derick W. and James B. Mayfield. "Democratic Governance in Iraq? Progress and Peril in Performing State-Society Relations." *Public Administration and Development*, 25 (2005) 1, 59–73.

Brinkerhoff, Derick W. "Building Local Governance in Iraq," in Louis A. Picard, Robert Groelsema, and Terry F. Buss (eds.), *Foreign Aid and Foreign Policy: Lessons for the Next Half-Century*. New York: M.E. Sharpe, 2008, 109–128.

Brinkley, Paul. "A Cause for Hope: Economic Revitalization in Iraq." *Military Review*, July–August 2007, 64–73.

Brownlee, Jason. "Can America Nation-Build?" *World Politics*, 59 (2007) 2, 315–340.

Burrows, Geoff and Phillip E. Cobban. "Financial Nation-Building in Iraq 1920–32," University of Melbourne, unpublished paper, June 2010.

Caan, Christina, Beth Cole, Paul Hughes, and Daniel P. Serwer. "Is This Any Way to Run an Occupation? Legitimacy, Governance, and Security in Post-Conflict Iraq," in Karen Guttieri and Jessical Piombo, (eds.), *Interim Governments*. Washington, DC: United States Institute of Peace, 2007, 319–343.

Caba-Perez, Carmen, Antonio M. López-Hernández, and David Ortiz-Rodríguez. "Governmental Financial Information Reforms and Changes in the Political System: The Argentina, Chile and Paraguay Experience." *Public Administration and Development*, 29 (2009) 5, 429–440.

Caiden, Naomi and Aaron Wildavsky. *Planning and Budgeting in Poor Countries*. New Brunswick: Transaction Publishers, 2003.

Carnahan, Michael and Clare Lockhart. "Peacebuilding and Public Finance," in Charles T. Call (ed), *Building States to Build Peace*. Boulder, CO: Lynne Rienner, 2008, 73–102.

Cave, Damien. "5 British Civilians Abducted from Iraqi Finance Ministry," *New York Times*, May 29, 2007. http://www.nytimes.com/2007/05/29/world/africa/29iht-Iraq.4.5915937.html?scp=3&sq=5%20british%20civilians%20abducted%20in%20iraq&st=cse/.

Center for Strategic and International Studies. "Task Force for Business and Stability Operations: Lessons Learned Final Project, Final Report on Lessons Learned." Washington, DC, November 6, 2009, 44.

Cetinsaya, Gokhan. *Ottoman Administration of Iraq, 1890–1980*. New York: Routledge, 2006,

Chandler, David. *International Statebuilding: The Rise of Post-Liberal Governance*. New York: Routledge, 2010.

Chandrasekaran, Rajiv. *Imperial Life in the Emerald City: Inside Iraq's Green Zone.* New York: Knopf, 2006.

Chandrasekaran, Rajiv. "Ties to GOP Trumped Know-How Among Staff Sent to Rebuild Iraq." *Washington Post*, September 16, 2006, A1.

Chandrasekaran, Rajiv. "Agencies Tangle on Efforts to Help Iraq." *Washington Post*, March 11, 2007, A1.

Chandrasekaran, Rajiv. "Defense Skirts State in Reviving Iraqi Industry." *Washington Post*, May 14, 2007, A1.

Chaudhry, Kiren Aziz. *The Price of Wealth: Economies and Institutions in the Middle East.* Ithaca, NY: Cornell University Press, 1997.

Coalition for International Justice. "Sources of Revenue for Saddam and Sons: A Primer on the Financial Underpinnings of the Regime in Baghdad." Coalition for International Justice, Washington, DC, September 2002.

Coalition Provisional Authority. "Memorandum 4, Contract and Grant Procedures Applicable to Vested and Seized Iraqi Property and the Development Fund for Iraq: Implementation of Regulation Number 3, Program Review Board." Baghdad, August 19, 2003.

Coalition Provisional Authority. "Order 1, De-Ba'athification of Iraqi Society." Baghdad, May 16, 2003.

Coalitional Provisional Authority. "Order 71, Local Governmental Powers." Baghdad, April 6, 2004.

Coalition Provisional Authority. "Order 77, Board of Supreme Audit." Baghdad, April 18, 2004.

Coalitional Provisional Authority. "Order 87, Public Contracts." Baghdad, May 14, 2004.

Coalition Provisional Authority. "Order 95, Financial Management Law and Public Debt Law." Baghdad, June 2, 2004.

Coalition Provisional Authority. *An Historic Review of CPA Accomplishments, 2003–2004.* Baghdad, 2004.

Collier, Paul. *The Bottom Billion: Why the Poorest Countries Are Failing and What Can be Done About It.* New York: Oxford University Press, 2007.

Collier, Paul. "Postconflict Economic Policy," in Charles T. Call (ed.), *Building States to Build Peace.* Boulder, CO: Lynne Rienner, 2008, 103–118.

Collins, Joseph J. "Planning Lessons from Afghanistan and Iraq." *Joint Forces Quarterly*, 41 (2006) 2, 10–14.

Commission on Wartime Contracting in Iraq and Afghanistan. "At What Cost? Contingency Contracting in Iraq and Afghanistan, Interim Report to Congress." Washington, DC, June 2009.

Cordova, Matthew. "A Whole of Government Approach to Stability." DIPNOTE, U.S. Department of State Official Blog, June 10, 2009, http://blogs.state.gov/index.php/entries/government_approach_stability/.

Cordsman, Anthony H. "The Quarterly Report on 'Measuring Stability and Security in Iraq:' Fact, Fallacy, and an Overall Grade of 'F.'" Washington, DC: Center for Strategic and International Studies, June 5, 2006.

Cosgel, Metin M. "Efficiency and Continuity in Public Finance: The Ottoman System of Taxation." *International Journal of Middle East Studies*, 37 (2005) 4, 567–586.

Cox, James. "BearingPoint Gets Contested Iraq Contract." *USA Today*, July 21, 2003. http://accounting.smartpros.com/x39807.xml/.

Crandlemire, Bruce N. "Memorandum from Bruce N. Crandlemire to Gordon H. West and Timothy Beans, 'USAID's Compliance with Federal Regulations in Awarding the Contract for Economic Recovery, Reform and Sustained Growth Contract in Iraq.'" (AIG/A Memorandum 04–005), Office of the Inspector General, USAID, Washington, DC, March 22, 2004.

Crane, Conrad C. and W.Andrew Terrill. "Reconstructing Iraq: Challenges and Missions for Military Forces in a Post-Conflict Scenario," Strategic Studies Institute, U.S. Army War College, January 29, 2003.

Crocker, Ryan C. "Testimony of Ambassador Ryan C. Crocker before the Senate Armed Services Committee." April 8, 2008, 8. http://www.defense.gov/pdf/Ambassador_Crocker_SFRC_Testimony.pdf/.

Darling, Linda T. "Public Finances: The Role of the Ottoman Centre," in Suraiya N. Faroqhi (ed.), *The Cambridge History of Turkey, Volume 3, The Later Ottoman Empire, 1603–1839*, Cambridge: Cambridge University Press, 2006, 118–131.

Davies, R. W. *The Development of the Soviet Budgetary System.* New York: Cambridge University Press, 1958.

Day, Kathleen. "BearingPoint Getting Close to Timely," *Washington Post*, July 9, 2007, D2.

del Castillo, Graciana. *Rebuilding War-Torn States: The Challenges of Post-Conflict Economic Reconstruction.* New York: Oxford University Press, 2008.

del Castillo, Graciana. "The Economics of Peace: Five Rules for Effective Reconstruction." *Special Report*, No. 286, Washington, DC: United States Institute of Peace, September 2011.

DeYoung, Karen. "U.S. Effort to Rebuild from War Criticized." *Washington Post*, April 18, 2008, A18.

DeYoung, Karen and Walter Pincus. "Corruption in Iraq'Pernicious,' State Dept. Official Says." *Washington Post*, October 16, 2007, A13.

Diamond, Larry. "What Went Wrong and Right in Iraq," in Francis Fukuyama (ed.), *Nation Building: Beyond Afghanistan and Iraq*, Baltimore. Johns Hopkins University Press, 2006, 173–195.

Dobbins, James F. "Towards a More Professional Approach to Nation-Building." *International Peacekeeping*, 15 (2008) 1, 67–83.

Dobbins, James F., John G. McGinn, Keith Craine, Seth G. Jones, Rollie Lal, Andrew Rathmell, Rachel Swanger, and Anga Timilsina. *America's Role in Nation-Building: From Germany to Iraq.* Santa Monica: Rand, 2003.

Dobbins, James F., Seth G. Jones, Benjamin Runkle, and Siddharth Mohandas. *Occupying Iraq: A History of the Coalition Provisional Authority.* Santa Monica: Rand, 2009.

Drolet, John D. "Provincial Reconstruction Teams: Afghanistan vs. Iraq: Should We Have a Standard Model?" Carlisle, PA: U.S. Army War College, May 2006.

Easterly, William. *The White Man's Burden: Why the West's Efforts to Aid the Rest Have Done So Much Ill and So Little Good.* New York: Penguin, 2006.

Eriksen, Stein Sundstol. "'State Failure' in Theory and Practice: The Idea of the State and the Contradictions of State Formation." *Review of International Studies*, 37 (2011), 229–247.

Feeny, Simon and Mark McGillivray. "Aid Allocation to Fragile States: Absorptive Capacity Constraints." *Journal of International Development*, 21 (2009) 5, 618–632.

Feldman, Noah. *What We Owe Iraq: War and the Ethics of Nation Building*. Princeton: Princeton University Press, 2004.

Ferguson, Charles H. *No End in Sight: Iraq's Descent into Chaos*. New York: Public Affairs, 2008.

Flavin, William. "US Doctrine for Peace Operations," *International Peacekeeping*, 15 (2008) 1, 35–50.

Flintoff, Corey. "Iraqi Watchdog Official Alleges High-Level Corruption." NPR, September 29, 2008. http://www.npr.org/templates/story/story.php?storyId=14245376&sc=emaf/.

Foley, Stephen. "Shock and Oil: Iraq's Billions and the White House Connection." *The Independent*, January 14, 2006. http://www.commondreams.org/cgi-bin/print.cgi?file=/headlines07/0114–02.html/.

Foote, Christopher, William Block, Keith Crane, and Simon Gray. "Economic Policy and Prospects in Iraq." *Journal of Economic Perspectives*, 18 (2004) 3, 47–70.

Forman, Johanna Mendelson. "Striking Out in Baghdad: How Postconflict Reconstruction Went Awry," in Francis Fukuyama (ed.), *Nation-Building: Beyond Afghanistan and Iraq*. Baltimore: Johns Hopkins University Press, 2006, 196–217.

Foster, Henry A. *The Making of Modern Iraq: A Product of World Forces*. Norman: University of Oklahoma Press, 1935.

Foust, Joshua. "Cutting through Pentagon Spin about Businesses in Iraq." *The Atlantic*, August, 2011. http://www.theatlantic.com/international/archive/2011/08/cutting-through-pentagon-spin-about-business-in-iraq/243773/.

Fozzard, Adrian and Mick Foster. "Changing Approaches to Public Expenditure Management in Low-Income Aid-Dependent Countries," in Tony Addison and Alan Roe (eds.), *Fiscal Policy for Development*. New York: Palgrave Macmillian, 2004, 97–129.

Fukuyama, Francis. *State-Building: Governance and World Order in the 21st Century*. New York: Cornell University Press, 2004.

Gazdar, Haris and Athar Hussain. "Crisis and Response: A Study of the Impact of Economic Sanctions in Iraq," in Kamil A. Mahdi (ed.), *Iraq's Economic Predicament*. Reading, UK: Garnet Publishing Ltd., 2002, 31–83.

Ghani, Ashraf and Clare Lockhart. *Fixing Failed States: A Framework for Rebuilding a Fractured World*. New York: Oxford University Press, 2008.

Ghani, Ashraf, Clare Lockhart, Nargis Nehan, and Baqer Massoud. "The Budget as the Linchpin of the State: Lessons from Afghanistan," in James K. Boyce and Madalene O'Donnell (eds.), *Peace and the Public Purse: Economic Policies for Postwar Statebuilding*. Boulder, CO: Lynne Rienner, 2007, 153–184.

Gibson, Clark C., Krister Andersson, Elinor Ostrom, and Sujai Shivakumar. *The Samaritan's Dilemma: The Political Economy of Development Aid*. New York: Cambridge University Press, 2005.

Glanz, James. "An Audit Sharply Criticizes Iraq's Bookkeeping." *New York Times*, August 12, 2006, A6.

Glanz, James. "Congress Told of Problems in Rebuilding Provinces." *Washington* Post, September 6, 2007, A8.

Glanz, James. "Provincial Ways Find Favor in Rebuilding Iraq." *International Herald Tribune*, October 2, 2007, 4.

Glanz, James. "As US Rebuilds, Iraq Won't Act on Finished Work." *New York Times*, July 28, 2007. http://www.nytimes.com/2007/07/28/world/middleeast/28reconstruct. html?scp=1/.

Glanz, James and Riyadh Mohammed. "Premier of Iraq is Quietly Firing Fraud Monitors." *New York Times*, November 18, 2008. http://www.nytimes.com/2008/ 11/18/world/middleeast/18maliki.html?/.

Gordon, Michael R. and Bernard E. Trainor. *Cobra II: The Inside Story of the Invasion and Occupation of Iraq*. New York: Vintage, 2006.

Gregory, Mark. "So, Mr. Bremer, Where Did All the Money Go?" BBC News, November 9, 2006, http://news.bbc.co.uk/2/hi/business/6129612.stm/.

Grier, Paul. "Record Number of US Contractors in Iraq." *Christian Science Monitor*, August 18, 2008. http://www.csmonitor.com/2008/0818/p02s01-usmi.html/.

Hafidh, Hassan. "Iraq Lost $24.7 Billion 04–06 on Sabotage, Lack of Investment-Study." Dow Jones Newswires, November 13, 2006.

Hallerberg, Mark. *Domestic Budgets in a United Europe*. Ithaca, NY: Cornell University Press, 2004.

Hamre, John J. and Gordon R. Sullivan. "Toward Postconflict Reconstruction." *The Washington Quarterly*, Autumn 2002, 85–96.

Hastings, Max. *Armageddon: The Battle for Germany, 1944–1945*. New York: Vintage Books, 2004.

Healy, Jack. "Iraqi Lawmakers Take on a Quixotic Quest." *International Herald Tribune*, May 13, 2011, 7.

Henderson, Anne Ellen. "The Coalition Provisional Authority's Experience with Economic Reconstruction in Iraq: Lessons Identified." *Special Report*, No. 138, Washington, DC: United States Institute of Peace, April 2005.

Herring, Eric. "Variegated Neo-Liberalization, Human Development and Resistance: Iraq in Global Context." *International Journal of Contemporary Iraqi Studies*, 5 (2011) 3, 337–355.

Herring, Eric and Glen Rangwala. *Iraq in Fragment: The Occupation and Its Legacy*. Ithaca, NY: Cornell University Press, 2006.

Hirschman, Albert O. *The Strategy of Economic Development*. New York: W.W. Norton, 1978.

Holt, Victoria K. and Michael G. Mackinnon. "The Origins and Evolution of US Policy Towards Peace Operations." *International Peacekeeping*, 15 (2008) 1, 18–34.

International Budget Partnership. "Open Budget Survey 2010." October 19, 2010. http:// internationalbudget.org/files/2010_Full_Report-English.pdf/.

International Monetary Fund, *General Government Statistics Manual*, Washington, DC, 2001.

International Monetary Fund. "Use of Fund Resources: Request for Emergency Post-Conflict Assistance." Washington, DC: Middle East and Central Asia Department, September 24, 2004.

International Monetary Fund. "Iraq: Letter of Intent, Memorandum of Economic and Financial Policies, and Technical Memorandum of Understanding." Baghdad, September 24, 2004.

International Monetary Fund. "Iraq: Request for Stand-By Arrangement – Staff Report; Staff Supplement; Press Release on the Executive Board Discussion; and Statement by the Executive Director for Iraq," International Monetary Fund, IMF Country Report No. 06/15, January 2006.

International Monetary Fund. *"First and Second Reviews Under the Stand-By Arrangement, Financing Assurances Review, and Request for Waiver of Nonobservance and Applicability of Performance Criteria."* Washington, DC: Middle East and Central Asia Department, July 17, 2006.

International Monetary Fund. "IMF Executive Board Completes Fifth Review of Financing Assurances Under Iraq's Stand-By Arrangement, and Approves Three-Month Extension of the Arrangement to December 2007." Press Release No. 07/175, Washington, DC, August 2, 2007.

Iraq Administrative Reports 1914–1932, Volume 1, 1914–1918. Cambridge: Cambridge Archive Editions, 1992.

Iraq Administrative Reports 1914–1932, Volume 5, 1920. Cambridge: Cambridge Archive Editions, 1992.

Iraq Administrative Reports 1914–1932, Volume 7, 1920–1924. Cambridge: Cambridge Archive Editions, 1992.

Iraq Administrative Reports 1914–1932, Volume 10, 1931–1932. Cambridge: Cambridge Archive Editions, 1992.

Jamrisko, Michelle. "Big Contractors May Lose Out as Federal Agencies Cut Back." *Washington Post*, July 18, 2011, A11.

Jiyad, Ahmed M. "The Development of Iraq's Foreign Debt: From Liquidity to Unsustainability," in Kamil A. Mahdi (ed.), *Iraq's Economic Predicament*, Reading, UK: Garnet Publishing Ltd., 2002, 85–137.

Johnson, Ian and Ethan Corbin. "Introduction – The US Role in Contemporary Peace Operations: A Double-Edged Sword?" *International Peacekeeping*, 15 (2008) 1, 1–17.

Johnson, Ronald W. and Ricardo Silva-Morales. "Budgeting Under Resource Abundance and Hesitant Steps to Decentralized Investment Planning and Budgeting in Iraq," in Charles E. Menifield (ed.), *Comparative Budgeting: A Global Perspective.* Sudbury: Jones & Bartlett Learning, 2011, 203–219.

Jones, James L. *The Report of the Independent Commission on the Security Forces of Iraq.* Washington, DC, September 6, 2007.

Juhasz, Antonia. *The Bu$h Agenda: Invading the World, One Economy at a Time.* New York: Regan Books, 2006.

Juul, Peter. "U.S. Military Strategy Shifts Focus." Center for American Progress, December 20, 2011. http://www.americanprogress.org/issues/2011/12/us_military_strategy.html/.

Kahler, Miles. "Statebuilding after Afghanistan and Iraq," in Roland Paris and Timothy D. Sisk (eds.), *The Dilemmas of Statebuilding: Confronting the Contradictions of Postwar Peace Operations.* New York: Routledge, 2009, 287–303.

Kang, Cecilia. "Obama Approves $795 Million to Expand Broadband." *Washington Post*, July 3, 2010, A14.

Karl, Terry Lynn. *The Paradox of Plenty: Oil Booms and Petro-States.* Berkeley: University of California Press, 1997.

Kaufmann, Greg (ed.). *Stability Operations and State-Building: Continuities and Contingencies.* Carlisle: Strategic Studies Institute, U.S. Army War College, October 2008.

King, Neil Jr. "Bush Officials Draft Plan for Free-Market Economy in Iraq." *Wall Street Journal*, May 1, 2003, A1.

Klein, Naomi. "Iraq: RTI Designing Government for Baghdad." *The Nation*, February 23, 2004. http://wwww.corpwatch.org/article.php?id=11151&printsafe=1/.

Knights, Michael and Eamon McCarthy. "Provincial Politics in Iraq: Fragmentation or New Awakening?" Policy Focus 81, Washington, DC: The Washington Institute for Near East Policy, April 2008, 1–52.

KPMG Bahrain. "Development Fund for Iraq: Report of Factual Findings in Connection with Disbursements for the Period 1 January to 28 June 2008." Kingdom of Bahrain, September 2004.

KPMG Bahrain. "Development Fund for Iraq, Appendix: Matters Noted Involving Internal Controls and Other Operational Issues During the Audit of the Fund for the Period to 31 December 2003." Kingdom of Bahrain, June 29, 2004.

Ktazman, Kenneth. "Iraq: Post-Saddam National Elections." RS21968, Washington, DC: Congressional Research Service, March 11, 2005.

Kushnirsky, Fyodor I. *Soviet Economic Planning, 1965–1980*. Boulder, CO: Westview Press, 1982.

Lake, David A. "Two Cheers for Bargaining Theory: Assessing Rationalist Explanations of the Iraq War. *International Security*, 35 (Winter 2010/11) 3, 7–52.

Lange, Oskar. "Planning Economic Development," in Gerald M. Meier (ed.), *Leading Issues in Economic Development*. New York: Oxford University Press, 1976, 804–808.

Laursen, Eric. "Privatizing Iraq," *In These Times*. http://www.inthesetimes.com/site/main/article/325/.

Lazo, Alejandro. "BearingPoint Seeks Bankruptcy Protection." *Washington Post*, February 19, 2009, D1.

Lee, Jr., Robert D. and Ronald W. Johnson. Public *Budgeting Systems*. Gaithersburg, MD: Aspen Publishers, 1998.

Lemer, Jeremy and Stephanie Kirchgaessner. "GE to Pay $23.5m to Settle Iraqi Bribe Allegations." *Financial Times*, July 28, 2010, 1.

Levi, Margaret. *Of Rule and Revenue*. Berkeley: University of California Press, 1988.

Lewarne, Stephen and David Snelbecker. "Lessons Learned about Economic Governance in War Torn Economies." PPC *Evaluation Brief* 14, PD-AGC-437, USAID Bureau for Policy Program Coordination, February 2006.

Lochhead, Carolyn. "Conflict in Iraq: Iraq Refugee Crisis Exploding." *San Francisco Chronicle*, January 16, 2007, A1.

Londono, Ernesto. "U.S. 'Money Weapon' Yields Mixed Results." *Washington Post*, July 27, 2009, A1.

Londono, Ernesto. "Barren Iraqi Parks Attests to U.S. Program Flaws." *Washington Post*, January 3, 2010, A1.

Londono, Ernesto. "Pentagon Faulted on Control of Fund." *Washington Post*, July 27, 2010, A15.

Longrigg, Stephen Hemsley. *Four Centuries of Modern Iraq*. Beirut: Lebanon Bookshop, 1968.

Looney, Robert. "The Neoliberal Model's Planned Role in Iraq's Economic Transition." *Middle East Journal*, 57 (2003) 4, 569–586.

Looney, Robert. "A Return to Baathist Economics? Escaping Vicious Circles in Iraq." *Strategic Insight*, 3, (July 2004) 7, 1–9.

Looney, Robert. "Reconstruction and Peacebuilding Under Extreme Adversity: The Problem of Pervasive Corruption in Iraq." *International Peacekeeping*, 15 (2008) 3, 424–440.

Lowi, Miriam R. *Oil Wealth and the Poverty of Politics: Algeria Compared.* New York: Cambridge University Press, 2010.

Mahdi, Kamil A. (ed.). *Iraq's Economic Predicament.* Reading, UK: Garnet Publishing Ltd., 2002.

Mahdi, Kamil A. and Haris Gazdar, "Introduction," in Kamil A. Mahdi (ed.), *Iraq's Economic Predicament*, Reading, UK: Garnet Publishing Ltd., 2002, 1–27.

Mahoney, James and Kathleen Thelen. "A Theory of Gradual Institutional Change," in James Mahoney and Kathleen Thelen (eds.), *Explaining Institutional Change: Ambiguity, Agency, and Power*, New York: Cambridge University Press, 2009, 1–37.

Makiya, Kanan. *Republic of Fear: Politics in Modern Iraq.* Berkeley: University of California Press, 1989.

Mangan, Alan. "Planning for Stabilization and Reconstruction Operations Without a Grand Strategy." Strategic Studies Institute, U.S. Army War College, March 2005.

Mansoor, Peter R. *Baghdad at Sunrise: A Brigade Commander's War in Iraq.* New Haven: Yale University Press, 2008.

Marbourg-Goodman, Jeffrey. "USAID's Iraq Procurement Contracts: Insider's View." Procurement Lawyer, 39 (2003) 1, 10–12.

Marr, Phebe. *The Modern History of Iraq.* Boulder, CO: Westview Press, 2012.

Martins, Mark S. "No Small Change of Soldiering: The Commander's Emergency Response Program (CERP) in Iraq and Afghanistan." *The Army Lawyer*, February 2004, 1–20.

Martins, Mark S. "The Commander's Emergency Response Program." *Joint Forces Quarterly*, 37 (April 2005), 46–52.

McCarthy, Ellen. "BearingPoint Thinks Global." *Washington Post*, October 3, 2005, D. 1.

McCaffery, Jerry L. and L. R. Jones. *Budgeting and Financial Management in the Federal Government.* Greenwich, CT: Information Age Publishing, 2001.

McLay, Sean C. "Provincial Reconstruction Teams (PRTs): A Panacea for What Ails Iraq?" Montgomery, AL: Air Command and Staff College, April 2007.

McNab, Robert M. and Edward Mason. "Reconstruction, the Long-Tail, and Decentralization: An Application to Iraq and Afghanistan." Monterey: Naval Postgraduate School, 2007.

Merza, Ali. "Oil Revenues, Public Expenditures and Saving/Stabilization Fund in Iraq," *International Journal of Contemporary Iraqi Studies*, 5 (2011) 1, 47–80.

Michaels, Jim. "Gen. Odierno: Iraqi Government Must Improve Services." *USA Today*, September 29, 2008. http://www.usatoday.com/news/world/iraq/2008-09-29-odierno_N.htm/.

Miles, Renanah. "The State Department, USAID, and the Flawed Mandate for Stabilization and Reconstruction." *Prism*, 3, December 2011, 1, 37–46.

Miller, T. Christian. *Blood Money: Wasted Billions, Lost Lives, and Corporate Greed in Iraq.* New York: Little Brown, 2006.

Miller, T. Christian. "Sometimes It's Not Your War, But You Sacrifice Anyway." *Washington Post*, August 16, 2009, B2.

Misconi, Humam. "Iraq's Capital Budget and Regional Development Fund: Review and Comments on Execution Capacity and Implications." *International Journal of Contemporary Iraqi Studies*, 2 (2008) 2, 271–291.

Moore, Galen. "Keane Plans BearingPoint Buyout." *Mass High Tech Business News*, July 9, 2009. http://www.masshightech.com/stories/2009/07/06/daily45-Keane-plans-BearingPoint-buyout.html/.

National Defense University. "Saddam Meeting with His Cabinet to Discuss the 1982 Budget," Conflict Records Research Center, National Defense University, CRRC Record Number SH-SHTP-A-000-635, Undated Document, circa 1982.

Natsios, Andrew S. "The Nine Principles of Reconstruction and Development." *Parameters*, 35 (2005) 3, 4–20.

Natsios, Andrew S. "Information Memo for the Secretary." August 31, 2005.

Natsios, Andrew S. "Time Lag and Sequencing Dilemmas of Postconflict Reconstruction." *Prism*, 1 (2009) 1, 63–76.

Natsois, Andrew S. "The Clash of the Counter-Bureaucracy and Development." Center for Global Development, Washington, DC, July 2010.

Nice, David C. *Public Budgeting*. Stamford, CT: Wadsworth, 2002.

North, Douglass C. *Institutions, Institutional Change and Economic Performance*. New York: Cambridge University Press, 1990.

O'Keefe, Ed. "Energy Dept. Stimulus Program Lags Behind Goals, Audit Says." *Washington Post*, September 8, 2011, A17.

OECD. "Improving Transparency within Government Procurement Procedures in Iraq: OECD Benchmark Report." Paris, March 5, 2010.

Office of the Special Inspector General for Iraq Reconstruction. "Audit Report: Oversight of Funds Provided to Iraqi Ministries through the National Budget Process." Report No. 05-004, Arlington, VA, January 30, 2005.

Office of the Special Inspector General for Iraq Reconstruction. "Status of the Provincial Reconstruction Team Program in Iraq." SIGIR-06-034, Arlington, VA, October 29, 2006.

Office of the Special Inspector General for Iraq Reconstruction. "Interim Report on Efforts and Further Actions Needed to Implement a Financial Management Information System in Iraq." SIGIR-08-001, Washington, DC, October 24, 2007.

Office of the Special Inspector General for Iraq Reconstruction. "Commander's Emergency Response Program in Iraq Funds Many Large-Scale Projects." SIGIR-08-006, Arlington, VA, January 25, 2008.

Office of the Special Inspector General for Iraq Reconstruction. "Transferring Reconstruction Projects to the Government of Iraq: Some Progress Made but Further Improvements Needed to Avoid Waste." SIGIR-08-017, Arlington, VA, April 28, 2008.

Office of the Special Inspector General for Iraq Reconstruction. "Most Iraq Economic Support Funds Have Been Obligated and Liquidated." SIGIR 10-018, Arlington, VA, July 21, 2010.

Office of the Special Inspector General for Iraq Reconstruction. "Development Fund for Iraq: Department of Defense Needs to Improve Financial and Management Controls." SIGIR-10-020, Arlington, VA, July 27, 2010.

Office of the Special Inspector General for Iraq Reconstruction. Hard Lessons: *The Iraq Reconstruction Experience*. Washington, DC: U.S. Government Printing Office, 2009.

Office of the Special Inspector General for Iraq Reconstruction. "Quarterly Report to the United States Congress." Arlington, VA, October 30, 2011.

Oliver, Dave. "Restarting the Iraqi Economy," November 2003, unpublished manuscript.

Orren, Karen and Stephen Skowronek, *The Search for American Political Development*, New York: Cambridge University Press, 2004.

Ottaway, Marina. "Rebuilding State Institutions in Collapsed States," in Jennifer Milliken (ed.), *State Failure, Collapse and Reconstruction*. Oxford: Blackwell, 2003, 245–266.

Packer, George. *The Assassins' Gate: America in Iraq*. New York: Farrar, Straus and Giroux, 2005.

Pam, Jeremiah S. "The Treasury Approach to State-Building and Institution Strengthening Assistance: Experience in Iraq and Broader Implications." *Special Report*, 216, Washington, DC: United States Institute of Peace, October 2008.

Pamuk, Sevket. "The Evolution of Fiscal Institutions in the Ottoman Empire." Unpublished manuscript, 2002.

Paris, Roland. "Peacebuilding and the Limits of Liberal Internationalism." *International Security*, 22 (1997) 2, 54–89.

Paris, Roland and Timothy D. Sisk. "Understanding the Contradictions of Postwar Statebuilding," in Roland Paris and Timothy D. Sisk (eds.), *The Dilemmas of Statebuilding*, New York: Routledge, 2009, 1–20.

Parker, Michelle. "The Role of the Defense Department in Provincial Reconstruction Teams." Santa Monica, CA: Rand Corporation, September 2007.

Parker, Jennifer. "Waste in War: Where Did All the Iraq Reconstruction Money Go?" ABC News, February 6, 2007, http://abcnews.go.com/Politics/print?id=2852426/.

Patrick, Stewart. "A Return to Realism? The United States and Global Peace Operations Since 9/11." *International Peacekeeping*, 15 (2008) 1, 133–148.

Pei, Mixin and Sara Kasper, "Lessons from the Past: The American Record on Nation Building." Carnegie Endowment for International Peace, *Policy Brief*, 24, May 2003, 1–8.

Pelofsky, Jeremy. "U.S. Sent Giant Pallets of Cash into Iraq." *Washington Post*, February 6, 2007, A1.

Penrose, Edith and E. F. *Iraq: International Relations and National Development*. London: Ernest Benn, 1978.

Perito, Robert. "The Coalition Provisional Authority's with Public Security in Iraq: Lessons Learned." *Special Report*, 137, Washington, DC: United States Institute for Peace, April 2005.

Perito, Robert M. "Provincial Reconstruction Teams in Iraq." *Special Report*, 185, Washington, DC: United States Institute for Peace, March 2007.

Perito, Robert. "Iraq's Interior Ministry: Frustrating Reform." *Peace Brief*, Washington, DC: United States Institute for Peace, May 2008.

Perito, Robert and Madeline Kristoff. "Iraq's Interior Ministry: The Key to Police Reform." *Special Briefing*, Washington, DC: United States Institute for Peace, July 2009.

Peters, B.Guy. *Institutional Theory in Political Science: The 'New Institutionalism,'* London: Continuum, 1999.

Philips, Kate, Shane Lauth, and Erin Schenk. "U.S. Military Operations in Iraq: Planning, Combat, and Occupation," in W. Andrew Terrill (ed.), Strategic Studies Institute, U.S. Army War College, April 2006.

Pierson, Paul. *Politics in Time: History, Institutions, and Social Analysis.* Princeton: Princeton University Press, 2004.

Pincus, Walter. "U.S. Targets Reform of Iraq's Civil Service." *Washington Post*, October 5, 2010, A13.

Pincus, Walter. "USAID Leader Outlines His Change in Strategy." *Washington Post*, January 25, 2011, A17.

Pincus, Walter. "U.S. Office Urges Halt in Funds for Iraq Security Institute." *Washington Post*, January 26, 2011, A4.

Pollack, Sheldon D. *War, Revenue, and State Building: Financing the Development of the American State.* Ithaca, NY: Cornell University Press, 2009.

Powell, Walter W. and Paul J. DiMaggio. "Introduction," in Walter W. Powell and Paul J. DiMaggio (eds.), *The New Institutionalism in Organizational Analysis*, Chicago: University of Chicago Press, 1991, 1–38.

Pringle, Evelyn. "When Bremer Ruled Baghdad: How Iraq Was Looted." *Counterpunch*, April 21, 2007. http://www.counterpunch.org/pringle04212007.html/.

Pryce-Jones, David. *The Closed Circle: An Interpretation of the Arabs.* Chicago: Ivan R. Dee, 2009.

Riggs, Fred W. "Bureaucrats and Political Development: A Paradoxical View," in Joseph LaPalombara (ed.), *Bureaucracy and Political Development.* Princeton: Princeton University Press, 1963, 120–168.

Rondinelli, Dennis A. and John D. Montgomery. "Regime Change and Nation Building: Can Donor's Restore Governance in Post-Conflict States?" *Public Administration and Development*, 25 (2005), 15–23.

Royal Institute of International Affairs. *The Middle East: A Political and Economic Survey.* London: The Royal Institute of International Affairs, 1952.

Rundell, Walter Jr. *Military Money: A Fiscal History of the US Army Overseas in World War II.* College Station: Texas A&M University Press, 1980.

Sachs, Jeffrey D. "Reforming US Foreign Assistance for a New Era." Senate Foreign Relations Committee Hearings on the Case for Reform: Foreign Aid and Development in a New Era, July 22, 2009.

Santora, Mark. "Pervasive Corruption Rattles Iraq's Fragile State." *New York Times*, October 29, 2009. http://www.nytimes.com/2009/10/29/world/middleeast/29corrupt.html/.

Savage, James D. *Balanced Budgets and American Politics.* Ithaca, NY: Cornell University Press, 1988.

Savage, James D. "The Origins of Budgetary Preferences: The Dodge Line and the Balanced Budget Norm in Japan." *Administration & Society*, 34 (2002) 3, 261–284.

Savage, James D. "Iraq's Budget as a Source of Political Stability," *Special Report*, 328, Washington, DC: United States Institute of Peace, March 2013.

Schramm, Carl J. "Expeditionary Economics: Spurring Growth After Conflicts and Disasters. *Foreign Affairs*, 89 (May/June 2010) 3, 89–99.

Schick, Allen. "Why Most Developing Countries Should Not Try New Zealand's Reforms." *The World Bank Research Observer*, 13 (1989) 1, 123–131.

Schooner, Steven. "Remember Them Too." *Washington Post*, May 25, 2009, A21.

Shabibi, Sinan and Ali Allawi. Letter from Dr. Sinan Shabibi and Dr. Ali Allawi to Mr. Rodrigo de Rato, Managing Director, International Monetary Fund, "Letter of Intent, Memorandum of Economic and Financial Policies and Technical Memorandum of Understanding," Baghdad, December 6, 2005. http://www.imf.org/external/np/loi/2005/irq/120605.pdf/.

Shadid, Anthony. "Letter from Iraq: 'People Woke Up, and They Were Gone." *Washington Post*, December 4, 2009, p. 1.

Shah, Anwar. *Participatory Budgeting*. Washington, DC: World Bank, 2007.

Sheridan, Mary Beth. "Leadership Vacancy Raises Fears About USAID's Future." *Washington Post*, August 5, 2009, A1.

Shimko, Keith L. *The Iraq Wars and America's Military Revolution*. New York: Cambridge University Press, 2010.

Silverstein, Ken. "The Minister of Civil War: Bayan Jabr, Paul Bremer, and the Rise of the Iraqi Death Squads." *Harper's Magazine*, August 2006, 67–73.

Stansfield, Gareth. "Governing Kurdistan: The Strengths of Division," in Brendan O'Leary, John McGarry, and Khaled Salih (eds.), *The Future of Kurdistan in Iraq*. Philadelphia: University of Pennsylvania Press, 2005, 195–218.

Stansfield, Gareth. *Iraq*. Cambridge: Polity Press, 2007.

Starkey, Jonathan. "BearingPoint Nears End of Difficult Run." *Washington Post*, September 25, 2009, A14.

Steinmo, Sven. "What Is Historical Institutionalism?" in Donatella Della Porta and Michael Keating (eds.), *Approaches in the Social Sciences*. Cambridge: Cambridge University Press, 2008, 118–138.

Steinmo, Sven. *The Evolution of Modern States: Sweden, Japan, and the United States*. New York: Cambridge University Press, 2010.

Stephenson, James. *Losing the Golden Hour*. Washington, DC: Potomac Books, Inc., 2007.

Susman, Tina and Saif Hameed. "Sunni Bloc Quits Iraqi Cabinet." *Los Angeles Times*, June 30, 2007, A6.

Szayna, Thomas S. Derek Eaton, and Amy Richardson. *Preparing the Army for Stability Operations*. Santa Monica: Rand, 2007.

Taecker, Kevin. *"Treasury/IRMO-FFA Staffing and Resources for Continuity of Coverage."* US Treasury Department Financial Attaché, Baghdad, January 3, 2006.

Tansey, Oisin. "The Concept and Practice of Democratic Regime-Building." *International Peacekeeping*, 14 (2007) 5, 633–646.

Taylor, John B. "Reconstruction in Iraq: Economic and Financial Issues." JS-452, Office of Public Affairs, United States Department of the Treasury, June 4, 2003, 2.

Taylor, John B. "Reconstruction of Iraq's Banking Sector." "A Briefing Sponsored by the Bankers Association for Finance and Trade and the Arab Bankers Association of North America," JS-895, Office of Public Affairs, United States Department of the Treasury, October 10, 2003.

Taylor, John B. *Global Financial Warriors: The Untold Story of International Finance in the Post-9/11 World*. New York: Norton, 2007.

Taylor, John B. "Iraq: Dollars for Dinars." *Hoover Digest*, Stanford University, 2, 2007. http://www.hoover.org/publications/hoover-digest/article/6078/.

Taylor, John B. "We Did Get the Money to Iraq." *International Herald Tribune*, February 27, 2007, 6.

Taylor, Leonard B. *Financial Management of the Vietnam Conflict, 1962–1972*. Department of the Army, Washington, DC, 1974.

Ter-Minassian, Teresa, Pedro P. Parenta, and Pedro Martinez-Mendez. "*Setting up a Treasury in Economies in Transition*." WP/95/16, International Monetary Fund, February 1995.

Thelen, Kathleen. *How Institutions Evolve: The Political Economy of Skills in Germany, Britain, the United States, and Japan*. New York: Cambridge University Press, 2004.

Tilly, Charles. "Reflections on the History of European State-Making," in Charles Tilly (ed.), *The Formation of National States in Western Europe*. Princeton: Princeton University Press, 1975, 3–83.

Todaro, Michael P. *Development Planning: Models and Methods*. Nairobi: Oxford University Press, 1983.

Torres, Lourdes. "Accounting and Accountability: Recent Developments in Government Financial Information Systems." *Public Administration and Development*, 24 (2004) 5, 447–456.

Tripp, Charles. *A History of Iraq*. New York: Cambridge University Press, 2007.

Tsalik, Svetlana. "Iraq's First Public Budget." *Revenue Watch*, Report No. 1, 2003.

Tsalik, Svetlana. "Keeping Secrets: America and Iraq's Public Finances." *Revenue Watch*, Report No. 3, October 2003.

Tyson, Justin. "Budget Implementation in Post-Conflict Countries: Iraq Case Study." 2006, unpublished manuscript.

Van Creveld, Martin. *The Rise and Decline of the State*. New York: Cambridge University Press, 1999.

Von Hippel, Karin. "State-Building After Saddam: Lessons Lost," in Brendan O'Leary, John McGarry, and Khaled Salih (eds.), *The Future of Kurdistan in Iraq*. Philadelphia: University of Pennsylvania Press, 2005, 251–267.

United States Institute of Peace and the US Army Peacekeeping and Stability Operations Institute. *Guiding Principles for Stabilization and Reconstruction*. Washington, DC, 2009.

United States Joint Forces Command. "Military Support to Stabilization, Security, Transition, and Reconstruction Operations Joint Operations Concept, Version 2.0. Arlington, VA: Department of Defense, December 2006

U.S. Central Intelligence Agency. *Comprehensive Report of the Special Advisor to the DCI on Iraq's WMD, Volume 1, Regime Finance and Procurement, Iraq's Budgetary Process, Annex C*. Langley, VA: Central Intelligence Agency, September 30, 2004.

U.S. Congressional Budget Office, "Contractors' Support of U.S. Operations in Iraq," Washington, DC, August 2008.

U.S. Department of the Army. "Stability Operations," Field Manual FM 3–07. Washington, DC: Headquarters, Department of the Army, October 2008.

U.S. Department of Defense. "Measuring Stability and Security in Iraq." Washington, DC: U.S. Department of Defense, October 2005.

U.S. Department of Defense. "Measuring Stability and Security in Iraq." Washington, DC: U.S. Department of Defense, February 2006.

U.S. Department of Defense. "Measuring Stability and Security in Iraq." Washington, DC: U.S. Department of Defense, August 2006.

U.S. Department of Defense. "Measuring Stability and Security in Iraq." Washington, DC: U.S. Department of Defense, June 2007.

U.S. Department of Defense. "Measuring Stability and Security in Iraq." Washington, DC: U.S. Department of Defense, September 2008.

U.S. Department of Defense. "Measuring Stability and Security in Iraq." Washington, DC: U.S. Department of Defense, July 23, 2009.

U.S. Department of Defense. "Measuring Stability and Security in Iraq." Washington, DC: U.S. Department of Defense, September 2009.

U.S. Department of Defense. "Measuring Stability and Security in Iraq." Washington, DC: U.S. Department of Defense, March 2010

U.S. Department of Defense. "Measuring Stability and Security in Iraq." Washington, DC: U.S. Department of Defense, June 2010.

U.S. Department of Defense. Office of the Inspector General, "Internal Controls over Payments Made in Iraq, Kuwait, and Egypt," Report No. D-2008-098, Washington, DC, May 28, 2008.

U.S. Department of Defense, Department of Defense Instruction. "Subject: Stability Operations," Number 3000.05, Office of the Under Secretary of Defense for Policy, November 16, 2009.

U.S. Department of State. Economy and Infrastructure (Public Finance) Working Group. "The Future of Iraq Project." Washington, DC: Department of State, 2002.

U.S. Department of State. *Leading Through Civilian Power: The First Quadrennial Diplomacy and Development Review.* Washington, DC, 2010.

U.S. Department of State and the Broadcasting Board of Governors, Office of Inspector General. "Report of Inspection: Survey of Anticorruption Programs, Embassy Baghdad, Iraq." Report No. ISP-IQO-06-50, August 2006.

U.S. Department of State Regional Embassy Office Hillah. Michael Chiaventone to U.S. Embassy Baghdad. "Babil's Budget Execution Rate High but Needs Improved Allocation from Central Government." September 19, 2008.

U.S. Department of the Treasury. Office of the Inspector General. "International Assistance Programs: Review of Treasury Activities for Iraq Reconstruction." Audit Report OIG-06-029, Washington, DC: Department of the Treasury, March 23, 2006.

U.S. Department of the Treasury. "The Iraqi Financial Management Information System, Briefing to Ambassador Tim Carney," April 11, 2007.

U.S. Department of the Treasury. "Action Memorandum to the Ambassador, 'Suspension of U.S.AID Project Support for the Iraqi Financial Management Information System (FMIS) and Conditions for Resumption of Project.'" July 3, 2007.

U.S. Embassy Baghdad. "Minister of Finance Signs MOU to Restart Implementation of the Iraqi Financial Management Information System (IFMIS)." January 16, 2008.

U.S. Government Accountability Office. "Rebuilding Iraq: Status of Funding and Reconstruction Efforts." GAO-05-876, Washington, DC, July 2005.

U.S. Government Accountability Office. "Securing, Stabilizing, and Rebuilding Iraq: Iraqi Government Has Not Met Most Legislative, Security, and Economic Benchmarks." GAO-07-1195, Washington, DC, September 2007.

U.S. Government Accountability Office. "Iraq Reconstruction: Better Data Needed to Assess Iraq's Budget Execution." GAO-08-153, Washington, DC, January 2008.

U.S. Government Accountability Office. "Securing, Stabilizing, and Rebuilding Iraq: Progress Report: Some Gains Made, Updated Strategy Needed." GAO-08-837, Washington, DC, June 2008.

U.S. Government Accountability Office. "Stabilizing and Rebuilding Iraq: Iraqi Revenues, Expenditures, and Surplus." GAO-08-1031, August, 2008.

U.S. Govenment Accountability Office. "Stabilizing and Rebuilding Iraq: Iraqi Revenues, Expenditures, and Surplus." GAO-08-1144T, Washington, DC, September 16, 2008.

U.S. Government Accountability Office. "Provincial Reconstruction Teams in Afghanistan and Iraq." GAO-08-905RSU, Washington, DC, October 1, 2008.

U.S. Government Accountability Office. "Contingency Contracting: Improvements Needed in Management of Contractors Supporting Contract and Grant Administration in Iraq and Afghanistan." GAO-10-357, Washington, DC, April 2010.

U.S. House of Representatives. Committee on Government Reform – Minority Staff, Special Investigations Division. "The Bush Administration Record: The Reconstruction of Iraq." Washington, DC, October 18, 2005.

U.S. House of Representatives. Committee on Armed Services, "Agency Stovepipes vs. Strategic Agility: Lessons We Need to Learn from Provincial Reconstruction Teams in Iraq and Afghanistan," Washington, DC, April 2008.

U.S. House of Representatives Committee on the Budget. "Iraq's Budget Surplus: Hearing Before the Committee on the Budget, House of Representatives." Serial 110–40, Washington, DC, September 16, 2008.

U.S.AID. *2005 U.S.AID Annual Report*, Section "U.S.AID/Iraq Economic Growth Projects." Washington, DC, 2005.

U.S.AID. "Lessons Learned About Economic Governance in War Torn Economies." PPC *Evaluation Brief* 14, PD-AGC-437, Washington, DC: U.S.AID Bureau for Policy Program Coordination, February 2006.

U.S.AID. "Republic of Iraq District Government Field Manual, Volume 1." Research Park, NC: RTI International, July 2007.

U.S.AID. "Writing the Future: Provincial Development Strategies in Iraq." Research Park, NC: RTI International, November 2007.

U.S.AID. "Iraq Financial Management Information System Situation Assessment, Executive Summary." Baghdad, Iraq, January 20, 2009.

U.S.AID. "Iraq Local Governance Program (LGP) 2007 Annual Report, October 1, 2006–December 31, 2007." Research Park, NC: RTI International, January 15, 2008.

U.S.AID Office of the Inspector General, "Audit of U.S.AID/Iraq's Participation in Provincial Reconstruction Teams in Iraq." Audit Report No. E-267-07-008-P, Washington, DC, September 27, 2007.

U.S.AID Office of Inspector General. "Iraq," "Audit of U.S.AID/Iraq's National Capacity Development Program." E-267-09-001-P, Washington, DC, November 25, 2008.

U.S.AID Office of Inspector General. "Audit of U.S.AID/IRAQ's Local Governance Program II Activities." Audit Report No. E-267-09-003-P, Baghdad, May 31, 2009.

U.S.AID Office of the Inspector General. "Audit of U.S.AID/Iraq's Economic Governance II Program." Audit Report No. E-267-09-004-P, Baghdad, Iraq, June 3, 2009.

U.S.AID Office of Inspector General. "Audit of U.S.AID/IRAQ'S Implementation of the Iraq Financial Management Information System." Audit Report No. E-267-10-002-P, Baghdad, July 19, 2010.

U.S.AID/Iraq. "U.S.AID/*Tatweer* Project: Developing National Capacity in Public Management, Annual Report, Year 1, September 2006–September 2007." Washington, DC: MSI, December 19, 2007.

U.S.AID/Iraq. "U.S.AID/*Tatweer* Program: Developing National Capacity in Public Management, Quarterly Progress Report, 11, January–March 2009." Washington, DC: MSI, April 30, 2009.

U.S.AID/Iraq. "U.S.AID/*Tatweer* Program: Developing National Capacity in Public Administration, Annual Report, Year 3, October 2008–September 2009." Washington, DC: MSI, October 30, 2009.

U.S.AID/Iraq. "Fact Sheet: National Capacity Development." Washington, DC: U.S.AID, April 2008.

U.S.AID/Iraq, "Legislative Strengthening Program, Quarterly Report, January–March 2010." Arlington: AECOM, March 31, 2010.

U.S.AID/Iraq. "*Tatweer* National Capacity Development Program Final Evaluation." Washington, DC: QED Group, April 2011.

U.S.AID/Iraq. "U.S.AID/*Tatweer*, Final Report." October 31, 2011.

Viernum, Robert J. "Understanding and Understandability: Post-Budget Review of the Iraqi Council of Representatives Involvement in the FY 2009 Federal Budget Process." Baghdad: USAID Iraq Legislative Strengthening Program, Baghdad, March 2009.

Waldner, David. "The Limits of Institutional Engineering: Lessons from Iraq." *Special Report*, 222, Washington, DC: United States Institute of Peace, May 2009.

Wanna, John, Lotte Jensen, and Jouke de Vries (eds.). *Controlling Public Expenditure: The Changing Roles of Central Budget Agencies – Better Guardians?* Cheltenham: Edward Elgar, 2003.

Ward, Celeste J. "The Coalition Provisional Authority's Experience with Governance in Iraq: Lessons Identified," *Special Report*, 139, Washington, DC: United States Institute of Peace, May 2005.

Watson, Brian G. "Reshaping the Expeditionary Army to Win Decisively: The Case for Greater Stabilization Capacity in the Modular Force." Strategic Studies Institute, U.S. Army War College, August, 2005.

White House, National Security Council. "National Security Presidential Directive/NSPD 44." Washington, DC, December 7, 2005.

White House, National Security Council. "Benchmark Assessment Report." Washington, DC, September 14, 2007.

White House, Office of the Press Secretary. "President's Address to the Nation," Washington, DC, January 10, 2007. http://georgewbush-whitehouse.archives.gov/news/releases/2007/01/20070110-7.html/.

Wildavsky, Aaron. *The Politics of the Budgetary Process*. Boston: Little, Brown and Company, 1984.

Williams, Timothy. "A Search for Blame in Reconstruction After War." *New York Times*, November 21–22, 2009, 4.

Williams, Timothy. "U.S. Fails to Complete, or Cuts Back, Iraqi Projects. *New York Times*, July 5, 2010, 5.

Williamson, John. "A Short History of the Washington Consensus," in Narcis Serra and Joseph E. Stiglitz (eds.), *The Washington Consensus Reconsidered: Towards a New Global Governance*. New York: Oxford University Press, 16–17.

Woodward, Bob. *Plan of Attack*. New York: Simon & Schuster, 2004.

World Bank. *Public Expenditure Management Handbook*. Washington, DC: The World Bank, 1998.

World Bank. "Rebuilding Iraq: Economic Reform and Transition." Washington, DC: Economic and Social Development Unit, February 2006.

World Bank. *Conditionality in Development Policy Lending*. New York, November 15, 2007.

World Bank. *Republic of Iraq: Public Expenditure Review*. Report No. 68682-IQ, Washington, DC, June 2012.

World Bank Iraq Trust Fund. "Update to IRFFI Donor Committee: Public Expenditure and Institutional Assessment, Key Issues in Public Financial Management." Washington, DC, February 18, 2009.

World Bank Iraq Trust Fund Public Finance Management. "Project Summary Sheet," (TF094552/TF094654-P110862), Washington, DC: World Bank, September 2010.

Wright, Donald P. and Timothy R. Reese. *On Point II: Transition to the New Campaign: The United States Army in Operation Iraqi Freedom, May 2003–January 2005*. Ft. Leavenworth, KS: United States Army Combat Studies Institute, 2008.

Yasui, Toshiyuki. "Occupying Japan. Five Myths and Realities: Economist's Eyes and Its Possible Implications to Iraq." JIAP Event "Occupying Iraq," April 23, 2003.

Zurbrigg, Sheila. "Economic Sanctions on Iraq: Tool for Peace, or Travesty," *Muslim World Journal of Human Rights*, 4 (2007) 2, Article 3.

Index